MARGOT

Daphne Bennett is the author of two highly praised biographies: of the Princess Royal (*Vicky*, 1971) and of Prince Albert (*King Without a Crown*, 1977). Her delightful portrait *Queen Victoria's Children* was published in 1980.

Mrs Bennett is married to the historian Ralph Bennett and lives in Cambridge.

MARGOT

A Life of the Countess of Oxford and Asquith

Daphne Bennett

An Arena Book
Published by Arrow Books Limited
62-65 Chandos Place, London WC2N 4NW

An imprint of Century Hutchinson Ltd

London Melbourne Sydney Auckland
Johannesburg and agencies throughout
the world

First published in Great Britain by Victor Gollancz Ltd 1984
Arena edition 1986

Printed and bound in Great Britain by
The Guernsey Press Co. Ltd,
Guernsey, C.I.

ISBN 0 09 942050 3

To Margot's half-sister
Katharine
Baroness Elliot of Harwood D.B.E.

CONTENTS

PART THREE: WAR AND THE AFTERMATH

PART FOUR: WIDOWHOOD

ILLUSTRATIONS

ACKNOWLEDGEMENTS

First I must thank Mr Mark Bonham Carter for allowing me to quote from Margot Asquith's unpublished letters, now scattered in various collections, of which he holds the copyright, and from her autobiography.

I must also thank Viscount Chandos and the Master and Fellows of Magdalene College, Cambridge for letting me quote from the Chandos Papers now in Churchill College Archives and from the manuscript of A. C. Benson's diary respectively.

Many people have kindly given me permission to consult and quote from papers which they have donated or deposited in libraries and archives, and I thank them most warmly: Lord Simon, Mr and Mrs W. A. Bell, Vice-Admiral Sir Ian Hogg, Mr A. D. Maclean, Messrs Walker, Martineau and Company, the Master and Fellows of Balliol College, Oxford, the Librarian, the Bodleian Library, Oxford, the Librarian, the British Library, the Syndics of the Fitzwilliam Museum, Cambridge, and the Warden and Fellows of New College, Oxford.

Lord Balfour of Inchrye, the Hon. Emma Tennant, Sir Basil Bartlett and Mrs Maud Radcliffe have kindly allowed me to see and quote from papers in their possession.

Baroness Elliot of Harwood, Margot's half-sister, has given me unstinted support and encouragement throughout, and has most generously allowed me to take up much of her valuable time. Her guidance has enabled me to avoid many mistakes. It has been an immense privilege to be able to rely on the advice of one who knew Margot so well, and I am truly grateful for it.

A very great number of Margot's letters are now in the Bodleian Library, Oxford, and I am much indebted to Mr Dennis Porter, the Senior Assistant Librarian, for drawing my attention to the various collections in his care. Without his help my work would have been well-nigh impossible, and I thank him warmly. His staff too were most helpful.

The assistance given me by Dr Michael Brock has been invaluable. Although under pressure to finish his edition of Asquith's letters to

Venetia Stanley, he very kindly made time to see me and answer my questions.

As always in the past, it has been to Dr Ronald Hyam that I have often turned for advice, this time particularly on South Africa, and I thank him for letting me take up so much of his time.

I am particularly grateful to Lord Crathorne, who discovered and photographed the painting by Edmond Dulac which appears on the dust-cover.

Lord Glenconner allowed me to visit The Glen to get a feeling of the environment in which Margot was brought up, and Sir Edgar Williams kindly conducted me round the Master's Lodgings at Balliol College, where she visited Jowett: I thank them both.

My thanks are also due to the late Sir Duncan Wilson, Dr Michael Hart and Mr Paul Chipchase for drawing my attention to papers which they had come across in the course of their own researches.

Lord Freyberg, Mr Robert Rhodes James MP, and Mr Philip Sinker have all contributed information which added considerably to my know-ledge of Margot's life.

I wish to thank the Master and Fellows of Balliol College, Oxford and the Master and Fellows of Churchill College Cambridge for allowing me to work on papers in their archives. At Churchill Miss Marion Stewart, the Archivist, and her assistant, Mr Alan Kucia, were always ready to help me when I encountered difficulties; I thank them both warmly.

As on previous occasions, the staff of the Manuscript Room at the British Library have been extremely kind and have made my work there easy.

My Editor, Mrs Margot Levy, has made many useful suggestions which have improved the presentation of my work, and I am very grateful for them.

Mrs Jo Wallace-Harrill has deciphered my difficult handwriting with great cheerfulness and skill, and has produced an immaculate typescript; she too has my very warm thanks.

                                                                      D.B.

PREFACE

'No one is likely to write a biography of me,' wrote Margot Asquith in 1933, 'but when I die someone is sure to write something about me in *The Times* because I was the wife of the Prime Minister who guided this country through times of historic difficulty.' Despite this modest disclaimer, Margot knew that she was worthy of a biography, but she would have preferred it to have been written in her lifetime while she watched over the author's shoulder, suggesting and correcting, for there was one condition she would have been certain to impose—she passionately wanted 'the truth' to be told, particularly about her 'glorious youth', and how she had always defied convention and yet remained at the centre of affairs, undisputed leader of society, the friend and confidante of the famous, known as 'Margot' throughout Britain, even by those who had never seen her.

A fortune-teller had once predicted that her nerves and emotions were 'too sensitive and incalculable . . .' and because of this she must pass through troubled waters that could easily overwhelm her. That she escaped this fate was due to her remarkably strong and resilient will that bent to the storm but never broke.

It was her destiny to live through three wars and to see change accelerating all round her, for she was born when Victoria was on the throne, Palmerston Prime Minister and the Crimean War a recent memory, and died in the reign of George VI, three months after Hitler committed suicide. During the greater part of this long life she kept in touch with family and friends by letter, writing every morning— sometimes as early as 3 a.m. if she could not sleep—always in pencil, usually in bed and wrapped in a huge shawl. There are hundreds of these letters in existence, some of great length, all either undated or with an incorrect date, for Margot was oblivious of figures. Some were dashed off under emotional stress in a kind of private verbal code that is almost impossible to penetrate. Since Margot was not a reticent woman and did not expect anyone but the eyes of the recipient to see them, the letters

ignored the laws of libel and the rules of punctuation and grammar
—anything that prevented her hand keeping up with the speed of her
mind. Nevertheless, despite this idiosyncrasy, the letters reveal the true
story of her life and personality far more accurately than do her books.
This biography, the first to be written of Margot Asquith, is primarily
based on these unpublished letters.

Those already familiar with Margot may wonder why I have not made
more of her reputation as a coiner of sharp and witty sayings. Some of
these sayings will be found in the pages that follow, but they were neither
so numerous nor so cruel as is commonly believed. None occur in her
letters, and there is scarcely a reference to them until late in her life. It
seems likely that the clever young men from Oxford whom Puffin brought
to The Wharf in the 1920s improved upon the undoubted wit of her
conversation when recounting their impressions of her, and thus gave
currency to *bons mots* which she never uttered. There is a cruelty about
most of these alleged remarks which is uncharacteristic of Margot.

'No two leaves on a linden tree
are exactly the same'

PART ONE

Childhood and Early Years

'The permanent happiness of my life, of which no man can rob me, has been my two homes—Glen before marriage and The Wharf after.'

CHAPTER 1

Always Mellow, Always Green

WHEN MARGOT TENNANT was five she summed up her father's character in four words: 'Papa is a genius!' Later on, when she began what she expected would be a successful career as a writer, she prided herself on her accurate character sketches, many of which are reproduced in her autobiography. Never again, however, was she to hit the mark so accurately or in so few words.

Charles Tennant's ability to make money did, indeed, amount to genius; everything he touched was successful: land, property, securities, gold and diamond mining in South Africa and numerous other deals across the world, all flourished under his hand. This was not merely because he was lucky to be born in an age of free trade and expansion but also because he possessed in full measure the instinct for successful enterprise, the confidence to back a hunch, and a cool and steady head for business. The wild rumours that circulated in the City in those days did not disturb him in the least, and once he had entered into a deal he stuck to it. Thus Charles was a millionaire when others who started at the same time were still struggling on the bottom rung of the ladder.

When Charles Tennant married Emma Winsloe in 1849 he was thought to be making the better match. Margot tells us that the Winsloes were of 'gentle birth', regularly taking Holy Orders, or serving in the army and the navy, while Emma's great-grandfather was Richard Walter, founder of *The Times* newspaper. The Winsloes naturally expected that this pretty and accomplished girl would choose a husband from a professional family. Instead she fell in love with a slender, attractive man of twenty-six, a partner in his father's chemical works, who after a serious illness happened to be taking the cure at Malvern, where Mrs Winsloe, a deserted wife with two children and small means, had settled after spending a few years in France.

Although Charles Tennant was not in one of the favoured professions but in commerce, he had had a thorough education and was always an eager pupil. Two excellent schools, Ayr Academy and Tillicoultry School (where a most unusual headmaster taught his pupils to think and act for themselves) had formed him. And like many a Scot, Charles went on learning long afterwards 'in the great school of life'. Well grounded though he was, Charles was expected to start at the bottom. At the age of sixteen he was apprenticed to his godfather, William Nevett, whose Liverpool office handled the sales of the Tennant chemical works. His progress was so rapid that after five years Mr Nevett offered to make him a partner. But Charles was destined for the family business and in 1843 his father, John Tennant, made him and his elder brother partners in Tennant, Clow and Co; Charles was to run the London office.

Margot liked to think, indeed often boasted, that her father was a self-made man. This was an exaggeration, for he came of a prosperous family with a small but well-established business run by sober, unambitious men in whom the gambling instinct which Charles possessed was conspicuously absent. Nevertheless John was proud of his go-ahead son and did nothing to hold him back, for at twenty-one Charles was already the best judge of indigo and madder dyes in the country. Wisely his father sent him to London, where there was more scope for the young man's talents. However, he did not allow him to go with empty pockets to make his way in the world and generously gave him an allowance of £400 a year and £2000 capital. With the help of a loan from Gurney's Bank, Charles immediately used the capital to buy shares in the Midland Railway Company. Those were the days of the astonishing railway boom, and Charles made enough profit to repay the loan in a matter of weeks. He used the resultant capital to invest in an Australian land company, a daring move which made him a rich man after a year, when the shares suddenly rose in value. He was still only twenty-nine. As he began so he went on, and before long he was spoken of in the City with awe. These early speculations were the foundation of the vast and prosperous Tennant empire that Margot was thinking of when she called her father a self-made man.[1]

Apart from his ability to make money, perhaps the most remarkable thing about Charles Tennant was that success did not change him; he never became hard, grasping or miserly. As Margot said, 'the striking thing about him was his freedom from suspicion. Thrown from his earliest days among common shrewd men of singularly unspiritual ideals

—most of them not only on the make, but I might almost say on the pounce—he advanced on his own lines rapidly and courageously, not at all secretively, almost confidently, yet he was rarely taken in'.[2] His daughter thought him a comic mixture of temperament, irritable and sunny by turns yet fundamentally sound, serene and high-minded in every sense. He was a man of action, full of vitality with the ability to make up his mind in a flash and a will that made others do his bidding. To quote Margot again: 'I think I understood my father better than the others did. I guessed his mood in a moment and in consequence could push further and say more to him when he was in a good humour.'[3] Margot was more like him than the others, too, and could therefore handle him better. She was also more like him in looks. Charles was a small man with long, finely chiselled features, a wide, sensitive mouth and large grey eyes which were humorous, lively and set well apart. His dark curly hair was worn after the fashion of the day, rather bushy over the ears but with neatly trimmed side-whiskers and beard and a clean shaven upper lip. As a young man he was always carefully but unpretentiously dressed; later he liked to look what he was—very prosperous indeed. This was shown in small but unostentatious ways—fur collar and lining to his overcoat, his hats from Lock's, his gloves and shoes also hand-made, and of course he always went to his office wearing top hat and frock coat and smoking a large cigar.

Although Charles Tennant kept horses he did not emulate his colleagues and ride to work but preferred to travel by hansom cab and later in his own brougham. The hurry and rush of the City, the constant excitement, were the breath of life to him and awoke afresh every day his bold and adventurous spirit. He knew everybody and was charming and kind no matter who they were. But London soon became more to him than just Lombard Street. He did not make money simply to let it pile up in stocks and shares, and as he grew richer, antique furniture and art galleries attracted his interest. On his way to the City he would call at Christie's saleroom as well as Agnew's and Duveen's, and soon discovered that it was worthwhile rising early to be on the spot when they opened, to have first pick of the pictures that were going so cheaply in those days. In this way he secured many a bargain and thus built up a fine collection of paintings, furniture and china.

Emma's first home was the only moderate-sized house she was ever to have. She loved 14 Craven Hill, Bayswater, dearly, for it possessed everything she liked best in a house. It was close to the park, with a garden and greenhouse where she spent many happy hours tending her plants. It was so quiet that Emma could imagine she was living in the country, which was where one day she hoped to be. In those days she not only had Charles home in good time every night but the company of her mother during the day. This was Charles's doing, for he was very fond of his mother-in-law and had insisted on her coming to live with them. The scheme worked admirably; Emma was never lonely, and at night Mrs Winsloe went early to bed, leaving the young husband and wife alone. Charles enjoyed his mother-in-law's company and excellent conversation; moreover, she was keenly interested in his work—far more than Emma, who hardly knew what her husband did beyond making more and more money. Unassuming, shy and timid, Emma was very different from her husband. All the Winsloes, according to Margot, were of 'low vitality'. In this they were the exact opposite of the Tennants, but Emma was the kind of wife Charles needed after exhausting days in the City, where he had to keep his wits constantly about him as he searched for the next profitable deal.[4]

Emma and Charles had twelve children, but four of them died young. Their first child, Janet, born in 1850, a year after their marriage, was followed rapidly by three sons. All three boys died before Margot was born and Janet when Margot was still an infant, and it was many years before she realized the effect of these tragedies on her mother. 'No true woman ever gets over the death of a child,' Margot was to write many years later. So it was with Emma. The loss of these children caused her to shrink into herself so that even to a close observer she seemed strangely detached from her family. Nevertheless she was the pivot round which their lives revolved. There were the three older girls, Pauline (Posie) born in 1855, Charlotte (Charty) and Lucy, the two older sons Eddy and Frank, the younger girls Laura and Margot, and finally Jack. Although Emma was often abroad at health spas with her three eldest daughters (all married women when Margot was still a child) the children felt her presence in the house just the same. This suggests that she had a stronger personality than her family gave her credit for. Charles was now so often away that his youngest son Jack once asked with unconscious irony: 'Is Papa really Papa, or only a kind of visitor?'[5] There were times when Emma felt like Jack. Although surrounded by sons and daughters she was a lonely woman with a husband often absent and no close women friends, afraid to love her children deeply in case they too should be snatched away. Her life might have been happier if she had married a poor man, for she would not have minded in the least if she had been forced to make both ends meet. Frugal by nature, she could not keep herself from turning off lights, damping down fires and turning old dresses because the material was too good to throw away. The economies she practised as a millionaire's wife caused Charles much amusement. If Charles's business had failed, if his health had become impaired by work and worry, Emma would have come into her own. But nothing Charles touched ever failed, and his health was always excellent.

Whatever Emma's shortcomings as a mother, all her children loved her dearly and saw her good qualities. 'She was a most gentle, lovable and beautiful woman,' her youngest child wrote after her death.[6]

Like all Scots who spend their working life away from their native land, Charles longed for a permanent connection with his old home. There was a side to his nature that loved and understood the country and he could throw off the cares of Lombard Street the moment he set foot in Scotland; fishing, shooting, walking over the moors and, later, playing golf revived his spirits and prepared him for another week's work. He started looking for a suitable country estate and in 1859, with the luck of the very rich, found exactly what he was looking for: a moderate-sized Georgian mansion situated in beautiful surroundings in Peeblesshire came on the market. The house was not large enough for Charles's growing family and his even more rapidly increasing art collection, so Bryce, the well-known architect, was employed to expand it into a turreted baronial castle. Four thousand acres went with it, and a well-stocked flower garden with greenhouses enough to rejoice Emma's heart. 'The Glen'—for Charles kept the old name—was before long celebrated for its pictures, its hospitality, but even more for the extraordinary family who lived there.

The house had a personality of its own, derived from the peace and beauty of its surroundings, which shrouded it in a mysterious glamour that most people felt but few bothered to define. Writing to George Curzon many years later, Margot described Glen as 'a place buried in the restful hills where the echoes of the burn are never heard, except by the peewit and the curlews and the moor mists wreathed round the sun'.[7]

It was in this enchanted setting that Emma Tennant gave birth to her eleventh child on 2 February 1864. Two months later the new baby, almost smothered in silk and lace, was christened Emma Alice Margaret by the pastor at Traquair Kirk, with water from the local burn. Janet held the baby at the font, while the other children clustered round their mother in a scene of perfect domestic happiness that would have gladdened the heart of Landseer, always at his best painting family scenes. He would have come willingly to Glen, had not Emma thought it needless extravagance.

Although Emma's confinements passed off well—she never lost a child at birth—none of her children was really strong. Margot, as the new baby was soon called, proved to be as difficult to rear as the others. Thin, because a poor feeder and therefore slow to gain weight, she also slept lightly and would awake screaming at the slightest sound. Her nurse said she was highly strung and she certainly cried enough for two. As she grew, her true temperament began to unfold: passionate and irascible yet sensitive and easily upset, she was the bane of mother and nurse alike. Never timid nor shy but bold as a lion, she attempted feats beyond her strength and screamed with frustration when she failed. These passions were redeemed by a loyal and affectionate nature, which remained constant throughout her long life, however many other traits were added or taken away.

There was in the Tennant family a ready-made companion for the new baby: eighteen-month-old Laura Mary Octavia, small and lively, but very delicate, a child with such winning ways that everyone admired her. The only anxiety was whether the more forceful Margot would try to dominate her and make her life difficult. In fact Margot loved Laura dearly and the story of her early life would not be complete without the elder sister's story too, so entwined were their two lives. This deep bond of affection did not mean that life in the nursery was peaceful, for they argued and quarrelled as children do who are close in age and have strong wills, driving the household half mad with their screams. Yet they were very close and nothing could ever change the depth of their love for each other.

From the start the two sisters shared everything—their bedroom, clothes, toys, books, even their occupations—but this did not prevent quarrels. Margot longed to become famous and one day announced that the way to do this was to write a novel. Laura said she wanted to be famous too and would also write a novel, and there and then dashed off a few pages at high speed about a little white house and the people who lived in it, which Margot scoffed at. A quarrel broke out, there were tears and recriminations, and their ambitions were forgotten in the fierceness of their argument.

Margot possessed a talent for dancing which Laura did not share, and was invited to join a class held in the nearby Innerleithen manse. But she scandalized the other children with her 'frenchified airs' by kicking her legs high in the can-can and showing her knickers. Yet when Charles persuaded Emma to take her to London for lessons from a famous dancing master, her behaviour was perfect. She was praised so highly and looked so charming in the traditional white muslin that Emma feared that she saw signs of a dawning vanity and in her alarm overlooked the important fact that, when interested, her rumbustious daughter invariably behaved well.

Emma's last child, Harold John (Jack), was born a year after Margot, leaving Emma exhausted. Jack was delicate too, so he occupied all his mother's attention, the other children being left very much to their own devices. Thus Margot became used to doing more or less what she liked, which she said was exactly right for one of her difficult nature. Any attempt to restrain her would only have made her more rebellious and difficult, which in turn would have led to even more dangerous acts of defiance that no amount of scoldings from angry governesses could have prevented.

In all her writings Margot refers again and again to her insistence on youthful freedom of a kind very unusual in any age. In her novel *Octavia* Margot's heroine says, 'I am determined to have a life of my own'. On another page the youthful Octavia, who is of course Margot herself, arrogantly claims 'no one was ever so alive to the present as I am'. Octavia is cocksure, defiant, wild and beautiful, but nevertheless everyone adores her; the only difference between authoress and heroine is that Octavia could influence people for good and Margot could not, hence her perpetual cry: 'Oh, if only I could influence people . . .' Margot's novel gives a far more revealing picture of herself than her autobiography, in which she hides her true self under a mass of supposedly 'stylish' writing and harsh comments meant to impress the reading public.

She called her youth 'glorious', because she said it was free and untrammelled like a gypsy's. She would never admit that her early life would have been more fruitful if it had been disciplined. As it was, her numerous talents were never harnessed to an activity that could bring her satisfaction, but instead were frittered away on unsubstantial dreams.

In many ways she was like her father, especially when it came to strength of character, but Charles was fortunate in having his character formed from his earliest days by wise and (in their simple way) worldly men who gave him a good education and saw that he made the right use of it. They taught him that it was not enough to be clever, and that achievements are won by discipline and hard work. Margot knew all about her father's determination to make something worthwhile of his life, because he talked of it perpetually. She wanted so much to do the same that it secretly worried her that without education her efforts might come to nothing. Her respect for education was so high that it often blinded her to faults of character in the educated, and brought in its wake disillusionment and hurt feelings. She never learnt to emulate Charles's robust view of people, which was realistic rather than cynical, and without which he would never have survived the City. Margot depended on other people too much. Without them, she could not recharge her vitality; gregarious to a fault, she longed for hosts of friends whom she could rely on, but she wanted them to be the way she imagined them. She liked to be different from other people, too. She believed that her mother loved her but did not understand her, and thought that this set her apart; in reality Emma understood her last daughter very well, and handled her with far more wisdom than Margot was to handle her own children.

Margot was told so often that she was plain that she came to believe it. Contemporary letters, diaries and autobiographies say otherwise. Mary Gladstone, paying her first visit to the Tennant family as a young girl, thought the eighteen-year-old Margot 'the prettiest of the lot, her hair curling darkly over her head, eyes large and deep, skin very pleasing without much colour and the most bewitching mouth'.[8] Ten years later, Arthur Benson, then a young master at Eton, thought Margot very pretty when they met on holiday at Pontresina, but changed his mind when she showed indifference to his shy overtures. Instead of a fulsome account of the pleasure of her company on their mountain walks, he noted in his diary that Margot's looks were 'spoilt by an upper lip that curls up, shows the teeth and gives a feeling of scorn'.[9] This short upper lip, the unfortunate result of a hunting accident in 1886 when she broke her nose, was perpetually to give those who did not know her the feeling that she was haughty and condescending, whereas in fact she felt nothing but goodwill towards the world in those days, blessed as she was with her full share of vivacity and bounce.

At Charles's large shooting parties Laura and Margot gave themselves the task of looking after their father's guests. When they heard the guns return they would rush downstairs, seize the best looking men and start talking with breathless haste as though time was passing too quickly for all they had to say. The impression they left was of 'the maddest merriest whirl from morn till night—wonderful quickness, wit and cleverness'.[10] To men used to more sedate female company, these two girls seemed the most extraordinary, lively and seductive little creatures they ever saw.

As the sisters grew older Charles's shoots were a life-line that not only joined them to the world beyond their own small horizons but drew that world to Glen. Charles was an excellent host, his hospitality lavish, his game plentiful, his house outstanding in every way for comfort, with Laura and Margot thrown in for entertainment.

Laura received her first serious proposal of marriage at one of these shooting parties when she was barely sixteen, and Margot when not much older. So bemused did the guests become that on several occasions the same man proposed to both girls in turn 'and we had to find out from each other what our intentions were'.[11] Both took it for granted that they would marry young; Laura hoped to find a serious, steady husband to counter the unbalance of her own passionate nature, for she understood herself very well. Margot could not decide what she wanted until she had her hand read by a gypsy who told her that she would marry a man who would one day become Prime Minister.

According to Margot the Tennants were not popular in Peeblesshire, partly because they had no country connections but chiefly because they were Liberals. In their household Mr Gladstone was looked on as the supreme politician. Home Rule and Free Trade were the two maxims by which Charles ordered his political life. He would read to the family passages from the *Daily Chronicle*—the popular Liberal newspaper—to prove how right Gladstone was, and how wrong those who did not follow his wise leadership. As a child Margot learned the useful habit of pretending to listen attentively while her thoughts were far away. Laura, however, although not in the least interested in politics, felt she had to give her father her whole attention; she hated to pretend anything in case she was found out, thus causing hurt feelings. Unlike Margot she never learned to dissemble and spare herself in any way, thereby putting undue strain on her fragile constitution. It was one of the qualities that made her so unusual. This was, perhaps, the greatest difference in the two sisters. A core of toughness in Margot helped her to hold part of herself back, enabling her to weather many a storm.

'Fashion' was slow to reach Peeblesshire and Laura and Margot were not in the least interested in clothes. They wore such an odd assortment of garments, dictated by the extreme cold of that part of Scotland, that they were sometimes mistaken for tinkers' children. Knickerbockers over bulky woollen combinations and liberty bodices, a blouse, a thick jersey topped by a covert coat. Stout boots were an absolute necessity to keep the feet dry, as well as hand-knitted stockings to keep them warm, and the whole was finished off by a scarf wound several times round head and neck. On extra cold days when a cruel 'Russian' wind blew strongly (straight from Siberia the children thought) they would wear a skirt over the knickerbockers for extra protection. 'We were too busy with life to be interested in our appearances'[12] was Margot's lofty explanation of the extraordinary figures they cut.

Margot hated to wear heavy garments, which put too much weight on her fragile bones, but no notice was taken of her complaints and she never remembered a time when she did not suffer discomfort when encased in thick wool day and night, for it itched abominably and made her skin red with heat spots. Winter and summer alike, they wore flannel petticoats and chamois leather lung protectors which restricted their narrow chests and slowed them down, causing unnecessary fatigue and lessening the natural exuberance of childhood. Thick blankets on the bed and windows tight shut made them awake heavy-eyed and miserable. It was Emma's unshakable belief that checked perspiration was the root cause of many serious illness. They were not allowed enough water to slake their thirst either, so that their tempers became brittle and tears were always near the surface.

The sea was not far away, yet they never knew the delights of bathing or the fun of playing barefoot on the sand. Margot kept herself in good health through her passion for riding: 'I love riding like I love existence,' she proclaimed.[13] She never remembered a time when she could not ride, but it was not until she was sixteen and staying with one of her married sisters, Lucy Graham-Smith, at Easton Grey that she went hunting for the first time. It was with the famous Beaufort pack and she distinguished herself by falling heavily, but she got up at once and proceeded to ride so daringly that she attracted the attention of the Master, the Duke of Beaufort, who asked her if she would like to wear the blue and buff habit of the Beaufort hunt. Not understanding that she was being honoured, she did not answer his question, but asked 'Do you always do this sort of thing when you meet anyone like me for the first time?' Amused, the Duke replied, 'Just as it is the first time that you have ever hunted, so it is the first time I have met anyone like you.'[14]

Flying through the air on a big and powerful horse which she could only just handle gave Margot the feeling that she was living life to the full. The excitement of jumping a tricky fence or out-riding everyone else was an experience that went to her head, and once she was heard to say that only fools refused to hunt. Edith (DD) Balfour was one such fool, and Margot looked on her friend's lack of enthusiasm as a serious flaw in her character. Over and over again Margot retold the delights of following hounds, refusing to give up hope that DD's resolution would one day crack and that she would come out with her. 'The pleasures of hunting I don't believe you have had the pleasure of,' she wrote to her friend in the curious style that she affected at that time:

> I cantered home down a grass road, Roman I believe, called the Foss, ten miles the other side, after hunting in the low evening sunlight with the trees lilac and the grass almost like it is in May—it was so delicious all alone. Not knowing my way I took my hat off . . . and like a vagrant who when asked on what principle he steered his way answered—'I always turn my back to the wind' . . . I felt like a caravan child, whistling away the departing day, letting my thoughts wander through a lot of loose matter in my head and settling on to nothing in particular.[15]

This carefully written letter, so unlike Margot's usual unpunctuated scrawl, was intended to show DD that a sporting life did not mean that one became insensitive to the poetic side of nature that DD thought so important.

Margot always considered herself uneducated and felt that this was the only thing that could put her at a disadvantage. She certainly had little formal education since the governesses Emma employed were of the very poorest quality. Their teaching was purgatory to an intelligent child; questions were dismissed as impertinent and time was wasted learning the

names and dates of the Kings and Queens of England and the principal
towns and rivers. Punishment for the slightest misdemeanour was swift
and painful—several raps over the knuckles with a sharp ruler that often
drew blood.

Neither Laura nor Margot would have learned anything at all if Charles
had not given them the run of his magnificent library when they were not
much more than eight or nine. At first they were bewildered by shelf upon
shelf of beautifully bound books and had little idea where to start. With
no one to guide them they dipped into the most indigestible matter and
understood not a word. The works of Rousseau and Lavater's physiog-
nomy did not make for enjoyable reading, volumes on witchcraft, ana-
tomy or astronomy (bought for their rarity) proved not much better and it
was not until they discovered the Brontës, George Eliot and Jane Austen
that they understood the point of reading and were suddenly lost in a
world that was new and exciting. When they discovered Shakespeare for
themselves they delighted so much in the sound of the Sonnets that they
learned some of them by heart, repeating the words to themselves as they
rode their ponies, tramped over the moors or lay sleepless in bed.
Margot's memory, always good, was formed in this way and proved
useful later on when she began to write. After-dinner games were then an
integral part of family life and every member of the household took part as
a matter of course. Since large families were the rule the games did not
depend on guests. 'Styles', 'Epigrams', 'Twenty Questions' and the
daringly frank 'Character Sketches' (which broke up many a friendship)
were amusements in which Laura and Margot excelled. There were, of
course, many others but the Tennant children were loyal to old favourites
which they changed and improved at will.

These games were good training and sharpened their wits, even helped
them to understand the books they read, but did not provide the kind of
hard learning they both pined for and were at just the right age to imbibe.
It is sad to think of two intelligent eager young girls planning a course of
education for themselves, but although haphazard, it had its merits. Their
enthusiasm drew their three married sisters into this ring of self-
education. Posie Gordon Duff was too delicate to do much but Charty
Ribblesdale had always longed to know more history and fired by Laura
and Margot asked George Curzon to recommend a comprehensive book
'that does not reach from here to Australia'.[16] Lucy Graham-Smith, made
to feel that her talent at drawing was not enough, hit upon the idea of

joining a correspondence course in English Literature organized by Glasgow University. Not to be outdone, Margot enrolled for a series of lectures given by Churton Collins, the literary critic, on his favourite poet, Lord Tennyson. She got to the lecture hall early, sat in the front row, took copious notes, and enjoyed herself hugely. Homework was a criticism of 'Maud', a poem Margot doted on, but when seated at her desk her mind was filled with nothing more erudite than half-remembered facts; where had she read that 'Maud' was based on 'a feeling for Shakespeare's Sonnets'? Confidence quickly melted away, so she wrote to George Curzon ('the best educated friend I have') telling him that she would 'like to write a good paper immensely, only doubt my powers'.[17] In 1884, the year before Laura married, the girls discovered Gibbon, but Laura was afraid people would think it shocking that they had come across the historian of the Roman Empire 'so late in life'.[18] They set a high standard for themselves and it paid well. When they began to mingle in London society, they shone more brightly, caused more of a stir and were more in demand than many a famous beauty whose whole existence was absorbed in practising the art of attracting admirers.

When it came to choosing a tutor for his sons Charles was no more astute than Emma, although he had a reputation in the City for being an excellent judge of character. He blithely handed them over to the care of men who turned out to be half-educated and sadistic and damaged the boys mentally and physically. Furious at seeing Frank knocked down by a tutor, Margot rushed to defend him and hit the man over the head with her fists, but got her ears boxed for her pains, while Laura was toppled to the ground. Because Frank Tennant was artistic, sensitive and quiet, he came in for the brunt of his tutor's displeasure and was hit so often that his development was retarded. Eddy and Jack were tougher and stood the beatings better. Margot suffered greatly on her brother's behalf and what she saw made her hate violence all her life. Some years later she wrote grimly: 'When I think of our violent teachers—both tutors and governesses—and what the brothers learned at Eton, I am surprised that we knew as much as we did and my parents' helplessness bewilders me.'[19] Her parents' blindness and lack of common sense in other respects puzzled her too. They worried because Eddy did not grow, but failed to realize that the fault might be theirs. Charles was so proud of his eldest son's prowess with a gun and of his incredible flair for billiards that he would encourage him to tramp miles over the moors at the age of ten 'so that his guests could see for themselves his excellence as a marksman'. Sometimes Charles would even awake him from sleep to give a display of his brilliance at billiards before his admiring friends. Margot felt helpless to protect the brother she adored and who more than the others shared her passion for Glen.

From her earliest years Margot worshipped the house, as did Laura, but not everyone shared their view. When Margot's new London friend, DD Balfour, first saw it she put her nose in the air and said in a superior voice that it was not the genuine thing at all but a modern castle of the most artificial kind. Happening then to look at Margot's stricken face, she added kindly, 'the hills are very lovely'.[20] Margot could just tolerate this, because she liked DD, but when she heard one of her father's guests remark of the Scottish baronial façade 'I hate turrets and tin men on top of them' she was furious.[21] Comfort came from Laura who explained that outsiders could not see what they were privileged to see. In her opinion it was 'the most beautiful place on the whole earth'.[22] But Margot's anger was slow to abate: she had no doubts that Glen was the most perfect home in the most perfect setting in the world; heaven must be like it, and those who did not think the same were fools. Margot was to love other houses passionately, but none save Glen was to be a refuge from the storms of life. Ill, worried, out of sorts with herself and the world, she would rush home to Glen even if it was empty, to be made well again. Her depressions would lift, her sleeplessness go away the moment she was back in her bed at the top of the house or lying on the sofa by the window, drinking in the sense of peace that came to her merely by staring at the great stretches of heather that swept right up to the garden walls. She called herself a child of the heather and liked to quote Emerson: 'Human nature is everywhere the same but the wilder it is the more virtuous.'[23]

Living in this wild and desolate spot, remote from civilization, she believed herself to be different from other children and of course better: she was Margot Tennant, a superior being, because she lived at Glen. She was a wild child, because of it, and she identified herself with the peasants and gypsies who roamed the moors, doing a bit of poaching here and there. She knew them all and would stop and talk, but she never betrayed them by a single hint, even if she saw them net a fish and shoot pheasants. They were her friends. Years later, when describing Glen, she said it was 'always mellow, always green' for, looking back over a long passage of time, this is how she remembered it; the 'wildness' had diminished. Yet frequently it was very wild indeed; the rain pelted against the window panes, making them rattle and shake and the fierce howling of the wind as it roared round the house sent shivers of delightful terror through Laura and Margot as they wondered if the roof would hold. It did, but the damage to trees and shrubs could be severe. At these times when Glen was lashed by storms, Margot would become almost uncontrollable, but it was partly an act, brought on perhaps by nerves jangled by the continual noise. Had she wished, she could easily have taken herself in hand; but she liked to behave as though she was as untamable as the wind. Her behaviour affected Laura, making her by contrast quiet and still. Nevertheless, their steadier brothers complained that they were 'more like lions than sisters'.[24]

All her life Margot was sincerely and deeply preoccupied with religion. It was quite natural for her to pray, often with intense fervour, whenever she felt like it, either alone or with Laura. If she did not go to church on Sunday, the omission weighed on her conscience, and at all great moments of her life she never failed to fall on her knees. This was all the more surprising since there was no religious teaching in the home, no Bible stories were read in the nursery and Emma did not follow the normal routine of most Victorian mothers, of hearing her children's nightly prayers. From her story books Margot knew this was done in most homes and it concerned her that perhaps her mother was different from other mothers, did not believe in prayer and never prayed herself. The idea shocked and upset her for she was afraid that this was the downward path to damnation, but she was too shy to say so and was comforted to find that Laura had never harboured such a dreadful thought. It was Laura who gave Margot her feeling of reverence and godliness. Not for nothing did a close friend say that Laura had one foot in heaven and the other on earth. Laura was, Margot says, 'the most truly spiritual person I have ever met, with a feeling of intimacy with the other world and the sense of love and wisdom of God and plan of life'.[25] Although she admired Laura's willingness to submit to misfortune, she could neither understand nor follow her example. If Laura was right and life on earth was transitory Margot privately decided that she must get everything out of it while she could.

To think of others before herself did not come naturally to Margot. She had to work at it or earn Laura's disapproval, whereas before Laura was sixteen she was teaching at a girls' Friendly Society, holding Sunday School classes for mill-girls in the housekeeper's room at Glen and visiting the old and sick in the village either with her mother or alone, without ever once being told to do so.

As children, the girls liked attending the Kirk at Traquair, sitting in the family pew each Sunday and listening to the sermon (although it was delivered in a dialect they could scarcely understand), while Charles brought shame on them by dozing peacefully like the sheepdogs that lay at their masters' feet. The conventions of Sunday were observed even at Glen. It was the gloomiest day of the week and Margot hated it. There was no ludo, draughts or chess, no exercising the horses and no rough games in the garden—not even quarrelling was allowed, but this was too tall an order to be kept. Yet Margot felt compelled to observe these taboos and she was upset to find that Charty and her husband regularly played tennis on a Sunday. Since Laura evidently did not think her younger sister's heart was in good works, Margot defiantly started a Sunday School class of her own and was quite happy until she chanced upon an unposted letter from Laura to Posie in the pocket of a dress of Laura's she was wearing: 'Does it not seem extraordinary that Margot should be teaching a Sunday class?' Bursting into tears, she rushed upstairs to hide in a small dark cupboard, her usual refuge when life overwhelmed her.[26] Margot admired Laura with all her heart and when she compared her sister's successful efforts to influence people for good with her own, she knew she fell far short of Laura's standards.

CHAPTER 2

A Taste of Freedom

IN 1879 AND 1880 two events occurred which were to open doors into the great world outside Glen. Charles was elected unopposed as Liberal MP for one of the Glasgow constituencies in 1879, and as a Member of Parliament he acquired a status he could never have achieved through his business interests alone. Allowing his natural acumen to compensate for his lack of political experience, he made his mark in politics as quickly as he had in business. Next year he was invited to stand for Peebles and Selkirk against a Tory who had held the seat for twenty-eight years, and won a remarkable victory; his plain, even blunt, oratory put across his Liberal views in language his audience could understand and his radicalism (he advocated an elective House of Lords) appealed wholeheartedly to the people.

This was the year in which Gladstone, who sat for the neighbouring constituency of Midlothian, conducted the famous campaign which became such a landmark in party history. There was great excitement in the Tennant family when Charles was asked to put up Mrs Gladstone and Lord Rosebery for the night before Gladstone was to speak at a meeting in Glasgow. Charles revered Gladstone almost as a god, and had impressed his uniqueness on the whole family.* Now he determined that his children should not miss the chance of hearing 'the greatest orator that ever lived, so that in years to come we would be able to tell our grandchildren of the event'.[1]

The mere idea that she was going to hear Mr Gladstone speak made

---

* Only once did Margot dare to oppose Gladstone's political opinions in her father's hearing. She and Laura were dining downstairs one night to help entertain Lord Spencer when Gladstone's views on Ireland came up in the conversation. In a clear voice Margot cut in with 'His Home Rule policy is a Balaclava blunder', for which she was banished to the business room to cure her cheek. There she took her revenge by smoking one of Charles's best cigars.

Margot tremble with excitement and she lay awake all night, every now and then leaning over to the next bed and poking the sleeping Laura so that they could talk. Yet despite her wakeful night she was bright and full of energy next morning, while Laura was pale and drawn.

The girls knew very well who Lord Rosebery was; the papers were frequently full of his parliamentary outbursts, for he had a reputation as a colourful character who attracted the limelight. That night when they were changing into their best dresses and Margot in her petticoat with a shawl round her shoulders was having her hair brushed, the door of the 'Doocot' (the girls' sitting-room) opened and in walked Lord Rosebery, his arms full of grapes and chocolates. Only for a moment were they taken aback, then they rushed at him, seized his arms and dragged him into the room. In a letter to Mary Gladstone soon after, he called Laura and Margot, 'little quaint romping girls, smuggling themselves into the public meeting at Glasgow and turning up with bright demure faces in un-expected places'.[2] Rosebery left to dine with the Lord Provost and presently they were in the carriage and away. St Andrew's Hall was packed to the doors, a notice 'Standing room only' outside. The dingy hall was transformed: the blue and yellow Liberal colours floated from lamps and pillars, the walls were plastered with slogans: 'Free Trade for all!' 'Home Rule for Ireland!' Lord Rosebery and Charles Tennant sported huge rosettes and two of these gorgeous emblems were handed to the girls. All of a sudden the hubbub died down and there was absolute silence as Mr Gladstone and his retinue processed slowly up the hall to the platform. Then just as suddenly the thunder of applause broke out and rose higher and higher until it seemed to the two excited girls as though the roof must fall in. The atmosphere was so charged with emotion that Laura and Margot were afraid to look at each other in case of bursting into tears. They were too dazed to take in a word of the speeches, although the voices of the speakers penetrated their minds like music, while the words hung in the air, mere meaningless notes.[3]

It was the first of many such meetings for Margot, who in due course became hardened to the cheers, the boos and hisses and rough heckling, but never again did she recapture the magic and delight of that first campaign.

'Why cannot Papa invite some young men to Glen?' was the perpetual wail of Laura and Margot, who had by now become thoroughly bored with helping to entertain their father's middle-aged friends. Charles refused to listen until Emma convinced him that unless he was willing for his daughters to marry grooms he must do as they asked and invite just a few eligible young men to his shoots. After that timely warning Margot noticed that at the next house-party the age of their guests had crept noticeably downwards. Thus began friendships with men who were later to be among the most distinguished in England: Arthur Balfour, George Wyndham, George Curzon, Mark Napier, the Lyttelton brothers and many others. As the years passed, 'Our standard of success was so high,' wrote Margot, 'that nothing short of Sir William Harcourt dancing or Lord Acton becoming spontaneous satisfied us.'[4] In such company the after-dinner games which had kept Laura and Margot amused for years took on a new lease of life and became a serious business that sharpened the wits, improved memory and increased imagination. It did much for the sisters' self-confidence to find that they could compete on equal terms with highly educated young men and even vanquish them.

For years it had been Emma's habit to go to bed punctually at eleven. Her departure was the signal for a general rush to the girls' quarters at the top of the house, where the stage was set for a discussion on books, politics, religion and current affairs. The sisters conducted the 'salon' sitting up in bed looking enchanting in lace bedjackets with ribbons in their hair. The lights were dimmed, the fire made up and the chintz curtains drawn against the night. Laura scattered cushions over the floor for their guests to sit on, since there were not nearly enough chairs to go round.

To begin with the men were taken aback by such extraordinary freedom but quickly adapted to it, and before long the lack of chaperonage even began to seem natural. Nobody came to interrupt these night sessions, to order lights out or to sweep the men from the rooms.[5] It was impossible to fault the girls' behaviour, and soon even the most timid and conventional of men were won over by Bohemianism that was as transparently innocent as it was socially daring. Everything was carefully stage-managed. Laura and Margot kept the conversation in their own hands, only talking about subjects they understood and seeking to impress by frequent literary allusions. Conversation never flagged and no one, however shy, was left out. Their chronicler, Adolphus Liddell, a quiet man by nature, drank it all in and described the scene in long letters to his sister: 'Books, hunting prints, a crucifix with a fald-stool beneath for prayer, a skull on a shelf and a collecting-box for the East End poor on a table between the two beds. An extraordinary mixture of sport, literature and virtue.'[6] The talk was so scintillating that Algernon West, Mr Gladstone's private secretary, actually thought of taking notes, but he was drawn so closely into the discussion that there was no time because 'life at Glen, though somewhat startling to an early Victorian, caused a joy of eventful living that I never thought could exist, except in a book'.[7]

It was the unanimous opinion that the girls were 'spontaneous, enthusiastic, warm and virtuous', although Margot liked to shock at times in order to give the impression that they would stop at nothing. Laura was uneasy after she had heard that they were considered 'fast'. But Margot told her not to be absurd and consulted an older friend, Godfrey Webb, who reassured her with an odd phrase: people who were easily shocked were like 'old women who sell stale pastry in Cathedral towns'. She wrote in her diary, 'he advised us to take no notice whatever of what people said',[8] sound sense that fitted in perfectly with Margot's inclinations. Some years later she gave what she felt to be sufficient explanation of the custom: 'It was unthinkable that men and women friends, who wanted to stay up, should not be allowed to join us.'[9]

To Margot, it was a new idea that people could be so unreasonable as to misunderstand their motives, and her only concern was that the slur on their characters made Laura tremble. But she put Laura's nervousness down to Mary Gladstone, who was fast becoming Laura's 'best friend'. The last time Mary had come to Glen, Margot had noticed a certain pursing of her lips to register disapproval of the sisters' conduct. Mary's upbringing was typical of her generation—conventional enough to make her narrow-minded. She wrote to her cousin Lavinia from Glen that it was 'strange after watching the girls show real piety at Kirk on Sunday, praying on their knees before the altar longer than anyone else, less than an hour later to come across a sketch of Margot, quite without drapery, openly displayed on a table in the drawing-room. "Isn't it beautiful" Laura exclaimed. "Margot did it from herself in the looking glass." '[10] As usual Laura and Margot reacted quite differently: Margot furious with indignation, Laura worried. Laura asked tremulously if the nude female figure was indecent? If so, why were classical statues always nude?

Since Mary showed a marked preference for Laura, it was not difficult for Margot to guess that she herself was supposed to be the bad influence. She did not mind in the least for she disliked many things about Mary and was never quite at ease in her presence, mainly because she felt that Mary was mentally criticizing her the whole time. That was why only Laura was invited to Hawarden, only Laura was invited to cruise with the Gladstones on Sir Daniel Currie's yacht, and why 'Auntie Pussy' (as the girls called Mrs Gladstone) encouraged her husband to take Margot to a quiet corner of the drawing-room for a 'little talk' when the Gladstones called at 35 Grosvenor Square, the house Charles had bought after his election to Parliament.[11] In fact the old man delighted in Margot's vivacity and charm and was never known to be averse to being dragged away from dreary conversation to enjoy Margot's 'wonderful quickness, wit and cleverness'.[12]

Only in 1889, after Laura's death, was Margot at last invited to Hawarden. She did not improve relations between herself and Mary when she cunningly manoeuvred to spend more time with Mr Gladstone than with the family. She was a fascinated spectator as he cut down trees and read mouse-like in his study when he worked on a speech or sat on his knee (she was twenty-five!) while he recited poetry. Under Margot's guidance he turned his hand to versifying and did so well that after her departure he sent her several stanzas all about herself. Here are two:

> When Parliament ceases and comes the recess
> And we seek in the country rest after distress
> As a rule upon visitors place an embargo
> But make an exception in favour of Margot.

> For she brings such a treasure of movement and life
> Fun, spirit and stir to folk weary of strife.
> Though young and though fair, who can hold such a cargo
> Of all the good qualities going as Margot.[13]

In 1881 Laura and Margot were separated for six months. Laura, now eighteen, was to have a London season, while the seventeen-year-old Margot went to study in Dresden. The decision to part them was due to a remark Godfrey Webb made in Emma's presence: 'the effect on London of the two of them would be devastating'.

When told of the plan Margot was desolate; she minded more than Laura, who was looking forward to her first taste of London society and never once said a word about missing her sister. If Margot found this hurtful, she never mentioned it, for she was always unselfish where Laura was concerned and now tried to enter enthusiastically into discussions about how many ball-gowns Laura would need, and how many new pairs of shoes—as though Laura was going to be married and this was her trousseau, Margot thought crossly.

The girls were not rivals in any sense; each longed for the other to succeed and Margot even managed to derive pleasure by thinking how her beautiful sister would take London by storm. Laura's appearance belied her strong character. Small, delicate and graceful, she was irresistible to women as well as men. Her large grey-blue eyes that easily filled with tears gave the impression to those who did not know her that she was very much in need of protection, which was not at all the case. Her nature was passionate and sexually mature. Possibly her high sexuality was related to the disease from which she suffered, but at this period her tuberculosis was still undiagnosed. Only one person understood exactly what Laura was like, and that was Margot, who feared for her sister in London without her protection. She knew, too, that Laura worried about this side of her character, which she was afraid that she might not be able to control one day. But the most she ever ventures to say about Laura in her writings is that she was 'no plaster saint'.[14]

Mary Gladstone, Laura's 'best friend', worried endlessly about her, and appointed herself her guardian angel. Unlike Margot, however, she only had half the puzzle in her hands and could not imagine the reason for the duality of this strange and enigmatic girl's nature, but could only describe her as 'one moment the life and soul of the party, the next an altered being with the curious inscrutable weird far-off look, so sad, so tearful, her face small and pale and pitiful as a suffering child's, you could simply cry by looking at her'.[15] After Laura's cruise with the Gladstones on the *Pembroke Castle* in 1882, Mary wrote of Laura to her cousin Lavinia Lyttelton: 'Her sense of fun and enthusiasm sometimes led her into daring expressions, dangerously near forbidden ground.'[16]

When she was able to put her worries about Laura behind her, Margot could not help feeling mounting excitement at the thought of living free and unfettered in a foreign town. She came to love Dresden and her life there, and it is surprising that she makes so little of it in her memoirs. The fun of real independence—her own friends, her own key, her own room—was very precious to her, because she knew it could not last. Even if she only learned a few halting words of German, it was worth going to Dresden for the feeling of complete freedom.

The plan to give Margot six months abroad was sounder than its execution. Excellent lodgings with a cultivated widow who had seen better days, Frau von Mach, were found for her by a German friend of her father's, but that was as far as 'arrangements' went. Her parents made no attempt to ask Frau von Mach to find a good teacher to provide German lessons, and it was left to the seventeen-year-old Margot to devise a timetable entirely for herself, so that her six months should not be wasted. The timetable included two hours' practice on the piano and violin every morning. If Frau von Mach had not spoken good English and had not had a band of jolly students staying in her house, Margot might have returned home as ignorant of the German language as she had come.

Her journey to Dresden was the first and last Margot ever enjoyed. She was never a great traveller, and in a list she once compiled of her pet hates she put her dislike of the sea first. She always felt ill on board ship, she said; Mary put this down to affectation, but her fear of the sea was real and painful and she could not overcome it. Yet on her first journey alone the moment she stepped off the boat train and walked up the gangway to the channel steamer, she never gave a thought to the seasickness, storms or drowning that so haunted her later on. Crossing the German frontier, where strange voices made unintelligible sounds, was pure delight. She fell in love with Dresden and all things German at first sight, a love affair that lasted all her life.

It was while in Germany that Margot began to develop an individual style of dressing that was very much her own. Striking and expensive, her clothes were the one thing she never grudged spending money on, saying very rightly that first impressions mattered.[17] In her widowhood, when she thought herself poor, she wore nothing but black dresses, usually expensively made, long and flowing with matching toques in which she looked remarkably regal. Her friends laughed when she said dressing that way was an enormous saving. But at seventeen and on her own in Dresden the thought of saving money never entered her head. One day she went into a dressmaking establishment on impulse and in her imperfect German ordered a full-length scarlet cloak. It never occurred to her that the outfit was daring and might give strangers a false impression. Walking home in the dark after a performance of *Die Meistersinger*, she was followed by an officer in the white uniform of the Prussian Guard whom she had noticed sitting in a box just opposite her.

I heard the even steps and the click of spurs . . . I should not have noticed this had I not halted under a lamp to pull on my hood which the wind had blown off. When I stopped the steps also stopped. I walked on wondering if it had been my imagination and again I heard the click of spurs coming nearer. The street being deserted, I was unable to endure it any longer; I turned round and there was the officer. His black cloak hanging loosely round his shoulders showed me the white uniform and silver belt. He saluted me and asked me in a curious Belgian French if he might accompany me home.[18]

She had been mistaken for a tart!

Margot had been in Dresden for some weeks before Emma woke up to the unpleasant thought that her daughter might fall in love and elope with one of the young Germans staying in Frau von Mach's lodging house. She wrote to Frau von Mach with the preposterous request that she should please not take any men lodgers while Margot was in her house. Emma had forgotten her own mother's lean times as a deserted wife on a small income and seemed to have no idea that taking lodgers was the German woman's only means of existence.[19] Margot was deeply distressed to find her kindly landlady in tears and wrote home forthwith in very plain terms. But the jolt showed her how wealth and ease of living can act as a cushion against the realities of life.

After her return to England Margot spent the summer at Glen, 'resting' in preparation for her first London season, which she had come to look on with distaste. She knew that its purpose was to catch a rich husband, for Charles had said, only half in fun, that he wanted the girls to marry millionaires who could keep them in the style to which they were accustomed. But at eighteen Margot had no intention of marrying for many years yet. Meanwhile she threw herself with zest into the familiar routine of life in the Scottish countryside, riding all day and sleeping well at night. Happily reunited with her sister, Margot relived for Laura all her adventures in Germany. To heighten the affect she exaggerated here and there. What harm was there in adding a little extra glamour to her picture of Dresden as a sophisticated city, the Mecca of the famous in the musical world? She possessed in full measure the dramatist's instinct to make a plain tale more exciting and it never occurred to her that exaggeration of this kind might be looked upon as a form of lying.

Poor Laura had a different tale to tell. Her season had been disappointing, invitations had been slow in coming because Mama knew too few people, and she had only glimpsed the glittering scene occasionally and from the outside. Although Margot knew nothing of London society, she refused to believe that it was unassailable. Secretly she felt Laura would have done better if she, Margot, had been allowed to manage her season instead of leaving everything to her mother. She had yet to learn that Society was just as Laura said: brilliant, rich, snobbish and enclosed. It was also exceedingly dull, an eternal round of pleasure within a small exclusive circle, where the same people met each other day·after day. The women were all supposed to be 'beauties', perfectly dressed, perfectly groomed and overloaded with jewels. They only had to appear for men to fall down and worship. 'Beauties' were to look at adoringly, they had no need to make the slightest effort. Few girls of seventeen and eighteen were allowed a look-in, and most of them quailed at the mere thought of competing with Lady de Grey, Lady Dudley, Lady Londonderry and Mrs Cornwallis-West. The Prince and Princess of Wales were the acknowledged leaders and gave lavish balls and receptions at Marlborough House to which Laura had not been invited, so that she was only too glad to return to the security of Glen.

The first few weeks in London did not go well for Margot either, despite her self-assurance and the company of Laura, who had come along to show her sister the ropes. Charles's magnificent dance for her was filled with too many of what Margot called 'middle-aged men' in their thirties and forties. Mr Gladstone opened the ball with her, an honour that did not exactly make Margot swoon with excitement. At her next ball she danced a quadrille 'with a mediocre member of Parliament' and for the rest of the evening she and Laura—who had fared no better—stood watching, wondering if they were always to be cast for the role of wallflowers. 'We did not mind being spectators, since we were together,' Margot wrote bravely in her diary. 'We had a great deal to discuss and observe in the gay illuminated crowd of beautiful strangers . . . I reminded Laura of those moments later on when she was the centre of almost universal attention.'[20] It was unthinkable that Margot would endure this treatment for long. Pleading lassitude from lack of exercise she persuaded her father to buy her a first-rate thoroughbred horse, so that she could ride every day in the Row and be noticed. Wearing a top hat and a jacket as tight-fitting as Mrs Langtry's, every morning at the fashionable hour of

eleven she trotted into the Row where her striking appearance quickly
drew the eyes of the crowd, who pressed their noses against the railings in
order to see her better. It was now that her hunting friends came in useful.
One morning Lady Waterford, the Duke of Beaufort's daughter, recognized the lone rider as the attractive stranger who had showed such
courage when hunting with the Beaufort, and invited Margot to dine the
following week. At the dinner she was placed between the Earl of
Pembroke and Mr Arthur Balfour. At once Balfour turned his quizzical
eyes on her, disconcerting her a little by saying in a bored voice that he
detested work, adored leisure and always left everything to chance,
adding that he found nothing so absorbing as his own health. She
managed to make some sort of a reply and summed him up accurately in
her diary that night as 'a self-indulgent man of simple tastes'. Lord
Pembroke was easier to get on with. Older, married and with children, he
indulgently gave Margot a chance to show off a little, talking to her about
books and music of which after Dresden she knew enough to be able to
sound quite knowledgeable, and after a rather poor start she managed to
hold the attention of both these sophisticated men throughout the rest of
dinner. It was an achievement few girls of her age could claim so early in
her first season. Lord Pembroke sent a note across the table to Blanche
Waterford asking her the name of 'the girl with red heels'.[21]

Her presentation day was not the high spot she had hoped for, although
she had taken trouble with her appearance and looked almost beautiful in
an off-the-shoulder dress of cream satin, which showed up the pearl
choker her father had given her. Nipped in at the waist, the dress had a
train caught up here and there with bunches of artificial snowdrops. Her
appearance gave her so much confidence that she was not at all upset
when, after a careful scrutiny, Emma said in a gloomy voice, 'Your dress is
not very becoming, but no one will notice you.' It was disappointing, after
she had taken so much trouble, to find the drawing-room tedious. The
young girls were nervous and the royal family looked bored, a sharp
contrast to the rest of the entertaining that season. Moreover, she felt
ridiculous dressed in elaborate evening clothes on a beautiful June
morning, merely in order to curtsey to a fat little old lady who never
smiled and looked as though she could not wait for the ceremony to be
over.

Suddenly invitations began to arrive at 35 Grosvenor Square. A new
friend, Frances Graham, who was organizing a bazaar, roped Margot in

to help raise money for charity. Margot worked so hard and was so successful that the older more disapproving members of society (who had heard of the bedroom sessions) were quite won over. An idea of hers that turned out to have a two-fold purpose was to write to well-known people asking for a signed photograph to sell at her stall. A disarming letter to each brought results. Who, after all, could resist a request that asked: 'Please send me your photo signed to sell at my stall. I am getting all my famous friends to give me their signatures.' To the poet Wilfrid Scawen Blunt she went further, flattering him blatantly by saying 'You are kind as well as clever, which is rare'—Margot never believed in half measures. To another she said that 'a photograph signed by you will sell well'. St Loe Strachey was asked to recommend 'a light little play for three women and four or five men. Do send me the names of a few that have movement and sparkle in them'. Evidently Strachey responded well, for a second letter invited him to Grosvenor Square for lunch at 2 o'clock although 'the house is all in curl papers, the service execrable but I have heard much about you and would like you to come'.[22] Curiosity, if no other reason, must have driven him to Grosvenor Square and its extraordinary inmates. Margot had a nose for interesting people and she never dropped those who had been kind and helpful in a charity project.

As the season wore on, Emma grew tired of acting chaperone and returned to her old habit of going to bed at eleven. For appearances' sake Margot's brother Eddy was asked to take her place. Eddy hated dances more than Emma and since both he and Margot had latch-keys he soon left Margot to look after herself. But Eddy had to promise to take her to Ascot. With some difficulty they obtained tickets for the Royal enclosure, where they met Lady Dalhousie who, knowing Margot's interest in horses, took her to the paddock. There she was presented to the Prince of Wales, who promptly said she must have luncheon with him.

He asked me if I would back my fancy for the Wokingham stakes and have a little bet with him on the races. We walked down to the rails and watched the horses gallop past. One of them went down in great form. I verified him by his colours and found he was called Wokingham. I told the Prince that he was a sure winner; but out of so many entries no one was more surprised than I was when my horse came romping in.[23]

The Prince sent her a gold cigarette case, but Margot was far more thrilled to discover that after that happy encounter in the paddock, she was invited as a matter of course to all the great houses, and that when the Prince of Wales was present (which was almost always) he never failed to talk and dance with her.[24]

Even by the standards of those days, when every fashionable woman changed at least three times between breakfast and dinner, Margot had a tremendous number of dresses for her first season. The juvenile and the merely pretty did not appeal to her, as it did to so many young girls. She filled her wardrobe with such striking garments that even if she had not been the personality she was, her clothes alone would have made her stand out. In a roomful of pale butterflies, she could not fail to catch the eye in her black tulle trimmed with red cherries, a diamond brooch pinned below one shoulder. The dress was cut in the new unfussy style (always much favoured by Margot) invented by Monsieur Worth, the rotund little designer who was just setting out on the career which transformed him from a shop-walker in Derry and Toms into the most sought-after couturier in Europe. It was a style that suited Margot's small angular figure, and gave her the delicious feeling that her dress was unlike any other in the room.

Only two of Worth's creations for her were in the traditional white, her presentation gown and the one she wore for the dance her parents gave for her in 35 Grosvenor Square. The others were mostly in dark colours, very unusual for young girls in those days: black chiffon and tulle worn with red shoes; grey with black spots and a wide-brimmed black hat with a huge red rose for Ascot; pale grey or white with a grey felt hat trimmed with white feathers; a dark red dress with puffed sleeves and low neck for an important dinner. These innovations heralded a change in fashion in England, brought about by an eighteen-year-old girl who could wear Worth's clothes with dash and style, as well as by the great man himself, who was fortunate to find so young and striking a figure able to show off his creations.

From the first Worth gave Margot the assurance with which to fight the domination of the great beauties, women who relied on their looks alone.[25] The black dress brought her a new acquaintance. Unknown to Margot, her diamond brooch fell from her shoulder during a spirited waltz and was picked up and restored to its owner by Prince George (later

George V) who knew at once whose it was because it had shown up so clearly against the dark material. He told her that a few days before he had noticed her riding in the Row.[26]

The intense desire to be noticed—pursued, it must be owned, with single-mindedness and tenacity—had brought its reward. Margot's dynamic and witty personality, Laura's sweetness and charm, soon made an enormous impression and long before the end of the season a party that did not include the Tennant sisters was unthinkable; as soon leave the bubble out of champagne. But some who did not know her well thought otherwise. For instance, Arthur Benson was scathing in his criticism of the Tennants, and talked of the girls 'screaming themselves into society'; 'there is something vulgar about the Tennants'.[27] Benson could not know that, apart from the delightful personalities of the girls themselves, Margot's début happened to coincide with social changes among the upper classes. Fashionable people were no less snobbish than of old, but in the last two decades of the century wealth was replacing birth as the criterion for social acceptance. Lady Frances Balfour, who was of the old school, shook her head sadly at the changes. Her views of society were very strictly defined: 'Good society was composed of people who knew how to behave, were well-bred and felt their obligations to live according to the position in which they were placed. Certain things were not done, certain people not received.' But stiff and old-fashioned though she was, she was also fair and generous when she wrote in 1884 her final word on the movement of change that undoubtedly came 'with a family highly gifted, of totally unconventional manners with no code of behaviour except their own good hearts, the young women of the Tennant family'.[28]

Chapter 3

Garish Flowers and Wild and Careless Weeds

Because they were now accepted members of society, in future Laura and Margot met everybody of importance as a matter of course. Henceforth Margot had more invitations than she could accept. She liked to go to tea-parties where only women were present and the talk no more than gossip, for she enjoyed the company of her own sex and always leaned heavily on her female friends when she was ill or upset. Many earlier acquaintanceships now began to take a new position of warmth and trust in her life. It was at a female tea-party in Belgrave Square that she met Maggie and Betty Ponsonby, the daughters of Queen Victoria's Private Secretary. Two years before, the girls had sat next to Margot at a political meeting in Glasgow when Charles was the principal speaker. But at sixteen Margot was too keen on riding, Maggie and Betty too wrapped up in their intellectual pursuits, for anything as positive as friendship to blossom. Since then Maggie had become an advanced Radical of decided views which she never hesitated to air, despite her father's closeness to the throne. Betty was more homely, did not care for furious debate and shrank from the merest hint of a quarrel. So it was natural that Maggie should pair off with Margot and Betty with Laura. It was the first time that Margot had a real friend of her own who was not her sister, a girl whose wit and humour she shared.

The Ponsonby sisters knew everybody and were only too happy to introduce Laura and Margot to their friends, among them a girl who was to become important in Margot's life. Frances Graham already knew Laura, for they had met while convalescing at St Moritz. The two families had dined together every night at the Kulm Hotel, danced into the early hours[1]—reckless behaviour that nevertheless brought about a cure.

Frances was already bored with the season and wanted to go home and do something serious with her life. She was a friend of William and Jane Morris, the Rossettis and Ruskin, favoured long flowing dresses, piled her uncurled hair naturally on top of her head, and wore no constricting garments of any kind.[2] She laughed in the kindest way at Margot spending so much money with M. Worth, but Margot strongly defended her extravagance, saying 'Clothes are the first thing to catch the eye'. Although Frances Graham was so different, Margot admired her very much, especially her determination not to allow her talents to run to seed. Her warmth of heart and strong character made a great appeal, as did her generosity of spirit. 'With most women,' Margot wrote, 'the impulse to crab is greater than to praise and grandeur of character is surprisingly absent from them; but Frances Horner* comprises all that is best in my sex.'[3]

Margot came to look on Frances as a sister and later the friendship was cemented by the marriage of Frances's daughter and Margot's eldest stepson Raymond.

When the season was over at the end of July Margot went to stay for a few days in the country with the well-known hostess Lady Manners and her husband 'Hoppy'. Lady Manners was much taken with Margot and tried to persuade her to spend the summer with them at Biarritz, but Margot refused; she longed, she said, to get back to Glen. But there was another reason for her refusal that she could not mention, and it shows how even at eighteen she had more than her share of steadiness and common sense: the Manners favoured the Prince of Wales's rich gambling set which bored Margot to distraction and of which she very much disapproved.

But she revelled in country-house parties, then such a feature of English social life. After the late nights and noise of London, the calm of a comfortable, well-run house soothed a nervous system which, she had come to realize, was too highly strung for comfort. At Gosford, Stanway or Clouds, no one ever raised their voices in anger, argued loudly, slammed doors or cried with vexation. Yet the guests were frequently people of decided views who had read widely and talked well. Influenced by the atmosphere of calm and amused tolerance, Margot was content to speak as quietly as the others and to refrain from argument, yet contribute very effectively to the conversation. The fact that she could appear detached yet forceful on any subject where she felt passionately, was a revelation to herself. Without competition she lost the desire to shout at

* Frances Graham had meanwhile married John Horner.

the top of her voice in order to get the better of her opponent, as she did with Laura.

In these surroundings, filled with sophisticated people who all knew each other well, she discovered she had a chance to reflect on her own feelings and in so doing learned another important fact about herself: she preferred older men and was more at ease with them than with boys of her own age. Totally unselfconscious, she was like a breath of fresh air to most world-weary men with too much leisure. Because she was not beautiful she knew she had to make greater efforts to be noticed. She did not expect attention without giving something in return, nor did she put on airs; on the contrary, she was natural, enthusiastic and intelligent. It was impossible to enjoy the kind of freedom Laura and Margot took for granted without causing talk, but once people got to know them criticism evaporated and invitations to Grosvenor Square and Glen were eagerly sought after. All that summer of 1882 admirers flocked to Peeblesshire so that half the time Emma did not know who was sitting at her table; but she had to accept what she was told by her husband, that their daughters' friends were among the most interesting in London. Lady Frances Balfour, now completely won over, wrote in her reminiscences that by the end of the season 'it was unnatural if every young man did not propose to Laura and Margot after a few hours' acquaintance', and that 'they got distinctly confused concerning the identity of those who had not proposed, but certainly enjoyed the delights of their society'.[4] Of course not everyone admired so wholeheartedly. The Earl of Pembroke, who was both old-fashioned and a little hidebound, had met Margot frequently in the course of the last six months and was appalled at her uninhibited ways, especially with men. He had noticed that she always travelled by train alone and did not take her maid with her on country-house visits. In his opinion she was allowed too much freedom of speech, for nothing lost friendships faster than plain speaking, a fact Margot never quite understood. Pembroke admired her lack of vanity, but she had yet to learn how much unhappiness could come from a lack of self-control. He wrote her a letter couched in sentimental, even romantic, terms, to warn her of those faults that he feared might bring unhappiness in their train:

Keep the outer borders of your heart's sweet garden free from garish flowers and wild and careless weeds, so that when your fairy godmother turns the prince's footsteps your way he may not, distrusting your nature or his own powers, and only half glancing at the treasure within, tear himself reluctantly away and pass sadly on without perhaps your ever knowing that he had been near.[5]

The warning was accepted good-naturedly, for Margot always said of herself that she was not touchy. She took his words to heart. ' "Garish flowers and wild and careless weeds" described my lack of pruning,' she wrote years later in a burst of honesty. She memorized the warning so charmingly couched and even copied it into her diary. But fearing that he might have offended the young girl, George Pembroke sent her a carefully chosen present to take the sting out of his words: Butcher and Lang's translation of the *Odyssey*. He hoped that this would show her that in spite of his severity he nevertheless thought highly of her intellect, and he wrote on the flyleaf: 'To Margot who most reminds me of Homeric days.'

Margot's relationship with Laura was the most intimate and perfect of her whole life. Generously she acknowledged that her sister was far prettier, cleverer and more fascinating than anyone she had ever met, an opinion that was shared by most people who knew them both. Although the younger of the two, Margot had an almost maternal instinct to protect Laura from the disappointments of the world, for she was often alarmed at the contradiction between Laura's emotions and her spirituality, a contradiction which often racked her body and troubled her mind, so that Margot hoped that she would marry some understanding young man who could be a safety-valve for her emotions.

Because Emma found it difficult to manage her two high-spirited daughters when she had them together at home, she separated them more and more from the time they entered their teens. Even birthdays, once so sacred, were now often spent apart. On Laura's twentieth birthday Margot was at Melbury, hunting in her usual daredevil fashion, but she did not forget her sister altogether.

Darling Sweet,
    It seems rather sad to think you are all alone. Twenty is such a nice age. In some ways the glamour of birthdays is over, it no longer means a red-letter day to oneself and others, but in some ways it means more and you dilate and glow with an inward satisfaction and your whole being at peace with God and man. I pray you may live to repeat many

birthdays and watch the last swallows dip round the snow and feel the
soft damp autumn air blow round your temples for many years to come
. . . Darling Laura, there is nothing new for me to wish you, you deserve
to be happy if any one does and I hope you always will be strong, useful,
active, influential and above all happy, happy, happy.[6]

Despite Laura's occasional ill health, which gave cause for concern to the
whole family, Margot was thoroughly content with her life. Later on, she
was to look back on these as the years which the locusts had eaten.
Enjoyment when it is excessive and without the balancing influence of
hard work becomes self-indulgence and begins to cloy, but at the time
Margot did not feel this. Nothing in her life had changed since childhood
and nothing had become stale to her. Autumn and winter were spent in
the saddle; she was out in the sun, wind and storm, and her skin, the pallor
of which had once been remarked on as one of her beauties, was becoming
quite weatherbeaten, but she had never given her appearance a thought.
Every spring, she and Laura moved from Glen with their parents to
Grosvenor Square for the season and more fun and enjoyment. 'And so we
spent four years of uninterrupted intimacy, discussing life, love and
literature, reading together, praying together, laughing and crying
together.'[7]

    This ideal existence could not go on for ever. Laura understood her own
nature very well and wanted to marry if she could find the right man, for
she did not intend to spend the rest of her life with a husband who was
frivolous and fell easily in and out of love. For four years she had indulged
in light affairs, feeling passion and excitement, but not love. It worried her
that she could not stop herself leading men on, often indulging in more
than one love affair at a time. She confessed to Margot that she knew that
this was wrong, but did not know what to do about it. Bluntly Margot
pointed out that she thought she saw qualities in the men she was
attracted to that were simply not there. 'I was more stolid and practical,'
Margot wrote, 'and took the feathers off her swans and turned them back
into geese, which they often were.'[8] The bedroom sessions they had once
held at Glen now worried Laura more than ever. Margot had recreated
them with great success at 40 Grosvenor Square* and even Mr Gladstone
did not disapprove. That was no comfort to Laura, who wondered if it

---

* The Grosvenor Square house had recently been renumbered.

could stop the 'right man' from proposing. Such nonsense made Margot scoff: only the prim and narrow-minded could think them improper and if any man held them against her it would show he was unworthy of her and Laura must drop him at once.

CHAPTER 4

Spirit, Fire and Dew

AT A DINNER given by Mrs Herbert Jekyll in the summer of 1884, Laura was placed next to a young man who at once immensely attracted her. Alfred Lyttelton, son of the fourth Baron Lyttelton and nephew of Mr Gladstone, was tall, good-looking, athletic and serious and Laura had heard nothing but good of him. The timing of the meeting could not have been more propitious, for Alfred, now twenty-five, was just beginning to feel it was time he married. As a hard-working barrister he had felt bound to establish himself first, and he was looking for a serious and yet womanly woman who would appreciate the great store he set by a marriage where there was both love and companionship.

Margot has left a picture of Alfred at that time that makes him sound every girl's dream: 'Everyone adored him. He combined the prowess at games of a good athlete with moral right-mindedness of a high order. He was neither a gamester nor an artist. He respected discipline but loathed asceticism.'[1] Asquith said that of all men of his generation, Alfred came nearest to the mould and ideal of manhood which every English father would like his son to aspire to and if possible to attain.[2]

Alfred was as deeply religious as Laura, went to church every Sunday and took holy communion regularly, and when he got to know Laura better, encouraged her to go with him. But with all his virtues, Alfred was unsympathetic towards the weaknesses of others, possessed a cruel sense of humour (considered quite normal in those days) and was insular in the extreme. He took it for granted that a black skin was inferior to a white one and treated all foreigners with contempt. Margot tells how he and his companions were convulsed with laughter when one day he threw a half-sucked orange out of the window of an Italian train at an old man standing on the platform, striking him full in the face.[3] Behaviour like this disgusted Margot, who had been brought up to treat foreigners and servants with courtesy, but it did not prevent Laura from falling seriously in love. She thought Alfred possessed all the qualities she had ever wanted in a husband in the most beautiful form. However, they did not have as much in common as Laura thought. Margot noticed early on that although they shared a great many interests like books, music and church-going, they did not laugh at the same things. Laura once remarked in a puzzled voice to Margot, 'Wouldn't you have thought that laughing as loud as the Lytteltons do, they would have loved Edward Lear? Alfred says that none of them think him a bit funny and was quite testy when I said his was the only family in the world that didn't.'[4]

At the time of their meeting Laura was thin and pale and far from well, and all that winter she coughed incessantly. In a curious way her ill-health made her more attractive, more spiritual than ever—at least that is what Alfred thought. He admired particularly her large luminous eyes with their peculiar upward turn of the underlids which gave pathos and charm to her strange little face. An admirer once said that Laura was made of 'spirit, fire and dew'.[5] Margot's own description of her sister was not very different: 'The most astonishing vitality and eagerness, nerves that were almost too high strung for every day tempers and a mind that knew no limits. She admired life and love and knew how to give them.'[6] Others said much the same. Since modern writers have repeated the sentimental exaggerations written after Laura's early death it has become almost sacrilege to criticize her. There is no doubt that she was unusual and talented, but she was also whimsical, over-religious and sentimental to a degree. She loved to write as though she was an infant lisping out the wonders of the world to a close friend. 'Little holy clouds lying in the lap of the sky with the sun in their eyes'[7] was for her quite a usual way to express herself. She talked, cried and wrote with a freedom that almost shocks a more prosaic age. Perhaps her tuberculosis, which even at the time of meeting Alfred already had her in its grip, helped her to see visions not discernible to others and made her more aware of the misery of life and the glory of death. She once said, 'I shall not live a long life, I shall wear out quick, I live too fast.'[8]

Alfred Lyttelton came to Glen in October 1884 for the first time, invited by Margot at the insistence of Laura, suddenly shy because she was attracted to him, but anxious to find out how deep his feelings were. The visit did not further Alfred's cause very much, for Laura was ill in bed and Margot had to deputise for her. Disappointment made Alfred glum and put Margot in a wicked mood so that she forced him to do all sorts of unconventional things. At Margot's suggestion they went for a long walk (Alfred referred to it as a ramble) and on the way back Margot pretended to fall into a burn and called to Alfred to rescue her. Then she pretended to get stuck up a tree which she had climbed to collect nuts and Alfred had to climb up too to help her down, barking his shins and tearing his best trousers. The return track to Glen was rough and stony, it started to rain and Alfred had no mackintosh. Nor had Margot, but after her training on the hunting field a wetting did not trouble her; besides she had plenty of clothes to change into. The crowning insult came when they returned to the house; Margot made Alfred carry her to her room, where he dumped her unceremoniously on the bed.

Why did Margot behave so badly to a guest that everyone liked? The probability is that she was trying to put him off Laura and to stop him coming again, since she suspected that the old carefree life with her sister might be over for ever. He did come again, a few months later, proposed and was accepted.

Her engagement made Laura happy, yet she was afraid '. . . Red dawns bring storms and tempest . . . shepherds like the grey mornings . . . ours so red . . . will that orange cloud grow less dark . . . will it get sinister and foreboding?'[9]

Margot was amazed that the idea of marriage to the man of her choice made Laura tearful and nervous, when she ought to be leaping over the moon. Indeed she lost so much weight that the family doctor ordered her abroad to the sun; the strain of becoming engaged had been almost too much for her, he said. Always emotional, she had reacted so violently that Charles and Emma began to think that the marriage would have to be postponed. Only Margot knew that Laura's morbidity, her strange dreams, her religious fervour, tore her mind to shreds and made her thinner and paler than ever. It was almost as though she was hearing voices like Joan of Arc, another consumptive of whom Laura loved to read.

Bordighera was chosen as the warmest and most cheerful spot for the ailing Laura and to Margot's irritation she was reckoned to be too much of a disturbing element to go with her sister, an injustice that hurt her deeply. In fact Margot's brisk and cheerful attitude to life, her laughter and teasing, were exactly what Laura needed to keep her spirits up. More than that, a holiday together would have given Margot an opportunity to look after Laura and would have helped her fight her jealousy that Laura loved Alfred more than her sister and companion of over twenty years. That this was natural did nothing to assuage her depression, but she accepted it as a hard fact of life.[10]

In Bordighera Laura lay in the sun all day and spent every evening with the writer George Macdonald and his family who had settled in the town. It is very probable that the religious discussions with Macdonald did her more harm than Margot's amusing sisterly chatter, and as far as one can tell from her letters, her morbidity increased in Italy. She wrote regularly to Margot, who could see that under Macdonald's influence Laura was having a dangerous flirtation with death. It was a problem far too big for Margot to solve and she began to dread Laura's letters and was chided for looking pale and subdued. Her mother put Margot's lifelessness down to the sorrow of losing Laura. For once Margot was too afraid to speak out because in her heart she was terrified that Laura was really going to die.[11] One of Laura's letters worried her so dreadfully that at first she hid it from her parents. It was all about a talk which Laura and Macdonald had had when they were alone one evening. Macdonald had said that 'the only way lovers can meet is in God and that in him alone they can be one'. This was the sort of language that a Mother Superior might use to a postulant nun, not that of a young girl in love, and Margot read it with mounting alarm. The letter went on to describe the funeral of an unknown young girl that Laura had seen that morning. She talked of the body 'as merely a window from which the soul leans out'. Laura developed this mawkish theme until she became lost in her own imagery.[12]

In April Laura wrote to Margot from Paris, a prosaic, ordinary little letter, which showed Margot how influenced her sister was by the atmosphere in which she happened to be, and with Laura's return to Glen—not exactly looking fit, but certainly better—Margot's fears vanished and that first night home they talked until dawn. 'We used to talk until the sun rose, often valuing each other's opinion. I think in those days my opinions were more decided and far less idealistic and sympathetic than hers.'[13] Unselfishly Margot made Laura believe that she had come to terms with the parting. 'She is so glad about it [the marriage],' Laura wrote to Alfred, 'that it makes me feel gladder.'[14]

Laura and Alfred were married on 21 May 1885 at St George's, Hanover Square. All the family were present except Posie Gordon Duff, who was in South Africa for her health. As she walked down the aisle on her father's arm, Laura looked 'white and small like a snowflake but radiant with happiness'. Mr Gladstone proposed the health of the bride and bridegroom at the reception at 40 Grosvenor Square, standing on a chair. But when it was all over, Margot sat at her desk to send a description to Posie.

> . . . My head is splitting, my eyes aching and my heart not inside me at all, but between the soles of my boots. It was all so real to me, so strange that I am fighting with my stupid tears all the time and in consequence my head aches, aches, aches. No one can take Laura's place in my heart but oh how many will take my place . . . even if she is faithful to me, nothing can take the place of a bedroom, bathroom intimacy. No one outside home can take the attitude of home people, see the worries, the pleasures, the trifles, the chiffons in the same light. It was all quite beautiful, here is a bit of her bouquet and veil . . . 400 presents and not many ugly. Some very beautiful . . . old Mrs Gladstone in blue velvet with white lace which she wears at every wedding . . . Laura's going away dress was the loveliest I ever saw . . .[15]

They were gone, and Margot was desolate and in tears. She unburdened herself of her unhappiness to George Curzon, the one friend she knew would understand.

> Oh George you were so nice to me, so sympathetic . . . you understand things so quickly and don't remind me of the fact. I can't help it, it may be selfish but it's true, I mind Laura's going, she's part of myself and I shall shriek at the empty bed now and work off what I wanted to say by biting my pillow and banging my head.[16]

Margot's turning for comfort to George Curzon on a day that brought happiness to Laura but loneliness to her, is all the stranger since he had just quarrelled with her about her opening a letter he had written to Laura when she was in Bordighera and Margot was acting as her secretary. With a lack of sensitivity that characterized him of occasions, Curzon had blasted Margot for opening other people's letters. Instead of being angry Margot was contrite: 'Laura . . . told me to open her letters but I quite forgot the other party might mind.'[17]

By November Laura was pregnant and the knowledge gave her a

premonition that she would not survive the birth. She did not tell Margot of her feelings nor that all the morbidness that made her so ill before her marriage had returned to torment her at a time when she should be feeling nothing but happiness. In Margot's presence she tried to be cheerful, but Margot knew Laura too well not to feel that something was very wrong. At the marriage of Mary Gladstone to Henry Drew, the curate of Hawarden, in February 1886, a friend of the family noticed how well Margot looked and how by contrast Laura seemed ill and oppressed. But the first to see that Laura's illness was mortal was a friend of Mary Drew's who called to see Alfred. Afterwards he wrote to Mary: 'They call Mrs Lyttelton a charming woman but none of them knows that she is dying under their noses.'[18]

When Laura's baby was due, Emma decided that Margot might be put off marriage and child-bearing if she was with Laura when the baby was born. Instead she was to stay with her sister Lucy in Badminton country for the hunting. Before leaving Margot went to see Laura and found her in a strange mood. She greeted Margot dolefully: 'I am sure I shall die when my baby is born.' Margot's brisk reply, 'I am just as likely to be killed out hunting,' did nothing to lift Laura's spirits. Feverishly she made Margot promise that if she did die, Margot would read her will to the family in the death chamber: 'Promise you will not forget?' Tenderly Margot took her sister's hand and they knelt and prayed together as they had so often done before 'that whether it is me or you who die first, if it is God's will one of us may come to the other here and tell us the truth about the next world and console us as much as possible in this'.[19]

It was not a good send-off, but Margot was young and healthy and soon all her cares blew away in the joy and excitement of the hunt. She began to test her skill at jumping and took unnecessary risks in a spirit of bravado, so that it was all the more unfortunate that she had what could have been a serious accident when cantering gently home through a wood. Spring was in the air, wild flowers were budding and Margot, like the good countrywoman she was, could smell the change in the air. Happy and content, her hands slackened on the reins; her horse stumbled and Margot fell heavily, hitting her head. She was half concussed, her nose and upper lip so torn that three painful stitches had to be inserted without an anaesthetic. Faint and dazed, she saw herself in a mirror and burst into tears.

A telegram arrived when she was in bed to say that Laura had given birth to a son and all was well. Next day a second telegram said that Laura was ill, then a third telegram summoned Margot to London. Weak and shaky Margot got up; the doctor forbade her to go—there was danger of erysipelas—but it was unthinkable that she should not be with Laura. Margot defied her doctor and went, her face bloated and red (a silk scarf covered as much of it as possible); it hurt abominably and made her feel cold and sick. When she reached Paddington, where Alfred awaited her with a brougham, she was just able to whisper: 'Is she dead?'—'No, but very ill.'

The house was crowded with friends calling to commiserate, to ask for news or to comfort Alfred. Charty had rushed up from the country and was in charge, calm, pale and heavy-eyed. Laura was unconscious and Margot was not allowed to see her that night. At dawn Margot woke and ran down to the sick room in her dressing-gown. In her memoirs she gives a poignant account of the scene:

> I opened the door and stood at the foot of the wooden bed and gazed at what was left of Laura. Her face had shrunk to the size of a child's, her lashes lay a blank wall on the whitest of cheeks, her hair was hanging dragged up from her square brow in heavy folds upon the pillow. Her mouth was tightly shut and a dark blood stain marked her chin. After a long silence she moved and muttered and opened her eyes. She fixed them on me and my heart stopped. I stretched my hands out towards her and said 'Laura'. But the sound died and she did not know me. I knew after that she could not live.[20]

Tragically, she took several days to die, days in which Margot suffered intensely but uncomplainingly, often lying quiet and still on the floor by Laura's bed, keeping a long agonizing vigil and determined not to sleep while Laura drifted slowly into eternity. Once she seemed to wake and Margot heard her say clearly, 'I think God has forgotten me.' She died with Margot's arms around her: 'I put my cheek against her shoulder and felt the sharpness of her spine. For a moment we lay close to each other while the sun . . . played upon the window blinds.'[21] An hour or two after Laura's death, Margot returned to the bedroom to gaze on her sister's face for the last time. Calmly and with steady hands she cut off some of Laura's hair to give to friends, hair that was soft and pretty still: 'The one thing I believe will remain after Laura's body has crumbled into dust.[22] Posie and

Margot wrapped a few strands of the hair in tissue paper and sent them off in little boxes like wedding cake, with labels in Posie's neat hand.

In her will Laura had asked that Alfred's sister Kathleen should have her 'little silver crucifix that opens, and Alfred must put in a little bit of my hair and Kathleen must keep it for my sake'.[23] Keepsakes, like promises, were sacred to Margot. All her life, relics from those who had gone meant much to her and she cherished among her jewels several locks of hair —each in separate envelopes—a leaf pressed between the pages of a book, a poem in the dead friend's hand, a lace handkerchief, a faded piece of orange blossom between the pages of her Bible. Not to forget: that was the important thing.

CHAPTER 5

Friends Illuminate Darkness

IN THE MONTHS after Laura's death Margot spent much of her time working in the East End of London. Social work had never much interested her; she lightly excused herself by saying others could do it better. In 1880 she had helped Laura start a crèche in the East End and had been bitten by fleas: mortified, she had had to hide away until the tell-tale bites on her face disappeared. Her social conscience had not troubled her unduly, even when going round Whitechapel she saw girls of her own generation in clogs slaving away at unrewarding work. For her teaching in an infants' school would not be right since she did not like the very young and would not know what to do with them, and she protested that to organize a working-girls' club would bore her. Yet she admired the way Laura had done all these things so well. With her frail physique Laura had possessed a will of iron, and it says much for Margot's loyalty to Laura's memory that she volunteered to work in the East End again.

Margot began her ministrations at Clifford's Box factory in Whitechapel after a tough battle with the owner, who had had enough of idle young ladies giving his girls ideas. After much persuasion he reluctantly allowed her to read to his employees during the lunch break, and for the next eight years she continued to visit his factory three days a week when she was in London. It may not have done Clifford's girls much good but it certainly helped Margot, who felt she was following in the footsteps of Laura, whose photograph she pinned on the wall behind the upturned box on which she sat to read.[1]

As the summer wore on, she began to long for green fields and clean air. One hot afternoon as she sat on her box, the air heavy with soot, it occurred to her how taxing this unhealthy atmosphere must have been for Laura. Had it helped to push her into an early grave? That decided her; she packed up and left for Glen.[2]

Her brother Eddy welcomed her back, as caring and affectionate as ever. Before daybreak she joined him in a wild-duck shoot, drawing health and strength from the country air. Eddy was the ideal companion. He shared her passion for Glen and realized better than anyone how among the hills and the heather she could find the peace of mind so necessary to her recovery. He asked no questions, but was silently companionable on the many expeditions they made together. His sense of humour kept up her flagging spirits when a well-remembered hill or dyke reminded her too painfully of the sister she had lost. If the male members of the family were of a 'cooler circulation' than the females, a time of sorrow and of mourning was a time to be glad of it.[3]

There was one solace that she never mentions in any of her writings: her correspondence at that time with a young Jewess whom she had met one night at the opera in Dresden. She and Elsa (Margot never told DD Balfour her surname and DD was the only one who knew of her existence) became close friends, played the piano together, sang duets and exchanged confidences as though they were sisters. Half-Russian, half-German, Elsa was reticent about her parents, although she talked of her stepfather, Julius Schulhoff the musician, whom she loved and admired. 'We knew none of each other's people and nothing of each other's lives, but books and ideas and occupations . . . form endless topics for letters and we are great pals.'[4]

Now, in 1886, Elsa became the recipient of all Margot's woes. No stranger to sorrow, Elsa knew how to brace and how to give hope for the future—exactly what Margot needed. They wrote to each other until the Second World War when Elsa disappeared. They only knew each other for four or five months in Dresden yet remained devoted friends for fifty years. Margot realized that Elsa was an exceptional woman, always loving, kind and intelligent, as well as an excellent influence on her own more mercurial nature. Margot was thinking of her when she wrote an essay 'True Friends' for DD. 'I confess to being devoted to people but they must be loving or one hurts oneself against them. I cannot do without them, however.'[5]

Ever since Laura's death, nightmares had haunted Margot's sleep: 'I woke up dreaming that I am lost and that Laura is crying,' she wrote to Mary Drew seven months afterwards.

I dream of her constantly, in fact nearly whenever I dream at all. Nothing curious or beautiful, but simple acts of our lives, travelling or eating or discussing. She is never married in my dreams but just Laura Tennant that I cared for and will all my life.[6]

The days at Glen passed undemandingly. Margot spent as much time out of doors as possible and when the weather was too rough to ride or walk she would sit in the 'Doocot' alone, reading a little or just watching the hours go by without regret that she had achieved nothing. She noticed without gratitude that she was no longer suffering in the old passionate, desperate way from her burning anger that someone as loved and needed as Laura should be taken. She wrote to Alfred Lyttelton that at last she had found strength to visit Traquair churchyard.

I went to the little grave and at first it seemed very dark but as my eyes grew accustomed to it, I saw the lambs huddled up against the tomb-stones . . . I thought of all you said on the hill top to me and I prayed that my now loosened grasp of the world may continue and not merely be a new departure born of tears and . . . mourning. Kneeling on the ground that covers Laura and feeling the same wind that blows over us both, I felt perhaps God was not far off and her spirit was near.[7]

'A loosened grasp of the world' had been the trouble with Laura. Margot had never experienced this mystical feeling before and erroneously mis-took lassitude and emotional exhaustion for spiritual exaltation, rejoicing in the belief that she was becoming more like her sister. 'Serenity fills my whole life,' she confided to Alfred in another letter. This was far from the truth; serene she never was nor could be. The best sign of hope, although she did not realize it, was that she was beginning to long for London and her friends.

In May 1886 Alfred had invited Margot and her youngest brother Jack to join him on a visit to America: his family hoped that a change of scene would speed his recovery. Although at first Margot liked the idea, she declined the invitation—she hated the sea, she hated travelling and could not face the effort of being pleasant to strangers. Before his departure Alfred came to see the Tennants and give them news of Laura's son Alfred Christopher, now four months old and thriving in Charty's care: 'The baby does well,' Alfred wrote, 'and I have seen looks of her in him at rare intervals.'[8] Surprisingly, Margot could not take an interest in Laura's child. She does not mention him in her memoirs or in anything she wrote for publication, but let her readers assume that the child had died at birth.

When Margot at last returned to London in June 1887 she was still torn between her natural longing to be happy and carefree again, and a belief that it was wrong to be dragged too quickly from her mourning. After clearing out some of Laura's drawers one day she wrote defeatedly to Mary Drew: 'Happiness is the worst possible training for misery.' Recently Mary had shown a sympathetic side that Margot had not seen before, and soon after Laura's funeral she sent the bereaved family all the letters Laura had written to her, hoping they might bring some consolation. 'They are enchanting but so infinitely sad,' Margot wrote in her letter of acknowledgment.[9]

A part of Margot believed that it was only right to go on grieving, but her intense desire for companionship proved too strong. Both Laura and Margot had collected friends as their father collected paintings, in large numbers, but whereas Laura had been thus drawn into other interests and occupations, Margot had stood aloof. At one time Maggie Ponsonby had tried to enlist her help in her campaign for the higher education of women, but in vain. Frances Graham (now Mrs Horner) had talked to her long and earnestly of the Pre-Raphaelite Brotherhood, but Margot told her frankly that young men so full of self-worship could not appeal to her. She admired Edward Burne-Jones, who she met frequently at her friends' houses, and she agreed that the Brotherhood was influential—for instance, they had quite changed the way women wore their clothes, did their hair, held their heads—but she could not share Frances's enthusiasm; 'they are too lacking in vitality', she had commented.

Margot might have disdained commitment in the past but now, without Laura, having close friends became for the first time very important to her, and she began to reflect on the nature of friendship. In later years, Margot wrote a good deal about friendship and her views are precise and very much her own: 'Friendship should be kept in good repair: written to [sic], remembered in one's prayers and generally made much of.' Although the life-span of a friendship was for ever, it was important to make new friends frequently: to keep ideas moving and boredom at bay, new acquaintances must be brought into the fold. Friends illuminated darkness and sorrow with light and the warm glow of life. Clever people must be warmly welcomed as friends, for they added an extra dimension to the mind by drawing one into the range of new mental observance of all kinds.[10] Perhaps her standards were unattainable, for she demanded absolute loyalty, fidelity and truth: 'I feel I could give my friends a good deal,' she wrote in 1889, 'no girl or woman has better friends than I have.'[11] Her own attitude to friends was rather naïve; she gave them her journals to read even though they held her innermost thoughts and feelings. Confidingly she handed over a recent suitor's love letters in order to show how his love had not been thrown away, because she had influenced him for good. Soon after meeting DD Balfour she told her:

> Friendship is of imperceptible growth and should not be looked at or into with any touch of consciousness or modern self-questioning—'Do I like you?'—'Yes a good deal'—or 'I don't know yet if I do' are all immense mistakes to my mind. One may be pretty sure there will be no questions when you do love your friend, though there may be ever so much criticism.[12]

Analysing the characters of her friends (one of the bad results of the Victorian passion for pencil games) was an infinite source of profit and pleasure to her: 'I love Pembroke, he is a great dear,' she wrote to one friend whom she did not know very well. 'He has not got quite enough to do to make friendship a recreation—it becomes an occupation which is a mistake, but I feel proud of counting him among my friends.'[13]

Not everyone believed Margot's oft-repeated theory that opposites make the best friends. She tried to impress this on DD, who at first was a little frightened of her: 'You say you are rather different. Do you think this against our becoming real friends? Of course I don't know, but when I look at my friends, they are all utterly different from me.'[14] Of course they were! As Katharine Horner said: 'Margot is unique.'

The moment she returned to London in June 1887 she began to pick up. Balls and receptions were taboo, for the period of mourning in those days was long and strict, and many of Laura's friends also denied themselves dancing and the theatre. The tragedy of her early death was felt by an extraordinarily wide circle of people, Frances Horner, George Curzon, Arthur Balfour, Mary Wemyss, Etty Desborough, Violet Rutland and George Pembroke* among them.[15] All felt that they wanted to withdraw

---

* The four last-named were respectively Countess of Wemyss, Countess of Desborough, Duchess of Rutland and Earl of Pembroke.

from society for a time and that they could the better keep Laura's memory fresh by meeting regularly in private to discuss topics in religion, literature, politics and poetry about which she had felt deeply.

In this small world of the rich and the leisured, all spoke the same language, had the same interests and understood each other's ways. The discussions were long and lively, as was to be expected: the men were clever and well educated and though the women were hardly educated at all they played their part with assurance and style, especially Margot who soon became the leader of the group. Moreover the women could be relied on to supply the lightness of touch, humour and laughter needed to soften male society, although they had their work cut out to cope with Arthur Balfour's sophisticated wit and Harry Cust's lightning epigrams. The preparation that the women undertook was rigorous. They learned pages of poetry by heart, devoured serious novels and works of history, biography and travel, everything that would make them better informed and more amusing. They set themselves essays to write on any subject that might be profitable, read them aloud to each other and accepted criticism without as much as a frown. Margot won acclaim for a discourse on the art of conversation. She had tried in vain to induce DD Balfour—'a new recruit'—to write one too and put it in for comparison, but DD was shy. Margot wrote to encourage her. 'I wish you had nothing to do, you could just sit down and without looking up any books or anecdotes, write what you think of the art of conversation. We are all going to do it and Curzon says he will too.'[16]

It was fortunate for Margot that she had been mixing with men of intelligence and assurance for years, and she was highly delighted at the idea of pitting her wits against them. She was often heard to say, 'If I had been born a man, I would be able to assess my intellect.'[17] Her critical faculty helped her to hold her own. But all the women were greatly helped by understanding what they were aiming for: high ideals, a feeling of obligation towards society to be repaid by good and entertaining conversation, a proper attention to the opinions of others, and good manners, even under trying circumstances.[18] Before long, many people began to look on this group of friends as an antidote to the smart racing and gambling set that followed the heir to the throne.

They were too well known not to be remarked upon. When their activities leaked out, Lord George Beresford (not one of their number) coined a name that he felt suited the group exactly: 'You are always talking about your souls,' he told the Duchess of Rutland. 'I shall call you "The Souls".'[19] At once Margot sensed the derision in the name, even a hint of mockery, and was indignant. Someone else suggested 'The Coterie' but when Margot pointed out that it smacked even more of the precious, it was dropped. Her own suggestion of 'The Gang' was rejected as too juvenile—they were not a bunch of school-children. They all agreed that whatever they were, they were certainly not 'souls'. Yet when she described the group in 1926 Margot wrote, 'Most of us had a depth of feeling, a moral and religious ambition which are entirely lacking in the clever young men and women of today.'[20] On the other hand, the High Priest of the group, Arthur Balfour, thought he had killed the name stone dead when he wrote: 'To me, the name "The Souls" seems meaningless and slightly ludicrous, it seems to imply some kind of organization of purpose where no kind of organization or purpose was dreamed of.'[21] Nevertheless the name stuck and they are known as 'The Souls' to this day.

Some of those who were not 'Souls' were of course jealous and criticized the group for its exclusiveness. Margot emphatically denied the charge; they did not open their doors to all and sundry because introducing new faces into a circle of old friends was something to be done with caution. 'The Souls' were not mere acquaintances, she said, and if they had a crest their motto would be 'loyalty, devotion, fidelity'. The misfortunes of one of them affected all and it was remarkable how the ranks closed when adversity struck. George Curzon, one of the leading lights, was found to have a patch on the lung and was ordered to Switzerland for a year, and at once there was a general feeling of anxiety amongst them all. As a last fling he gave a banquet at the Bachelors' Club and to make it unforgettable (in case he did not return) he composed a short verse to each member which he declaimed while standing on a chair. The ones to Margot and her sisters ran thus:

> Here a trio we meet
> Whom you never will beat
> Tho' wide you may wander and far go
> From what wonderful art
> Of the gallant old Bart*
> Sprang Charty and Lucy and Margot.

* Charles Tennant had been made a baronet in 1885.

To Lucy he gave
The wiles that enslave
Heart and tongue of an angel to Charty
To Margot the wit
And the wielding of it
To make her the joy of a party.[22]

The Souls wrote to each other frequently when apart, gushing, sentimental letters all froth and bubble, insubstantial but not insincere. They poured out their feelings in a torrent of words they fancied to be poetic. Some years later Margot was told that 'lean writing is the highest thing to aim for' if she wanted to get her work published. But if she changed her mind about the art of writing she stuck furiously to the belief that the Souls had an enormous influence in the world of politics, although there is nothing to back this up. For instance, the Souls deplored the socially divisive effect of the current controversies over Home Rule and tried to mitigate them, but quite without effect. Margot gave a luncheon party at 40 Grosvenor Square to which she invited Mr Gladstone and Lord Randolph Churchill, who were locked in bitter argument over the Home Rule Bill and had not spoken amicably to each other for a very long time. To Margot's joy all went smoothly, conversation flowed and neither man showed the slightest sign of animosity. It was disappointing to read next day in the *Daily Chronicle* that back in the House they were at each other's throats as usual. But the news of the luncheon party leaked out (Margot gave it a vigorous push or two) and she was the heroine of the hour for daring to invite these old enemies together.

The Souls great mistake was to overrate their influence. Arthur Balfour wrote, 'No history of our time will be complete, unless the influence of the "Souls" upon society is accurately and dispassionately recorded.'[23] Margot went a stage further. She sincerely believed that ' "The Souls" made London the centre of the most interesting society in the world and gave men of different tempers and opposite beliefs an opportunity of discussing without heat and without reporters. There is no individual or group among us powerful enough to succeed in running a salon of that kind today'.[24] When Margot wrote these words in 1920 the world was changing rapidly and leisure on the old scale was a luxury that had ceased to exist.

CHAPTER 6

Breadth of Vision

WHEN ALFRED LYTTELTON became a widower he found he preferred the company of the extrovert Tennants to that of his own family, who encouraged him to suppress his feelings and to look on his loss as God's will. With Margot and her family he was able to give way to his emotions and find relief and consolation. Charty Ribblesdale had kindheartedly undertaken to bring up his child with her own and it was her idea that Alfred should move from the house in Brook Street which he had shared with Laura to a flat in Mount Street where he could more easily learn to live alone. For the next few years Alfred spent every anniversary (Christmas, Easter, Laura's death) at Glen where he and Margot would make a pilgrimage to Laura's grave and, kneeling on the grass, pray together.

In the autumn after Laura died Margot persuaded Alfred to take up hunting under her tutelage, in the hope that physical exercise would help him to sleep. He soon became competent in a cool, detached way but was no match for Margot, whom he began to see in a different and not altogether complimentary light. She too had her small disillusionments when he told her after an exhilarating day's sport that it was a pity that hunting was not as exciting as cricket.

That Christmas Alfred brought his baby, Alfred Christopher, to Glen where the child was made much of by Charles and Emma. Alfred adored this pretty, intelligent but highly excitable little boy: 'He makes a large difference in the feeling of isolation which I experienced in the new flat before he joined me there,' he wrote to his sister Lavinia, 'he has got to know me a little and is beginning to throw a beam upon my life.'[1] Then quite suddenly Alfred Christopher developed tubercular meningitis, became seriously ill and died on 19 May 1888. No one was more shaken than Margot; she wrote to DD:

I have clung to the idea that the baby was Laura's legacy, a sort of angel messenger from Heaven to keep us good, but now I see that Heaven was incomplete without her sweet. The little white funeral was yesterday (Laura and Alfred's wedding day) and we stood with lilies in our hands crying, crying with our hearts heavy with memories. He was laid near his little girl mother and all the village children threw posies on the coffin—oh DD life is not meant to be happy—quite, is it?[2]

At the graveside Margot took Alfred's arm; they both derived some solace from the beauty of the service for so young a child. '. . . Everything in the funeral service aided me,' Alfred wrote to Lavinia, 'for almost unlike every other funeral service, I recollect not one jarring note struck in the utter beauty and pathos of it all . . . the dreadful thought is the future without the point and centre which he could have made . . . I am so fearfully discouraged.'[3]

After the funeral the Tennants' practical nature came to Alfred's rescue again. Without delay Charty moved him to another flat where there was nothing to remind him of the past, and Margot helped with suggestions to take his mind off his grief: more hunting and shooting, stalking (which Alfred had never tried) in Scotland. Alfred was pathetically grateful.

It has often been said that Alfred had once had difficulty in deciding which sister to choose for a wife. This was not true at all. Admittedly, Margot corresponded with him using terms that to modern eyes seem to suggest one lover writing to another, but this was nothing more than the extravagant language of the time, when it was considered natural even for men to address each other in highly affectionate terms. In sorrow they had turned to each other for comfort and thus their need for each other had grown until they were very close in the kind of relationship not uncommon in those days but which nowadays scarcely exists outside marriage or between lovers. They had shared happy memories so precious to the Victorians, but despite Margot's extravagant letters (which all the Souls indulged in) she never was, nor could be, in love with Alfred, nor he with her.

But her dependence on him worried her more and more. She did not want to cut the tie but merely to loosen it. 'You must let me go, Alfred,' she wrote imploringly,

I cling to you just now with passionate longing and complete happiness, for your directness of nature, your uncomplex morality, your star of success and healthy life-giving—be patient with me and don't condemn me if I don't immediately fulfil your hopes. Be tender if I turn to your sheltering arms and if anything give me a little more love just now at this parting of the ways.[4]

With Alfred's help, Margot was compiling a scrap book (known as 'my white book') from letters and cuttings telling the story of Laura's life. But Alfred was reluctant to hand over Laura's diaries and love letters. In her will Laura had left her girlhood diaries to Margot and afterwards Alfred had begged for them, but Margot was firm: 'I can't give you Laura's diaries, they would be of no sort of use to you, I think Laura would not like any human being to see them.' Later her better feelings overcame her scruples and she sent Alfred the diaries: 'Of course I give them to you,' she wrote a little crossly, 'as she and all of her seems to be your own sad right.'[5] When she found that she could not continue the 'white book' without the diaries, she had to ask for them back again, and added a plea for the letters. 'You can trust me absolutely,'[6] she wrote. But Alfred feared that Margot might let her close friends see some of the letters and obstinately refused to give them up. She could not see that some things have to be private. 'You can refuse your letters if you like,' she wrote ungraciously, 'but the diaries I think you may lend me. No eyes but mine and hers had ever seen them before and I gave them to you. I sometimes wonder whether I ought to have given them to you for there are some impulsive nonsense passages which are only written to contradict afterwards.'[7] A week later the diaries arrived without even a note inside, but the love letters remained in Alfred's keeping. Immediately he lost prestige in Margot's eyes for lack of trust towards an old friend, and after this a coolness sprang up between them. Margot's insensitivity when crossed shows that the sentimentality of her other letters did not go deep.

The friendship between Margot and DD Balfour had ripened slowly into a real affection that Margot was wise enough to cherish, for DD's quiet nature went well with her more rumbustious Tennant temperament. When one went up in the air like a rocket, the other remained cool and collected, feet on the ground. To be able to remain calm and slow to anger in a dispute were qualities that mystified Margot, but she admired those that had them all the same. There was not always harmony between the two friends, for although of a peace-loving disposition DD had a mind of her own and, like many quiet people, she could be stubborn. Perhaps she was a little too quick to criticize some of Margot's faults, but Margot liked her too much and understood her too well to take umbrage and once when she thought that DD might have misunderstood her reaction to some severe strictures her friend had thought fit to administer, she wrote at once to explain:

> I should not like you to think I did not agree with you when we were talking and you said one should forget oneself and in losing one's life gain it. If I took it in a little sullenly, it was only because I wanted to defend such self-centredness I felt perhaps you were accusing me of.[8]

There was not another woman from whom Margot could take so much correction, except her mother or sisters. It upset DD to hear Margot anger people by careless words uttered through sheer thoughtlessness; yet she had also noticed that Margot could be diplomatic on occasion. Her true friends knew her generosity and many acts of kindness, but her enemies remembered only her lapses—her strong, sharp remarks calculated to startle, her over-concentration on herself, her bragging about her prowess on the hunting field. Slowly DD had come to understand that Margot was quite unaware of her own shortcomings and that even at her worst she still retained a certain disarming quality. So DD could not prevent herself admiring Margot and was happy to count her amongst her closest friends. In return Margot showed how she appreciated DD's trust by opening her heart to her in a way she had never been able to do before to anyone but her family.

Margot and DD did not move in quite the same world. DD did not hunt and had no interest in the never-ending round of pleasure in which London society indulged and which so attracted Margot. This is partly why Margot found DD so interesting, even in some ways mysterious, for DD kept her interests and aspirations very much to herself. Therefore she was all the more surprised when she found that Alfred Lyttelton and DD knew each other. But it never occurred to her that it was a friendship that could turn to love, although she says that she did not expect Alfred to remain single for ever. So she took their friendship lightly, thinking little of it. Moreover, dozens of girls had thought themselves in love with

Alfred, indeed, it had almost become a fashion, for he looked like a Greek god or an Olympic athlete.

At Christmas 1891 Margot received a letter from Mary Drew hinting that Alfred had fallen in love with DD Balfour and would probably marry her. Mary had not missed Margot's proprietorial air towards Alfred and the way she gushed over him whenever they were together. She thought such conduct deplorable in a sister-in-law and it gave her much inward satisfaction to know it must soon cease. In marked contrast to Mary's letter Margot's reply was calm and frank: 'I shall try to be what is worthiest and best when Alfred does think fit to marry again, but I could not pretend not to mind.'[9] Unfortunately Mary misunderstood the letter. It was not of herself that Margot was thinking, but of another woman taking Laura's place, and that upset her very much. Naturally the news of Alfred's remarriage was a shock, but she would have to adjust to it, and she was never very good at adjusting to circumstances beyond her control. In the New Year of 1892 Alfred himself wrote and confirmed Mary's hints. He was lonely in his bachelor flat and longed for family life again. He had fallen in love with DD and had asked her to be his wife.[10]

As soon as the forthcoming marriage was announced Margot wrote again to Mary Drew, an open honest letter for she had nothing to hide.

> Alfred's engagement is naturally a shock, to break old ties a wrench and I am bound to say from my point of view that they are broken now in two. The Laura part which Charty and I carried on is all gone quickly, steadily into the past and has suddenly disappeared, the old life with its aspirations dethroned. New life and love springs up, and we are among the spectators. It is quite right, quite true and natural and DD and he will be entirely happy, suitable, respectable and prosperous, much approved of by all his relations and friends and all of hers . . . but there are reflections that cannot be kept out, there are memories that spring open when the lock is touched and there is no place for them among the rejoicings.[11]

It was more difficult to answer DD's short letter with its bald statement of her engagement, but after many attempts Margot managed it well enough. She did not try to hide her feelings, friendship would not be worth anything unless based on a foundation of truth.

Your letter brought blinding tears to my eyes and a kind of muffled ache to my heart. It is not difficult to love you, but I felt in gaining Alfred's love you are independent of all else and on these occasions little loves get merged in the greater ones . . . I am sure you must be very happy for such love as I have had from Alfred has lightened every dull hour and strengthened every weak one in my life . . . I always want to keep more than I dare own and there is loneliness in my life which few suspect.[12]

The letter to Alfred was harder to write but she could not rest until it was done and done properly and above all honestly. She could never understand that honesty is not always the best policy and that there are poignant moments in life when the heart cries out to say one thing while the mind demands caution. According to Margot's standards, caution was as bad as hypocrisy. Fortunately DD understood this and remained a life-long friend despite much 'honesty' on Margot's part, for she knew and trusted the kind heart that never failed to hold out a helping hand.

The links with the past were now severed. If she refused to go to the wedding it was only because the image of Laura and Alfred cutting the cake and laughing together was still, even after seven years, too fresh and clear. It was certainly not pique, as Mary Drew thought. After Margot became used to the sight of Alfred with DD on his arm at Glen, she came to rejoice, even share in their happiness.

For some years past Margot's life had been darkened by the ill health of her other sisters, who all suffered from various types of consumption, each one in a different stage. Her earliest childhood memories were of her mother and the three eldest girls going off to the pure air of Switzerland to avoid the damp and fog of an English winter. Posie, the eldest, spent the year 1886 basking in the sun of Cape Town, the guest of a distant cousin Sir David Tennant, but had returned home uncured. Charty and Lucy frequented Davos because it was closer to home, husbands and children, and to winter there became a regular part of their lives. At five Margot understood, without being told, that these 'holidays' abroad were part of the elusive search for health and were not pleasure trips in any sense of the word. In the winter of 1882 when Margot was eighteen and staying with the Ribblesdales for a hunt ball, Charty suddenly developed a hacking cough and had to leave hurriedly for Switzerland. 'I feel very low at the thought of Ribblesdale and Charty going abroad' Margot wrote to a friend, 'Poor, poor sweets, and Posie is ill too. I wonder how long it will last? The uncertainties that life holds out for me make me hide my face in my hands. My happiness is nothing, even if it never comes . . . I see us planting more *immortelles* for graves we love.'[13]

In those days Davos was considered the best health resort in Europe. There the three ailing Tennant girls and their equally sick sister-in-law, Helen, went in search of a cure in 1887. They took it for granted that Margot, the only really healthy one and the youngest girl, should go with them as companion and nurse. Margot went meekly enough, although weeks in attendance on invalids had a lowering effect on her spirits and triggered off nervousness and those bouts of insomnia that became the bane of her life. 'This place has a curious effect on one,' she wrote to Mary Drew from Switzerland, 'it loosens one's hold on life if one is ill, as the air gives life and vitality and certainly inspires one. Death lives here and is friendly with everyone. He passes so often that even I have a nodding acquaintance with him.'[14] The danger to Margot's own health was very great, living as she was in close contact with consumptives; but in those days no one realized that the disease was contagious. Eating with the invalids, breathing the same air, and sleeping in the same room when they were too sick to be left, it was a miracle that she did not become infected. But an instinct for survival kept Margot out of doors as much as possible, even though she disliked the joyless pursuit of tramping through the snow without a companion to talk to. She thought with a sigh of her friends in Leicestershire enjoying the excitement of hunting and longed to be with them. Yet she showed a cheerful and uncomplaining face to her sisters who were so taken up with themselves that they had no time to spare for their young amateur nurse.

A year later, when she was again in Davos, this time only with Posie, her kindness to her sister was rewarded in a most unexpected way. Not long after her arrival she was introduced to John Addington Symonds, the historian of Italy, a happy contact that made her stay in Davos infinitely more pleasurable. Every evening, after putting Posie to bed, she climbed the winding road that led up the hill to 'Am Hof', the Symonds' villa, her way lit only by the stars, until the lantern Symonds placed in the porch to guide her shone out in the darkness.

The delightful thing about this friendship was the ease with which it developed. In the conversations she and Symonds had together Margot felt neither inferior nor self-conscious. There was no question of Symonds patronizing her; from the beginning he established her intelligence, and she might have been a literary figure of established importance to judge by the way he deferred to her opinion or paused for comment when he read her his latest work. He broadened her mind amazingly by introducing her to a wide variety of authors: Plato, Swift, Voltaire, Browning, Walt Whitman and Robert Louis Stevenson, who was his great friend. Margot never knew what he would talk about, but whatever it was she lapped it up like a thirsty kitten. Her own contribution was to give Symonds an essay she had written on Gladstone and to ask for his criticisms. But he had none to make—it was 'excellent and could be of great literary value in the future'.[15] Descriptions of Symonds and of other evenings at the villa made her letters home very different from those she had written the year before: 'I delight in him, his humour and his mysticism combine to make him original and he is more in earnest than anyone I have ever met. I feel as though I have known him a long time . . .'[16]

There was a romantic flavour to these evenings, congenial to them both in spite of the disparity in their ages: the drawn blinds, the roaring wood fire, warm and welcoming after the cold and stillness outside, the elderly scholar with his thinning hair, spectacles on the end of his nose, bending over his book, Margot all attention on a stool at his feet. Symonds was small and insignificant in build, but made up for his lack of presence by his bright alert eyes and beautiful voice. As midnight scholarship gave way to the picturesque when they were joined by the postman and woodman who drank wine with much clinking of glasses before continuing on their round. Symonds and Margot would walk with them to the door, the icy air stinging their faces as they listened to the yodelling of their departing guests.[17]

When she returned to England Margot put Symonds' own copy of a book of Stevenson's, which he had given her as a parting present, on her bedside table as a 'remembrance'. The following year Symonds showed his appreciation of Margot's intelligence by dedicating his latest book of essays to her. Unfortunately they did not sell and in his typically modest way Symonds wrote to her humbly, 'I am sorry that the Essays dedicated to you are a failure . . . to judge by the opinion of the Press. I wanted, when I wrote them, only to say the simple truth of what I thought and felt in the simplest language I could find.'[18]

Before she left Davos, Symonds gave her many messages to take to his friend Lord Tennyson. Margot had never met the ageing genius, but she had adored his writings ever since she could remember: her black leather copy of his works was shabby with use and she prided herself on her ability to quote from them without hesitation or mistake. The poet's son Lionel was one of the Souls, an untidy and somewhat uncouth man (fastidious herself, Margot could tolerate such faults only in the great, never in the mediocre). He had sent her his verses, and when he asked her what she would like for a birthday present she promptly replied: 'If you want to give me pleasure, take me down to your father's country-house for a Saturday to Monday.'[19]

Three days later they went down to Haslemere, Margot resplendent in a scarlet cloak trimmed with black cock's feathers and a black tricorn hat. The first sight of Tennyson fulfilled all her expectations—he was magnificent to look at, possessed of height, figure, carriage, features and expression. His conversation, however, was disconcerting. 'Are you as clever and spurty as your sister Laura?' was his greeting, and when they sat down to tea he asked whether she wanted him to dress for dinner, adding, 'Your sister said of me that I was both untidy and dirty.' Did Margot agree? 'You are very handsome,' she managed to answer. 'I can see by that remark that you think I am,' Tennyson went on. 'Very well then, I will dress for dinner.' They discussed Jane Carlyle's letters. Margot said she thought them excellent but that it seemed a pity that Jane had married Carlyle. 'With anyone but each other they might have been perfectly happy.' Tennyson shook his head. 'By any other arrangement four people would have been unhappy instead of two.'[20]

Following his usual hours, Tennyson went up to bed after an early dinner and came downstairs at ten o'clock to read his poetry to the company until midnight. Margot had by now regained her confidence, and finding a blue paperbound volume of 'Maud' among the piles of books on the floor, she asked him to read from it to her. He began with 'Birds in the High Hill Garden' and all her embarrassment at the poet's brusqueness was forgotten. His voice had 'the lilt, the tenderness and the rhythm that make music in the soul. It was neither singing, nor chanting, nor speaking, but a subtle mixture of the three . . .'; its haunting harmonies left her profoundly moved. When he had finished he pulled her towards him and said, 'Many have written as well as that, but nothing that ever sounds so well.'

She took back to London the copy of 'Maud' from which the poet had read, inscribed with her name and a line of poetry. In the last year she had begun to appreciate what George Curzon had meant when he came to Glen for the first time and talked to a young and ignorant girl of 'breadth of vision'.

CHAPTER 7

Indian Summer of an Oxford Don

IN OCTOBER 1890 Margot received a letter from a new but already
valued friend, Dr Benjamin Jowett, Master of Balliol College, Oxford. He
was returning Margot's commonplace book, lent so that Jowett could
criticize her short essays on well-known people, among them the one on
Gladstone which Symonds had praised: 'I return the book you entrusted
to me,' Jowett wrote, 'I am very much interested in it. The sketch of
Gladstone is excellent. Pray write some more of it some time. I understand
him better after reading it.'[1] These flattering words from so good a judge
went a little to Margot's head, for they came from a man she esteemed
above all others and whose praises she craved.

They had met in the autumn of 1888. There had been a large shooting
party at Gosford, the home of Lord and Lady Wemyss, where the sport
was second only to that at Glen. The women did not shoot, and when the
guns went out, Margot and the others occupied themselves until the men
returned, usually in time for tea. It had become the habit for Margot to
dance after tea to entertain Lord Wemyss. She would put on an accordion-
pleated skirt designed for the purpose, and go down to the marble hall to
await the men's arrival. On this particular day someone was playing the
piano softly. Margot kicked off her shoes and was weaving in and out of
the chairs when she suddenly caught her heel in the skirt and fell at the feet
of an elderly clergyman sitting by the window. Before she could stop
herself she uttered a loud oath of the kind common on the hunting field.
Ashamed, she stood up, full of contrition and apologized: 'I am afraid I
have shocked you,' but he answered politely, 'Not at all' and begged her to
continue. Did she know that the man at whose feet she fell was the famous
Dr Jowett? She told the family that she supposed him to be the minister of
Aberlady, but this is hard to believe; she could not have been at Gosford
five minutes without knowing that the Master of Balliol was expected and

his identity must have been revealed by a process of elimination, for she knew everyone else in the house.

Almost immediately she sensed a sympathy between herself and Jowett. Here was a man whom she could respect and admire but never be afraid of, a man who might even teach her much that she longed to know. It was the start of one of the happiest periods of Margot's life; under Jowett's firm but affectionate paternal discipline, she abandoned all pretence, all conceit and all striving after effect.

> . . . I was young and he was old . . . but I never felt this difference. I do not think I was a good judge of age, as I have always liked older people than myself, and I imagine that it was because of this unconsciousness that we became such wonderful friends. Jowett was younger than half the young people I know now and we understood each other perfectly.[2]

Jowett was a bachelor, but as an experienced Oxford don he understood the young very well and knew exactly how to handle them. He sized up Margot without difficulty, met her direct gaze without blinking so that Margot knew instinctively that she had better not try to swamp him with her personality after her customary fashion. When she was placed next to him at dinner and began to talk in her quick, confident way, she noticed that Jowett listened, putting in a word here and there to indicate that he was interested and to spur her on. It took no time at all for her to learn how he had been twice passed over for the Mastership before he was elected, because of the alleged rationalism of his views, and how Pusey (of the Oxford Movement) had attacked his essay on the interpretation of scripture. Symonds had recently read Plato's *Republic* to Margot, painstakingly explaining everything she did not understand—which was most of it. It was from Symonds that she had learned that Jowett was in the process of translating the whole of Plato, a monumental task that left even Symonds amazed. Thus she came to the friendship better equipped than Jowett, for she knew a great deal about him and he nothing of her. In the circumstances she could hardly fail to make an impression on a lonely old man, a little soured by the treatment he had received at Oxford.

Jowett was a silent man who had no wish to earn a reputation as a conversationalist. Margot did not mind this in the least. Talk poured out of her, revealing her personality and showing she could be lively, inquisitive, sympathetic and passionate, as she gave Jowett the benefit of the

curious patchwork of her mind. If Jowett was silent, it was not from
boredom; by contrast Margot threw reticence to the winds as she told him
the story of her life. To become the friend of such a learned man and one,
moreover, from that elitist society, late Victorian academic Oxford (of
which she had heard so much from Symonds) and to be allowed to talk to
him on serious matters, was a form of bliss that had hitherto always
eluded her. And when the Master did see fit to instruct her, Margot
listened without once interrupting and that very night while the words
were still fresh in her head she wrote them down in her diary.

Early in the acquaintanceship Margot coaxed Jowett into talking to her
about religion. She sensed that the depth and sincerity of his religious
belief was expressed by his character, which only those close to him were
allowed to glimpse: 'Humility, freedom from self, moral courage and the
ability to live, were all there for me to profit from. He had an ennobling
influence on my life.'[3] These were not idle words, but written with the
deepest sincerity in Margot's old age when she was able to look back and
assess her past.

Like Margot, but in a very different way, Jowett took his religion
seriously and he was afraid that a young girl's emotions were too
unbridled to discuss such matters calmly. Besides he was afraid he might
influence her, he said, and that therefore his feelings on the subject must be
muted. However, he had no objection to discussing 'academic religion',
for that was quite a different matter. But Margot had no such inhibitions
and begged him to explain about miracles. Jowett replied:

> There need be no trouble about dogmas, which are hardly intelligible to
> us, nor ought there to be trouble about historical facts including
> miracles, on which the view of the world has naturally altered in the
> course of ages. I include in this such questions as whether our Lord rose
> from the dead in any natural sense of the word. It is quite a different
> question whether we shall imitate him in this life. I am glad you think
> about these questions and shall be pleased to talk to you about them.[4]

Jowett threw the wonders of his mind wide open for Margot to see and
enabled her to talk of matters she had never touched on before, a most
extraordinary experience. They discussed everything from the Athana-
sian creed to Disestablishment. When a remark struck her as particularly
apt she wrote it down at once. There was one she liked very much: 'Most

individuals have always been better than churches!'—eight little words that to her contained the wisdom of the ages.

Jowett very quickly divined that Margot not only thirsted for knowledge but also for occupation. He guessed that though she was alert and intelligent her mind was crammed full of worthless facts which she mistook for learning and yet left her unsatisfied. The long letters he sent her suggest that he understood that she was crying out for instruction, discipline and orderliness, but did not know where to look for them. On impulse he gave her his translation of Plato's *Republic* and then regretted it. Would it confuse her? Was it too complicated? 'I hardly know whether it was an appropriate present,' he wrote to her afterwards, 'at any rate I do not expect you to read it.' But she read it avidly. Already she had read Jowett's book of sermons, which she kept on her bedside table to read when she could not sleep: 'I always feel you leave some touch of yourself and your work near to help me.'[5] Jowett's heart was touched; never before had he met a young person who worked so hard to learn.

To her credit Margot cherished every letter Jowett wrote to her and when he admonished her, which he did whenever he thought it necessary, she took her scolding like a lamb and was pleased that her sex was no protection from the Master's strictures. If he did not approve of something she had said or done, he told her so. He had been outspoken far too long when dealing with his pupils to have any qualms now. If Margot defended herself it was because she wished to stand well in his eyes. Her smoking shocked him and after one of her visits to Balliol he wrote to her not without humour:

> The Symonds girls at Davos told me you smoked, at which I am shocked because it is not the manner of ladies in England. I always imagine you with a long hookah, puffing, puffing, since I heard this; give it up, my dear Margaret, it will get you a bad name.[6]

Although she was hurt, she accepted what he said without offence, an excellent mark in her favour which he noticed with pleasure. But she could startle him more than anyone, even when it was not her intention. One evening when staying in Oxford she took with her to Balliol a large packet, tied together with ribbon; it contained letters from her admirers which she wanted to read to him. He rebuked her, but kindly, and after she returned to London sent her some advice:

Shall I give you a small piece of counsel? That it is better for you and a duty to them that these disappointed persons should never be known to a single person, for as you are well aware one confidante means everybody and the good natured world, who are of course very jealous of you, will call you cruel and a breaker of hearts etc.[7]

This was news to Margot. Who could be jealous of her? For self-assured though she was, in some ways she was very humble and without vanity. In fact, as she told the Master at their next meeting, so unconscious was she of herself that when she parted from her acquaintances she never thought 'what do they think of me, but always, what do I think of them?'. She pondered on this new thought of jealousy. How could even someone so ordinary as she (well, perhaps not exactly *ordinary*) make people jealous or envious of her? She asked Jowett to tell her, which made him smile broadly. He thought the picture she had of herself to be so juvenile as to be very touching.

When she returned to London that night she sat at her desk in her dressing-gown, composing a character sketch of herself. When it was finished she put it in an envelope with a short note asking for Jowett's comments. It was a challenge which he met with perfect composure and sweetened the answer with just a little flattery, natural in an old man to a sprightly young girl whom he liked and who so openly admired him. But it was the waste of her talents which he found alarming:

The young lady's portrait of herself is quite beautiful and not at all flattered. Shall I add a trait or two? She is very sincere and extremely clever, indeed her cleverness almost amounts to genius. She might be a distinguished authoress if she would, but she wastes her time and her temperament, scampering about the world and going from one country house to another in a manner not pleasant to look upon and still less pleasant to think of twenty years hence when youth will have made itself wings and fled away.[8]

Tears of dismay filled Margot's eyes as she read his letter but on the whole she took it in good part, for she knew Jowett was really fond of her and that his criticisms were meant for her benefit. Her reply was brisk and gave no hint of her private tears: Did he want to make a Sister of Charity out of her?[9] Back came his reply with all speed:

Certainly not (although there are worse occupations) nor do I desire to make anything. But your talking about plans of life does lead me to think of what would be best and happiest for you. I do not object to the hunting and going to Florence and Rome, but should there not be some higher end to which these are the steps? I think that you might happily fill up a great portion of your life with literature (I am convinced that you have considerable talent and might become eminent) and a small portion of works of benevolence, just to keep us in love and charity with our poor neighbours and the rest I do not grudge to society and hunting . . . You see that I cannot bear to think of you hunting and ballet dancing when you are fair, fat and forty-five. Do prepare yourself for that awful age.[10]

From time to time, Jowett continued not only to scold her gently for misusing her time and for indulging in profitless pursuits, but also to give her good advice which she eagerly sought but seldom followed, he noticed with a sigh. Nevertheless she longed for his good opinion: 'I am glad you do not think me frivolous,' she wrote after one happy weekend. 'You do not know how much I try to be good and intelligent, full of life with energy and interest. I shall never never forget how much you have done for me.'[11]

By a lucky stroke Jowett had picked on the one talent that might some day be of great solace to her—writing. But he made the mistake of letting her think she could write easily and without much effort, an error he would have avoided when dealing with his pupils. Margot's personality had won this taciturn man over and there were moments when he felt he had been too harsh with her. Without in the least intending it, he gave Margot the impression that her talent was so great that she could sit down and produce a masterpiece at the drop of a hat. He did not realize that he was preaching to the converted by talking extravagantly.

Margot had known Jowett for some months before he invited her to one of his famous weekends. She was puzzled as to the reason since he had many women friends who stayed in the Lodgings, among them the strait-laced Mrs Humphry Ward. In the end she asked him why she was left out, and was told that he did not care for her to stay in the home of a bachelor without a chaperone, but that if she would bring one with her, she should have an invitation for the very next Friday to Monday. Peals of laughter greeted this announcement. She told him (between gales of mirth) that she had never gone anywhere in her life with a chaperone, and that if he wanted her as his guest he must take her without one. Defeated, Jowett gave in and Margot was on such good form and helped her host so much with his older women guests that before long she was regularly acting as his hostess, sitting opposite him at the ugly long mahogany table with its heavy silver, and afterwards sweeping the women off to her sitting-room. Although so much younger than the others she behaved with perfect grace and dignity, keeping the conversation going in a most becoming fashion, flushed with pleasure at Jowett's pride in her.

It was one of the Master's habits to conduct his guests across the quadrangle after dinner, no matter what the weather, merely to hear indifferent music played in hall by Balliol undergraduates. Margot viewed the prospect of walking over the cobblestones in her trailing skirt and thin shoes (often in the rain) with dismay, and made up her mind that it was her duty to put a stop to such nonsense. The following weekend she convinced Jowett that it was much more profitable to spend the hour or two after dinner in conversation, an arrangement he found so agreeable that all thought of amateur music was quickly forgotten. Very soon Jowett dropped into the habit of consulting Margot about his guest list, and in this way she met many cultured and well-known people, among them some of the most noted scientists of the day. Scientists had never come Margot's way before and she was quite unused to their strange behaviour, until she found herself sitting between Sir Alfred Lyle and T. H. Huxley at one of Jowett's Saturday dinners. It was heavy going. Next time they came to Balliol she did a little better. The talk turned on religion and Huxley challenged her to name one man of action who had been influenced by religion. Promptly Margot said 'General Gordon' and Huxley declared himself defeated. After this splendid start Margot expected a discussion on Gordon between them, but in the manner of academics, his duty done, Huxley turned his back on her indicating that the conversation was closed.[12]

Determined never to be snubbed again, Margot read a great deal about subjects she was interested in and a few months later when she and Huxley met again, she adroitly turned the conversation her way, making herself appear both clever and well-informed, thus captivating her neighbour completely. It was an old trick she and Laura had learned when preparing for those bedroom sessions at Glen. This time she only did it to shine in Jowett's eyes because she had become devoted to him; but she did not care a fig for Huxley himself, nor for the other guests if it came to that, and said so in a letter to the Master which shook him a little:

> . . . as for being influenced by the world and its opinion of me, I have trampled it under my feet all my life. I should like to see it cast me off! I assure you it never will. Society is after all but a slippery stepping stone to other far more important things and once one finds one's footing and knows it is slippery one does not slip . . . I have never gone to the world and asked anything of it and it has come to me and always will, because I am independent of it.[13]

This letter followed a week-end that had not been wholly successful. Jowett had invited an old friend, Lady Tavistock, and because of his ignorance of the reaction of woman to woman he felt sure that she and Margot would get on well together, but they did not. Perhaps jealousy to be first in the affections of the innocent, well-meaning old man, was the cause of the antagonism. Lady Tavistock complained that Margot did not know how to treat an older woman, which Jowett knew to be true, but only in the sense that Margot never thought about age and behaved in the same way to young and old alike—'I did not think people should be treated differently because they are old.' When Jowett told her what Lady Tavistock had said and scolded her gently, Margot was furious and said that Lady Tavistock could no more understand her than a Presbyterian the good in breaking the Sabbath. For this bit of sauce, a rebuke came by return of post—Margot did not treat her friends properly.

To do her justice Margot had never once thought of Lady Tavistock as a friend, but she knew very well that what Jowett really meant was that she had been guilty of rudeness to a guest in his house. Tears filled her eyes at the havoc caused between this dear friend and herself by that hateful woman: 'I minded your letter of this morning,' she wrote.

> Although I would rather be corrected by you than anyone. I could not stand it from anyone else. It is all very well for other women to have very different natures and impulses to criticize, they can never understand or interest me. They do not understand life, they understand etiquette, and very respectable too, which I know enough about to mix in what is called the 'best society'. Seriously I hate you thinking this about me. I try to work and be good much more than you think and I am alive to my

fingertips with a desire to serve God and, through the best in man, make
the best of myself. Write me one word more like your very own kindest
self, the self that is not severe or influenced by anything but your real
affection for me—it saddens me terribly to think of losing you. I cannot
bear it and I would give you a long slice of my life if it would keep you
here and help everyone like you always do.[14]

This was too much for Jowett's kind heart. Full of remorse he sent her a
telegram (unfortunately now lost) and Margot's reply is another relic that
he could not consign to the flames: 'Your telegram and sweet messages
warmed my heart—I hope my letter did not vex you.'[15]

When it came to experience of the world, Margot sometimes had
something to teach Jowett, who did not have his feet planted as firmly on
the ground as his young friend. Margot could not help laughing heartily at
the Master's simple faith in certain sections of society, whose foibles she
had discovered years ago. She would chide him for his pathetic belief in
'the fine manners, high tone and wide education and lofty example given
by the British aristocracy. It shocked him that I did not share it'.[16] Neither
Jowett nor Margot had been born into the uppermost ranks of society.
Margot had joined them, but joining them had made her cynical, for they
were not all they appeared to be.

It was difficult to say which of them bloomed the more during the short
years of this strange friendship. Margot felt Balliol to be her second home,
and when Jowett was busy on college business, she would take her books
and read in a large leather chair by the window in the drawing-room that
looked out on the tree-filled quadrangle below. He had assured her that
she was never in the way and that it comforted him to come in and find her
happily occupied as he liked the young to be. A man who has lived among
men all his life and who has seen more than one generation pass before his
eyes but has formed no deep attachment to anyone is bound to feel he has
missed something as he approaches old age. The friendship was not
one-sided. Not only did Margot bring her own sparkling personality with
her, she also gave a lonely old man a new absorbing interest, a new role
almost, as mentor and adviser to a lively and clever young girl.

Teaching was second nature to Jowett and it is as a teacher that he will
be remembered, as well as for his dominant personality. Subtly he started
educating Margot from the moment they met; books became something
more than leisure reading and she began to see old favourites like Jane

Austen, George Eliot and the Brontës in a new light and noted much that she had passed over before. The same is true of her reading of history; it was like wearing spectacles after having been short-sighted for years. In the discussions together she began daringly to make comments which she had been afraid to make in Jowett's presence before. He quite understood her longing to be better educated and put himself out to help her, while at the same time restraining her from attending lectures and discussions she might not fully understand, since 'they are only a waste of time'.

Early in 1893 Jowett was seriously ill and while he was still able to do so, composed farewell letters to all his friends, dictating them to his housekeeper and secretary, Maria Knight. Margot was at Glen when she received hers but refused to take the illness seriously; the letter had been sent in a fit of depression she felt sure. At once she telegraphed back: 'I refuse to accept your farewell letter to me: you have been listening to some silly woman and believing what she says.'

The telegram had a magical effect, she says; from that moment Jowett got steadily better. It was probably as Margot sensed, that he was merely depressed and not dying at all and that her telegram made him laugh. If that was so she did do him much good. Margot always believed that her brisk message cheered him up enough to give him a few more months of life. Later in the year Jowett really did begin to fail. His biographer says he suffered from a prolonged malaise that defied diagnosis.[17] Maria Knight wrote to tell Margot how things were and at once Margot dropped everything and travelled to Oxford. She went quite alone, for she could not bear that anyone should see her grief and for once in her life talk seemed out of place. Had she meant anything to this man who had meant so much to her? She did not know, yet from Jowett's letters to her it is not difficult to discern deep affection, though camouflaged by advice and not a little scolding. She pondered on this on the way to Oxford, a journey she had done many times in the five years she had known Jowett.

Towards the end of her own long life, Jowett often came back into Margot's thoughts as she tried to assess what his friendship meant to her. She came to the conclusion that his guidance and admonitions had done her more good than all the praise of her other friends put together. For the first time she had seen herself through another's eyes and realized that he was serious when he said that she was wasting her talents on trivialities. How easy it had been to reform with Jowett on hand to guide, advise and love her.

For the last three days she ever spent at Balliol there were no other guests. Both Jowett and Margot knew that this was the end, but there was no sadness or tears for Margot wanted nothing to spoil this time together. Jowett still got up for part of the day, and after a simple dinner Margot took his arm and helped him back to his study, a room smelling of beeswax and old books which Margot loved. When he sat in his big leather armchair she noticed how small he had become and kneeling by his side she silently gave thanks for having known him and for all the richness he had brought into her life. Very early next morning Margot left for London and never saw her beloved old friend again. The following Sunday he wrote to her for the last time:

> I shall look forward to your coming to see me if I am seriously ill—'be with me when the light is low'. But I don't think that this illness which I at present have is serious enough to make any of my friends anxious, and it would be rather awkward for my friends to come and take leave of me if I recovered, which I mean to do, for what I think a good reason—because I *still* have a great deal to do.[18]

On 23 September 1893 Jowett could not get out of bed and on 1 October he died peacefully. The faithful Maria Knight informed Margot of his death by telegram, but Margot does not mention the fact in her autobiography. As when Laura died, the pain went too deep for words.

Chapter 8

A Winter Love

EVER SINCE SHE could remember, Margot had been in and out of love. In her first season she had managed, almost without thinking about it, to get herself engaged to a most unsuitable man who was forbidden the house by her irate father. At the time Margot was furious and contemplated running away and getting married at Gretna Green, but Scottish common sense came to her rescue just in time. Years later, when writing her autobiography, she wanted to describe this love affair, but could not even remember her fiancé's name. Charles had repeatedly told his girls he was not going to allow any Tom, Dick or Harry to marry them, and that they must choose men as rich as he was in order to keep them in the style to which they were accustomed. 'You must marry your superior', was Emma's motherly advice (which meant much the same thing) after Margot had produced two unsuitable prospective husbands from among her acquaintances in the hunting field. Yet when it came to the point, both Charles and Emma allowed all their daughters to marry the men of their choice.

With Peter Flower it was different. Margot was nineteen when she first met him, and on her side it was love at first sight. It happened at Ranelagh in 1883 on a golden summer day. Peter Flower was sitting at a table with her sister Charty Ribblesdale eating ices and looking so wonderfully handsome and carefree that Margot caught her breath with amazement. It seems that Peter Flower noticed her at once too, for as Margot walked slowly towards him, a tiny figure in grey muslin with a wide black sash and hat to match, Peter Flower asked in a voice carefully calculated for her to overhear, 'Is that the one who rides so well?' It was a splendid start for Margot, who could not fail to notice the admiration in his voice. Nevertheless after they were introduced he turned his back on her and soon wandered away. He did not forget her, however, and so began a long and ardent love affair that was to bring Margot little joy.

That Margot fell madly in love is not surprising. Peter Flower, the younger brother of Lord Battersea, had been breaking hearts for years and when Margot met him he was no longer in his first youth, although in other respects quite unchanged. Some called him a bounder and a cad, others an attractive dare-devil, with his peculiar animal grace, powerful sloping shoulders, fascinating laugh and infectious vitality.[1] Margot always noticed how men wore their clothes and judged them accordingly; she saw at once that Peter Flower was the best-dressed man she had ever seen: 'I do not know who could have worn his clothes when they were new,' Margot wrote, 'but certainly he never did.'[2]

Although usually so critical and demanding, Margot was soon so in love that she did not notice Peter's lack of humour, his sullen temper and his unreliable nature. When they first met she did not know that Peter borrowed freely from his friends and never paid them back (Margot may have lent him considerable sums of money herself, for she had a large allowance which her father did not ask her to account for). Women, servants and the lower orders in general were there to serve him. Over and over again Margot had scolded George Curzon for his rudeness to servants, yet she was not in the least put out when Peter Flower spoke offensively to his patient groom or forced a tired horse over a difficult fence merely to show off. She knew that he lived like an emperor but had never done a day's work in his life, and that when England became too hot to hold him he got out of trouble by disappearing to India to hunt big game until his outraged creditors cooled off or his brother paid his debts; but all this made no difference. Before he met Margot his love affairs had always been with married women and it was quite usual for him to have two or even more mistresses at a time, for the sheer excitement of preventing one getting to know about the other. He was notorious for the number of husbands who threatened to horsewhip him. He probably would never have looked at Margot if she had not ridden even more boldly than he did.

Attraction developed into a serious passion and before long Margot was wildly, uncritically in love and grudged every moment spent apart from the adored. Yet she kept him away from her intellectual friends (he had never been known to read a book in his life) and never took him with her to a 'Souls' house-party. At nineteen she was already too experienced a woman of the world not to know that Peter would be a fish out of water in such company.

In her novel *Octavia* Margot idealized Peter as the hero Greville, the lover and eventually the husband of the heroine. In this tempestuous love affair there are tears, recriminations, threats, partings and sweet reconciliations, until Octavia almost dies in childbirth when Greville, on his knees, asks for forgiveness. Although some of the incidents are substantially exaggerated, most of the novel is autobiographical and tells in essence the story of her affair with Peter Flower. One aspect of this love of hers still mystifies. Why did a girl of such spirit put up with so much rough treatment? Peter had a terrible temper and when Margot once kept him waiting he deliberately smashed a Chippendale mirror and, as if that was not enough, seized a valuable chair and broke it in half. A besotted Margot forgave him because Peter had such charm, so she let him stay instead of sending him packing.

In spite of all this, it is curious how much they had in common to hold them together. Both admired great recklessness, which meant to them living life at its best. Once Peter dared her to ride his half-broken horse, Havoc, which only he could manage. Margot could not resist a dare so she mounted him and it was only a few minutes before she was thrown, the violence of the fall knocking her unconscious. All she says of the incident was that it was bliss to wake up and find Peter rubbing her feet, a look of concern on his face.[3]

Margot wasted the best years of her youth in imagining herself in love with Peter Flower: 'His power lies in love-making not in loving' was one of the truest things she ever said of him. But like every Victorian girl with a wastrel on her conscience, Margot deceived herself into believing that her love improved him. Years later, when the scales had fallen from her eyes, she wrote to a new friend she had met at Balliol, Alfred Milner: 'Peter was born without ambition, either moral or intellectual, tho' I poured all I possessed into stimulating and caring for him and believing in him. I found I had not the power to change him.'[4]

They had long periods of separation when Peter was in hiding in India. At these times Margot imagined herself cured, but the first sight of the prodigal on his return, brown and lean, sent her again head over heels in love. She was not only in love with him, but completely under his influence and obediently did everything he asked. After one of his Indian visits he came to her with a very long face: in his absence his brother had sold his hunters, so that he had not a single horse to ride. He begged Margot to borrow some for him. Alfred Lyttelton was not using his horses at the moment but since he neither liked Peter nor the way he treated his own hunters, could Margot persuade him? 'Peter is in London,' she wrote to Alfred, 'and he knows nothing of my request, but I thought as he has only a few days hunting since he got back, if you weren't using your horses, they could train [go by train] a little way and be at the hunt next Saturday . . . it is a small county and Peter is the gentlest rider . . .'[5] 'Gentlest rider indeed!' Alfred read between the lines all too accurately and promptly wrote refusing Margot's request.

Alfred had heard about the Peter Flower affair from Margot's sisters, who were beside themselves with worry over the affair. If she married Peter, her father would certainly cut her off with a shilling, for he had no intention of supporting such a spendthrift. Charty, the eldest surviving sister since Posie's death in 1888, undertook to talk seriously to Margot when she visited them in Leicestershire for the hunting. Bluntly she pointed out that Peter was not only worthless, but twenty years her senior, and would never marry her: 'except for hunting, you have no mutual interests'.

'Mine is a winter love,' Margot replied mournfully, dramatizing herself as she often did when Peter was mentioned. Charty briskly put her down. 'Nonsense, there is no such thing as winter love; if you are not careful, no decent man will ever marry you.'[6]

Something of Margot's ambivalent feelings for Peter Flower can be gauged from the fact that he never accompanied her to Balliol, although Jowett had encouraged her to invite her friends whenever she liked. Instinctively she knew that Jowett and Peter would not have taken to each other. But Jowett had a favourite pupil whom he invited especially to meet Margot, leaving them alone together during a quiet weekend so that they should have a chance to talk without interruption. Alfred Milner was ten years older than Margot, a fellow of New College and a barrister, one of those clever men whom Jowett was able to turn into stars. Just before they met he had been appointed private secretary to George Goschen, the Chancellor of the Exchequer, a wonderful chance for a man interested in politics. Jowett predicted a great future for him. Whether he was deliberately match-making when he threw Margot and Alfred together cannot be known but Jowett sensed that Milner was attracted and thereafter, for those weekends when they were both with him, the wily old man let Margot see Alfred in the sort of company where he could shine. No one understood the art of conversation better than Milner, who had that lightness of touch added to great knowledge that made him a delight to listen to; when he and Jowett got going together on a subject they both enjoyed, no one could keep up with them.

As Jowett guessed, Margot was enthralled. She admired Milner's looks too. He was not provocatively handsome like Peter Flower, but interesting, with his dark skin, melancholy but highly expressive brown eyes, and a humorous mouth. In those days he laughed easily, and Margot had forgotten how infectious genuine laughter could be. It made her feel happy simply to hear it. Jowett slyly fostered this new interest, extolling Milner's learning—he had won the Craven and Hertford prizes—and telling her what a joy he had been to teach. He told her that Milner did not smoke, gamble, hunt or play golf, although not in the least a prig but the most enjoyable company in the world. Here is a man of substance, she told herself, my superior in every way. The problem was to know if she was attracted because she was flattered by the attentions of such a clever man, whose company she so much enjoyed, or whether it was because he was so completely different from Peter. She told herself that his friendship was valuable to her and that she did not wish to lose it. Was she in love with two men at the same time? In July 1891 (a rare dated letter) she wrote to Milner thus: 'I want you to like me always. I feel as if I could give my friends a good deal—perhaps this is over confident, but I truly think I have a great deal of affection and interest to give anyone who cares to learn about me, if I care for them.'[7] This is a naïve letter for a girl of almost twenty-eight. The obligations of friendship were very clear to her, but she showed too plainly that she was over-anxious to keep her friends. Even if she did not love Milner, she nevertheless wanted him to remain close by her side.

The winter of 1891 found Margot once again in Davos after a lapse of three years, this time with her sister Lucy Graham-Smith, whose love-life had been almost as tangled as her own. Although married for some time, she had allowed herself to have a flirtation with the irresistible Harry Cust, a 'Soul' and one of the most self-indulgent men alive. The ending of it had sent Lucy into a decline, so out of pity Margot had taken her to Switzerland, where in the sunshine and the snow they had both licked their wounds in silence.

Determined not to think about Peter Flower, Margot spent too much of her time brooding on him. They had built up nothing together except a long series of quarrels, too ugly to remember. A few stray thoughts went to Alfred Milner—had he forgotten he had a friend called Margot? Walking in the glare of the Swiss sun made her long for the gloom of England. Even John Addington Symonds, waiting eagerly in the villa 'Am Hof' to read his latest work, had lost his charms. After a week his lack of manliness began to bore her—the luxury of Jowett's conversation, the rich storehouse of his mind, made Margot intolerant of lesser men. Jowett's thoughts never dwelt on his own feelings like Symonds', nor did he constantly think of his health. He had influenced so many by the sheer force of his personality, among them her new friend Alfred Milner, who was himself a strong character, and she began to realize how much she had gained in stature from the interest Jowett had taken in her. Unfairly she now forgot how much she owed to Symonds as well, and it was wrong of her to say that his friendship left no mark. She would keep comparing Symonds with Jowett to the former's disadvantage; he no longer improved her mind and she began to think him not as clever as she had supposed.

Lucy rapidly improved but Margot caught a cold which turned into a hard, dry cough, and made her think she had consumption. With obliging sweetness, Charty took her place as nurse when Margot went to Pontresina to convalesce. She knew no one there but she soon saw a face she recognized, Arthur Benson, the bachelor schoolmaster who had taught her brothers at Eton. They talked and dined and went climbing together for they were staying by chance in the same hotel. Benson felt Margot liked him and knowing a little of her conquests, was delighted with his success. He wrote in his diary: 'My weeks at Pontresina came like a light in the cloud. I was well and happy there and a rapid friendship formed with Margot Tennant was a great pleasure and delight. But I do not think it can be kept up.'[8] How cross he would have been could he have read what Margot wrote about the stuffiness of his views to Alfred Milner: 'It bores me to find people nailed to their opinions, it always means weakness.'[9] Little did Benson guess how far away Margot's thoughts had been on those walks they took together.

On the second morning while climbing a steep slope, Margot had such a dreadful fit of coughing that she thought the end had come. It passed, but it left her too weak to move. The fright was salutary, for it made her decide once and for all to let Peter go. Jowett had told her that she had a dual personality: Peter appealed to one side, Alfred Milner to the other. Which was stronger? Perhaps when she went home Jowett would help her to decide. He had said half in fun that she was 'the most educated uneducated woman' he ever knew. If she married Peter the educated part of her would be lost for ever, she reflected, but if she chose Milner with his quick mind and lightning wit, her intellectual side would be safe. For some months, although she had not recognized it, she had been moving towards Milner and away from Peter, so her decision was not as sudden as she thought. In the autumn she had spent a week at Bayreuth with a party of friends she had met at Oxford, and had enjoyed their company. All day there was fascinating conversation, laced with the wit and humour she loved so much, and she knew for certain that she could not exclude people like these from her life. They did not hunt, nor did they care in the least if Margot rode boldly or not—it was after all only a sport. Instead of this irritating her she found it refreshing and not once did the image of Peter flying over high fences in Leicestershire distract her thoughts. She wanted to tell Alfred Milner how she felt and to give him some hint of her release. But did she know him well enough? Perhaps she could give him a book and the manuscript of a story she had written with Laura as the heroine. The manuscript was illustrated with a sketch she had drawn of 'Laura in Heaven holding my heart strings' and with this she added a short note, hopeful yet enigmatic: 'You must come out to meet a new love and a new life and I shall help you to find it.'[10]

To her disappointment, he could not join her either at Bayreuth or at Davos, for he was about to be sent to Egypt as Financial Secretary to Sir Evelyn Baring. Her feeling of dejection surprised her and she was flat for days afterwards. Somehow she had thought that she had only to decide to give up Peter Flower, and Alfred Milner would step into his shoes. Was she to lose him too, she asked herself? To make certain that he would not forget her, she wrote to him again, although there was little to say, except for some trite words of congratulation and regret that he could not come.

Was she playing with fire? Alfred Milner was a shy, sensitive man unused to women, and although thirty-eight at the time he met Margot he had never been so attracted to a woman before. Her letters gave him hope, for he did not understand that Margot wrote in the extravagant fashion adopted by the 'Souls', who used words of endearment with far less than their ordinary meaning. On one or two occasions Margot had handled him roughly, not realizing at all that he was the kind of man who feared rebuff, especially from a woman as sought after as Margot. When things went wrong he would retire into his shell and could not be prised out easily. Up to that date Margot had not been very good with such men.

That she missed him was genuine enough, for she had assessed his value in her life very accurately, and the fact that her beloved Dr Jowett thought highly of him gave him added glamour. That Milner liked her she knew, but would this liking turn to love with both of them? She sent him a lock of her hair, a very intimate thing to do, then a book with a poem written in her own hand on the fly-leaf. In return Milner asked permission to dedicate his latest book to her. Then without warning, she did an astonishingly stupid thing: she sent the meagre pack of letters Peter Flower had written to her for him to read. Milner was even more shocked than Jowett had been. At once he became wary. Did she show her friends the letters he wrote her? The next time he wrote he made a stiff reference to her indiscretion, but Margot defended herself, albeit lamely: 'I wanted to prove to you that in not marrying Peter, it was not before he himself acknowledged that it could not work.'[11]

One day in late July 1891, without previous warning, Emma announced calmly to Charles and Margot that she wanted to see Egypt before she died. She begged them both not to put up any opposition for she had made up her mind to go and to go soon: 'She loved Glen, knew Paris, disliked London and wanted to see the East.'[12] Hastily Charles and Margot thought up a thousand reasons why they could not go that summer; Charles pleaded pressure of work—he could not be spared from his office—while Margot reminded her mother how ill foreign travel always made her and that she would only be an encumbrance.

They both knew their excuses were useless for Emma had made up her mind and went about her business as though the matter was already decided, and all that was left to settle was the date. Afterwards Margot told her father in a surprised voice that she never thought sweet, quiet Mama could be so overbearing and selfish as to bounce them into a foreign holiday they did not want; it was nothing short of downright bullying to force them to leave home against their wills. That she was doing it for her daughter's sake Margot never suspected for a moment, nor that in a subtle, quiet way Alfred Milner had put her up to it.

While Margot was still in Davos with Lucy, and Charles too was away, Alfred had come to Glen to talk to Emma before taking up his new post. He had met Emma briefly several times in London and she, knowing of his passion for the country, had invited him to Scotland—a most uncharacteristic thing for her to do, but she saw in Alfred many excellent qualities that would counterbalance the bad ones in Margot. For three days the two of them had a happy time together, discussing gardening, inspecting the greenhouse—Alfred suggested she should grow more rare plants—and spending the evenings in talk by the fire, for Peeblesshire in July was chilly. It did not take Emma long to discover that Alfred was deeply attracted to her ebullient and reckless daughter and that he wanted her help. In a flash of inspiration Emma saw a way to remove Margot from the clutches of 'that horse-coper' Peter Flower. She touched lightly on the possibility of their making a European tour and perhaps ending up in Egypt. What was the climate like? Alfred took up the idea enthusiastically; if they came out he would see that they were entertained and looked after. She must leave it all to him.

It was not easy for Emma to manage a long journey with two unwilling companions, especially since she had never done anything of the sort before. Belief in her cause gave her the ability to cope and she managed it; it even surprised her how devious she could be when set on something that mattered to her. In order to disguise the real reason for the trip she announced that the holiday was to start with a leisurely overland trip through France and Italy, so that it would seem that European art and culture were the primary objectives and the visit to Egypt a mere after-thought. She hoped this might please her art-loving husband and perhaps propitiate her sulky daughter a little.

Right up to the last minute Charles vowed he would not go and put every obstacle in Emma's way; it was only on the last day that he admitted he was beaten. Arthur Balfour, who called the day before to say goodbye, asked Charles how he felt, only to be told 'as well as a man going to be executed can'.[13] On 13 November 1891 a gloomy little party left 40 Grosvenor Square for Victoria Station; when the train was late starting Charles announced in a satisfied voice that the boat would not wait, and that they might give up the idea of going altogether. One look at Emma's determined face dashed his hopes. She took no notice but without fuss began to count the mountains of trunks, baskets, rugs and wraps that made up their luggage, giving instructions to the courier and check-ing the tickets as though she had been travelling every day of her life. Margot watched her mother with amazement, not realizing that she was seeing a woman who believed herself fighting for her daughter's happiness.

The crossing was uneventful and Margot was not sick. She even enjoyed sight-seeing in Rheims, was enchanted by Lucerne, bought silk and visited the cathedral in Milan and showed such indefatigable energy that Emma smiled to herself with satisfaction. Because she saw Rome for the first time on a cloudy day, Margot thought it a 'sad city'. Then its treasures amazed her: 'Every bronze is a masterpiece and can appeal to quite common people ... Even criticism is silenced and you can only wonder at people ever tolerating anything ugly near them.'[14]

Friends resident in Rome appeared as though conjured out of thin air to act as guides and mentors: Rennell Rodd, Harry Cust, Lord Dufferin. The last took Margot aside to give her a bit of advice: 'You must marry, but you must never marry because but in spite of being in love. You are far too clever, my dear Margot, not to be helping some man.'[15] She was introduced to Dr Axel Munthe, the famous Swedish surgeon, and was nearly as delighted with him as he was with her. 'He took me to the Pantheon which I thought hideous inside,' and immediately a kind of flirtation started between them which added a touch of excitement to everything they did together. He told her that she had 'flown across his path like a brilliant little bird that comes quite close and then flies away', but added censoriously that she was 'dreadfully spoilt and that he wished he had met her before she was so spoilt'.[16] Harry Cust and Rennell Rodd took her to Pompeii, where she was delighted to find a rose tree in full bloom amidst all the evidence of destruction and at its roots some maidenhair fern which she picked as a souvenir.[17] At Brindisi they embarked for Alexandria in a noisy and uncomfortable ship. The food was vile and Margot was ill: 'I felt I was in hell.' Alexandria she thought loathsome—'all Egyptian screams and perspiration'. She thought it about time she wrote to Alfred Milner. 'I am with uninteresting people so I don't read and don't speak to anyone—you will be surprised to hear I don't—no one takes any notice of me.'[18] It was a poor letter, but she felt sick and her brain had stopped functioning. Part of her trouble was lack of exercise. Never before had she suffered the sheer misery of days of inactivity, cooped up in a small boat with nothing to do. The experience so enervated her that she soon ceased to read but lay on her bed, torpid and inert: 'the ship was so hot, the cabin so stuffy, that I took off all my clothes in the afternoon and lay in my chemise,' she wrote to Mary Drew. But at the very first glimpse the Nile was 'the most beautiful river in the world and the sunsets thrilled into my very soul'.[19]

Letters from England were waiting and one from Cairo which she opened first. Life suddenly took on a rosier hue, for the letter was quickly followed by Alfred Milner in person, full of plans for her entertainment. Margot found she was surprisingly tongue-tied, but excused this to herself on the grounds that 'Alfred makes me feel a little too dependent on information to talk well . . . the fact is I do not know enough and all the imaginative insight in the world will not serve me instead of knowledge . . .'[20] After a few hours in his company she changed her tune: 'Alfred Milner has gravity and charm,' she wrote in the journal she was keeping of the trip. 'I delight in talking to him . . . He has a very rare mind,' she went on. 'Without being a humorous man, he has a very fine sense of humour.'[21]

One evening, as the light was fading, they rode along together near the Pyramids, cool at last after a hot and gruelling day. Exhilarated by the excellent performance of her arab mare and the company of an attractive male who was so obviously in love with her, Margot was radiant with the joy of living, looking almost beautiful in her white jacket that showed off her small figure. Abruptly Alfred reined in his horse and dismounted; lifting Margot down he kissed her with great passion and proposed marriage. The spell was broken: a love affair was one thing, marriage another. When she got her breath back Margot played for time, neither accepting nor rejecting him. After a long and tempestuous affair with Peter Flower, she was not ready to love again so soon, but she did not want to lose him altogether and made an astonishing suggestion—could she not do something in return for his love?[22]

Parting from Alfred (the Tennants' Egyptian holiday was drawing to an end) was painful, and tears filled her eyes when she kissed him good-bye. Once alone in her cabin, she flung herself on her bunk and wept copiously. What was the matter with her? Why were her feelings so ambivalent? She wanted him close to her but that did not mean she needed the intimacy and permanence of marriage. In her mind the two were different. Yet, lonely without him on the boat, she wrote him a tender letter: 'I have . . . flung myself into the safest, strongest, and dearest protection any woman can have or hope to have.'[23]

The journey home in the *Gironde* was faster but just as uncomfortable as going out. The disgusting food and the smell of rotten apples combined with the violent motion of the boat made Margot sick again. Three more days of rough seas and her own company (Emma and Charles kept to their cabin) brought on a cooler mood and she wrote a letter that shocked the suitor she had left behind. Margot claimed that it was 'only honest' to let Alfred know of her changed feelings, overlooking the fact that she ought to have been sensitive enough to let him down gently: 'I am especially blessed by your love,' she wrote, 'but every hour I live I am more certain that we ought not to marry; we have too many of the same faults, love of life and joy of impulse.'[24]

Of course they were not in the least alike really, and Alfred was far too perceptive not to guess that her love was waning. Only a few days before, sitting on the desert sand as they rested their horses, Alfred's arm round her waist, her head on his shoulder, she had stressed how *opposite* their natures were and taken this for a good sign. She had ticked their differences off on their fingers: she was extrovert, demanding, selfish and cheerful; he was shy, melancholic, clever, serious and selfless and so on. It was all said lightly, with much laughter and banter and at the time Margot had been sincere. But once at home, facing the gloom of a delayed spring, she knew for certain that although Alfred's friendship was precious to her, she did not want him for a husband. Among other things, his caresses were far more passionate than she cared for and she could not respond to them. It was largely because Peter Flower had been a cool lover that she had felt safe and had allowed the affair to drift on for years.

The familiar surroundings of 40 Grosvenor Square helped her to think rationally again and she began to analyse her feelings in earnest. The rides in the desert, Alfred's declaration of love and her agony of indecision were like a dream and fading just as quickly. While she was with him she enjoyed keeping him in a state of suspense between hope and despair, but this was crueller with a man of far more sensitive feelings than Peter Flower. Furthermore, she could never live out of England. Where else was the hunting so good? Every time she wanted to come home she would have to endure the agonizing fear and discomfort of crossing the sea, and she would want to come home often.

She had been right from the beginning; the Egyptian trip had been a waste of time. Looking at herself in the glass the very first day home, she noticed how yellow her skin had become, how sunken her cheeks and how bloodshot her eyes. Her hair felt dry and stiff like wire and despite many washes she fancied she could still feel sand on her scalp. What would happen to her if she had to live in a hot climate for the rest of her life? Besides, her interest in foreign countries was minimal. Yet despite all these disadvantages, she could not quite let go of Alfred and she continued to play out the charade of still caring for him, by post.

Her account of the Egyptian holiday written in the form of a journal was to be privately printed, the copy for Alfred to have a special inscription, for the Egyptian past belonged to him. Re-reading the journal awoke sentimental feelings she had begun to think quite gone, and she had to fight down words of endearment when writing to him: 'I don't think you know or have any idea how intimate I feel with you—we are close, close friends' ran one letter, and another started out well but ended in an impossible fashion so that Alfred did not know where he stood.

> I have been living in the saddle Friday and Saturday with beautiful rides home along the Tay . . . Such a great open growing country I love every field in it and I ride better this year than I ever did . . . good-bye dear blessing, I am your restless, hopeless, intensely happy, passionately unhappy, always loving Margot.[25]

It was spring, and Charty wanted Margot to come to Gisborne, ostensibly to see how her nephews and nieces had grown but really for a quite different reason. No one in the family knew whether to welcome Alfred as Margot's prospective husband or not, and they could not be left in ignorance any longer. Besides, it would do Margot no harm to have a taste of family life in the company of bright and friendly children. In this way she might see what she was missing. Despite little experience, Margot was good with Charty's children. She romped with them, read to them and showed them how to paint. Full as her days were, she did not forget Alfred: 'We have been out of doors with every sort of animal, horses, pet lambs, goats and kids. We read out loud in the evenings.' Casually she mentioned that the Member of Parliament for East Fife, Mr Asquith, whom she had met once, months ago, was coming to stay with the Ribblesdales for a political meeting: 'I look forward to hearing him speak.'[26]

She even wrote to Alfred regularly, indeed she could not have written to him more often if they had been engaged. Not once did it strike her that she was unkind to lead him on. In her own mind the matter had been settled and she expected that Alfred would understand this; it was a bore to tell him in so many words. It was always to be her great failing that she could not dismiss a lover when love had disappeared but wanted to keep them and their devotion as trophies of past triumphs.

In the summer Alfred's book on Egypt was published and was an instant success. It was dedicated to Margot and was the occasion of a rare letter from Peter Flower: 'I am reading Milner's book, it has a fresh sort of swinging style about it.' Margot delighted in that phrase. Perhaps Alfred himself had a sort of 'swinging style' about him and that was the reason for his fascination for her. She loved the book, read it from cover to cover then lent it to her friends and made such a fuss about it that everyone believed it was a prelude to an announcement.

lian face. I thought then, as I do now, that he had a way of putting you not only at your ease but at your best when talking to him . . .'[1] He was different from the rest in other ways too, and although unfashionably dressed, he had so much personality that Margot made up her mind on the spot that this was the man who could help her and who would understand everything.

When dinner was over they had walked together on the terrace and despite Lord Battersea's efforts to elbow him out Asquith stayed by her side, eventually guiding her to the darkest corner where 'we gazed into the river and talked far into the night'.[2] At this first meeting they did, in fact, talk until dawn and each learned much about the other. Asquith had been at Balliol with Milner, knew and liked him, and was full of admiration for Jowett. This was an excellent beginning, perhaps a good omen. Protected by the dark and the interest in Asquith's voice Margot held little back, and it seems almost certain (since she felt so at ease with this stranger) that Margot gave him her life story there and then, including her affair with Peter Flower. She may even have told him (for she was desperately in need of a father confessor) of a very clandestine affair—of which she was more than a little ashamed—with Evan Charteris, the son of her friend Lady Wemyss, an undergraduate at Oxford whom Margot regarded as being of a different generation. It was to him that she had sent the sprig of maidenhair fern from Pompeii to make amends for a petulant letter.[3] She excused the lapse to herself by pretending that it would not have happened if she had not been bothered and wearied by her prolonged affair with Peter Flower. All she had done was to show that she enjoyed Evan's conversation and it never occurred to her that he could fall in love with so little encouragement, for she had made it known that she preferred older men and never gave the young ones any rope whatsoever. At the time, Evan had been a comfort, but a few weeks later when she had tired of him she was angry with herself for not managing her life better.

Compared with Evan, even compared with Alfred Milner, Asquith seemed to Margot a much more experienced man of the world. A Yorkshireman of humble origins, he had carried off all the important prizes while at Oxford. His early life had been a struggle, and he had continued practising at the Bar after entering Parliament in order to provide for his large family; hence he had little time for social life, which is why Margot had never heard of him. She was fascinated by the amount he had packed into only forty years. They found they had much in common in the love of books, and Asquith promised to advise her with her reading, especially poetry which he loved.

As she drove home to 40 Grosvenor Square in the early morning she felt happy, almost released, for the first time in months. Asquith's appearance in her life at that precise moment was heaven-sent. He poured healing oil into her wounds, drove away her self-pity, and gave her hope for the future. Already after only a few hours she looked on him as an anchor in a storm-tossed world, but it made her laugh to think that she was attracted to a man who played no games (in middle age he took to playing a little bad golf), did not hunt and did not even like riding. Yet he epitomized her ideal. Perhaps it was necessary for one of her nature to suffer deeply in order to appreciate a man of Asquith's calibre. If that was so, the bad times had been worthwhile.

A few days later they met again at a dinner party given by Sir Algernon West, Mr Gladstone's Private Secretary, who had been persuaded into inviting Asquith by Margot, on fire to meet her new friend again and make sure she was not exaggerating his good points. They were placed next to each other and both were delighted to discover they could pick up the conversation of the first meeting as though it had never broken off. That night she noticed things about him she had passed over before: he was a little gauche, a little awkward in movement and blushed frequently, was modest and shy but not easily embarrassed. Everything she had read, he had read too, and a great deal more besides. He enjoyed the theatre, dining out (although he seldom had the time for either) and staying up late, for it was only then that he had time for reading.

It made no difference to Margot that he was married and had a large family, nor did she feel guilty that by seeing him again she might be depriving them of his company. But she could not help herself being curious about his wife. When they did meet Margot was struck by the difference between Helen Asquith's nature and her own: Helen looked 'fulfilled', the kind of wife a man would be happy to go home to after a grinding day at the Bar or the House. Yet Margot knew she had the power to keep Asquith talking to her when he ought to have been in Hampstead with his family. Once she tentatively mentioned this to Asquith who replied that Helen did not like gadding about but preferred to stay quietly at home with the children.

Pretty, composed and homely, Helen Asquith gave Margot the impression that her own feelings were unimportant and that her family was her whole life. To a woman as restless as Margot the happy peace that Helen generated all round her was difficult to understand. Now that they had met, Margot did begin to feel a stab of conscience that she was keeping Helen's husband away from her for many a long evening, simply because he did her so much good, and yet this alone seemed to justify her action. Mr Asquith (as she still called him) was important to her; his wife had the children and could not mind his absence. It was very easy indeed thus to excuse her conduct to herself.[4] However, she was still outwardly kindly: 'I do hope, Mrs Asquith, you have not minded your husband dining here without you,' she asked the first time he brought her to dine at 40 Grosvenor Square, 'but I rather gathered that Hampstead is too far away for him to get back to you from the House of Commons. You must always let me know and come with him whenever it suits you.'[5]

Well said but not well meant. Margot guessed that Helen was too shy and too proud to ask any favours of her, since she knew very well she would be in the way. Writing many years later Margot wanted her readers to believe that there was no sting in her invitation and that she really meant what she said.

Asquith did not have enough leisure at this period of his life to see Margot as often as she would have liked, although when they could not meet they corresponded. She longed to see how her friends would take to him, so arranged for Lady Desborough to invite both the Asquiths to Taplow for one of Asquith's rare free week-ends. Did Margot hope that Helen would not come? If so she was disappointed, for wisely Helen accepted. The visit was a success. Everyone liked the young and pretty Mrs Asquith, who did not push herself forward but was content to listen to the conversation, although ready to speak up if her opinion was asked. How different from Margot, who was not happy unless the centre of attention! Later Helen admitted to Margot that although she had enjoyed herself 'she would not care to live in the sort of society that I loved'.[6] This confession filled Margot with amazement: she was even more taken aback when, after pointing out to Helen that she had a remarkable husband who might reach the highest pinnacle as a politician, Helen replied quietly that the 'highest pinnacle' was not what she coveted for him.[7]

In September 1891 Helen Asquith died of typhoid fever while on holiday with her family on the Isle of Arran. A month later Margot left for the Egyptian holiday. On her return it hit her suddenly that circumstances had changed dramatically. Only now that her love for Alfred had bloomed and quickly faded did she take in the full significance of the fact that Asquith was now a free man. At first it had not struck Margot that Helen's death would make any difference for she had never looked on the wife in the background as an obstacle to the friendship with her husband. All that concerned her was the realization that at last she had met a man who could satisfy her completely and that she badly needed his friendship, companionship and advice, which she was coming more and more to believe that he was willing to give. That this was taking away from Helen Asquith a very important part of marriage she did not seem to understand. She only saw this new friendship through her own eyes, her own feelings. She called the days spent in Asquith's company a 'great awakening for me'. Only once before, in Dr Jowett, had she met these great qualities of wisdom, tranquillity and perfect honesty all combined in one man. Like Jowett, Asquith was her intellectual superior, she could look up to him, feel safe with him, two elements essential for her if love was to last. She had been half afraid that Asquith would forget her when she was far away in Egypt, and that was partly why she was reluctant to go. But he sent her a 'parcel of books for your amusement' to await her arrival in Cairo and the nicest of letters which she read many times:

> The more I think of the flight into Egypt, the more I dislike the prospect ... but when you once get there you are bound to be interested in what you see ... and the tedium will be alleviated by the society of Milner and other well informed persons ... I curse the whole thing. But of course you are right and I love you for going.[8]

It was not a typical heartbroken widower's letter, but it had the effect Asquith intended; although Margot was only intermittently aware of it as yet, from that moment Milner's fate was sealed. In another letter Asquith's jealousy of Alfred Milner is scarcely veiled:

> Milner has been my friend for twenty years, which makes me more sensitive to what he says and I can't help noting a certain commonplaceness, a slight indefinable want of depth and delicacy, a lack as it were of flavour and fragrance both in the sentiment and the expression of what he writes. Am I wrong? I would not say so to anyone but you, for I know him to be a true and loyal friend.[9]

Margot would have treated any other man's denigration of his friend with contempt, but in Asquith's case she took the opposite line and began to see flaws in Milner which she had not noticed before; nor did she censure Asquith's lack of sympathy for Milner's difficulties. He had just taken up a new and exacting financial post which presented a hundred problems, and which were bound to make him abstracted at times. But she made no allowance for this. In Asquith's eyes Milner had committed the unforgivable sin of having the opportunity to see Margot every day under ideal conditions, something that was denied to himself. In him he saw a rival not only for Margot's love (though perhaps unconsciously) but also for the public eminence which was undoubtedly already his own goal.[10]

It was fortunate that Asquith was the kind of practical man who could put grief behind him with reasonable speed. He and his wife Helen had experienced eighteen years of perfect happiness and there is much evidence that Asquith did love her. Yet even before her death he had begun to move imperceptibly away from the life she wanted for him—a quiet day-to-day family life centred round the children, their illnesses and their successes. Asquith had been content with this too before he tasted the delights of society and the flattery and adulation of beautiful women. If Helen had lived and tried to hold his ambitions back, she might have suffered much misery.

Asquith's letters to Margot continued all through 1892–3. Whenever they did not meet the letters became long, hopeful and lover-like, and Margot replied to each one. This does not mean that Alfred Milner was neglected; she wrote regularly to him too. These letters gave Alfred hope: 'Home Rule separates Mr Asquith and me,' ran one letter that brightened his day, for it ended on a tender note: 'Good-bye dear blessing.'[11] In gloomy moments he wondered if Margot was playing them off against each other. Such coquetry was against her nature, however, which was always to proceed steadily towards the object of her desire. Nevertheless she was building up a dilemma for herself. Which man did she love?

Suddenly Asquith declared himself openly and sketched out his plans for their life together:

> I can conceive of no future of which you are not the centre . . . I know that there are moments when you picture to yourself with a shudder a life drained of movement and colour. I would rather be blotted out of your thoughts and even your memory than be the means of shutting you

off from the sunlight and the free air which you need, and in which alone your nature can put forth its incomparable radiance. I will give you everything that is in me to give—shelter, devotion, unshakable loyalty, timeless trust and homage, and I will take from you nothing but your love. The way of your life shall be as you determine it and your choice shall be my law.[12]

Margot's literal character took 'your choice shall be my law' to mean exactly what it said—she was to enjoy the privileges of a married woman yet be completely free and her own mistress. As it happened it was a most unwise letter for Asquith to write, and when she took it literally and spent each winter away from London for the hunting, it kept them apart mentally and physically for the first few years of their married life. However, his letter brought matters to a head; she knew at last that she could not go on hesitating for ever but must make up her mind. Yet this was the one thing she did not want to do.

Margot wrote to Jowett to ask him to help her decide, but wisely the old man would not do this; all he did was to weigh up the pros and cons and leave the decision to her:

The real doubt about the affair is the family. The other day you were at a masked ball, as you told me . . . and a few months hence you will have or rather may be having the care of five children with all the ailments and miseries and disagreeables of children . . . and not your own, although you will have to be a mother to them . . . I know that it is, as you said, a nobler manner of living, but are you equal to such a struggle? . . . I would not have you disguise from yourself the nature of the trial, . . . On the other hand you have at your feet a man of outstanding ability and high character who has attained an extraordinary position [Asquith had just been made Home Secretary] . . . and you can render him the most material help by your abilities and knowledge of the world . . . You may lead a much higher life if you are yourself equal to it.[13]

The letter gave Margot food for thought; she pondered on it long and earnestly but could come to no conclusion. She asked Jowett if she could bring Asquith to Balliol, and in those surroundings she saw him with new eyes, for Asquith shone in donnish company. It was obvious that Jowett was fond of his old pupil and between them they almost cut Margot out, but for once she did not mind. Jowett always wrote to her in glowing terms of 'Mr Asquith': 'He is a capital fellow and has abilities which may rise to the highest things in the law and politics . . . and not at all puffed up with his great office.' But he could not find it in his heart to allow Margot to forget Alfred Milner entirely: 'I have been reading Mr Milner's book with great satisfaction—most interesting and very important.'[14]

Before she could resolve her dilemma Jowett died and Margot was in despair at the loss of this adored friend. Like a child she had not expected him to die while she still needed him. Who will help me now? she moaned. Two men wanted to marry her and she did not know which she should choose. Peter Flower, too, was part of her life still and Evan Charteris had a strange hold on her. She thought herself bowed down with insoluble problems, began to feel ill, could not sleep and had such headaches that she had to lie down in a darkened room, sometimes even in the mornings. Then one day on impulse she packed a bag and took the night train to Glen; in the peace of the country she might be able to make up her mind, but at the sight of all that was familiar and dear she completely collapsed and had to be put to bed. For years she had talked of her nature as extrovert, yet she was just as capable as other people of suppressing her fears and worries and the bigger they were the more she refused to talk about them. This suppressed inner voice made itself heard in moments of strain like the present.

Unfortunately, though, there were guests at Glen, all healthy, all noisily enjoying themselves when Margot demanded perfect quiet. Lying with the curtains drawn, with a wet towel round her head, she heard doors banging, laughter and whispering on the stairs. One morning she woke to the sound of horses and going to the window saw a jolly party start off for an all-day expedition of the kind she used to love. She burst into tears and rushed back to bed sobbing her heart out.

Of course the whole household was worried about her. Her behaviour was irrational; weeping, refusing to eat or talk, and turning her face to the wall every time poor Emma begged to know what was wrong. She became hypersensitive and began to resent the fact that she was hardly ever left alone. Exhausted after crying, she would fall asleep and awake to find someone sitting in her room. She was a prisoner now and her jailers took it in turn to keep guard over her. What did they think she was going to do? Throw herself out of the window? When she asked with something of her old spirit why they were there, the watchers by the bed would lie 'because we want you all to ourselves, Margot'. Exasperated, Margot would mutter 'How dense people are'.[15]

Alfred and DD Lyttelton were in the neighbourhood and came hurrying over. Privately DD thought Margot was making a fuss about nothing, but could not help feeling sorry for her when she cried out dramatically:

How shall I be able to do this thing [marry Asquith and send Alfred away]? Never again before God will I place myself in this teasing, weary, tangle of doubt between two again. I feel every day now that life is closing in on me, not fettered by Asquith but by the now overbearing sense that I must put out to sea.[16]

Asquith wrote often and Margot found his letters a consolation. 'To know and to love you has been the best gift of my life . . . I know that in all the rushing interests of your life today and every day that there is at the back of your mind, a place for me. And that I am—shall I say content?'[17]

Asquith had been pleading for some time to be allowed to come to Glen, and when Margot felt well enough to see him he caught the overnight express and arrived for breakfast, but so worried about his prospects that by the time he reached Scotland he felt certain that Margot was going to refuse him. The sight of her thin and pale shocked him, for he had no idea of the agony of mind she had gone through. He had not realized that her recent nervous collapse was the consequence of a tug-of-war in her mind between her love for Milner and for himself. He had thought her illness a cold or a chill, perhaps an excuse to get away by herself and think. Now he felt bewildered. Why had she not said her illness was serious? He had thought that they were close; she had once said that there was nothing she could not tell him. He knew little of the life of the young woman he wanted to marry. If he had known more he might have understood what was holding her back: 'The future seems so veiled in haze,' he wrote in one of the letters he sent her at Glen, 'which may hide either sunshine or storm, that I cannot even form a guess of what may lie before me.'[18]

At first Margot received him coolly, but as the day wore on she began to unbend, won over by his lively conversation and good company. He was delighted with Glen and praised the scenery, the surrounding country and the good fresh air, so different from London. Margot knew he was not a man sensitive to visual beauty (it was only later on when he had more time

on his hands that, under her influence, he became very fond of pictures),
and she was touched that he should notice so much for her sake.

They walked hand in hand to Laura's grave and Margot achieved the
improbable feat of making him kneel down and pray with her in the peace
of the little churchyard. Kneeling in prayer was not a self-conscious act to
Margot, but came as naturally to her as breathing. She and Laura used to
drop on to their knees whenever the mood took them and the habit
remained with her. Once, after a mere half-hour's acquaintance, she
prayed with General Booth of the Salvation Army in a railway carriage
which they happened to be sharing. But that the conventional Home
Secretary of Her Majesty's Government should do so without demur
shows the hold Margot had gained over him.

Unfortunately for his peace of mind, Asquith left Glen without realizing
that Margot's reserve was cracking, for when he reached London he
wrote her a gloomy letter:

> I left Glen very sad at heart, for you almost blew out the candle of hope.
> It has often been very near extinction, but you could always by a touch
> of your finger make it blaze up again. As you know . . . it has been all the
> light of my day. You are not going to leave me in the dark, are you?[19]

Since the declaration of his love did not seem to move her, he tried, in a
desperate attempt to get back on to a companionable footing, to make a
suggestion that

> . . . it would be rather nice, as I can't see you, if we were to read some
> things together?—I mean read them at the same time and then ex-
> change ideas . . . we could begin with Keats' 'Hyperion'. Do you know
> it well? I haven't read it since I was a schoolboy. After all these things
> are better going over and over again than most of the new books . . .[20]

It was a move in the right direction, almost an inspired move and appealed
at once to the intellectual side of Margot, as well as having a calming
effect. Her fear of physical love subsided as she busily wrote Asquith an
essay on what she thought of Keats.

Sooner than she dared expect Margot felt strong enough to leave the
solitude of Glen and return to London. Her rapid recovery was as
mysterious as her decline. Perhaps by now in her heart she had decided to

marry Asquith and put her past behind her, but she told no one, although a letter to DD suggests this:

> Do not grow weary by thinking over me and my affairs, they must smooth out some day ... do not think it is selfishness this endless deliberation. I could not have married before, I was not free in my heart. Things must come from inside and somehow till I had quite released myself in a hundred little ways which live between one's heart and one's conscience I could not have felt honest in even speculating on an immediate marriage. I will do the best I can . . .[21]

All her doubts and fears were not yet resolved, but the biggest decision of her life was almost (although not quite) taken. As she travelled back to London the wheels of the train seemed to echo Asquith's last letter: 'I miss you, love you, live for you.' Unlike Peter Flower, who had a barely concealed contempt for women, Asquith revered women, and Margot felt the difference. What more could she want? She could find no flaws in Asquith; he had all those qualities important in a marriage that her other suitors lacked. Alfred Milner came nearest to him, but he could not relax and had already made work his god. Nevertheless she could not stop herself still regretting him. Each man that she had loved possessed something in his nature that cried out to hers, but none had everything. She told a friend: 'I often want help more than I dare own and there is loneliness in my life which few suspect.'[22]

CHAPTER 10

I should like to make something of my Life

A FEW HOURS after returning to London she wrote to tell Asquith that she would marry him: of her doubts she never said a word. Asquith was touchingly grateful that she had at long last come to a decision. Since he was one of those men who express themselves best on paper, he did not rush round to 40 Grosvenor Square but wrote a letter by return that moved Margot to tears:

> Almost the first time in my life I feel as though I could not distinguish dreams from realities. The thing has come which I have most longed for, waited for, prayed for, willed as I never did with any other aim or object in my life. And yet it seems at one moment so strange and at another so familiar and natural that my whole mental vision is out of perspective and I cannot describe because I cannot see.[1]

When they met his joy was so great that once again she feared to spoil it by telling him that she still had reservations, but on one point she would not give way. She did not want the announcement of their engagement to be made just yet; it would help if she could just get used to the idea a little.

Margot was grateful for his understanding; she knew perfectly well that people were talking about them, and wondering whether now that Asquith was Home Secretary she would have him. One or two said it to her face, and did not believe her when she replied that she preferred him when he was 'a less great man. If I marry Asquith it will be for one reason and one alone—because I admire his character'.[2] She even went to great lengths to hide her engaged state, by saying she and Asquith had little in common. 'He has none of my country tastes and life, I lean towards him more by strong approval than by love . . .'[3] Yet she had to admit that Asquith had proved more considerate and tender than any of her friends. The year before when E. F. Benson (son of the Archbishop and brother of

Arthur) published his novel *Dodo*, everyone took the heroine, 'a pretentious donkey with the heart and brains of a linnet' to be none other than Margot herself. Asquith was the only one who noticed her distress and did not mention the book to her, making it seem that he did not care a fig who Dodo was modelled on. It was only some years later that he told her that Lord Rosebery had used the heroine of the novel to warn him against her: 'If you want to know what Miss Tennant is like read *Dodo*.'[4]

Asquith was eager for her to meet his children and she agreed, though dreading it. The knowledge that she was to see them at last made her wonder what would happen if she disliked them. Would it sow dissension between her and Henry and spoil Henry's life? More easily than she had expected she had dropped 'Mr Asquith' and started to call him 'Henry' although he was 'Herbert' (a name she thought rather common) to his first wife and to all his friends: 'I must learn to call him "Henry",' she wrote to DD, and once the deed was done she wondered why she had been shy. To Asquith it was a sign that he was making progress.

Before the announcement of their engagement he took her to Redhill, where his children lived in the care of a governess. The meeting with these five extraordinary children (ranging in age from sixteen down to three) did not go well, yet it proved better than Margot expected. They were so different from the children of her friends, from Charty's children, from herself and Laura when young. She was nervous, they withdrawn. Raymond, the eldest, who was his father's great hope for the future, she had met three years before with his mother, and had thought him a jolly little boy. Now he seemed self-possessed, mature and over-polite. At sixteen he perfectly understood what a stepmother was and showed by his coolness that he did not care for the idea. Margot too was unnaturally stiff. If only Asquith had not told her so often of their intellectual brilliance, she would have been more herself, talked more naturally and gone some way towards winning them over by her friendliness and sparkle. As it was she felt defenceless, without a weapon to penetrate the armour of their suspicion.

Many years later she wrote in her autobiography:

I do not think if you had ransacked the world you could have found natures so opposite in temper, temperament, and outlook as myself and my stepchildren when I first knew them . . . Tennants believed in appealing to the hearts of men, firing their imagination and penetrating and vivifying their inmost lives. They had a little loose love to give to the whole world. The Asquiths—without mental flurry and with perfect self-mastery—believed in the free application of intellect to every human emotion: no event could have given heightened expression to their feelings. Shy, self-engaged, critical and controversial, nothing surprised them and nothing upset them.[5]

Could the gap be bridged? As though he divined her thoughts Henry wrote afterwards: 'You have put your hand in mine and you will not draw it back because you have faith and hope.'[6] If only it could be with the children as it was with the father. If she was to play the difficult role of a stepmother with any success it was absolutely necessary to start off on the right foot whatever her private feelings. She sensed that Raymond would be the hardest to win over, and in order that there should be no misunderstanding between them she wrote him a letter remarkable for its sympathy and tenderness. Its coaxing tone was just right for a boy of his age, who felt himself in charge of the motherless family:

> I only want to say one thing. You must not think that I could *imagine* even a possibility of filling your mother's (and my friend's) place. I only ask you to let me be your companion . . . if need be your helpmate. There is room for every one in life if they have the power to love. I shall count upon your help in making my way with Violet and your brothers . . . I should like you to let me gradually and without effort, take my place among you, and if I cannot—as indeed I would not—take your mother's place in any way, you must at least allow me to share with you her beautiful memory.[7]

Since Margot's letters were usually dashed off carelessly with a faint pencil and without punctuation and dates, this letter to Raymond shows unusual care and preparation, thus revealing how much store she set by his approval. Raymond's reply, although typical of a schoolboy's unemotional bluntness, did something to comfort Margot: 'I am sure we shall all like you very much and you will get on very well with us and I will do my best to help you, though I don't think you will need much help with the others, especially Violet and Cis.'[8]

Time was passing but still Margot begged Henry to let her keep their engagement secret. If she was to marry with a clear conscience there were some matters outstanding, and a lot of explaining to be done to a lot of people, notably Alfred Milner. In the end she took the line that honesty was the best method in a matter as delicate as this:

> I do not want you to learn anything of my affairs from the papers . . . but I want you to know I am going to marry Asquith. I have walked very slowly and deliberately up to this decision, and I suppose it depends on myself to make happiness out of it. Asquith has shown concentrated and very great devotion in wanting to share his life and to marry me . . . I hope in some measure to deserve it. You know me so well and what I dreamt of having, but I *would never have found it* and this is the best I expect. In any case it is too good for me . . . it seems strange and even hazardous but I should like to make something of my life, if I could.[9]

There was not one word of regret for putting him in a false position, not one word of comfort for the pain she had caused him, no mention even of the happiness they had shared in Egypt; it is a chillingly self-centred letter. Yet Margot did not intend to be unkind. She merely wanted to get the unpleasant business over and done with as quickly and in as few words as possible. Besides, she had always found it difficult to put herself in someone else's place. Much had once passed between them and she hoped that by writing in a cool constrained way she could wipe it out at a stroke. The brusque way she broke the news could have destroyed their friendship for ever and it says much for Milner's generosity of heart that it did not quite do that, although it affected him deeply.

Henry had written that he wanted their marriage to be an expanding and enriching of their lives. Margot wanted that too but could not bring herself to say so enthusiastically, so said nothing. He had also told her to try and relax. 'Don't strain,' he wrote anxiously, 'or make any effort, but try to feel at rest.' Wise advice, but not easy for one of Margot's temperament to accept.[10]

That her engagement lacked excitement was not surprising. She had felt seedy for several days and had in the end to go to bed with colitis. In bed she brooded on her difficulties, magnifying them and wallowing in self-pity. She neither missed Henry nor longed to see him, while he wrote encouraging and loving letters. One of them runs:

How could I ever tell you that you have been to me at once the hope and despair of my life, so near and so far from me, revealing to me the unseen and unattained, now opening, now seeming to shut the gate of paradise . . . now you have given me the key which you can't and won't take back again. I swear you shall never repent it. Whatever happiness the will, the tenderness, the worship of a man can bring shall encircle you. To this I pledge my soul and devote my life.[11]

Never before had she received love letters like this. They ought to have thrilled her and gladdened her heart, yet there was still a barrier between them; she could not bring herself to tell her future husband of her innermost thoughts and feelings without fears of being misunderstood. Her close friend DD knew only too well the perplexities of Margot's life, many self-created, but none the less painful for that. When she felt stronger, Margot wrote to DD, a letter that seemed nothing but one long wail:

I should like to be happy too, but I don't see my way to it clearly . . . I am sure if I could see quite clearly and not swim with one foot on the ground, I should realize I am a very lucky girl to be so loved . . . I may have seemed self-absorbed but I am not really . . . I simply long for once to spread my wings like a winter swallow . . .[12]

A winter love, a winter swallow; Margot was quite determined to wring every ounce of misery out of what should have been a very happy period of her life.

At the end of February Margot went to Cold Overton to convalesce. At least she told herself this was the reason but in reality it was to postpone still further the announcement of her engagement: 'I should rather that the whisper and talk went on than that the rumour should be confirmed,' she wrote to Alfred Milner, who must have been thinking that he had had a lucky escape. To Henry she wrote promising not to delay much longer, at the same time pleading that she was 'not fit for London or shopping yet'.[13] Her wedding gown must be made in Paris and she needed several more dresses as she had nothing fit to wear as his wife, but she had made no plans to get on with the other preparations for their marriage. She excused her reluctance to Alfred Milner ('I want to get well quietly down here and possess my soul in peace'[14]) but she was, as Henry suspected, perfectly well. Her parents, her sister Charty and her close friends all said, 'Now you have made up your mind, get on with it,' while Margot complainingly asked why people tugged at her so; her marriage was her own business and it would come off in time—but her time.

Henry had written to say he wanted a long honeymoon, he was tired out, needed a holiday and looked forward to having Margot all to himself. Margot replied that long honeymoons were bad things; they might get bored with each other. She turned to Alfred Lyttelton for reassurance and comfort:

> Ten days is long enough for a wedding tour, is it not? You are coming down here, thank heaven, with your horses so we can talk together (I shall be riding in two or three weeks . . .), but I should like to say one thing to you before I stop this letter—Why do I marry Asquith? —because I have the deepest knowledge and admiration for his character and love for me . . . If at times my nerves and wild independence shrink from the weight of the undertaking, at others perhaps the best times bring me deeper knowledge than following my own inclination . . . I am sure we shall be happy, and even if I am not quite happy I have had thirty years of glorious life and I shall never, never complain or think of myself or allow myself to be pitied.[15]

If she sounds selfish she believed she had good reason, for she knew her fears were caused by herself alone and not by Asquith. She was terrified of failing with the children too; what would happen if she became sharp and unkind to the motherless five?

It was fortunate that Asquith was not as surprised at Margot's attitude as her family and friends, and he went on quietly making preparations to start married life again as though everything was settled. 'A wild horse cannot be tamed in a day,' he said. 'I don't want you to alter,' he wrote. '. . . You will have to give up much—every wife has: but the things you sacrifice shall be as few in number and as unessential and unvital to your nature as I can make them . . . the only other thing I ask you today is that you should feel free . . .'[16] In another letter he wrote that she should have the 'overruling voice'. This was not the treatment she needed or wanted. Frightened of losing her, he began to plead and give way not only to her every wish but to many she had never even thought of. When they had first met she sensed at once that here was her superior; he seemed to have mastery not only over her but over others too and this delighted her—she had met her match. But from the moment Asquith fell deeply in love, he let her get away with everything. He did not tell her he disapproved of her smoking so heavily, or that he hated her making fun of the weaknesses of politicians, among them his own friends. If Asquith had taken a tough line and rebuked her for behaving like a spoilt child, she would probably have married him sooner. He should have set the date for the marriage and made her stick to it. When she stretched out her hand for guidance, her future husband gave her freedom instead.

Asquith was not a man of the world, and his knowledge of women was limited. As a youth he had married his first love, the girl next door. His friends were all male and most of those who came to the house in Hampstead were bachelors. Margot was an enigma to him; he had never met anyone like her and was afraid that if he handled her roughly she would let herself be snapped up by somebody else. But close contact with this volatile creature taught him something he had not realized about himself: that he liked women and that they were absolutely necessary to his happiness.

Asquith's naïvety astonished Queen Victoria. When her Private Secretary, Sir Henry Ponsonby, showed her a letter from him asking whether as a Privy Councillor he need seek the Queen's consent to his marriage, she wrote on the back: 'How curious that he should ask if my consent is required to his marriage. If this was required, the Queen would not give it as she thinks her most unfit for a Cabinet Minister's wife.—V.R.I.'[17] Gossip about Margot's exploits had travelled far, and friends were not always as loyal as she thought. When Arthur Balfour was once asked if he was going to marry Margot Tennant he replied unkindly that he was thinking of 'having a career of my own'. Those who were really fond of her regretted she had broadcast her love affairs so widely, but it never occurred to her to keep such things private; it enhanced the cast-off suitors, she thought, if the world knew that she had once been in love with them.

On 4 April the engagement was announced at last. Every paper carried the news, there were photographs galore and both of them were besieged by the press wanting more details and by telegrams and letters. Their first dinner party as an engaged couple was at the house of another minister, the Secretary of State for War, Sir Henry Campbell-Bannerman. It was not a very successful evening. When the ladies left the room after dinner old Mrs Gladstone, supported by a body of political wives, clustered round Margot like a lot of interfering hens and began to harangue her on the duties of the wife of a possible future Prime Minister. It was pitiless and ill-timed, and although Margot understood that they meant well and only wanted to prevent her from making mistakes that could affect her husband's career, she could not conceal her anger. By the time they were found by the men tears were not far away and Margot's nerves were racing round like 'squirrels in a cage'.[18] Catching sight of Mr Gladstone, she seized his arm and guiding him to a secluded corner, poured her troubles into his ears. Was she really to give up everything she enjoyed the moment she married Henry simply because one day he might be Prime Minister? With the easy conscience of the male (he had arranged with his wife that she should be the one 'to speak to Margot') Gladstone patted her hand and said he knew of no one fitter to be the wife of a great politician than she was. He followed up this comforting remark (no doubt in case Margot impetuously rushed off to tell his wife that her husband did not agree with her) with a short homily on the wisdom of taking advice.

When she cooled down, next day, Margot was sorry she had been rude to Mrs Gladstone and wrote her a spontaneous letter of apology:

Dearest Aunt Pussy,
    I dare say I was a little out of spirits last night at the Campbell-Bannermans'. I thought you were lecturing me too severely, but I am sure you know I value all you say. I feel so deeply . . . your sorrow of retiring from so long and beautiful a public life; it will be a lasting example to me to remember your courage and devotion.[19]

But to her friend Lady Harcourt she showed her real feelings: 'It falls on me to be advised and misunderstood as if I were a heartless, selfish girl. I happen to be neither, though I like to be as good as my loving understanding friends think me.'[20]

It was not only the women who proffered advice. Many of her men friends (doubtless pushed into it by their wives) wagged their fingers at her and said she must reform; it was enough to put her off altogether, but in fact it strengthened her resolution. She had put her hand to the plough and no matter how unfit they thought her or how serious the criticism of her past life she would not now draw back. But there was another side to the

PART TWO

Marriage

'It is said that there is a chance of Asquith marrying Margot. To be a Cabinet Minister and the husband of Miss Margot in one year would indeed be to widen his experience of the world.'

CHAPTER 11

The Way of your Life shall be as you determine it

IN THE END everything had to be done in a rush, for Margot had decided that a quiet wedding would not do; all her friends must be asked. Her wedding dress had been ordered from Worth and she dashed over to Paris for fittings, leaving others to settle on the bridesmaids' dresses and to make endless other arrangements. For a woman who had been too ill until recently to do anything at all except put off the date of her marriage, Margot showed remarkable energy.

Where they were to live was a problem Charles solved in a day: he read that an imposing house, 20 Cavendish Square, was for sale and bought it on the spot. It was the very place for an important member of the Government and a possible future Prime Minister. He and Emma had taken Asquith to their hearts, with relief that after all the trouble and worry she had given them, their youngest daughter was putting herself in safe hands. When she walked down the aisle of St George's, Hanover Square on her father's arm on 10 May 1894 to become the second Mrs Asquith, Margot felt deeply emotional. Her thoughts were with Laura, married in that very church, kneeling as she was soon to do on the self same spot, so full of hope for a future that was denied her. Her own past with its freedom from responsibility flashed through her mind briefly too and as she joined Henry at the altar she prayed that she might make something worthwhile of her life.[1]

There had been no time for a rehearsal, so the child bridesmaids did not quite understand what they were to do and the four-year-old Dorothy Drew got left behind. There were too few ushers and no one knew where they were expected to sit. Mr and Mrs Gladstone arrived late and were 'jostled into a pew', but Margot hoped it made no difference to their enjoyment.[2] Four Prime Ministers, past, present and future, signed the register—Gladstone, Rosebery, Balfour and the bridegroom himself. The church was packed, the crowds outside so immense ('a gentleman with a carnation in his buttonhole' offered Charty's old nurse £10 for her seat—Margot wondered if it could have been Peter Flower) that the driver of the bridal carriage had difficulty in getting the newly-married couple to 40 Grosvenor Square where the reception was to be held. Mr Gladstone proposed the health of the bride and groom, as he had done at Laura's wedding, for Margot felt that one word from him 'would send me off hopefully on my way'. Everybody was so kind that more than once Margot had difficulty in restraining her tears; 'but I felt it would have been like a wineglass in a sea, so deep was my emotion'. She managed to hold back her tears until Charty, who had come to the station with a crowd of well-wishers to see her off, kissed her in the train and an old servant pressed her hand so hard that her new wedding ring cut into her finger: 'And even I felt, it was all over, and with a wave and a gasp I sank back in the train knowing I was married.'[3]

The week's honeymoon at Mells Manor, lent by the Horners, was followed by ten days at Clovelly, the home of an old friend of Margot's, Mrs Hamlyn. Henry had had to abandon all idea of a longer honeymoon, for Margot had refused to consider it. However the fortnight together was as serene as most honeymoons and Margot did not feel as uneasy in her newly-married state as she had expected. Henry's cheerfulness and good temper went a long way to lift her spirits. 'You are the best I have ever known,' he had written to her shortly before their marriage, and now he set out to prove that he meant it. Margot's letter to Mary Drew sounded surprisingly happy after the agonizing weeks of indecision:

It has been quite heavenly down here and I never saw such a thrilling lovely place, for tho' I had seen it often, it will now remain with me for life. I also am human enough to like hearing that I looked nice. I was in such a state that I did not notice a soul. . . .[4]

Asquith's anxieties about finance had been lifted shortly before the wedding when Charles had settled £5,000 a year on Margot. This seemed at the time to mean that they could live in some style, but neither Charles nor Margot herself had stopped to consider that, although 20 Cavendish Square was a most beautiful early eighteenth-century house, it was not only extremely inconvenient but very expensive to run. Friends like Osbert Sitwell envied her the fine panelled dining-room, long blue draw-ing-room, beautiful staircase, and walls frescoed by Sir James Thornhill, but it did not occur to him or to her other friends that it was a house which needed at least fourteen servants to keep it going if they were to live in any comfort and to entertain on the lavish scale to which Margot was accustomed. It is doubtful if she even saw inside the house before Charles purchased it; even if she did, it is most unlikely that she went into the kitchen quarters or saw how draughty and old-fashioned they would be to work in. All the food had to be carried to the dining-room across an uncovered courtyard from a mews kitchen at the back, a terrible trial for the servants in winter. Margot loved to fill her house with relations and guests, which meant that cans of hot water had to be carried upstairs to the bedrooms several times a day. It was fortunate that Margot was an excellent and considerate mistress and that her servants stayed for years despite the heavy work.

In one respect the house was just right; it could accommodate all five of the Asquith children and three governesses, and it had huge nursery quarters for the children Margot might have. Another advantage for Margot was that it was close to 40 Grosvenor Square, for despite her demand for freedom she did not want to live too far away from her family.

It was strange that Margot took so little interest in making the house habitable. Asquith had been living in a bachelor flat in Mount Street and was longing to have wife and children round him again, but Margot was so insistent on altering everything except the dining-room and drawing-room that they had to camp in three rooms while the children remained in Redhill with their governess. Yet long before it was ready Margot gave large luncheon parties several times a week. Dinner parties were a little less frequent, but only because Asquith disliked the English habit of the ladies leaving the table before the men, because all-male conversation bored him. In any case he much preferred inviting just a few friends to dinner for bridge afterwards; this was his way of relaxing after a hard day in the House of Commons. From the start, they were seldom alone.

Margot's friends did not find Asquith at all like the man they had expected her husband to be. To begin with, he wore his clothes badly and this was accentuated by his build: he was stocky, of medium height but looked shorter because of his broad shoulders. At forty-two he was already heavier than he ought to have been and with good living was soon to become more so. His official biographers describe his head, neck and shoulders as 'massive',[5] and at any rate in later years his appearance in photographs justifies that description. These photographs also show that his indifference to clothes continued, despite Margot's efforts to improve his appearance.

The contrast with Margot could not have been greater. To her clothes mattered, and she did everything possible when Henry became Prime Minister to encourage the wives of other politicians to dress stylishly. When they moved into 10 Downing Street she allowed a fashion parade to be held in her drawing-room with all the garments designed by the couturier Poiret, an innovation that created quite a stir, not all of it favourable. As for Margot's own appearance, this highly coloured passage in Sir Osbert Sitwell's autobiography is apt: 'The indefinable and clear-cut style of her individuality permeated the whole of her outward appearance and carried her through errors of judgement and high exaggeration to a singular sort of perfection. . . .'[6]

In the autumn Margot went hunting in Leicestershire, leaving Henry in the half-finished house. If he was lonely he did not spoil her pleasure by telling her so, for he had guessed, as soon as summer turned into autumn, that she was thirsty for sport. Had he not said 'the way of your life shall be as you determine it, and your choice shall be my law'?[7]

What a stern lesson Jowett would have read Margot on her wifely duties, had he still been alive. Afterwards he would have left her alone to battle with her conscience. As it was she did not feel in the least conscience-stricken as she leapt happily into the train that was to take her to her paradise. But old Mrs Gladstone's lips snapped together when she heard that the bride of only five months was hunting as usual. There were head-shakings in political quarters too, where it was known that Henry would be too busy to join her at weekends since a General Election was due in a few months' time.

Two weeks later Margot's fun was abruptly cut short by an urgent letter from her father, summoning her home to Glen. Emma was seriously ill. She had not looked well at the wedding, but Margot had put her pallor and languid air down to fatigue and the strain of two years' delay while she herself made up her mind. Now it appeared that it had been ill health all along. But she did not feel too anxious as she travelled to Peeblesshire; her father always became nervous whenever her mother was in the least indisposed and wanted his family round him for reassurance. In the train Margot thought more of her home than of her mother—beautiful, magical Glen that always tugged at her heart strings.

When she arrived Charty and Lucy were already there. Running to greet them, her joy swiftly turned to anguish when she saw in their faces that their mother was dying. 'Neither she nor my father know the awful name of her illness,' Margot wrote to Alfred Milner whom she now turned to in her distress. 'But we know it is cancer and I cannot tell you it breaks me to my heart. She has been in bed since September . . . and is full of pluck.'[8]

Christmas came, but without the usual festivities. Margot wrote to Henry that it was scarcely worth while returning to London since they had been warned that Emma might take a turn for the worse at any moment, so Asquith's first Christmas after his marriage was as lonely as the one before it. There was an added complication too: Margot was pregnant and far from well. She had realized that this might be the case when hunting, but had continued to ride as recklessly as usual. Child or no child, she was not going to forgo the feeling of exhilaration that invariably came to her when jumping high fences: 'I am not in the best of conditions to bear anything now,' she confided to Alfred Milner who had become once again a 'dear, dear friend': 'I expect to be confined in April. I am not a good subject for domestic burdens, though I hope I shall be worthy to bear the mystery and trouble that other women have borne and it may add to the richer experience of life, if I live through it.'[9] Pregnancy made her depressed, all she could think of was her mother's illness; she was not looking forward to the child and had not even begun to make preparations for it. The thought of Laura dying in giving birth to her son haunted her day and night and was to do so with every pregnancy, making the waiting period hideous with fear.

New Year's Day dawned black and wet, making even Glen look dismal. But Emma was no worse and Margot again hoped that the doctors might be mistaken. With hope came renewed energy and she wrote to DD telling her of the coming child. She had delayed telling this close friend till now, for DD was very maternal and would have promptly rebuked Margot for riding at all, let alone hunting recklessly with no thought of the dangers to herself or the baby. Now she had to know before she heard the news from someone else and was hurt. It was a quite extraordinary letter:

> . . . I am still very small so I can only hope it may be a girl and that I may live through it. One ought not to think one will die but at any rate I have had a good time of it as far as it went. I am not owed much. I don't feel

now that everything has so changed for me that it will matter so much if I die. I don't care for London, I am not wrapped up in my stepchildren, my beloved home here is breaking up, my nerves will very likely go and I believe in the goodness of God, so death after all may not be so terrible. Except to Henry my life is not valuable. Mumsy can't live very long and she would mind most. Mary Drew would doubtless think I deserved it for being so hideously frivolous (instead of serious) over my marriage and Charty and Lucy will have suffered so much over Mama's approaching leave-taking that I shall only be an extra sorrow . . .[10]

This gloom was the result of becoming pregnant before she was used to marriage. Although almost thirty-one she was still in some ways immature. At home with parents and sisters it was not difficult for her to go back in time and imagine herself a child again, the youngest girl and the spoilt pet of the family. Because of this Emma's illness hit her hardest of all after Charles.

At the end of the day when the house slept the sisters would creep out of bed and congregate in the 'Doocot', still just as it was when Laura and Margot shared it, but full of ghosts. These talks with her sisters were very precious to Margot, for they calmed her restless spirit and soothed her troubled mind. One night Margot asked Charty to promise that if she died in childbirth, she would bring up the baby with her own, as she had done Laura's boy. As soon as that was settled she was more at peace than she had been for months.

While at Glen—her stay there was in the end prolonged until February —she corresponded more with Alfred Milner than with anyone and never once did she say that she missed Henry or that the separation so soon after marriage was hard on him. In some curious way she thought Alfred might compensate for her absence and she asked him to go to 20 Cavendish Square where the pictures were still stacked against the wall and the books lay in heaps on the floor, waiting for the mistress of the house to arrange them. 'His goodness is very great,' she wrote to Alfred of Henry.[11] Everyone in London saw that Asquith needed a wife much more than Margot needed a husband and something in her cool attitude towards him and their marriage may bear out Alfred Milner's charge that she was frigid. Of course she had plenty of excuses for staying at Glen; her mother was dying, her father distraught and two sisters far from well. Yet during December or the early days of January she could have risked taking a sleeper to London for a few days. The idea never entered her head, for she had none of the overwhelming longing of most brides to be with their husband.

Henry tried to keep in touch with Margot through books: could they repeat what they had done before their marriage, read the same book at the same time every day? They might begin with the newly published life of Lord Randolph Churchill by his son. Unhappily it did not work out as satisfactorily as before. Margot was too bowed down with grief, and Henry too busy gathering the Liberals together for the coming election. His children, too, needed his attention. This was the job he thought in his innocence that Margot would take over and do well, yet he did not reproach her when, both before and after her absence at Glen, she did not manage it. This was not entirely Margot's fault, nor the children's for being what they were, polite but reserved; the root of the trouble was that they were not used to taking their problems to a stranger, nor she to making overtures to children. When asked how she got on with her stepchildren Margot's reply was always the same—they could not be kinder, but she did not add that they were loving or even mildly affectionate. On Christmas Eve she had written rather pathetically to Alfred: 'I can't love to order, and my stepchildren are merely duty and effort up till now. To be fair I have seen very little of them.'[12] If one has been sunned through and through like an apricot on a wall from earliest days, one is bound to be over-sensitive to the withdrawal of heat.

Emma was weakening daily. She encouraged neither tears nor sentiment and watching her awful sufferings Margot prayed for her to die peacefully in her sleep. But Emma never slept now without a heavy dose of morphine, while at all hours husband and children clustered round her bed trying to show how much they loved her. Fate had not been altogether kind to this quiet, loving mother who only asked that her children should enjoy good health. She had been granted everything in life but that. In her unobtrusive way she had been the sheet-anchor of the family; she never interfered, but when her children needed her she was always at hand and could be found either tending her plants, an old straw hat on her head, or relaxing in her sitting-room with one of the books that were piled high on a table by her favourite chair. It astonished Margot that her mother was so well-read and yet made not the slightest parade of it. If only Emma could get well, 'I would be perfectly happy living at Glen, even separated from Henry. None of my books have been moved, so I hardly feel as if I had left home,'[13] she told Alfred, to whom she was now writing more and more. She wrote to Henry too, of course, but when after his death she looked for these letters from Glen in 1894–5 she could not find them anywhere and came to the conclusion he had destroyed them, although Alfred Milner had kept all his.

One morning in early February, a day of frost and crisp, invigorating air, Margot went at eight o'clock as she always did to kiss her mother and lift her thin, wasted body higher on her pillows—a simple job but one Emma said Margot performed with more gentleness than any of the others. At first she thought her mother still asleep, then suddenly Margot realized that she must have only just that moment died, for she was warm though completely lifeless and still. She could hear the nurse in the room next door preparing the invalid's breakfast; she did not call her but said her own good-bye alone, kneeling by the bed and kissing her mother's almost transparent hands, so thin that her wedding ring fell off. She was grateful that her ordeal was over at last.

Later that morning she walked to Traquair to watch the workmen opening the family grave to receive her mother's coffin. At that moment she felt nothing but relief. As she always did when in that churchyard, she knelt by Laura's grave and prayed. Would she be the next, she wondered. She did not think she would mind being laid to rest in that peaceful spot with those she loved if, as she fully expected, she died when her baby was born.

As soon as she could after the funeral, she left for London. The family let her go, knowing she had made no preparations for the birth which was to be in the still half-furnished home in Cavendish Square. For the only time in her life she was glad to leave Glen. She wrote to Mary Drew the night before she left:

> The death of one's mother is the end of one's youth and what with my new house and new prospects and strange sensations I feel all the effort of a new beginning without quite the spirit or activity to undertake it cheerfully. Feeling as I do I am very glad to be quiet.[14]

Almost a year before when Margot was recovering from her collapse she had gone the round of the cottages with Emma and was surprised how well her mother understood the trials and tribulations of the village people and how fond they seemed of her. Margot had marvelled at the quiet way Emma carried on her life and how little she and her sisters really knew her.[15] Curiously enough Margot needed her now as never before since she was nervous of returning to London and starting married life again with a husband who after many months' absence seemed somewhat remote. It did not help to have three of her stepsons away at school, and just Violet and little Cis and their nurse in the house. Henry had written to tell her this with the best will in the world, saying that he had arranged it so that she should not be lonely. The prospect of only two children without the rest to act as buffers made Margot tremble. She had told DD in a confidential letter that she found six-year-old Violet a difficult child. This was because Violet adored her father passionately, and stuck to him like glue whenever he was at home, something which Margot suspected Henry of encouraging. It was impossible to have any private conversation until Violet went to bed or to be alone with Henry for five minutes if he happened to be at home during the day. Violet said little, indeed was not in the least noisy or bad mannered, but Margot in her highly strung state imagined she looked at her stepmother reproachfully, even with dislike, and this made Margot nervous and uncomfortable.

As the train neared London, it came to her at last that she had not been very successful in conveying to her husband how much she had missed him all these weeks. Instead she had told DD and, illogical though it was at the time, she thought that enough. 'It seems dreadful to leave him for so long and absolutely a mistake after his warm emotion when I hinted at it [that it might be some time before she returned home]. He has written daily how much he misses me.'[16] Henry greeted her rapturously—almost, as she told him laughingly, as though he had become a Tennant and did not care a rap who saw his pleasure. There were no reproaches, no hint that Henry felt he had been ill-used, only anxious enquiries about her health. She did not look well and except for the bulk made by the baby, she was thinner than ever.

CHAPTER 12

Small Things Lead to Bigger Ones

POLITICS HAD TAKEN over since Margot was last at home. All day Liberal Members of Parliament were in and out of the house, closeted in Henry's study for hours on end. Deprived of their veteran leader, the Liberals were in disarray. Even in old age, Gladstone had still possessed the vigour to promote Home Rule for Ireland, and the magnetism to attract votes. In March 1894 he had retired from office and on Margot's wedding day two months later Arthur Benson had noted in his diary: 'The G.O.M. very talkative and hairless and old. He talked long to A. Balfour on the vestry stairs with the pathetic reverence of old age for youth and success.'[1]

What would happen to Home Rule without Gladstone's leadership? Under Jowett's influence, Margot had begun to see it was not the mistake she had supposed. He had written to her in 1892:

Some think that the Home Rule Bill will be pushed to the second reading, then dropped and a new shuffle to the cards will take place under Lord Rosebery. This seems to me very likely. The Ministry . . . are not gaining ground and the English are beginning to hate the Irish and the priests.[2]

Gladstone had been succeeded as Prime Minister by Lord Rosebery, who lacked the qualities of a leader and could not hold the balance within the party. After receiving a gloomy letter from Henry at Glen, Margot lamented to Alfred Milner:

How our political fortunes seem to have fallen and what a disappointment Rosebery is. I have as you know never been a Radical, so more than ever would stick to the party so as to modify it. As for the Rule, Alfred [Lyttelton] was always a very old Home Ruler and snubbed my head off when I said it was a dream or a madness. If our side were strong obstinate Home Rulers, I should be on the other side, but are they? Is the Rule really alive? I think not, except in the minds of fanatics.[3]

In May 1895 Margot gave birth to a daughter at 20 Cavendish Square after a long and agonizing confinement in which she nearly lost her life. The baby was born alive but scarcely breathed and it died after a few hours, plunging Margot into the depths of despair. Not once during her pregnancy had she felt well; she put this down to anxiety about her mother, but it prevented her looking forward to the child. She had fully expected to die at its birth, and it was with surprise that she heard Henry say that she was going to live. The doctors made the mistake of refusing to allow her to see the infant while it was still alive. At once she jumped to the conclusion that she had produced a monster, and this troubled her more than its death and caused a recurrence of the painful nightmares that she had experienced after Laura's death. She would fall asleep and awake crying and soaked with sweat, not knowing where she was or what had happened to her.[4] Trivial things bothered her, but she did not ask the doctors the one important question—why did this awful thing happen? A wall of silence arose between her and them, and she was afraid to break it down in case it would reveal something terrible that she might not be able to face. But since pre-natal care with its examinations and tests did not exist in those days, her question might have been unanswerable—perhaps the child's death would have been called an act of God, and that her religious faith would not allow her to believe. It is strange that she did not seek help from the Hospital for Women where Elizabeth Garrett Anderson had until recently been senior physician. Hers was exactly the kind of mind that was capable of pursuing these inquiries relentlessly. Instead she simply accepted this tragic thing that had happened to her and was to happen again, leaving her shattered every time.

Phlebitis made her recovery miserably slow and it was three months before she left her room. Lost in a world of dread and horror she clung to her chief doctor, Sir John Williams, whose sympathy and Celtic imagination were useful in helping her over the worst of the crisis. Some good came out of this cruel ordeal: Margot saw her husband in a new light. A few weeks before her confinement, much tormented by memories of what had happened to Laura, she had felt so certain that she would die that she wrote Henry a farewell letter. It was more open and honest, she says, than any she had written before, so it is sad that it does not survive. Although in the same house, Henry wrote a reply which Margot kept. It is a tender letter, full of deep feeling. He calls Margot's letter 'the dearest tribute that has ever been paid me by woman or man and I shall carry it with me as a blessing and an inspiration until I die'.[5]

The phlebitis eventually responded to treatment and physically Margot seemed to be improving, but what her doctors called neurasthenia —probably an acute form of post-natal depression—got her in its grip and she could not fight against it.

Skin and bone and a bundle of nerves, she bravely tried to take an interest in Henry's work, but could not. When her five-year-old stepson Cis was brought to see her she burst into tears, alarming the little boy and putting yet another barrier between herself and Henry's children. Queen Victoria's heart was touched when she heard of Margot's sufferings. She had been subject to post-natal depression herself and she wrote to Asquith more than once to ask for a progress report, her early opposition to the marriage quite forgotten. In front of Henry Margot tried to put on a good face but to Alfred Milner she gave the true facts:

> . . . I have been so unhappy and had such a terribly agonizing time that I can hardly face life and only have echoes of happiness and that in the health and happiness of other people—I wondered if you had felt for me? I always said I was unfitted for married life, but when I said it I never knew how true it was except as regards Henry whose carefulness and tenderness have been wonderful.

She begged him to come and see her: 'So if you see me very reduced and discouraged, don't leave me right out—it has all turned out so sad.'[6]

Sleeplessness set in. It was a scourge that was to plague her on and off for the rest of her life. Later she learned how to deal with it, more or less, but in 1895 'I never sleep' was a refrain that was becoming all too familiar to her nearest and dearest and made her at times very difficult to live with. The visits of her friends made life more bearable for her; their sympathy and companionship proved a solace in her invalid state. They arrived loaded with books and flowers, bringing a breath of the world outside that was very salutary. Old Mr Gladstone tottered up the stairs, a little breathless, a little bent, but as full of amazingly interesting talk as ever, and was among the first to bring her hope. Richard Haldane came,

Augustine Birrell, John Morley, the Archbishop of Canterbury (who prayed by Margot's bedside), even Arthur Balfour, a man who hated illness in any shape or form, and although he did not stay long Margot took his visit as a real act of friendship. When Harcourt called one afternoon he seized a hunting crop hanging on the wall, remarking that he was glad to see it: 'Asquith will be able to beat you if you play fast and loose with him. That little tight mouth of his convinces me he has the capacity for it.' It was like a gathering of the 'Souls' to bring messages of hope and comfort to one of their brightest spirits in her distress.

Margot was dismayed to find her recovery so slow that there was little hope that she could play her part as Henry's wife in the general election, due in the autumn of 1895. They had discussed the possibility of an early election on their honeymoon and Henry had expatiated on the asset of an attractive wife who could canvass on his behalf. She could win many votes for the party, he told her, explaining that they had never needed them more. Most of all he wanted her to concentrate on the women so that they could influence their husbands, convincing them of the improvement in their lives Liberal policies would bring. The prospect of doing something real and tangible for Henry buoyed her up on her bad days when she had little to make her feel cheerful. She remembered with pleasure how in Glasgow in 1892 'Mr Asquith' had spoken for her brother Eddy, who was trying to win the Partick district. Asquith had surprised Margot by the enthusiasm he had generated in the audience despite a rather mediocre speech, his twenty-fourth in a week. He felt quite stale, he told Margot, but she could see even then that he had the right qualities for a great speaker.[7]

However, despite all Asquith's efforts the Tories won the election of 1895 comfortably. The Liberals had done so badly that Margot worried whether they would ever be in office again. Sir William Harcourt reassured her: 'Your man is a man of the future.'

Meanwhile, having lost office—and with it the Home Secretary's salary—Asquith made plans to return to the Bar where at least he would be assured of a steady income. A somewhat plodding advocate with little jury appeal, he never had a fashionable practice. Yet he was a past-master at arguing pure facts of law[8] and managed in good times to earn £10,000 a year, a considerable help with a large house and several children to support. This way of earning a living was to appeal less and less as Margot's world captivated him increasingly. In the end it was to be a battle between ambition and his inclination for the pleasures of society, which had been denied him hitherto.

His biographers are unanimous in stressing that Asquith was ambitious and had every intention of becoming Prime Minister if he could, but that in opposition he did not strain himself in the Commons. There were critics who thought he ought to have done more. In January 1899, Arthur Acland, a successful Minister of Education in Gladstone's last government, wrote Asquith a two-edged letter, ostensibly complaining of Harcourt's lazy leadership in the House of Commons: '. . . and you and he might do a good bit [in the House] if you have time to spare from law and society and he from his country pursuits.'[9] There were some who said Asquith's lack of energy was entirely due to a wife who sapped it; he was a different man since his second marriage. There was a grain of truth in this, although Margot was not much to blame. The real explanation was that he had been sadly disappointed and distressed at the prolonged delicacy of Margot's health, which to a vigorous man who had never been ill in his life must have seemed interminable. Moreover, the pangs of disappointment were aggravated by a secret fear that Margot might become a permanent invalid and that he must learn to ask little of her. He would have been less than human if he had not made golden plans for the future after Margot promised to marry him. With his ambition and her money, where might they not go together? Or was her ill health now to prevent them?

Asquith had told Margot that the Liberals were crying out for leadership, 'and all they get is a rattle of Harcourtian fireworks, and a sawdust programme from Newcastle'. In a burst of enthusiasm he had added, 'with you by my side we will some day drive the machine along at a pace with results that the world will feel'.[10] Margot was every bit as ambitious as Asquith and wanted to be able to help him reach the top, although she protested that she hardly knew what the word ambition meant. Early in their acquaintance, when discussing his eldest son Raymond, Asquith said that he was remarkably clever, and that he had hoped that he was also ambitious. To hear him say this, Margot says, was a surprise to her as she had always been told that ambition was wicked.[11] However, when Lord Randolph Churchill asked her whether she knew any politicians she promptly silenced him with her answer: 'I told him that with the exception of himself, I knew them all intimately.'[12] It had not occurred to her that without the driving force of ambition she would not have known any.

As the wife of a leading politician her world now expanded to include the whole 'machinery' of politics, that is party agents and constituents, with whom she got on very well, treating them all equally whoever they were, and without the slightest touch of patronage. She would have done this in any case, even if her husband had not impressed on her that those who made the party work ('the machinery') could not be ignored in a struggle to the top.

Some good came out of the long invalidism that followed her confinement: Margot began to take a little more interest in her stepchildren. Perhaps because he was only two years old when his mother died the youngest boy needed affection more than the others. One day when she was lying disconsolate on her sofa, wondering if her life was over, Cis came to her room, a book in his hand, and shyly asked her if she would read to him. From that it followed naturally that she should be the one to hear him say his prayers, tuck him up in bed and give him a good-night kiss. Small things in themselves, but to the love-starved little boy, longing for someone to notice him, they meant a great deal. Not only did her newly-awakened affection benefit the child, but it hastened her own recovery as well, by helping to take her out of herself. She began to look forward to his visits and to telling him stories of Glen and of all the things she and Laura did as children, promising to take him to her old home as soon as she was well and strong again. To Margot's amazement she enjoyed giving Cis these motherly attentions and found that having him around did her good.

She was also surprised to discover another strong link between her and Cis in the child's natural religious feeling which was very like her own, entirely self-cultivated. When she got to know him better Margot noticed this: 'We shared a certain spiritual foundation and moral aspiration that solder people together through life.'[13]

As Cis grew older he began to understand that Margot longed above all to be shown demonstrative affection and when his shyness vanished he was able to do this. One day when he was seventeen and he and Margot were discussing life and religion, he showed insight into her character when he said: 'It must be curious for you, Margot, seeing all of us laughing at things that make you cry.'[14] A closeness sprang up between them that she failed to achieve with the others, although she never gave up hope that it might come. The eldest, Raymond, was the most difficult to get to know and Margot sometimes wondered how far he influenced the other three.

He was very skilful at keeping her at arm's length, always polite though sometimes sailing near the wind, mocking, cynical and clever. At Winchester he learned to cultivate the supercilious manner of the intelligent schoolboy who wants the world to think he cares nothing for it. Margot had never met this before in one so youthful (her Etonian brothers never had a trace of it) and although as a rule so quick and witty, she did not know how to parry such talk and mistakenly thought it directed only at her.

In August 1895 she and Henry took a house in North Berwick, hoping that the bracing Scottish air would restore her to full health again. It did, but more came out of this holiday than good health. They took to the links as a family and discovered the joys and aggravations of golf. It amazed Margot to see the long drives the boys achieved with no apparent effort, while she and Henry merely topped the ball. Still the difficulties increased the fun: 'I'm improving at golf,' she told DD, 'and the boys love it.'[15] Reserve melted in the warmth of her praise.

Although remarkably well-read, the Asquith children had never scribbled verse as Margot and her friends did; good, bad or indifferent, it was all wonderful fun. She encouraged the children to try but they were reluctant. To show them how easy it was she recited the verses Gladstone had composed about her after her first visit to Hawarden, verses in which the words 'young and fair' occur. They had never thought of Margot like that: with the arrogance of youth, they looked on her as old, or at least ageing, but now they were being given a different view by someone they knew their father had greatly respected. She told them how Tennyson too had composed a short poem about her first visit to his house, then she recited all she could remember of Curzon's rhymes on the 'Souls'. They were incredulous when she explained how often poetry—or what passed for it—was used in her youth when there was leisure and how she had had many impromptu verses left on her desk by men friends who had called when she was out.

The Asquith children had never played pencil games and Margot thoroughly enjoyed teaching them how it was done, all sitting at a round table, the children eagerly trying to follow her instructions. The speed with which they became adept quite awed her. These simple pastimes bred a warm camaraderie between Margot and her stepchildren; it was not, alas, permanent, but it showed them all how much happier they would be if they could act as a family more often.

Margot had learned to her cost that it was better to keep off books, for the young Asquiths had read so much more than she had, and had understood everything far better. They laughed when she told them in all seriousness that Mrs Humphry Ward's *Robert Ellesmere* was considered 'advanced' in her day and that *Condemnation of Alcohol* was thought so shocking that no one would admit to having read either. Now they were on every bookshelf. When Margot told them she had known George Moore they were all attention; 'What was he like, Margot?' 'Very deaf and a bit too much of a prima donna for me!'

Asquith had promised never to interfere in Margot's life, and she kept him to that promise. By November 1895 she felt so well that the mad urge to go hunting overcame her good intentions. Off she went to Leicestershire again despite a severe warning from her doctor, Sir John Williams. Her departure caused much talk, and even her close friends called her headstrong and rash, but she ignored them too. It was also extravagant, for the expense of keeping a string of horses was enormous, and Asquith was now out of office. Many thought it unfair to leave him alone again after all he had gone through when she was ill, but the old Margot was back and careless of what people thought. Furthermore, it was not so unusual, even in the 1890s, for women of means to please themselves. Money bought liberty if the woman in question was determined.

Asquith did not object at first—indeed he snatched a few days away from the Commons to visit Margot at Melton—and although time hung heavy on his hands when she was out chasing foxes, he did not complain. But when in early December they were invited to stay with Lord Rosebery at Dalmeny and Margot took it for granted that Henry would not expect her to interrupt her hunting for a mere country-house visit, Henry put his foot down and told her in a voice that brooked no argument that he needed her with him and that Rosebery expected her: she could hunt later if she liked.[16] He had a compelling reason for his attitude. Without warning Rosebery had announced that he was going to resign as leader of the Party after a mere eighteen months and would shortly quit politics altogether. The visit to Dalmeny was to try to dissuade Rosebery from taking this drastic step, and Henry hoped that as an old friend Margot might be able to get him to think again.[17] So much Henry was able to tell Margot as they travelled to Scotland, and the look on her husband's face told her more plainly than words that if she wanted to hold his affections by considering his feelings before her own, now was the moment.

They reached Edinburgh just in time to hear Rosebery make his resignation speech in the Empire Theatre before an excited audience, all agog for some startling revelation. But there was no revelation, only a report that Gladstone was threatening to return to public life, which would, Rosebery said, make his position untenable. Margot told Henry it was a great to-do about nothing; Rosebery had always had a streak of exhibitionism in his nature, was easily bored and had probably announced his retirement simply to liven things up. For a short time he would be the centre of attention, which would please him. He was a man with too much of everything; Dr Jowett had put his finger on the trouble when he said Rosebery was 'overloaded with wealth and fine houses'.[18] Next day the papers were full of lamentations; all reported Rosebery's speech in full and carried photographs, as though he had just died and this was his obituary, Margot said, laughing. Before they left Dalmeny, Rosebery took Margot aside and told her that he wanted Asquith to become the next leader of the Liberals in his place. He had mentioned it to him but he was reluctant. For once Margot was silent. Was her dearest wish for Henry to come true so soon? Henry did not want the leadership just yet, he told her; the timing was not right, to be leader in opposition wore out the nerves without giving anything in return. Another reason weighed heavily with him too and showed he was no mere self-seeker: Sir William Harcourt was Rosebery's natural successor and had very nearly become leader of the Liberals the previous year; Harcourt's feelings must be considered, and Henry could not be easy in his conscience if he stepped out of line. With this Margot had to be content.

It was a surprise to her to find the few days at Dalmeny very rewarding. Henry was relaxed and in a companionable mood and they walked and talked together as they had not done since their honeymoon. Lord Rosebery was an excellent host and although he had not committed himself in any way, Margot got the feeling that their visit had done some good. It was very sweet, too, to bask in Henry's praise. He thanked her for her unselfishness in giving up her hunting for his sake and said that without her the visit might have taken quite a different turn.

Although the weather was just right for hunting, Margot did not return to Melton but to London with Henry. It was a decision taken with her usual speed—one moment she was composing a telegram telling her hunting friends when to expect her, the next she was tearing it into little pieces and shouting to Henry in the next room that hunting had lost its charm and that she wanted to go home.

It had occurred to her to try to persuade her father to join them for a family Christmas in London. He was expecting her to bring everybody to Glen, but without her mother the soul had gone out of the place. She had only been back once since Emma's death and had not liked the experience at all. Again and again she would think of something to say to her mother and start off to find her before she remembered. Her father looked desolate, showing how deeply he missed the light and warmth that Emma's steady personality had put into his life.

To tear him away from Glen was not too difficult and the festivities went off better than she dared hope, mainly because of the way her stepchildren entered into the fun.[19] Their enthusiasm and laughter created a proper Christmas spirit which in turn affected Margot. She arranged a servants' ball—once a great feature of life at Glen—which proved a huge success. Margot danced until 1.30 and Henry too bumped his way round the floor, treading on his partners' toes and causing his children to split their sides with laughter. Afterwards he rather pathetically asked Margot to teach him how to dance. In the New Year she sent him off to a proper dancing school with his sons—the competition, she said, would be good for him. 'I was so amused at his delightful keenness and jolly awkwardness,' she told DD. It was beginning to dawn on her at last that it was fun having a ready-made family.

After Christmas Margot invited the old Gladstones to stay for a few days to keep Charles company, then later regretted it, for despite Gladstone's vigour and Mrs Gladstone's sprightliness, they were demanding and crotchety. Everything had to be just as it was at home, and Margot was worn out protecting the servants. Gladstone was seething with indignation at Rosebery's behaviour and Margot got the impression that he expected nothing would be right now he was no longer at the helm. Pity tempered her irritation, especially when she remembered that one day she might be in Aunty Pussy's place. Poor old thing, she told a friend, she looked as though she had reached the end of everything.[20]

CHAPTER 13

Think Imperially

THE ASQUITHS WERE still in London in the New Year of 1896 when the news of the Jameson raid broke. On the night of 30 December 1895 Dr Starr Jameson, the pioneer administrator of the Chartered Company in Rhodesia and Cecil Rhodes's right-hand man, led a raiding party of five hundred men on Johannesburg to precipitate a rising of the Uitlanders against President Kruger's government in the Transvaal. The Uitlanders (foreigners) had settled in the Rand in order to work the gold mines but had been denied full political rights in Kruger's republic. The raid was a fiasco. Jameson and his companions were captured before even reaching Johannesburg and Alfred Milner later told Margot that Jameson's foolish act of bravado did more harm than good.[1] Not only was he quickly captured, but his action risked creating a disturbance in the whole of South Africa and very nearly caused an international incident when on 2 January 1896 the Kaiser sent a telegram to Kruger congratulating him on his speed in scotching the raid without appealing for the help of friendly powers.

In England, opinions on the raid were mixed. Politicians like Asquith were outraged at Jameson's folly, calling it a dastardly act that would lead to war; but there were others whose imaginations were stirred by his daring. With greater insight than her husband, Margot felt that the real villains were Jameson's backers, the millionaires Cecil Rhodes and Alfred Beit, who quickly retired into the shadows when Jameson was captured. As for 'Dr Jim', Margot had difficulty in holding out against the clamour to turn him into a hero. She had always admired nerve no matter to what use it was put (that was part of the hold Peter Flower had had over her), and the dare-devil spirit showed by Jameson thrilled her as it did many other women who allowed themselves to be captivated by the romantic side of the exploit.

London was full of rumours: Dr Jim was captured; he had escaped; he was in England, hidden no one knew where. Many women began to believe that they had spotted him in the street or even at private functions, so heady did imagination become. However ludicrous this kind of nonsense was, the matter was delicate and Henry warned Margot to tread warily and say as little as possible, although she was constantly bombarded with questions.

Then, out of the blue, the Countess of Warwick, a member of the new Independent Labour Party, stole the limelight with a letter to *The Times* extolling Jameson: 'There is a large-minded Englishman in South Africa upon whose resolute personality our hearts and hopes rely.'[2] The letter gave the impression that the Countess knew more than Margot did and the interest shifted from her to Daisy Warwick. Margot was incensed: how dare she presume to air opinions about something that was 'none of her business', and when they happened to meet soon afterwards Margot took care to irritate her by calling her 'Comrade Warwick' in public and condemning the raid, Jameson, Rhodes and Beit to her face. After this she rushed home and burst into tears. It was too bad that Henry had asked her to be silent. Where the Countess of Warwick led, others followed—Alfred Austin the Poet Laureate with a poem, published by *The Times* on 11 January 1896. He called it 'Jameson's Ride'.

> Wrong? Is it wrong? Well maybe
> But I'm going, boys, all the same.
> Do they think me a burgher's baby
> To be scared by a scolding name?
> They may argue and prate and order,
> Go tell them to save their breath.
> Then over the Transvaal border
> And gallop for life or death.

There were three more verses and Margot thought them all quite dreadful (she had condemned Lord Salisbury's appointment of Alfred Austin as Poet Laureate as 'cynical'), but secretly she found the poem rousing and felt dishonest in not coming out in the open and saying so.

Jameson was handed over to the British for trial and when he reached London society went wild: so magnetic was his personality that every woman who met him fell at his feet. J. B. Robinson, a Rand magnate who was renting Dudley House for the season, told Margot that 'Dr Jim was a

man in a million, he is absolutely straight'. Colonel Kitchener (whom
Margot had met in Egypt) endorsed Robinson's words. 'Dr Jim is the only
one of the lot who could have made a fortune, but never owned a shilling.
He was a really fine fellow.'[3] Curiosity overcoming discretion, she invited
Jameson to dine.

At this strange dinner party of three (the smallest Margot had ever
given), Jameson talked freely of the plot that had failed, astonishing
Margot by the naïvety of his plan—he had hoped to kidnap Kruger and
hold him to ransom. He had courage and charm in abundance but Margot
wondered if he was clever enough to be a leader of men. He was an
idealist, a dreamer and a romantic and studying his face while he spoke,
she thought what a success he would have made of his life had he chosen
to be a faith healer.[4] She was filled with indignation at the part she was
certain Cecil Rhodes had played in destroying this delightful young man
and did not hesitate to say so. To speak out at last made up for the
'dishonesty' of the indifference she had previously affected, and that
evening she did her best to cheer him up; but Jameson was perfectly
resigned as to what was to come. When he rose Margot felt choked with
emotion to think that next day he would be standing in the dock accused
of treason.

Today it would be impossible to keep Jameson's dinner with a leading
member of the opposition and his wife secret: television cameramen
would have greeted him as he rang the bell of 20 Cavendish Square and
Asquith would perhaps have been dropped from the shadow cabinet. But
in 1896 nothing was leaked and no harm was done.

The sentence passed on Dr Jim by Lord Chief Justice Russell was a light
one—fifteen months in Wormwood Scrubs. Even so Margot could not
bear to think of a young man used to fresh air and open space shut up for
that length of time. He had completely captured her heart.

The Raid brought South Africa to the forefront; everyone began to
discuss its problems, whereas before many would not have known where
to find the Transvaal on the map. The slogan 'think imperially', attributed
to Cecil Rhodes, captured the public imagination, for in these last years of
the nineteenth century many people believed that Britain had a divine
right to rule and were willing to back Rhodes to the hilt without asking
questions. Margot refused to join them; Rhodes was a lion she did not
trust. Something about him repelled her and some years later she refused
to be introduced to him at a reception given in his honour at 10 Downing

Street by Arthur Balfour, then Prime Minister. She gave Balfour her reasons for her refusal: he was 'a man of coarse fibre with no integrity and filled with conceit'. She took it as a bad sign too that he did not mingle with the guests but lolled enthroned like a king surrounded by adoring women. 'He sat like a great bronze gong among them and I had not the spirit to disturb their worship.'[5]

When autumn came round again, Margot's longing to hunt overwhelmed her once more and she began to plan where she would stay, how many horses she would take and how long she would be away. It did not seem to her that it was at all odd to indulge her whims as though she was still a single woman. Her sister Charty told her plainly that such selfishness could not be justified while her house was still not in proper order, her husband and stepchildren not catered for. Margot had her answer ready; her good health depended on hunting and without those glorious hours in the fresh air, her nerves would be strained and her marriage would suffer.[6] Margot always talked of her nerves as though they were something special to her, but in fact 'nerves' was the fashionable complaint, and from Queen Victoria down most women who could afford to indulge themselves used their nerves as an excuse for almost anything. Margot was as bad as the rest, but she often felt dreadfully ill with a nameless malaise that was both real and painful. Her doctor told her that her body recovered quickly from all her illnesses but that it was her nerves that kept her on the sofa and that she must try and avoid 'nervous strain' as much as possible or she might become a semi-invalid. Her sister Charty did suggest that perhaps lying for hours on end either in bed or on her sofa might be the worst antidote for depression, but Margot preferred to believe her doctor: 'I am not old enough to acquiesce in the loss of health and I feel as though I were too young to die,'[7] she wrote soon after her marriage. Of course she loved dramatizing herself and without realizing what she was doing she found ill health of use in getting her own way. Headstrong, she refused to listen to reason when it contradicted her wishes, and unconsciously made herself ill. When friends scolded her for hunting in a pregnant condition, she sought sympathy from Alfred Milner, who she knew would not rebuke her. She made great play about loss of weight, hair falling out and talking to herself: 'Sitting and doing nothing for nine months is not my style—blast all moderation.'[8]

It never seems to have occurred to her that riding the kind of horses she loved best—too big for her frail physique and more often than not unmanageable—she might equally well be killed on the hunting field as giving birth to a child. Her nerves, so often made ragged by humans, were proof against anything that a horse might do. When she complained to Lord Esher that she needed exercise in order to keep fit and that her only sport was hunting, and he suggested she might try skiing in Switzerland, which had the added advantage that she could take her stepchildren, she was not very enthusiastic: 'I know nothing of winter sports,' she said. 'Are they safe . . . ?'[9]—a strange query when the previous summer her passion for horses had brought her near death on at least two occasions. While at Swindon trying out hunters she had been thrown heavily and it was only luck that prevented her being trampled on by her mount. On another occasion a dealer, over-anxious for a sale, let her try out a horse that was only half broken. It bolted as soon as she sat on its back, throwing her to the ground; her nerves were quite unaffected by her fall, although she was bruised all over and had difficulty in walking for days.

Hunting had become her insignia of freedom; it took precedence over all else. She was hunting when she discovered another baby was on the way, and even with the example of her first disastrous pregnancy she was enjoying herself so much that she could not give up and go home. She was now thirty-two years old and married for two years, but did not yet feel it was her duty to undertake the responsibilities of a wife. She still knew very little about running a home and showed no inclination to learn; nor had she inherited Emma's sense of order. When she looked at her half-finished house and knew that nothing could be done to it unless she gave instructions, she longed to run away; hunting was the only escape she had. When DD scolded her gently, she confessed she lacked the energy 'to choose wallpapers and give orders about hanging curtains'.[10] Her books from Glen had arrived but were still in crates and she made no attempt to put Henry's study in order, although she knew he hated untidiness. If he had insisted she would have done so at once, but Asquith was always over-indulgent with the women in his house and he had not yet got over the wonder that this dazzling creature, the darling of society, was really his wife.

Margot was worried about her father. He was lost without Emma and, lonely and nervous, had begun to think that his investments (on which they all depended) were unsound and that bankruptcy stared him in the face. This unaccustomed anxiety made him testy. For the first time in his life he lacked proper occupation and had no idea what to do with his leisure.

In late August Margot took her stepchildren to Glen for the first time, more for her father's sake than for theirs. Both Charles and Margot were amazed to find these town children entranced by the natural beauty of the place. They delighted in the purple of the heather, the changing colour of the hills, the enormous variety of trees and wild flowers. Glen itself entranced them too. They ran all over it, liking each room better than the last, warming Margot's heart by their enthusiasm. She showed them the trap-door in the roof and the ladder which she used to climb to get out to the turrets, and even let them do it themselves if they promised to be careful. The boys begged to be taught to shoot and all wanted to learn to ride which pleased Charles, who fostered their requests with his cheque book.

One day Margot innocently remarked to Raymond that she had had no idea that they would like the country so much, at once turning his new friendliness back into the indifferent scorn of a schoolboy who was bored with everything but the company of his own kind. He had developed a habit of picking up the book she was reading and catechizing her on its contents, which he usually knew very much better than she did. Only his undisguised sadness at leaving gave Margot a glimpse into his real feelings—she began to wonder whether perhaps his sneers were no more than a façade for his uncertainties.[11] Long ago she had guessed that Raymond would be the most awkward of her stepchildren, the most difficult to please; she longed for his approval but did not know how to win it. Alone with him, she felt self-conscious and tongue-tied, unable to stop herself saying the wrong thing, and she would ponder on how he would have behaved to his real mother. Was she too set in her ways to learn how to handle this adolescent boy? Was she too old-fashioned, too out-of-date, or too old? She flew to her dressing table, searching for tell-tale wrinkles and the grey hairs which crept on one unawares. Henry's hair had turned quite white with anxiety when she had nearly died in her first confinement, but it did not make him look old, only more distinguished.

Her present pregnancy was going well. She was not nearly so sick as last time and Sir John Williams was hopeful. If only her nerves would stand up better to the advice her friends bombarded her with. For years she had assured all of them that she was not touchy, that she did not mind criticism; now she was paying a heavy price for the boast. In her bossy fashion Mary Drew had volunteered to be the one to speak to Margot on the correct way for a mother-to-be to conduct herself if she wished to give birth to a healthy child, as though that disastrous first confinement had been her fault. There was no better authority than Mary, who now had three bouncing babies to prove it.

Mary could have been a great influence for good in Margot's life if she had been less censorious and less critical of the wrong things, and if she had showed just a little more sympathy. Margot knew that she was a woman with many qualities, and wanted to be friendly with Laura's best friend: that was the only link between them, but to Margot it was a sacred one. It upset her that Mary did not feel so deeply about this as she did and not long before her wedding she had written to tell Mary how she felt, hoping that this was the way to strengthen the relationship. '. . . You must be true to me, even if you don't quite care for me. Believe in me and then we shall be real friends . . . I don't expect love . . . but I expect loyalty.'[12] Because hers was not a jealous nature Margot did not understand that the one obstacle in the way to their friendship was Mary's jealousy of her father's affection for Margot who, she said, did not mind 'wasting Papa's precious time'. However, there was more to it than that: Mary had not failed to notice how her father enjoyed the spontaneous way Margot flung her arms round his neck, sat on his knees or on a stool at his feet, wheedling him into composing a rhyme or two about some trivial thing that had occurred to her. And old Mr Gladstone seemed to enjoy this performance and of course did just as he was asked. One afternoon in London Margot's smart little phaeton went flashing past Mary with Margot in the driving seat and next to her Mary's papa, obviously enjoying himself hugely. Mary mistakenly thought that it was just a joy-ride, but in fact Margot was only taking Mr Gladstone along the quickest route to the House of Commons so that he should not miss the beginning of a debate.

In her heart Mary knew that Margot loved Gladstone dearly and looked up to him in exactly the way Mary approved of. Nevertheless jealousy nagged her. When Margot heard that he was seriously ill she burst into tears in public. When he died of cancer in 1898 she was overcome with grief, although she had known that the end was expected, for Mary had kept her informed of each state of this terrible illness, describing with merciless accuracy her father's agonizing spasms and the doctors' fruitless efforts to relieve them, thus distressing Margot almost beyond endurance. It brought back to her all too vividly the terrible agony of her mother's last days and made her burst out in distress: 'I am sure we shall all die of it.'[13] She could only find comfort in re-reading the letters Gladstone had sent her over the years when he had seemed immortal. She put the letters carefully away: 'They are my most valuable legacy.'[14] Gladstone's death affected her deeply and in order to prevent a bad fit of depression, Charty took Margot to Paris to raise her spirits. She had hardly been home an hour when a scolding letter arrived from Mary which for once Margot answered in the mildest terms: 'I feel all the awe and hope of my condition very much indeed . . . I have been wonderfully well these 5½ months . . . my doctors think I shall be all right.'[15]

Why could not these two women get on better? Why did Margot have to describe as 'humbug' Mary's praying on her knees longer than anyone else and never missing a church service? Why did Margot's 'honesty' provoke Mary so much? Why could not Margot understand that it was unkind to begin a letter to Mary on her engagement to an obscure clergyman: 'I have never heard of Mr Drew . . .'?[16] Many years later Margot tried to analyse the reasons why she and Mary did not get on: 'There was something in her nature which did not harmonize with mine. At the time of my marriage she expressed her disapproval with such vigour both to my face and to my friends that she hurt me.'[17]

Mary had indeed hurt her very much when she said Margot was not worthy of the devotion of a man like Asquith. Margot too feared that she might not be worthy of him, but naturally resented her friends saying so: 'When you are sharing something of the same opinion you need the support and not the censure of your friends.'[18]

CHAPTER 14

Happiness Just Develops

ON 26 FEBRUARY 1897 Margot gave birth to a daughter at 20 Cavendish Square. She had been in pain all the previous day and although everything was going normally, she refused to eat or drink, but sat moaning in a chair while Charty rubbed her hands and back, and urged her to be brave. It was not until two o'clock in the morning that the baby was born. Sir John Williams told her that labour would have taken half the time if her nerves had not let her down.

In the last few weeks of her pregnancy, although surprisingly well, she had become morbid, made her will and passed the time writing farewell notes to her friends, all stamped and ready to be sent off after her demise. On her better days she amused herself by working out theories on the education of the young and composed quite a clever little treatise on the subject,[1] but too theoretical to be of much use in dealing with a flesh and blood child, especially one as strong-willed as the new baby turned out to be.

Margot had hoped for a girl and had the names ready: Elizabeth Charlotte Lucy (to be called Elizabeth), because during the last days of her pregnancy she had been reading a life of Goethe and Elizabeth was his mother's name: 'It is reminiscent of old houses, finely mown lawns and valueless pictures and has a kind of square grace which will look well in the future whether she is plain or pretty.'[2]

Small and thin, the new baby was as light as a feather (babies were not weighed in those days) and just as fragile. After a few days of anxiety she began to thrive enough for plans to go ahead for her christening in St Margaret's, Westminster. Except for Godfrey Webb and Lady Manners, two of Margot's oldest friends, the godparents were to be all family—her eldest brother Eddy and sisters Charty and Lucy, the three people Margot trusted to look after the child should anything happen to her. To Margot's dismay, Eddy could not attend the christening, but to make up for his absence he wrote Margot a typically Tennant letter which delighted her: 'Elizabeth shall have all she wants in life and Glen shall be to her what it was to us. She will learn to love all that we have loved and I will take her by the hand and talk to her. God bless you and her.'[3]

Very soon Margot was well enough to receive visitors, looking charming in a pale-blue chiffon and lace bed jacket, a matching boudoir cap on her head. Her face had lost that tight look of anxiety and was smiling and relaxed. All the old crowd came flocking to her room and there were not enough vases to hold the flowers they brought or tables for the books and magazines. Even busy politicians like Lord Rosebery and George Curzon looked in, while Arthur Balfour's affection for Margot overcame his distaste for fulfilled maternity, as he stood by her bedside giving her the gossip of the day.

Henry sat with her when he came home from the House and chatted of the things Margot liked to hear, saying his prayers by her bedside before he went to his room. Margot had never felt so happy and in her imagination long years of contented motherhood stretched before her; now that she had achieved the miracle once, she could do so again. On the few occasions when she was alone, she loved to day-dream: Elizabeth was to be everything she was not, while she would be the perfect mother, always at hand when needed, especially at bedtime to read to her and hear her say her prayers. In this way she would influence her in many subtle ways, for Elizabeth was sure to be clever like all Asquith children. Because she had been successful in producing a live baby Margot felt ready for motherhood in a way that she had never done before, and her love for her infant was so great as to be almost overwhelming, arousing in her tender, protective feelings that she genuinely believed she had always possessed. She once wrote that she had a passion for babies and young children but in fact she never showed any sign of it.

With the birth of her daughter a lot of Margot's restlessness had disappeared, although for the first year or two anxiety for the baby's health was never far away. While she pretended at first to be cool with the infant, she delighted in playing with her child, making her smile and then laugh and was soon in danger of becoming the kind of woman she most despised, the woman who is never happier than when she can bring her child into the conversation. Having a child of her own helped her to understand her stepchildren much better, and for the first time she realized what a shock it must have been to be deprived of a mother so suddenly.

At last she believed that she was tasting real happiness for the first time. In 1892 she had written to Mary a forlorn letter:

> I don't think there is much real happiness in life . . . happiness grows apart from every external thing and cannot be found or experienced, it just develops with suffering and goodness and love in its purest and highest form . . . I, for one, hardly expect to realize what I properly understand by the word. We must live very near God and not mind things with as much personal passion as I do and not resent so bitterly some of the divine adjustment.[4]

She had found happiness where she least expected it, in her child. She had married Henry Asquith because she admired, respected and felt safe with him; love did not enter into her calculations. Now all that had changed too, and she was content with her world. 'My life with Henry is happier than I can describe,' she wrote to Mary a few weeks after her safe delivery. 'Constant interest and company, endless discussions and a sort of easy 3 or 4 to dinner at which time we have capital talks.'[5]

After the baby's birth Margot's health had so improved that she was able to pick up many old threads that she had allowed to drop through illness and inertia. Saturday-to-Monday parties at Stanway (the Elchoes), Taplow (the Desboroughs), Mells (the Horners) and Clouds (the Percy Wyndhams) saw Margot once again as one of the leading lights, sparkling, talkative and happy, with a husband who enjoyed this form of relaxation from his parliamentary duties. There was one new face: a quiet American whom Margot knew slightly before her marriage, but had taken little notice of, had since become the greatest literary lion of his day. No country-house party was complete without Henry James; everyone read his novels. Margot put down the fact that she had passed over a writer of such importance to her preoccupation with hunting.

Seeing Margot in this setting, so at home, so delighted with everything, it is difficult to understand the strange duality of her nature that made her equally happy and at ease with her hunting friends, where nothing more intellectual than horseflesh or the day's sport was discussed. One curious and to Margot gratifying fact was the remarkably friendly way her hunting companions accepted Asquith. It had never entered her head that they had anything in common, so she had kept them apart, not wishing to embarrass the one or bore the other. The year before when he had managed to join her at Melton for a few days, she was forced to introduce him. Henry was quickly the centre of an admiring group, listening to him reeling off the names and dates of Derby winners for years back.

The summer after Elizabeth's arrival they rented a house at Littlestone-on-Sea in Kent, and all of them enjoyed the golf and the swimming while Asquith derived great pleasure from watching them behaving as a family and Margot learned that even cool, clever children are not so formidable when one is not so conscious of their cleverness. Even Raymond admitted that Margot had her uses when he hurt his eye on a rock while swimming and she knew exactly what to do and promptly came to his rescue.[6]

In the autumn she went hunting in Leicestershire as usual but to her surprise she did not enjoy herself despite the fact that she was riding better than ever. Her thoughts would keep returning to her nursery and school-room—was baby Elizabeth eating properly? Was Cis happy at his new school? 'I feel my life too full to spend so much time hunting as I like,' she wrote to Alfred Milner.

> It is an awful bore as I feel so well and happy and love hunting. But children always with servants is not right and my baby is so clever and out of the way sweet and pretty that I feel I must turn my thoughts to bringing her up in a way no nurse could.[7]

She never hunted on this scale again and in 1906 abandoned it for good and sold her horses.

In the last few weeks of 1898 an event occurred that gravely threatened the Asquiths' financial future. At the age of seventy-five Sir Charles Tennant announced his engagement to a neighbour's daughter, Marguerite Miles, forty-five years his junior and whom he had first met four months earlier. They were married on 25 November and the first of their three daughters was born before the end of 1899. Although the sudden-ness of the affair was a shock, Margot was genuinely glad that her father was happy and would have someone to look after him in his old age. Nevertheless the implications of the marriage could not fail to strike her: 'Papa is horribly in love,' she told Alfred Milner, 'so nothing can be expected from him—Henry has to make some more money.'[8] Charles had been Margot's security, her insurance should they ever be in need of help and she had passed on this confidence to Henry. Now suddenly their growing financial embarrassment was made really serious by Charles's remarriage.

Margot's way of life was not cheap. Hunters, numerous servants, good clothes, frequent holidays and visits to country-houses, were all to her the necessities of life; it never once occurred to her to cut back, even if only until the Liberals were again in office. Besides, her nature was generous, and the news of her arrival at a house-party sent the servants into ecstasies, for her tips far exceeded those of any other guest.

Shortly before her marriage Charles had taken Margot on one side and advised her to have her money in her own name, sensible advice that was indignantly rejected. What was hers must be Henry's too, she said, the account must be in their joint names. This meant that she never really knew what she had to spend, nor exactly where the money went, and she found it boring to ask Henry to show her his accounts. She had always had money in the past and she saw no reason why she should not continue to have it in the future. Even Henry, once so frugal and careful, was becoming just as casual. With his second marriage he discovered that he enjoyed the good things of life just as much as Margot and quickly accepted high living as normal. The Hampstead days had receded very far into the background.

Charles and his bride were still on honeymoon when a crisis in the Liberal Party placed Asquith in a cruel dilemma. Sir William Harcourt resigned and Asquith was offered the leadership, a position Margot longed for him to have, for it would be but one jump away from the chief post of all—that of Queen's first minister. To her great chagrin Henry declined.

One of the conditions of the acceptance was that he should relinquish his practice at the Bar, something he could not do with Raymond at Oxford, two more sons at Winchester, and his other huge expenses. Margot thought that to refuse the leadership because of money was ridiculous, saying that the extra money could easily be found if needed. It was her philosophy to leap first and look round for ways and means second. It had worked well for her in the past, but as Henry said she had not had six children to worry about. He recorded in a memorandum at the time:

. . . On personal grounds it is impossible for me without a great and unforgivable sacrifice of the interests of my family to take a position which . . . would cut me off from my profession and leave me poor and pecuniarily dependent. . . . From every point of view I thought that the best choice our party could make was Campbell-Bannerman.[9]

Campbell-Bannerman had equal or better claims to the succession, and Asquith knew that to pass over the senior man now would jeopardize his own chances. Nor would Asquith fall in with the proposal that Harcourt should be persuaded to keep the leadership until he himself could take over.

Margot thought this a good idea, for she longed for Henry to grasp the nettle in case the chance might not come again. She confided in Alfred Milner, 'I strongly feel "C.B." is not the man to lead us.'[10] But Milner agreed with Henry; her husband was doing the right thing. Try as she might, she was never able to influence Henry in politics if he thought his actions were the right ones.

Margot did not know C.B. very well so did not realize that there was more in him than met the eye. Because he was neither a prima donna like Rosebery nor quarrelsome like Harcourt, she was inclined to dismiss him as a nonentity, but his friends knew he was steady, and possessed of a much more forceful personality than many gave him credit for. His aims too were the right ones: 'To preserve intact the unity of the party until those better days when he could guide it back to the promised land.'[11]

Ever since the Jameson Raid relations with the Transvaal had been uneasy. The lenient sentence passed on 'Dr Jim' had made Kruger furiously angry, an anger that was directed against the British people. In November 1897 Alfred Milner had gone out to South Africa as High Commissioner and from there he had written freely to Margot about the warlike atmosphere among the Boers, telling her that far from disliking the prospect of a conflict with the British, they had been hoping for it for some time and the raid had given them the excuse they wanted. Even before he left England Milner had said that war would come sooner or later and predicted the former.[12] Asquith thought him over-pessimistic; he was sure that the Boers did not want conflict. Eighteen months later, when Milner came back to England for consultations with the government, he called briefly on Margot before returning to South Africa and they were able to talk privately in her sitting-room. When he had gone she wrote in her diary a short description of his 'worried air' and how he seemed bowed down with anxiety and could talk of nothing but the worsening situation and his efforts to keep the peace. She felt that he must be exaggerating and it made her sad too to see that he had aged; the climate did not suit his constitution, which needed the invigorating tonic of crisp, cold air, not the scorching sun of an African summer. Moreover, the lack of the softening influence of a wife was beginning to tell now he was over forty. Margot was more than ever sure that Alfred's warnings were unnecessary when in the summer of 1899 she accompanied Henry on a tour of the Liberal constituencies and listened to his reassuring message: 'We are not alarmed by the irresponsible clamour for war which we hear from some familiar quarters.'[13]

Life was peaceful for Margot that year. Happy and untroubled, she wanted nothing to disturb the harmony of her home, so shut her ears to anything that might upset her. After a holiday in Scotland with the younger children she went in high spirits to Gosford for a few days. She was still there in October when Kruger's ultimatum arrived to shatter the hope that the Boers would not fight. She hurried home with all speed; how would a war in South Africa affect Henry, who had been so sure that it would not come?

To her surprise she found herself defending not Henry but Milner, who was being blamed for the 'mess' he had got Britain into—had he not said 'war is the only solution'?[14] Some of Margot's friends owned gold mines in the Rand and feared that a war would make them worthless, and with their money in jeopardy they wanted to tear Milner limb from limb. Although Margot had not heard from Alfred for some time, she did not believe a word that was said against him; she was convinced that he did not want war and had done nothing to provoke it.

When war did break out in October 1899, Margot felt with all her friends that it could not last more than a few weeks: the Boers were untrained, had few guns and lived scattered over a wide area. Therefore, when during the early months the British were losing ground (Henry explained to her that the strength of the Boers had been greatly underestimated), Margot's spirits sank lower with every adverse report. She knew nothing of colonial politics or the issues at stake between the British and the Dutch, but nevertheless had her own opinion of the cause of the conflict and aired it freely—it was greed. The disastrous discovery of gold on the Rand had led to the deaths of hundreds of people, a simple philosophy that held more than a grain of truth: 'The search for money that dominates South Africa is repulsive.'[15]

When shiploads of wounded began to arrive Margot toured the hospitals, speaking to the men and learning what was happening. Their stories varied little: inefficiency made life at the front wretched, as many died from infected wounds as from the Boers' guns. To be told this by mere boys 'with no arms or legs and agonizing wounds' all begging her to do what she could to stop the war, made her feel helpless and inadequate and tears came into her eyes as she listened. It was pitiful to be told that in many cases no plans had been made to receive the reinforcements when they arrived from England, so that they were given wrong instructions and were left wandering about in the darkness, leaderless, lost and hungry, sometimes to be shot by the Boers before they reached their units. A committee was sent out to investigate this mismanagement but, as Margot commented: 'By the time they reach South Africa all will be over and dead men tell no tales.'[16]

CHAPTER 15

Free Traditions are not Moonshine

IN THE AUTUMN of 1900 the Conservative government had sought to make capital out of the South African situation by calling the 'Khaki election'. Margot thought this contemptible sharp practice, and although she felt certain that Henry would be safe at East Fife (he was returned with an increased majority), she feared that it might go hard with lesser Liberals like her eldest brother Eddy, who was standing for his father's old seat in Glasgow. Her affection for this companion of her youth was so great that she was willing to make all sorts of sacrifices to see him win. Door-to-door canvassing she found embarrassing, speaking in public terrified her, but she undertook to show her enthusiasm and even offered to sell her jewels to pay his expenses. But he was not an inspiring candidate, for Margot found, although good and conscientious in every way, 'Eddy lacks drive, and as Pamela [his wife] is born without it . . . they are not people to conquer votes with'.[1] For the first time in her life, Margot was disillusioned by the Scots. Everyone in Scotland seemed to have detached themselves from the war—as soon as a politician mentioned South Africa interest melted away.

The huge Conservative victory did not surprise her, but she was increasingly apprehensive about the conduct of the war. Margot had distrusted Joseph Chamberlain, the Colonial Secretary, ever since he had been implicated in the Jameson raid (after that she labelled him 'mediocre and no gentleman'), and she feared that when peace came the Conservatives would not treat the Boers well, so that resentment against the British might smoulder on as it did in Ireland.

But in the summer of 1901 horror stories were pouring into England of concentration camps set up by the British to house in a rough and ready fashion the women and children left homeless as a result of Kitchener's scorched earth policy: to burn the homesteads to the ground was Kitchener's reply to the Boers' commando tactics. Reports of this ruthless action shocked people in England profoundly. Margot was full of indignation when she read of mothers watching helplessly while their children died in these terrible conditions where disease quickly spread and there were no doctors or medical supplies. Margot's voice was heard everywhere loud and clear, calling for this outrage to be stopped at once. All she got in return were insults—Margot Asquith was pro-Boer.[2]

Margot had heard a good deal to the discredit of Sir Redvers Buller and Lord Kitchener: one had lost his nerve, the other his humanity. Lord Crewe told her that he knew Kitchener 'inside out' and that it would be fatal for such a man to help Milner in the peace settlement when it eventually came. At Christmas 1901, with this information in her pocket, Margot tried to persuade Henry to listen to all Milner had written to her in a private letter: to get rid of Kitchener—he was loathed by the men and Milner wanted him replaced.[3]

But it was the Government that negotiated the peace, and as Margot had expected the treaty of Vereeniging which ended the war on 31 May 1902 did not mean the end of the trouble. Cries of revenge came from all sides and many in England were hotly in favour of reprisals, 'otherwise our men will have died in vain'. But the Boers had suffered too and Margot's heart was filled with admiration for Henry when he agreed that they too would need all the help England could give them to restart their lives. Fair play was essential after a war in which no one could rejoice and which had left much bitterness and hatred behind.[4]

The war had taught Margot one important thing—not to put too much emphasis on popularity or reverses and that the fortunes of public men were very much swayed by the winds of change. Alfred Milner had been most unpopular at the beginning of the conflict with the Boers; how Margot's friends had railed at everything he had done. While he was in South Africa his enemies had even spread a rumour that he had been summoned home to be dismissed in disgrace, a rumour that was killed stone dead when he did return in May 1901 for consultations with the government, and was met at the station by the entire cabinet and escorted straight to the King, who created him a peer on the spot.[5] At the end of the war Milner's name stood high and he was praised for his moderation and his refusal to countenance revenge. He had told Margot that his only desire was to see South Africa enjoy peace and prosperity again; he wanted nothing for himself, not even the vice-royalty of India, which he refused in 1905.

Margot's triumph at the rightness of her championship of Alfred Milner—'he was incapable of a dishonourable act'—was abruptly cut short when she read about his scheme to get the economy in the Transvaal going again by restarting the mines in the Rand with all speed and importing Chinese labour to work them, while forbidding the men to bring their families. Indignantly Margot accused Alfred of allowing power and success to make him cynical, and she warned him that acceding to this plan of 'digging up wealth for the few' meant that he set human life at nought. She wrote to ask him if he realized the suffering caused by his scheme. To separate husbands from wives for years on end and cut out family life was cruel; how could he do this dreadful thing and have a clear conscience?

Once Alfred Milner had been very close to her; she had loved him and seriously considered marrying him. Had he hidden this harsh side from her, or had she been so bemused in Egypt that she had not even sensed it? The idea that there were two sides to his nature so disturbed her that she found it difficult to write in the cool and controlled way which Henry had taught her was the only effective means to put an important point across:

> If they are as industrious as people say and sober and clever they should have fewer restrictions and be allowed to settle with their families. South Africa can never be a white man's country completely.[6]

She gave the letter to Henry to read and though he agreed with her, he remained cooler than she would have liked. When she begged him to 'put a stop to this horrible scheme at once', he answered her mildly: 'The House, as the trustee of the liberty of the subject throughout the Empire, had not yet seen the regulations.'[7] He omitted to tell her that some time ago he had promised Milner Liberal support and was now trying to stick to his promise. Margot would not let the matter drop, telling him that she never expected to see a Liberal supporting 'slavery under the British flag', a slogan being bandied about in London, now that the scheme was public knowledge.

In the end she got her way—it was the only time she ever did on a political issue—and when he denounced the Chinese labour scheme in the House of Commons she believed that he had changed his mind because of the justice of her case. But his enemies attributed his change of heart to Margot's ambition: they said that she had persuaded him that he was backing the wrong horse by supporting an unpopular measure which might do him great harm when the question of the leadership came up again. 'I do not think you had got Asquith straight on the point,' Leo Amery wrote to Milner. 'The temptation with office looming so near and the wallpaper for 10 Downing Street already selected by Mrs A. was too much for him . . .'[8] Astute though he was, Amery misconceived Margot's motives. There is not a word in any of her letters to suggest that she had Henry's future career in mind when she denounced the plan to use Chinese labour. It was not ambition for Henry that moved her but outrage at the inhumanity of the scheme. Her imagination was often too vivid for comfort and it was not difficult for her to feel with great intensity the misery of the coolies. Once having felt it, she could not rest until she had done all she could to right a great wrong. When she tried to enlist Lord Selborne's help, she ended her letter on as cool a note as she could manage and with her fury well in hand. 'No one can say it is a good principle to start a new country on . . . living without much freedom and not any women.'[9]

Her old confidence in Milner was shattered. In July 1906 she wrote Alfred Milner's epitaph in another letter to Lord Selborne: 'He does not believe in a conquered race having a hand in their own self-government. He does not believe in God or in man . . . and he thinks the free tradition that has been the making of us all moonshine . . .'[10]

Early in 1900 Margot lost a second baby and was again very ill. Over and over again she asked herself: 'What is it that went wrong?' It could not be her nerves which she knew to be tightly strung, for her doctors had assured her that her inability to produce strong, healthy children had nothing to do with the nervous system. Her women friends were her greatest comfort: Ettie Desborough and Helen Vincent, who had suffered in the same way, sat by her bedside holding her hand, giving support through their own unhappiness.

Cossetted and spoilt all her life, Margot now bewailed the fact that she had not been better prepared for these tragedies, indeed for all the tragedies of her life: 'For you it is different,' she wrote to Mary Drew. 'You have lived in a better atmosphere of preparation. I have had none. Happiness is the worst preparation for misery.'[11] She wrote to DD, whose sympathy (mixed as it was with firmness) always did her good:

I won't write about my baby. She was mine for seven hours, then they took her away and she is buried at Wansborough. Henry carried the little coffin all the way in his arms. He sobbed in front of the doctors and nurses on his knees by the tiny cradle. I had such agonizing pains. I was not allowed to see it alive—they filled me with morphine and made me sleep. Dear old Williams cried quietly while he injected morphine to give me rest. He says I am a wild animal, not a woman at all; my body recovers so instantly, but my nerves are horribly shaken. It is so maddening as I can hardly stop crying at the tiniest things and Elizabeth's littlest tears and smallest ailment fills me with despair. I pray and pray I may have one more and soon.[12]

Again Margot is separating her 'body' from her 'nerves' and in this she is probably only repeating what her doctors said. Not one doctor seems to have treated her body in order to strengthen her nervous system. No one seems to have realized that she was suffering from malnutrition among other things. After every confinement she had difficulty in eating. Her diet consisted of cups of tea and minute morsels of meat and vegetables which often had to be spooned into her by a nurse. When her childbearing days were over and she was again unwell, her ailment was diagnosed as anaemia of the brain, and she was ordered constant nips of brandy to prevent her from fainting. Much sport was made of this behind her back, especially by her daughter-in-law Cynthia who hinted that Margot's ailment was merely an excuse for secret drinking. Margot never cared much for alcohol and all these small doses achieved was to make her dizzier than ever and take the edge off her appetite, so that she ate less than before. No fashionable doctor treating the rich ever thought that the lack of three square meals a day could possibly be the cause of depression, faintness, headaches, palpitation of the heart and fatigue. Henry ate heartily, but Margot merely nibbled. It is possible too that she might have been suffering from a form of latent tuberculosis; indeed she often wondered how she had escaped this disease. She hardly ever mentioned what she called 'the curse of our family' but this did not mean that she forgot about it.

In the summer when Margot was on her feet again Asquith rented a huge house in North Berwick and because she was ordered plenty of fresh air and exercise she bravely struggled on to the golf links to play a round with Henry and her stepchildren. The boys would soon be miles ahead, intent on improving their game, leaving Margot, a tiny thin figure, far behind. When the boys returned to Oxford and to school, she took Violet and the three-year-old Elizabeth to Glen. From her room there Margot would stare at the landscape and in her imagination see her mother, a straw hat on the back of her head, a trowel in her hand while the young Margot with Laura and their brothers rushed about all over the place. Such nostalgia was not healing for it held too much of regret and bred dissatisfaction with the present. At North Berwick Margot had steadily improved, eaten more and slept better, but at Glen the old symptoms returned: 'I am weepy and nervous with deep personal grief,' she wrote to DD '. . . but I should be called quite well by most people, I suppose.'[13] Yet she had one healthy living child, who was fast becoming the pet of the family, especially of Violet, whom the little girl adored. In the old days that blessing alone would have been a reason for thankfulness.

When in the New Year 1902 DD and Alfred Lyttelton's two-year-old son Anthony died suddenly, her sorrow for these great friends was real and deep, but all her own grief for her own children came flooding back.

Margot felt this child's death all the more deeply because she was again pregnant and in a highly nervous state. Usually she laughed at superstition and would have nothing to do with it but, upset as she was, she began to wonder if the death of this child was a bad omen. If her baby turned out to be a boy and lived she would call him after the dead child to propitiate the gods. When in November she did give birth prematurely to a son, who fortunately survived, she had him christened Anthony, although he was always known as 'Puffin'.

At first Anthony did give cause for anxiety, but he possessed a strong will to live and although he was never robust, he was not ill. In one way his delicacy acted as a safeguard for, fearing the old curse (consumption), she kept him out of doors as much as possible, and when he developed a cold or a cough or even a slight temperature took instant action. She worried endlessly about this adored child who, his father declared, had inherited the best qualities of both Asquiths and Tennants. He was quick, intelligent and highly musical, but was slow in learning to dress himself, tie his shoes or even brush his hair and drove the household mad by eating at a snail-like pace. Motherhood had come late to Margot and she felt its responsibilities all the more keenly for being more mature. She could never forget that she had lost two children, so the two that lived were all the more precious to her.

In the summer of 1902 Lord Salisbury resigned as Prime Minister and was succeeded by Arthur Balfour.

Balfour was not only one of Margot's oldest friends but had been a prominent 'Soul', looked up to and admired as one of the most sophisticated men of his time. Nevertheless the cool, aloof qualities that so captivated every member of that élite society were not the ones to make a successful Prime Minister, and Margot knew it. All Tories were to her 'indescribable idiots' and under the Balfour government Tory misrule would continue just as it had done for far too long already.

As the years wore on Margot saw faults in Balfour that she had not noticed when she was younger and the occasional sharp criticism began to creep into her conversation and letters. He could be disengaged to the point of coolness, nothing moved him to passion; he hated the fatigue of quarrelling, and the argumentative atmosphere of the Commons was abhorrent to him because it did not suit the refinement of his temperament, but most important of all he lacked leadership quality. His first speech as Prime Minister rang with epigrams and lofty phrases, but said nothing at all, Margot noticed. Very soon he declared that his government would support Protection, but he did not fight for the cause he believed in as Margot thought he ought to have done. Instead he sat on the fence, saying blandly that there was something to be said for Free Trade too. Margot complained to Lord Selborne that Balfour's real weakness was his desire to keep on good terms with everyone: 'I can't forgive politically his aversions, his over-modelled sense of truth, his slight want of moral fibre—I believe in facing the music myself . . .'[14] Thoroughly irritated by Balfour, Margot could not stop herself thinking how much better Henry would do the job: his impassioned speeches at East Fife showed his constituents how deeply he cared. It dismayed her to hear Balfour say, in conversation with Henry, that the majority of the country was quite content with Unionist rule and that it was not inconceivable that they would stay in power for years. He warned her to have patience, an essential quality in politics, and that it was useless to say that if a government was doing no good it should go.

Searching for comfort, Margot thought she could discern several signs of coming Conservative unpopularity. Then suddenly it seemed as though there was a ray of hope. One morning in May 1903 Henry came into her bedroom, *The Times* in his hand. 'Wonderful news today,' he said, 'and it is only a question of time when we shall sweep this country.'[15] Joseph Chamberlain had made a speech in Manchester advocating 'naked Protection', calling for imperial preference and protective tariffs and rejecting the hallowed doctrine of Free Trade. Nothing could have been better timed to put a stop to Liberal quarrelling and get them to turn as one man on the Government. The Unionist Cabinet was itself divided: 'Would Balfour repudiate Joe or go to the country on Protection?' Margot wondered. When he did neither she was highly indignant—Arthur was up to his old tricks, doing nothing as usual. He ought to resign, it was the only honourable thing. But it was Chamberlain who resigned to lead the campaign for Tariff Reform, and two years of intense public debate ensued until in November 1905 Balfour at last relinquished office. Had Asquith's chance come at last?

In one way Balfour's resignation came at an inopportune moment for the Asquiths. Henry was just about to start for Egypt to represent the Khedive's family in an important lawsuit concerning land, for which he had already been given a fee of £10,000. To go, and earn the much-needed money, would be to miss the chance of a place in a new Liberal Cabinet. Margot was emphatic: money should never stand in the way of opportunity, so he should send it back. But she had an even bigger anxiety: Was Campbell-Bannerman bound to be Prime Minister simply because he was Leader of the Liberal Party? In opposition he had been no match for the speed and subtlety of Balfour's mind, as she had observed from her seat in the Ladies' Gallery.

When Edward Grey came to dinner, Margot was delighted to discover that he thought as she did. C.B. would not make a good Prime Minister; he should go to the Lords, leaving Henry to lead in the Commons. In fact, while the Asquiths were staying at Glen in September, Henry had met Grey and Haldane at Relugas, where Grey was fishing, and agreed that unless C.B. stood down to make way for Asquith all three would refuse to serve under him.[16] Since Margot could think of no reason for C.B. to refuse, to her the deed was as good as done. She reminded Grey that C.B. was not a fit man, and that his wife was far from well: he was a patriot and would put his party before self. That this could work two ways had not occurred to her. Shrewd though she often was in judging other people's characters, she sometimes made serious mistakes when she wanted something badly enough. She had got it into her head that Campbell-Bannerman was weak. For his part, C.B. underestimated Margot. He thought her merely a tiresome woman of no account politically, but one who was very ambitious for her husband.

One evening when Margot was having her hair washed Henry came to her bedroom and told her he had seen C.B. and discussed a future Liberal Cabinet. Filled with excitement Margot tied a scarf over her head and ran down to the library where they could talk in private. C.B., Henry said, had asked what post he would like. 'The Exchequer I suppose'—'I said nothing'.—'Or the Home Office?'—'I said certainly not'. C.B. then said 'Of course if you want legal promotion, what about the Woolsack?' —'No'—'Well then it comes back to the Exchequer.' He then said that Haldane had suggested that he (C.B.) should go to the Lords, 'a place for which I have neither liking, training nor ambition', adding that he could make no decision until his wife returned from Scotland that night. Before they parted Asquith made one stipulation: he would not serve unless Grey was given the Foreign Office.[17]

Listening carefully, Margot got the firm impression that C.B. was wavering about the Lords, and when Edward Grey told Asquith that he would call on C.B. at home and put a pistol to his head by making this a condition of his own acceptance of the Foreign Office she felt quite sure of it.

The Asquiths had been invited to Hatfield for a fancy dress ball that night and Margot with Violet had to go ahead while Henry waited in London for C.B.'s decision. When he arrived in time for dinner, Margot could barely hide her impatience to get him alone. His news was a bitter disappointment. Lady Campbell-Bannerman had been adamant. 'No surrender', her husband must not go to the Lords.[18] Henry told her everything and although his news was not what Margot had hoped for, she tried not to show it, for Henry looked worn out. At dinner she felt proud that he could put on such a good face before the huge crowd gathered at Hatfield that night, throwing himself into the dancing with a zest that belied his real feelings.

They returned to London next day to find Haldane sulking because he had been offered the War Office instead of the office of Lord Chancellor which he coveted, and Grey refusing to serve under C.B. at all, although he knew he was indispensable at the Foreign Office and that Asquith would not serve without him.

Margot's common sense, which so often came to her rescue in moments of crisis, told her that if Henry did not insist to the contrary Grey would give in—indeed, would have done so long ago—and Haldane would quickly follow suit. And so it proved. When Henry gave up, Grey followed his lead and all was well. Margot indulged in tears of relief as she wrote in her diary: 'We are all in, but not one of us has got what we wanted.'[19]

The general election of 1906 was an overwhelming victory for the Liberals, just as Asquith had predicted.

It was Margot's first taste of electioneering with Henry (she had been ill last time) and whenever he spoke she was a prominent figure on the platform, travelling all over the country with him, cheerful and friendly with everyone and, as he told her, a real support. In those days constituents expected prodigiously long speeches, and a prospective candidate who spoke for a mere hour was dismissed as no good; to one of Margot's restless temperament to sit still for so long was a trial, but she would willingly pay the price if it bought success.

Asquith's main weapon was the prospect of Protection under the Tories and the misery it would bring in its wake. ('Tax the poor man's loaf —never'.) After that he touched on the three questions that were troubling him: the Education and Licensing Bills and Old Age Pensions. On Home Rule he kept a low profile. At the outset he had decided to concentrate on a few simple issues which the people would understand and not to underestimate the difficulties in the way of a Liberal government: 'There is a lot of country still to traverse, steep hills to climb and stiff fences to take, deep and even turbulent streams to cross before we come to the end of our journey; but we know where we are going and we shall not lose our way.'[20]

In the new Parliament Asquith was Chancellor of the Exchequer and deputy leader as well, which Margot hoped augured well for the future. The usual home of the Chancellor of the Exchequer, 11 Downing Street, was not large enough; Margot could not see how she could squeeze a nursery and a school-room into such cramped quarters. Promptly Charles came to the rescue. Delighted at the elevation of his son-in-law, he said he would give them the rent which they would have received had they let 20 Cavendish Square, so that they could continue to live there in comfort. (11 Downing Street was lent to the Herbert Gladstones, who had no London House.) Charles hoped, he said, to live long enough to see Henry Prime Minister.

But on 3 June 1906 Charles died at the house he had bought after marrying his second wife, 'Broadoaks' in Weybridge. Margot and Henry travelled overnight to Glen to attend the funeral at Traquair and on a still, misty morning of the kind that Charles loved best, they followed the coffin the quarter-mile to the churchyard to place Charles next to Emma and close to those of his children who had predeceased him. It was a spot greatly loved by Margot, and although it was so often swept by cold winds and was bare of trees and flowers, it never failed to hold her captive.

'I can't believe Papa is gone', Margot wrote next day to DD.

> The centre of our lives; the vigorous keen darling heart, so self-willed and unique, so generous and simple. It was amazingly characteristic and sad, the beautiful misty Friday morning, the whole family waiting at Innerleithen Station for the Glen people . . . Poor Marguerite! She, Charty, Lucy and I were together and we wept at this his last return to Glen since it was burnt.* I'm glad he never saw it. The walls are just the same but the inside quite new . . . hardly a fault that I could find, tho' my heart was heavy as I started to go over it all with Lucy and Charty after the funeral. Poor Papa, he wanted to live very much.[21]

Arthur Balfour was in Margot's black books for not visiting Charles when he was ill, after promising to do so. She hated broken promises and felt Balfour's defection bitterly. 'How selfish Arthur Balfour is,' she wrote, 'he promised me that he would go and see papa, and the old angel looked forward so eagerly to his visit. Knowing Arthur's self-indulgent memory I wrote it down for him, but of course he never went and has not sent a line of any sort to any one of us. Strip Arthur of his charm and you'll find a poor creature . . . I have no illusions about deep feelings which are never shown. He ought to have said he could not go and did not want to'.[22]

Charles's will was a shock: he left his vast fortune to his three sons and nothing at all to the three surviving daughters of his first marriage, except the incomes he had settled on them as their dowry. It had been Margot's hope that because her sister, Lucy Graham-Smith, was crippled with arthritis and was married to a sort of maniac—harmless and kind, but very mad—he would have left her something extra. Charles had settled only £3,000 a year on Lucy since she had no children, much less than

---

* There had been a serious fire at Glen in 1905.

on Charty (who had five) while Margot had seven children (counting her stepchildren) and was expecting another baby in January.[23] They would all have to make the best of things, but it was hard to have no prospects.

Asquith was reaching the peak of his career and enjoying the experience. His constitution was excellent—he had hardly suffered a day's illness in his life—and under Margot's guidance he had become much more sure of himself socially. The realization that she was living in exciting times had come suddenly to Margot when one afternoon during the height of the election campaign a woman constituent told her that she and many of her friends envied Margot her position as the wife of England's coming man, for she was involved in the making of history. Margot had always wanted to be part of Henry's career (she had already begun to say 'we' when talking of the government) and she hoped very much that he would talk things over with her and benefit from her advice. It was disappointing, therefore, that Henry did not tell her anything that went on in Cabinet meetings nor asked her opinion of his colleagues, most of whom she had known longer than he. It was even more disappointing that the price she had to pay for his advancement was that she saw so little of him, and even less when he was preparing his first Budget speech. The press dismissed the speech as humdrum, much to her indignation. Henry had only been in office four months and could not be responsible for the finances of the previous years in which he had no hand.

In order to carry out her resolve to become a part of Henry's career Margot started a habit that remained unbroken for the next fifteen years. She went most days to the Ladies' Gallery especially when C.B. or Henry spoke. She enjoyed comparing them to C.B.'s disadvantage. These visits to the House of Commons, begun out of a sense of duty and curiosity, showed Margot another side of Henry, a new authoritative side which she found most attractive: 'No one speaks quite like Henry,' she wrote in her diary after listening to him delivering his budget speech. 'He seems to run rather a bigger show . . . he gives a feeling of power rather than grace or charm and has a very happy choice of words.'[24] This was a very different assessment of Henry's public manner from the first time she had heard him speak in Scotland in 1892: 'There is a harsh quality in his enuncia-tion,' she had written in her diary that night, '. . . as a speech it was good but no more.'[25] Thereafter she never found fault with a single speech, and thought even the Budget speech inspiring: 'Not a word wasted, not a word too much.'[26]

The summer of 1906 was stiflingly hot and Margot felt that they must get out of London as soon as the recess came and regain lost energy in the fresh air of the country. Now, and for the next six years, Margot's brother Frank lent them Archerfield, a beautiful Adam house situated on the coast between Edinburgh and North Berwick. It was large, comfortable and convenient, so close to sea and excellent links that they were all in heaven there. They loved the place so much and the climate suited Margot so well that it became usual for them to stay on until after Christmas, sometimes enjoying a picnic in the woods on New Year's Day. When Raymond condescended to visit his family, even he could find no fault with the place and seemed as happy there as the others.

Margot was pregnant again, her health very precarious as always. The baby was due early in February 1907, but even so she stayed on at Archerfield with the younger children until the last minute, resting and taking short walks in the astonishingly mild air. She reached London just in time, for labour began as her maid was settling her in bed. The whole household dreaded Margot's confinements. At one time Sir John Williams had thought the difficulty was to be found in Margot's nerves—she 'kept the baby back' through sheer fright—but now he had begun to wonder whether there was not some organic malformation and that as she had two living children she ought to have no more.

This birth was the old sad story all over again; the baby lived two days and was buried with the others. According to J. A. Spender, who saw Margot a few days later, she was reduced to a mere shadow and hardly able to lift her head from the pillow. When she was once asked why she had married so late, she answered with some truth, 'because I did not want to sign my own death warrant'—a reference to the terrible hazards of childbirth in those days. Post-natal depression, for which there was no alleviation except time, brought on the insomnia of which she was so afraid. Once again she entered the long, dark and lonely tunnel in which fear, pain and despair were her only companions.

This time the doctors were firm: there must be no more children, not the slightest risk must be taken. So blunt a statement can hardly have come as a surprise to Asquith but it must have caused him utter dismay neverthe-less. He was only fifty-five, healthy and vigorous, wanting to live life to the full, and not old enough to take such deprivation philosophically. On the other hand sexual love meant relatively little to Margot, so the sacrifice to her was nothing like so great. It was affection that meant everything to her. There were plenty of people who thought Margot highly sexed, yet she certainly was not. In their youth she and Laura were called 'fast', a word which could mean anything, but was certainly not meant kindly. She talked of Peter Flower as her 'lover' (the word did not then have its modern meaning, of course) and her letters to men of whom she was fond often read like an invitation to share her bed. Yet although not exactly frigid, she was content with giving and receiving affection: physical expression of love she neither sought nor particularly needed.

Henceforth, she and Henry had separate rooms, so in one respect their marriage ended in 1907. Yet so deep had her love for her husband become that the marriage endured, despite the rough winds that were so soon to blow over it.

CHAPTER 16

A Moment to Remember

IN THE SUMMER of 1906 Raymond fell seriously in love with Katharine Horner, the only daughter of Margot's old friend Frances Horner of Mells Manor. But Raymond, who had left Oxford in 1902, was now a struggling barrister with no private income, so Katharine's parents did not look favourably on the match. The unhappy couple were told they would have to wait until Raymond earned enough to keep a wife. Since large incomes were the perquisite of judges and elderly barristers, Raymond said bitterly that he would be waiting for his bride for ever.

Without hesitation, Margot came to the rescue. In spite of his caustic remarks, which she endured with as much good humour as she could muster, she believed that underneath his affectations Raymond was really fond of her. Moreover she was deeply touched by the signs of real love between Raymond and Katharine: 'He and Katharine are the most perfect combination of inloveness and friendship, marrying at the right age after the right knowledge of each other that I have ever known.'[1]

It was typical of Margot that her generosity was in no way affected by her recent disappointment over her father's will, or by the fact that Raymond was only her stepson. She knew she would miss the money she was settling on Raymond (about £400 a year, an important addition to his earnings) but that did not deter her in the least. All that mattered was that Raymond was in love and it would be cruel if he were prevented from marrying.

The wedding was on 23 July 1907, from Cavendish Square, with Margot footing the bills. She so enjoyed the fun of arranging her first wedding and helping Katharine choose her trousseau that the last vestiges of her depression vanished in activity and interest: 'At last, thank God, I've taken a real turn,' she wrote to DD after waving the happy couple good-bye. 'I feel like a person reprieved . . . to real freedom.'[2]

The Asquiths left for Archerfield immediately after the wedding, to avoid the awful anti-climax that occurs after the departure of the bride and bridegroom, and for Margot to get peace and fresh air. For 20 Cavendish Square was not a quiet house. Not only did the children and their friends fill the place with laughter and noise, but the constant comings and goings of Henry's political colleagues made it difficult for Margot to rest. She always said that rest did her no good, but the doctors said it was the only cure for her nerves. In fact a woman of Margot's temperament sank deeper into introspection and depression when left alone in idleness, while activity and work were the making of her. Nevertheless she often lacked the will to fight against her doctors and gave in to treatment that she suspected did her harm. She seldom suffered from nerves at Archerfield and while the children were young she thought nothing of spending six months at a time there, with Henry joining them whenever he could. There, in her native Scottish air, she ate and slept comparatively well and what with young children round her all day and regular golf she hardly had time to think of herself.

They returned to London in February 1908 with Margot so improved in health that they were full of hope for the future. They little knew as they settled into their sleeping cars on the night express that they were on the eve of momentous happenings.

During the previous autumn Sir Henry Campbell-Bannerman had suffered a sudden heart attack but after a holiday at Biarritz he seemed to have recovered completely and was soon back at work, cheerful and benign as ever. On 12 February 1908 he made a long and important speech in the Commons, but that night he had another heart attack and by the morning his condition was grave. Although critically ill, he lingered on, too sick to attend to his duties, but because he believed he would recover (as he had done before) he refused to resign. His doctors told Asquith privately that any mention of resignation might have fatal consequences and was not to be thought of in the interests of the patient.

Margot had not been home long when she heard that her sister Lucy was seriously ill and needed her. She travelled at once to Easton Grey, first making Henry promise to keep her informed of everything that happened, for although Asquith was C.B.'s rightful successor Margot was too worldly not to know that nothing was certain until it was done.

The King was about to leave for a spring holiday in Biarritz but before he went he received Asquith who wrote to Margot on 4 March that 'the

King said that he had quite made up his mind to send for me at once in the event of anything happening to C.B. . . .'[3] Then on 1 April, without consulting his colleagues, C.B. resigned, after realizing that he could never recover.

The moment Margot had been waiting for, the golden future which the gypsy had foreseen for her, had come at last, although she did not care for the idea that her dearest wish was to be realized because C.B. was a dying man. At once she sent him flowers with a warm and kindly note, telling him how well she understood what he was going through and that he must not give up hope.[4] Perhaps for a brief moment they came nearer to understanding each other than ever before.

On 4 April the King invited Asquith to form a government, after telegraphing from Biarritz an order for him to come out and kiss hands on appointment for, despite the entreaties of Francis Knollys, his Private Secretary, Edward flatly refused to interrupt his holiday for a mere change of premier. (Henry later told Margot how angry he had been at the King's lack of respect for protocol and how at first he was not at all sure that he would go. Margot reassured him; he had done the right thing even if the King had not. It mattered little where he kissed hands as long as the deed was done.)

At once Asquith made arrangements to leave England, and to keep his plans as secret as possible he left Cavendish Square for Charing Cross in an ordinary hansom and quite alone. Rumours of C.B.'s resignation were beginning to circulate and he had had to slip out of the servants' entrance to avoid the journalists who were lying in wait at the front door. He caught the continental express for Paris wearing what he hoped was sufficient disguise; a thick overcoat and a travelling cap pulled well down over his eyes.[5]

His return on 10 April was very different: the red carpet and officials were waiting, so was Margot with Raymond and Violet. As she walked to the car on Henry's arm, the huge crowd outside the station burst into cheers.

They did not go straight home, but stopped at 10 Downing Street so that the dying Campbell-Bannerman should learn of the events of the last few days from his successor, while Margot waited in the car.

According to Margot, the meeting was a moving one. C.B. was facing death with supreme courage, amazing Asquith by telling him that he had arranged the details for his funeral, even the text for his tombstone. All this he spoke of quite calmly, without a trace of self-pity, as though it was an everyday occurrence. Tears filled Asquith's eyes when C.B. praised him for being 'a wonderful colleague, so loyal, so disinterested, so able'.[6] When they reached home and Henry gave Margot an account of the interview, they both broke down: 'I put my arms round his shoulders and we cried together.'[7]

On the way back from Biarritz, the new premier had spent his time composing his Cabinet. In stature and brilliance its members were reminiscent of Aberdeen's Ministry of All the Talents, fifty years before, but were to prove far more effective. Many on the list were Margot's friends: Haldane, Ripon, Morley, Grey and Augustine Birrell as well as Herbert Gladstone. One of Asquith's most striking appointments was that of the young Winston Churchill, who had crossed the floor to join the Liberals only in 1904. Inexperienced and brash, he was very much an individualist even in those days, and Margot's feelings about him were always ambivalent. When in 1899 his first attempt to gain a seat in Parliament failed, Margot's comment had been 'he will be all the better for his defeat',[8] and she quoted with approval Morley's remark, à propos of Churchill reading a biography of Napoleon, that 'he would do better to study the drab heroes of life. Forming oneself upon Napoleon has proved a danger to many a young man before him'.[9] But now, knowing that he had coveted the Colonial Office but had instead been offered the Presidency of the Board of Trade, Margot wrote him a warm and sympathetic letter:

Dear Winston,

There are a few moments in life when unwelcome decisions seem forced on one. I know them well they make one feel sick & rebellious but I've had luck with mine. I knocked a great love out of my life to make room for a great character & do you suppose we ever regretted it? *Never*.

I was very touched by yr loyalty & sweetness when you said you wd give of yr best—I know you will & I believe it will be through you if we win in two or three years the Gen. Election . . .[10]

Henry and Margot dreaded the move to Downing Street but managed it rapidly. Despite lack of interest in the early days of her marriage, Margot had since made 20 Cavendish Square comfortable and attractive. Asquith was particularly delighted with his study, which Margot had furnished with great taste: red leather armchairs, a spacious desk and the walls lined with books. Everything was to hand: in summer his armchair was placed close to the window which looked out on to a paved courtyard; in winter it was moved to a spot in front of the fire. To uproot themselves to a smaller and inconvenient official house was a daunting prospect.

The interior of 10 Downing Street was well known to Margot. She had dined there as the guest of four Prime Ministers and thought the place drab and inferior. The Gladstones had no taste (and thought the expense of redecorating unnecessary), the Salisburys were too grand. Balfour was a bachelor and Campbell-Bannerman's wife was ill for the whole of his premiership, and in consequence little had been done to improve its appearance for at least forty years. The chintzes and flowered cretonnes tolerated by former Prime Ministers' wives covered the house from attic to cellar and had greatly amused Margot at one of the receptions she had attended there before her marriage. Yet she had seen its possibilities, and now she was the mistress of this historic house, she did the job so well that even Mrs Belloc-Lowndes, half-French and usually so scathing of English taste, recorded admiringly in her diary that Margot had completely altered the whole look of the house, turning it into one of the most elegant homes in London.[11]

She took infinite pleasure in entertaining those who had known 10 Downing Street in the old days, and in seeing their start of surprise at the improvements. Entertaining went on fast and furiously and Margot's luncheon and dinner parties were soon famous for good food and interesting people: every politician of renown was to be found at her table. Nor did she neglect the young and unknown, but encouraged her stepchildren's friends to invite themselves. She set out to make Downing Street known to the whole of London, whereas before, she said, hardly a single taxi-driver knew where it was.[12]

Not content with refusing to leave Biarritz when Campbell-Bannerman resigned, the King now demanded that his new Prime Minister should bring his Cabinet to the Crillon Hotel in Paris to receive their seals of office. Francis Knollys was frantic, Asquith adamant that such an important and historic constitutional ceremony should take place on English soil. Faced with fierce opposition, the King at last grumblingly gave way and returned to Windsor Castle.

It has been said that relations between King Edward and his first minister were never very close. More than once Edward had heard Asquith described as 'brilliantly clever' and as a result was wary of him. It was fortunate that Francis Knollys was the perfect go-between who always managed to smoothe his master's ruffled feathers—and they ruffled very easily when he did not understand. The other perfect go-between was, of course, Margot, who here proved to be the greatest help to her husband, since she well knew the limitations of her sovereign's mind and how he could turn without warning from smiles to anger. Diplomacy of a special kind was required. If the King was obstinate and objected to some proposal, it was essential to persuade him that the original idea had come from him and very good it was too. By using tact and her knowledge of human nature, Margot got on very well with the King, although privately she had no great opinion of him. Whenever she was with him she adopted a mixture of coquetry and demureness to which she sometimes added an amused and teasing manner that kept just within the confines of respect, and she was careful to appear not in the least clever, asking his opinion with great frequency. However, she was not afraid of showing she could be firm if it was necessary. His temper did not move her and when irritability looked like turning into a towering rage she knew how to nip it in the bud with a light word that by some magic process always seemed to work. Since Margot was not the type of woman Edward usually liked this needed wits as well as insight. Nevertheless, even the King could be dazzled by such a popular figure who, although not pretty, knew how to make heads turn. Apart from that, the King had the greatest respect for Charles Tennant's ability to make money, while on her side Margot had a similar respect for the monarchy and would never belittle the role her sovereign had to play.

The first session of Parliament with Asquith as Prime Minister ended with the Old Age Pensions Bill passing the Commons without trouble. It was a measure which delighted Margot, who had seen the privations undergone by many old and deserving people in the neighbourhood of her Scottish home. She was deeply proud to think it was Henry who carried through this humane act.

The Asquiths fitted into their new role as though they had never done anything else. Every Wednesday morning Henry held Cabinet meetings and Margot often had a chance of a word or two with his colleagues before they disappeared into the Cabinet room. She sometimes had further conversation with them when they came out, but not a word of what had gone on passed their lips. This rather impressed her.

To begin with Asquith wrote detailed accounts of these Cabinet meetings for the King, but they were too long and explanatory for Edward to take in and it was soon plain that he never bothered to read a word of his premier's painstaking essays. After discussing the matter with Margot, who knew exactly how far the King's intellect would stretch, Asquith tried writing in a simple way that would interest rather than inform him. Margot showed Henry the short letters he had written to her before her marriage, all of them childishly expressed, and with these in mind explained that he would have to use nothing but simple language— 'everything must be short and simple and no long words', and to abbreviate whenever possible.[13]

In June 1908 the Asquiths were invited to Windsor Castle. Twice before when they were asked (once in Queen Victoria's day) Margot had been too ill after a bad confinement to accompany Henry, who had to go alone. Unfortunately she never met Queen Victoria, so we are deprived of what might have been one of the best character studies of an extraordinary woman. The royal era only began for her with the reign of Edward VII, but the Windsor Castle which had so impressed Asquith by its beauty and comfort was Victorian. By the time Margot saw it for herself Edward had been on the throne for some years and many things had changed. She was, she says, taken aback by the drabness of the Prime Minister's apartments and the indifferent portraits of Henry's predecessors—Melbourne, Peel, Disraeli and Gladstone seemed to glower at them from the walls, giving the place the air of a superior lodging house. The only redeeming features in the rooms were the wonderful flowers and the enormous number of newspapers laid out for them to read.[14] By far the most beautiful thing in the castle was Queen Alexandra herself: 'She looked divine,' Margot wrote with her usual lack of jealousy for the good looks of other women. 'She wore a raven's wing dress contrasting with the beautiful blue of the garter and her little head a blaze of diamonds.'[15] Margot's own dress —Parma violet satin with net overskirt and silver sashes—was elegant too, but as she once remarked, Queen Alexandra always made other women look common.

The next day was Sunday and Margot looked forward eagerly to a service in St George's Chapel, but much to her disappointment Morning

Prayer was held in a room in the Castle instead: 'Although the sermon was a fine one,' she wrote, 'the service lacked the sense of worship that comes to one naturally in an ancient and hallowed chapel.'[16] For such a formal age there was surprisingly little formality. The women wore neither hats nor gloves and the service was soon over. Margot supposed that the lack of ceremony meant that it was 'done after the Danish fashion', but she disapproved: 'Sunday worship was not a duty to be got through quickly simply to avoid boredom.'

She disapproved even more of the whole atmosphere surrounding these pleasure-loving, self-indulgent royals. No one was quite at their ease in their presence and the conversation was trivial. The Edwardian court was a far cry from the unostentatious gatherings of Victoria and Albert's day, where respect for brains and good talk took precedence over less important matters. It was more reminiscent of that of Napoleon III and Eugénie but without the glittering splendour which made that court a byword for luxurious living throughout Europe. Instead the castle was pervaded by an aura of middle-class prosperity which eschewed anything that hinted at the 'intellectual': the superficial conversation, the fat cigars, the bridge and the rich guests whom Margot barely knew, for they did not belong to her world. When the King's mistress was an honoured guest, Margot felt that the whole atmosphere was alien to the climate of the times, which was one of industrial deprivation and unemployment.

However, no one could possibly have guessed at the boredom which Margot hid under an agreeable manner and an air of attention. When the Asquiths went for the first time together to Sandringham in 1911, she seemed to be overjoyed at being there. In fact she was taken aback at the hideousness of the interior with its yellow polished oak panelling relieved only by bad portraits and by chairs and sofas upholstered in striped red and blue linen, the colours of the Brigade of Guards. At tea in a cold, draughty hall Margot met the King's grandson, the future Edward VIII. Small for his age, nervous and shy, the fourteen-year-old prince hardly said a word, and Margot put this down to his grandfather's unmerciful teasing. Even here the company was not congenial to her. Quick though she was as a rule, she could not bridge the long and awkward silences that made her so uncomfortable. Royalty, she decided, made bad listeners.[17]

The next time they were invited it was to meet the King and Queen of Denmark. To Margot's dismay it was a very small party but the Danish royals were surprisingly easy to talk to. They spoke excellent English, were well-read and deeply interested in all the important questions of the day. Even Edward listened attentively and every now and again made his views known. Women's suffrage was beginning to take the place of Home Rule as a source of controversy. The King loudly declared that he was against it, protesting that 'it might open doors to developments that were unthinkable'. Lloyd George, he said, made him angry; what right had a minister of the crown to attend a meeting in the Albert Hall on women's suffrage? This sort of nonsense put him in a corner. Only a few days before he was asked to consent to the appointment of two ladies as members of a Royal Commission on the marriage laws. If females were allowed to meddle in public affairs where would it end?

It was on that first visit, in November 1908, that Margot saw that Edward and Alexandra could be of use to Henry if he could be persuaded to look on them as 'ambassadors extraordinary'. Not once since he ascended the throne had Edward been asked to do something of real use for his country on one of those trips to the continent he made many times a year. He always went without his family, in holiday mood, and it never seems to have occurred to a single member of the government to make even the smallest demand on his time. Although Lord Hardinge always went with him, politics were seldom discussed between Edward and whichever of his relations he happened to be staying with. As Sir Edward Grey made clear: 'If a Sovereign or foreign minister wished to make use of the King's visit, it was he [Hardinge] who dealt with these matters and not the King.'[18]

Margot had heard that the Kaiser had been sulking ever since he had been prevented from bringing his fleet with him on a State visit to England the year before. When later King Edward met his cousin at Homberg where both were taking the waters, the Kaiser was barely civil. Kaiser William was now harbouring another grudge against England. In 1907, when Edward had been cavorting on the continent with another cousin, Tsar Nicholas, he had, in a weak moment, made him an Admiral of the British Fleet without consulting the government or realizing that the Kaiser might be piqued on hearing that his Russian cousin had a rank superior to his own. The Kaiser was incensed at this apparent slight of himself.[19] To undo the harm Edward had done, Margot suggested to Henry that the King and Queen should pay a visit to Germany and charm Kaiser William back into a good humour. But she had reckoned without Queen Alexandra, who did not like the Kaiser and detested Germany (she had never forgotten that Bismarck had deprived her native Denmark of the territory of Schleswig-Holstein) and refused point blank to go. Ordinarily Alexandra took little interest in politics and when approached by Asquith she was astonished that he could ask them to go on a friendly visit to Germany after the interview the Kaiser had given to the *Daily Telegraph* in which he barely disguised his dislike of England. She certainly would not go. But Margot urged Henry to try again, advising him to drop personalities and to place all the emphasis on duty. Affairs on the continent were becoming graver every day and it was essential to be on good terms with Germany; so Asquith returned to the Palace and begged the Queen to put aside old grievances and to think only of her country. No one, he told her, knew how to get round the Kaiser better than she did. He whispered in her ear that he too disliked Kaiser William and had always agreed with his predecessor (C.B.) in thinking him 'a restless, dangerous, mischief-making man'.[20]

At once Queen Alexandra agreed to go, and on 9 February 1909 they sailed for Germany. The visit was a huge success and the Asquiths were jubilant. It was Margot's first attempt to influence politics at the highest level and it brought about a temporary truce between the German Emperor and the King of England that was important at that particular time—although it did not, of course, diminish in any way the Kaiser's deep-rooted jealousy of England.

CHAPTER 17

Firm as a Rock

IN THE AUTUMN of 1908 Margot had caught a cold which quickly developed into a painful cough, and because of her family history of tuberculosis her doctor ordered her to Switzerland. It was a wrench to leave Henry and the children and the prospect of perhaps many weeks of separation filled her with dismay, but she took the sensible line that if she became seriously ill she would be no good to the children and a burden on a husband who already had so much on his mind.

The Liberals' policy had reduced naval expenditure to pay for social services, and only four new Dreadnoughts were to be built in each of the next two years. Revelations that the German shipbuilding programme threatened to outstrip the British navy created a public furore and the cry arose 'we want eight and we won't wait!'. The Cabinet was split between those determined to ignore the clamour—led by Churchill and Lloyd George—and those who thought that extra ships were essential to meet the growing threat.

Henry had promised to keep Margot informed of everything that was happening, for he had learned over the years that to keep her in the dark meant that she would fear the worst and become nervous and upset. He wrote to her in Davos on 20 February 1909:

There is considerable underground rumbling and agitation over the navy. The economists are in a state of wild alarm and Winston and Lloyd George by their combined machinations have got the bulk of the Liberal press into the same camp . . . they go about hinting darkly at resignation (which is bluff) and there will in any case be a lot of steam let off and at least a temporary revival of the old pro-Boer animus. I am able to keep a cool head amidst it all but there are moments when I am disposed summarily to cashier them both.[1]

Winston Churchill had, in the words of his daughter, 'taken up the cause of social reform with ardour and determination and was now pushing forward the schemes for the Board of Trade which would attack the exploitation of sweated labour, and of Labour Exchanges to control the scourge of unemployment'.[2] It was not only these fiery progressive ministers who needed reining in, but other members of the Cabinet too. Asquith strove hard to keep his team together and managed it with some success. Soon he was able to give Margot better news:

We had our final Cabinet on the navy yesterday and I was quite prepared for a row and possible disruption. A sudden curve developed itself of which I took immediate advantage with the result that strangely enough we came to a conclusion that satisfied McKenna and Grey and also Lloyd George and Winston. The effect will be to make us stronger in 1912 than McKenna's original proposal could have done.[*][3]

Margot's heart leaped for joy when she read the letter; Henry had won as she knew he would. It amazed her that a man of Lloyd George's brains and political acumen should oppose Henry in the first place. At Winston Churchill's conduct, she was not at all surprised, 'all part and parcel of his erratic temperament and lack of judgement'.[4]

In the early summer Margot returned home fit and well and even a little fatter. The whole household were glad to see her and it warmed her heart to know that she had been missed. On 9 November 1909, a day of clear skies and gusty winds, a radiant Margot launched the first of the Dreadnoughts. She had always loved an occasion and this was one of double celebration: a victory for Henry and for his steadfastness in the face of tough opposition, and her own first real victory over ill-health.

She threw economy to the winds, and went to Lucille, who dressed her in the newly fashionable biscuit-coloured cloth that would stand out against the dark-blue naval uniforms and was the last word in elegance, with a tight skirt, string blouse and winged hat.

The reception from the crowds who lined the streets of Devonport all the way to the dockyard was loud and friendly. Margot took this as a well

* Instead of Asquith's first shipbuilding scheme, four Dreadnoughts at once and four more the following year, the extra four were laid down in July of the same year and five more Dreadnoughts were to be added in each of the two following years, making a total of eighteen, the number the Admiralty had originally demanded.

deserved tribute to Henry. The ceremony began fittingly with the hymn 'Eternal father strong to save' in which Margot—who loved hymns —sang heartily. Although she was self-possessed and cool, knowing what she had to do, the function did not pass off entirely without incident. Beside himself with nerves, the constructor tried to help her wield the hammer and chisel that were to sever the ropes which held the ship and almost succeeded in severing her wrist. However, she had not won her spurs on the hunting field for nothing. Although in great pain she acted quickly, wrenched the hammer from the constructor's hands, raised it above her head, and said in a slow loud voice: 'I name you *Collingwood*. God bless you and all who sail in you,' then with a 'violent blow cut the four ropes that released the galley and the ship slid without a splash into the sea'.[5] Everybody heard her voice clearly and distinctly and it gave her immense pleasure to be told that it was rare for a voice to be audible on these occasions.

Slowly, in the years after her marriage, Margot's character had been changing. She had always thought of herself as a liberated woman, untrammelled by the conventions of Victorian society; she had sailed through the vicissitudes of growing up, of love affairs and marriage, even the responsibilities of children, unaffected by gossip or the good advice her older friends did not hesitate to give her and just a little contemptuous of those who were bound hand and foot by the opinions of others. But as her admiration and love for her husband increased, so her wilfulness and independence decreased in equal measure. She had sold her hunters in 1906 and with them had gone the wish to be free. The move to Downing Street had completed the process of change. This was most noticeable in her attitude to Henry: she would not express a political opinion that he had not voiced first and everything he said was gospel. No longer did she criticize or argue fiercely with him, stubbornly holding to her own opinion, refusing to be shaken if she believed enough in what she said. His academic attainments and his rapid parliamentary rise, the high opinion Jowett and others had of him, all combined to create in Margot's mind the picture of a man of great learning and wisdom. She had always over-venerated education and was too apt to think that highly educated men must always be right. In the controversy over the Dreadnoughts, Henry's frank letters to her in Switzerland made her furious. Could not the idiots in Parliament see he was right? Her relief when he managed to get agreement was so profound that she felt as though she had been saved from some severe but unnamed illness. When he was proved right she was openly jubilant.

In this respect she was not the helpmate Asquith so much needed. The brisk and open criticism that only a wife can give was now sadly lacking and Margot ought perhaps to have realized this and used her privileged position to tell him occasionally where he went wrong and point out errors of tact and judgement—but how could she, when now she thought Henry was omniscient? She began, too, to dislike anyone who opposed him and lost many friends by being rude to them because they were lukewarm in their support of the Prime Minister. How dare they, when they knew that Henry was cleverer than they were? Asquith himself—the kindest of men where the women of his family were concerned—took this uncritical attitude as perfectly right and proper and praised Margot fondly for defending him. When Lady Londonderry dared to make a disparaging remark about a speech of the Prime Minister's, Margot fiercely took up the cudgels on his behalf and both women were soon lost in a public slanging match 'like two fish-wives'.[6]

She was unwise, too, in not softening his opinion of people and events, but would relate to him unkind remarks she had picked up in the Ladies' Gallery, infecting him with her own anger, for Asquith was not as placid as people were apt to think. She could have done more for his health if she had persuaded him to go to bed before his habitual 3 a.m., and although she did later on make an attempt to stop him drinking so much by watering the brandy bottle, she never talked to him openly and seriously about it. Nor did she ever try to inject a little of her own devil into him and thus help him lose his temper when there was need for anger and not sweet reasonableness. When he was accused of idleness during the Great War, it would have been sensible to warn him that he should not only work but be seen to do so, but she had become so blind to his faults that she said nothing. Her loyalty, always unshakeable to those she loved, would have been better employed for his good if she had recognized to herself that Henry had human frailties like everyone else.

From the start the Asquith government's programme of social reform had aroused the opposition of the Conservative majority in the House of Lords and this became even more marked when the necessity of paying for social reform and eighteen Dreadnoughts at the same time made it imperative to raise taxes (income tax was increased from 9d to 1s 2d in the pound). The conflict between the two Houses reached new heights when in December 1909 the Lords rejected Lloyd George's Budget, an action which Asquith declared 'a breach of the Constitution and a usurpation of the rights of the Commons'. Asquith said it was the land tax proposals in the Budget which 'set the heather on fire', and wealthy landowners saw in these measures 'a potential instrument for almost unlimited confiscation',[7] since they came after an increase in the tax on unearned income and so many other Liberal measures which Asquith and Lloyd George had introduced in turn as Chancellors of the Exchequer during these last three years.

The Lords had also rejected the Licensing Bill, which Margot welcomed as a humane measure which might save many a poor man's home and family from ruin. She had an antipathy to alcohol which was strengthened by reading the novels of Mrs Humphry Ward (the high priestess of teetotalism) woven round the evils of drink. 'Except for rare cases of fraud,' Margot wrote, 'our prisons are full of men detained for crimes of violence and all induced through drink.'[8] She urged Henry 'to do something' otherwise the Liberals would no longer be able to call themselves the party of progress. But he replied: 'My time will come,' and it did when the Lords threw out the Budget. 'The House of Lords has deliberately chosen its ground,' Asquith wrote, 'they have elected to set at naught in regard to finance the unwritten but time-honoured conventions of our constitution.'[9] This time Asquith knew he could break the Lords, and he impressed Margot by the audacity of his scheme to curb their obstinacy —he would ask the King to create enough new peers to swamp the Tory majority in the Upper House.

As soon as his course was clear Asquith was in great spirits. George Curzon told Margot that her husband was 'firm as a rock', because of the support he was getting in his home. And Margot did support him completely, unselfishly travelling round the country with him, sitting for hours on hard wooden seats on makeshift platforms, stared at and criticized, as Henry made speech after speech to rally Liberals to do their duty in the general election which was due in January 1910. Even as the struggle grew more intense (causing Asquith much anguish at quarrelling with his friends) there were light-hearted moments to ease the tension that gave the Asquiths much amusement: one aged peer wrote to *The Times* to say that if the Budget were passed he would be compelled to reduce his annual subscription to the London Hospital from £5 to £3—while in the same issue Margot read that he had bought a yacht that would cost him £1000 a month to run.[10]

Later that same year she braved the December cold to be by Henry's side in the second General Election campaign, when she heard him speak the solemn words that were to have such a far-reaching effect: 'This is a crisis of the greatest magnitude. Amendment by the Lords is out of the question, rejection by the Lords is equally out of the question, that way revolution lies!'[11]

In order to expedite matters Lord Knollys was asked to explain to the King what was happening, but even so Edward rejected Asquith's proposals as amounting to the deliberate destruction of the Upper House, and was extremely displeased. He summoned Asquith to Windsor immediately, and although it was highly inconvenient he had to go. Fortunately Margot was also asked, so the strain was eased, and they had just time enough while travelling by special train to plan the best and simplest way for Henry to present his scheme to his sovereign.

The audience with the King was more trying than the bitter wrangling with the Lords: Edward did not understand at all. While Asquith was going over the matter for the second time, Edward burst out with his own grievances against the peers—they kept him in the dark, told him nothing: 'I know no more than the man in the street,' and was taken aback when his Prime Minister explained to him very clearly that the peers were under no obligation to let him know anything at all.[12] Asquith did his work so well that the King insisted that they stay another day so that Margot could attend her first Garter investiture, that of the King of Portugal. It was a lucky chance that she had told her maid at the last minute to pack one of her grandest Worth dresses of silver tissue with a cornflower-blue sash that suited her so well. As she looked at herself in the glass she had the satisfaction of knowing that no one, not even Queen Alexandra herself, could be better dressed.

The second election of 1910 did not give the Liberals a secure enough majority to ask the King to create enough peers to outvote the Conservative majority in the Lords. Asquith had always made it clear that he did not wish to abolish the Upper Chamber, only its absolute veto. Now, without a Liberal majority, he would have to look to Irish support to push the Bill through. It disturbed Margot that the government was more or less dependent on the Irish vote, whose goodwill in turn depended on the passing of the Home Rule Bill. To be subservient to Irish interest merely to stay in office made Margot nervous, for it spelt danger for Henry's government: 'We can't bargain with the Irish!' Margot wrote to Lord Selborne.

> I hear they are furious with Henry, but he has always said the same. He is in favour of giving Irish, Scottish and Welsh power over their affairs subject to the imperial parliament. This will have to be done if any Prime Minister is to have a life of his own, the work is too heavy for anyone as it is and even Henry who has the strongest nerves and temper ... was too tired this year when he joined us for Christmas.[13]

Indeed Henry had continued exhausted, and before the start of the new Parliament he snatched a few days' holiday in Cannes. After he had gone Margot found a tender note on her pillow, thanking her for her support, that touched her deeply: 'All through these trying weeks you have been more than anyone sympathetic and understanding, loyal and loving. I have felt it much.'[14]

Meanwhile the King had returned from a holiday in Biarritz jovial and in good health. The papers filled their pages with pictures of him at various functions and in the best of spirits: at Covent Garden for *Rigoletto*, at the Royal Academy, at Newmarket, at an audience in the Palace and boarding a train for a few days at Sandringham. Shortly after Asquith's return from the continent the Prime Minister and his wife received a request to dine and sleep at Windsor Castle, but both were so worn out with worry that they forgot to go, thereby not unnaturally earning the King's extreme displeasure. He was so furious that he refused to meet Asquith to discuss the veto, the Irish or anything else, and Francis Knollys had to use tact and humour to induce him to forgive and forget. It could not have happened at a worse time. Asquith needed the King's support and to forfeit his goodwill simply because fatigue had caused carelessness made Margot furious with herself.

It was only the beginning of a series of misfortunes. Charty Ribblesdale was taken ill, and hardly had Margot reached her bedside when she was recalled to London to attend to Violet who had suddenly developed appendicitis. 10 Downing Street had become a veritable hospital in her absence, for Elizabeth, too, had a high temperature and Puffin was swathed in bandages after cutting his head badly while falling from a tree. Thus Margot happened to be at home when on 6 May Francis Knollys rang 10 Downing Street to say that the King was seriously ill with bronchitis.

Edward had often suffered from this illness before and had got over it, but feeling more than usually anxious Margot walked to the Palace next morning to see for herself how ill he really was. The bulletin on the gate was not reassuring, for it said that the King's condition was causing grave concern and the long queue of anxious faces waiting to sign the visitors' book made Margot fear the worst.

Henry was away again, cruising on the Admiralty yacht *Enchantress*, and Margot feared that he had not been told of the King's illness. She was right: astonishingly, no one had thought of recalling him, so Margot telegraphed him to be ready to return. The one and only official notice Asquith received was to inform him that the King was dead.

On the last day of Edward VII's life Margot gave her usual luncheon party. It turned out to be a dismal affair, for everyone was restless and talked of nothing but the King's grave condition. Lord Kitchener, home on leave from Egypt, was one of the guests and between courses he would get up and walk to the window where the flag on Buckingham Palace could be clearly seen, reporting to his breathless audience that it was not yet at half-mast. Such unseemly curiosity got on Margot's nerves and she coldly reminded Kitchener that he was in the Prime Minister's house and that they would be the first to hear when the King expired.

The moment her guests had gone Margot rushed to her desk and wrote a short note to Francis Knollys begging him to call in Kingston Fowler, the great authority on complaints of the chest, 'for court doctors were not necessarily the best'.[15] She longed for Henry in a crisis of this magnitude and felt lost without him. How soon could he get home? So great was her faith in her husband that she half believed that his arrival would cure the sick King. The day dragged on and still there was no fresh news. When it was time for Elizabeth and Puffin to go to bed, she joined them in the nursery where mother, nurse and children dropped to their knees to pray for the King's recovery, all of them crying copiously—so ridiculously overcharged was the sentimentality of the age.

Margot had never had a high opinion of Edward, yet he was the symbol of stability to the nation at large, which knew little of their King except as a jovial personality pictured in the papers. Margot feared and hated change, and with the passing of the monarch and a new reign there were bound to be momentous changes. She could indeed be crying as much for herself as for the King.

That night she was too restless to sleep, and slipping on a cloak she walked round to the Hardinges where she knew Edward Grey was dining. He told her that the suddenness of the King's illness was 'a terrible shock' and that he was now in a coma. Buckingham Palace was not far away, so before going home, Margot walked to the gates to read that the King was sinking; before the night was over he was dead.[16] When dawn broke Margot, wrapped in a shawl, went to her desk. She wrote to Queen Alexandra, Lord Knollys and many others, becoming, as she wrote, illegible with emotion. The shock of Prince Eddy's death in 1892 came back to her with peculiar vividness. The son who should be succeeding his father now had been dead and gone for many years. This 'sweet, awkward and timid boy' had been adored by his mother who hated the ill-judged chaff with which his father treated him.[17] Now the father too was gone.

The day was spent with mourning friends, all in deepest black, all recalling their last conversation with the dead King, greatly embellished. That night at dinner with Mrs George Cornwallis-West (Lady Randolph Churchill had remarried), Margot sat next to Winston Churchill, who angered her by his lack of sympathy when he drank the health of the new King, as though he was proposing a toast at a wedding.

Asquith received the news of the King's death at sea. 'I went up on deck and I remember well that the first sight that met my eyes was Halley's comet blazing in the sky. It was the only time that any of us saw it during the voyage. I felt bewildered and indeed stunned.'[18]

Edward VII was buried at Windsor on 20 May 1910. It was a long and trying day but except for a short nap in St George's Chapel (where there were many nodding heads) Margot was alert and interested all through the slow procession to Paddington led by nine Kings and the service that preceded interment. Her eyes were drawn repeatedly to the figure of the Kaiser, first on horseback riding next to the Duke of Connaught, his withered arm carefully concealed, and later in St George's where she was ideally placed to study his face. The fanatical eyes, disdainful, cruel mouth and general air of haughtiness made her shudder.

CHAPTER 18

Minds large enough for Trifles to look small in

ASQUITH RESUMED HIS cruise on the *Enchantress* immediately after the funeral and did not return to London until Parliament reassembled in June.

Under the new King the two pressing political questions of the day, Home Rule and the prerogative of the peers, became much more difficult, and without delay Asquith and his colleagues met the opposition to discuss the questions that divided them in an all-party constitutional conference; but it broke up with nothing settled. The Liberals were adamant that they would not give way on anything, for their morale had been boosted by the passing by a large majority of the bitterly contested Liberal Budget a week before Edward VII's death. In this belligerent mood they were more than ever determined to break the power of the House of Lords to veto legislation passed by the Commons.

Margot was in Scotland when Henry telephoned the news that the Round Table conference was a failure—*tout est fini*—and she knew at once that a General Election must follow. But she had no fears about the result, since the Unionists had no programme and were divided among themselves.[1] Thus it was quite a shock when Margot returned home and saw at once that Henry was far from confident—'the future has a nasty way of turning up surprises'.

Parliament was dissolved on 28 November 1910 after Henry had wrung from a reluctant King George V a pledge that if the Liberals won the election and the Lords obstructed the Parliament Bill, he would create a sufficient number of peers to ensure the passing of the measure in the Upper House. With the King's pledge in his pocket and a confident Margot by his side, Henry felt able to face electioneering in a far more confident mood. In *More Memories* Margot wrote of Henry that '. . . no one could have shown more tolerance but no one could deflect his invincible determination'. Success bred success. When it looked as though

Henry was going to win the day more and more people came over to his side. In later years Margot liked to remember with pleasure a small bet Henry had with 'Lulu' Harcourt, who had said that it would be two years before any government would change the attitude of the Lords. 'At which Henry took a diary from his pocket and wrote down the month in which his Bill would be put upon the statute book'—which turned out to be correct.[2]

The bitter battle that Asquith was fighting with the peers was distasteful to him. It was the kind of wrangling, dangerous and stifling to the real business of the House, that he detested. It was with a sense of wonder not unmixed with bewilderment that he noticed how much his young colleague Winston Churchill relished the thought that the Liberals showed no fear of creating five hundred peers, loudly asserting that such an action could only be in the interest of the Liberals but a disaster for the Conservative Party.[3]

Despite pressures on all sides, some ill health and many children, Margot was happy because busily occupied during the early years of Asquith's premiership. She was now on good terms with every Liberal Member of Parliament, especially the young back-benchers whom she made a point of getting to know in order to spot some special talent that might be of service to Henry. It was not unusual for her to have twenty of her husband's colleagues at her luncheon table after a Cabinet committee meeting. She liked to be able to ask them about the important questions of the day, airing her own views with great freedom: it was fortunate that more often than not they were Henry's views too. Throughout the controversy with the peers, she repeatedly addressed letters—or rather lectures—to members of the Cabinet. That to Sir John Simon, the Attorney General, for instance, discussed fundamentals: 'What I miss so much in our party is minds large enough for trifles to look small in. No government can get along without making mistakes and no doubt we have made mistakes . . .'[4] If it is surprising that Margot wrote like this, it is quite baffling that ministers not only took her views seriously but replied with the greatest care, setting out their own opinions with equal freedom.

'Our party', 'our mistakes' and 'we' (meaning the Liberal government) were so often on her lips that nobody thought anything of it. By 1910 Margot was writing to Henry's colleagues on House of Commons paper, several sheets of which were always in her handbag together with an assortment of pencils ready for emergencies. If a minister to whom she particularly wanted to speak was in the Chamber she never hesitated to send him one of her peremptory commands (requests they never were) to 'come to the Prime Minister's room any time you are bored this afternoon and send someone up to the Speaker's gallery for me—I'd like to see you soon'.[5] Not everyone took this in good part; some put it about that she was getting too big for her boots, and considered herself the Prime Minister's Private Secretary and confidential adviser-in-chief, but in those days their voices were not loud enough to be heard.

Correspondingly, politicians found Margot useful as a go-between when Asquith was difficult to get hold of. Happening to meet her in the lobby of the House one day, Winston Churchill asked her if she would see that the Prime Minister got the Parliament Bill over and done with before the coronation, now fixed for 22 June 1911. Margot promised to urge Henry to speed things up. She knew the new King disliked the Bill, and that it was almost too much for him to swallow so early in his reign. Moreover, she had sensed a coolness by the Palace towards the occupants of 10 Downing Street which she wanted removed as quickly as possible. Despite her criticisms and a certain amount of boredom, she had no intention of being crossed off the royal list; such a thing would be unseemly for a Prime Minister and his wife. At the time of Edward VII's death, she had written in her diary that she and Henry had known and loved the Prince of Wales, now George V, since boyhood.[6] This was not so at all. Their few meetings had been on formal occasions and then only brief and never at London society functions which the Sailor King, unlike his father, detested. She had expected that with the election over and won by the Liberals in December ('it could not have been won without my husband'), a royal invitation would soon have been forthcoming, and when it was not she grumbled to Henry, who said, 'thank God'. He was too worn out to be pleasant to anyone at that moment. He disliked controversy and loathed the bitterness which the Parliament Bill evoked, necessary though it was. Margot was quite unaware that he had told a friend that he did not know how much longer he could stand the uncertainty.

The Parliament Bill went forward from February to July but despite large majorities in the Commons, the House of Lords threw it out every time.

Having previously informed the leaders of the Unionist party on 21 July, Asquith at last released to the Press the King's pledge to create enough new Liberal peers to enable the Bill to pass into law.

On a hot and sultry summer afternoon, Margot drove with Henry from Downing Street to the House of Commons in an open carriage; cheering crowds lined the route. Despite the heat she looked cool and collected in a grey chiffon dress and large black hat. Inside the Chamber the atmosphere was very different: the Prime Minister was greeted with chilly silence broken only by some half-hearted cheers from a small handful of supporters. The Unionists, angered beyond bounds by what they regarded as an unconstitutional threat, were determined not to allow the Prime Minister to be heard: 'I saw in a moment that the opposition was furious,' Margot wrote in her diary that night, 'and I could hear an occasional shout of "traitor".'[7] Suddenly she felt afraid as cries of 'Who killed the King?' came from all quarters when Asquith rose to speak. Catcalls, led by F. E. Smith and Lord Hugh Cecil, continued for half an hour, while the Prime Minister stood at the box unable to make himself heard. Asquith was derided, scorned, insulted, the *Standard* newspaper reported next day, while another paper pointed out that the demonstration had the double effect of venting anger against the Prime Minister and stiffening the Unionist leaders who were contemplating surrender.[8] Agitated beyond endurance, Margot took a piece of paper from her handbag and scribbled a few lines to Edward Grey: 'They will listen to you, so for God's sake defend him . . .'

When Grey rose to speak there was silence. It was the shortest speech ever made in the Commons: 'If arguments are not to be listened to from the Prime Minister, there is not one of us who will attempt to take his place.'[9] The chamber suddenly went quiet and Margot breathed a sigh of relief, as she sat back on her seat, weak and spent. Thank God Henry still had friends.

As she was leaving Margot caught sight of Edward Grey and rushing up to him, too choked with emotion to speak, she seized his hand and kissed it. Three weeks later from her seat in the Ladies' Gallery she listened to Henry, in answer to a Unionist motion of censure, make a completely effective defence of his action: 'It was a speech that will live in history,' Margot wrote triumphantly in her diary, 'as he built up his case in orderly sequence the ranks of the Conservatives looked shattered and broken.'[10] The final act of the drama was played out in the House of Lords on 10

August. Not until the last moment would many of the Unionists believe that the threat to create peers was no Liberal bluff but that the King would in fact use his prerogative to ensure the passing of the Parliament Bill, but when it came to the vote enough of them abstained to ensure a majority of seventeen in favour of it.

The day the Bill became law, Margot wrote: 'Thus was accomplished the greatest constitutional reform since 1688, a success due to the patience, ability and foresight of one man and that the Prime Minister.'[11] It had been a struggle to the death and Henry had known it, yet never once had he lost his temper or appeared ruffled; throughout it, Margot's fierce support and love had never failed him and he had learned that he could count on that absolutely.

When all was safely over there was a reaction. Asquith had been suffering from a sore throat for some days, laryngitis set in and he had to take to his bed, but Margot, who had been living on her nerves during the whole of the crisis, remained in good health. Perhaps her role of emotionally involved bystander was the harder, but she had been too anxious to think of herself and thus had come through unscathed.

Of course there were post-mortems, some of them painful. It had been impossible to keep discussions on a high level when strong feelings were aroused, despite Asquith's efforts to do so. The sharp passages of arms between old friends left their mark. A coolness sprang up between Asquith and the leader of the Unionist opposition, Arthur Balfour, which Margot tried to smooth over, but words spoken in the heat of the moment rankled. No sooner was the Parliament Bill passed than they crossed swords again over Home Rule before Asquith could either savour his triumph or lick his wounds. Despite Margot's pleadings, Henry (now quite without fight) could not forgive Balfour and in a weak moment permitted Lewis Harcourt to turn his defence of Asquith's Home Rule Bill into a personal vendetta against Balfour.[12]

This was one of those rare occasions when Margot kept her balance better than Henry. Baiting Balfour was unworthy of Harcourt, she told him, it only caused trouble: 'Make it up and let the matter drop,' she pleaded. She had a secret fear that Henry had put Harcourt up to it and that Balfour too suspected this. Besides, Balfour's friendship was valuable to her, too much so to be kicked aside like an old shoe. On the other hand, Harcourt had his uses too and often told her things that Henry never mentioned and which Balfour would never dream of discussing with her. On impulse she decided to write to Harcourt and tick him off.

She ought, of course, to have remained aloof and done nothing at all, but all her life her heart was to overrule her head and get her into trouble. She scribbled a mild rebuke that nevertheless should not have been administered by her:

> I know you will forgive my writing because we are seriously fond of each other and my sole motive is real and loving friendship. I am *so* keen that you should not be personal in your speeches. I did not like what you said of Arthur Balfour . . . so I am dreadfully keen you should avoid personalities, as much as possible. The coming months are sure to produce some bitterness; don't let any of us add to social disagreeables we may have to encounter in London or elsewhere.[13]

When no reply came in the next two days, she began to fear that she was to lose two friends instead of one. 'Lulu', she remembered, could be surprisingly touchy at times. Impulsive again, she sent off a second letter to put the first one right: 'I am so dreadfully afraid you will have thought my letter impertinent, and think it may have hurt or vexed you. . . .'[14]

A month later, when Asquith was well again, Margot invited Balfour and Harcourt to dine. The food was so good, the conversation so excellent and Margot fussed so equally over both that all was forgiven.

The coronation of George V had taken place on 22 June 1911 in the middle of the crisis over the Parliament Bill. The celebrations were on a reduced scale and not nearly as much fun, Margot thought, as when Edward VII was crowned. The new King and Queen were shy and retiring and did not care for balls and receptions, did what was expected of them and left it at that.

The unavoidable royal progresses round the East End of London were a far greater success than a dinner Margot attended at Buckingham Palace, which was such a poor affair that she nearly fell asleep with boredom. The quality of the guests had declined and Margot wondered where on earth those bucolic squires and their dowdy wives had been hiding all these years. It amazed her that two such kindly people as King George and Queen Mary could have such a profoundly depressing effect on people whom she had always looked on as excellent value. In the presence of their sovereign they dried up and the conversation became a game of pat ball, trite and monotonous in the extreme.

When the season was winding towards its end, the Kaiser delivered a neat bombshell that quite disrupted his cousin's innocent festivities. Without warning he despatched a gunboat to Agadir in Morocco as a German challenge to French claims, and it suddenly looked as though war might break out any moment. Warnings that 'England's attitude could not be a disinterested one'[15] were ignored. On 31 July, in a carefully prepared speech at the Mansion House, Lloyd George made it clear that if Germany wanted war she would have to reckon with England, while Asquith made much the same statement in the Commons. The Kaiser backed down and the moment of danger passed.

While the Agadir crisis was at its height Asquith became very worried about Irish reaction. If one gunboat should turn into a fleet, which way would Ireland jump? Margot's fear was quite different: if the Irish joined the Tories against the Liberals, Henry would have to resign. Why, she wondered, did such impossible people have so much power? Ever watchful where her husband's interests were concerned, Margot wrote defending Henry's attitude towards the Irish to Lord Selborne; a repetition of a letter she had sent earlier to Sir John Simon and Lewis Harcourt.[16] She had come to have a bee in her bonnet about Henry refusing to defend himself, so at every opportunity she did the job for him, but often so badly that she made matters worse.

But as soon as Germany climbed down, the Irish ceased to be important. Unlike Winston Churchill and Lloyd George, whose pulses raced at the prospect of battle, Asquith shrank from war. By training and inclination he was essentially a man of peace. His great talent was for social legislation and the betterment of the condition of the people, and it was with an enormous sense of relief that he heard that the gunboat had gone home.

His feeling of security was short-lived. No sooner was the Agadir crisis over than strikes broke out in Wales and the London docks and the railwaymen threatened to follow suit. At one of Margot's luncheon parties Marie Belloc-Lowndes noticed with some perturbation that the Prime Minister was quite unlike himself: he looked ill and harassed and took little part in the conversation. Margot, however, was in great form, shocking them all by declaring that she for one was on the side of the strikers, because 'they have real grievances'. In front of them all she begged Henry not to appear 'harsher than he felt' but to show some sympathy: 'The days are gone when the workers can be cowed, they have their trade unions behind them now.'[17] This praise for trade unions shows how far Margot had departed from the politics of the old Glen days. Charles had hated the unions and would get choleric at the mention of the word.[18]

Happily the strikes were short-lived, thanks to Lloyd George who brought them to an end by reasoning with the men without causing ill-feeling. It was galling to Margot's pride to hear Lloyd George's praises sung on all sides. She did not care for so much adulation for a subordinate of Henry's at all—these things were never the work of one man alone. Of course Lloyd George publicly praised the Prime Minister for his support, nevertheless Margot was unreasonably suspicious that Lloyd George might intend harm to 'us'. She was even more displeased when the King sent Lloyd George his warmest congratulations but not one word of thanks to Henry.

Somehow or other her feeling grew that Lloyd George had insinuated himself into undue prominence and that the criticisms of Henry in the newspapers had all been 'set up'. This was the beginning of Margot's distrust of Lloyd George, which was to culminate five years later in a real hatred of the man who supplanted her husband in the premiership.

CHAPTER 19

A Little Breathless and a Little Cold

IN AUGUST MARGOT went to Scotland while Henry joined a party of friends for another cruise on the *Enchantress*. By 1911 separate holidays had already become quite usual. Asquith loved sailing and the company of a chosen few who enjoyed the luxury and excitement of life on a yacht. Only once did Margot accompany him, but she still hated the sea so much that she swore nothing would make her repeat the experience. Of course there was talk about these separate holidays: it was the general opinion that Asquith simply had to have a rest from Margot or go mad, but this was not the case. He would have liked to have her with him on *Enchantress*, but he had to accept the hard fact that she returned from these sea-trips in worse shape than when she started. She much preferred Scotland where the air suited her and she could give the children her undivided attention.

To everyone's surprise Margot had become a devoted mother, some thought an over-possessive one, for she wanted a hand in everything her children did; she called it taking an interest. It was plain to everyone but Margot that the fourteen-year-old Elizabeth resented so much interference and was accordingly driven into herself and became quiet and withdrawn. There is no evidence that Puffin disliked Margot's constant supervision, but he lived so much in a world of his own that he hardly noticed. She never looked back into her own untrammelled childhood nor learned from Emma's cool attitude towards her family. In this respect her stepchildren were better off than her own. She says she was not clever with them, yet in fact, considering the difficulties facing her, she handled them very well, all except Raymond whose affection she much wanted. She was too sensitive to his moods and took far too much trouble about such things as getting exactly the right Christmas and birthday presents. One year she bought him two first editions of Browning without knowing that he despised Browning and never read him. His offhand thanks hurt her deeply. Yet as the years wore on he saw her many good points and softened towards her although his marriage did nothing to bring them closer. The very fact that he could not have married at all without her money was a barrier between them. Raymond hated to be grateful, although Margot never once reminded him of what she had done for him.

Raymond often spoke of Margot's 'worldliness' and he did not mean it as a compliment. Yet it was this very worldliness that turned out to be such an asset to the Asquith children. Their father's second marriage to Margot Tennant lifted them into her own exciting world. Because of Margot all doors automatically opened to them, and society, snobbish and exclusive as it was in those days, took the children to its heart. There is no doubt that they quickly came to adore Margot's world and to feel perfectly at home in it; it suited them so much better than that into which they had been born. Nevertheless Raymond, at least, made great fun of Margot's intellectual pretensions and her respect for cleverness and learning, showing little sympathy for her constant efforts to improve her own mind. By the time he was at the Bar, he had come to take for granted the many opportunities that she had opened up for him, including his happy marriage to Katharine Horner.

Asquith's second marriage was of most service to Violet. This tall and pretty girl was well-read, poised and intelligent with a remarkably quick wit. Although she was not a beauty Margot dressed her in such good taste that she had no difficulty in attracting attention when she came out in 1906, at a ball Charles and his second wife Marguerite gave for her at 40 Grosvenor Square. Margot had taken great pains to choose good governesses for her stepdaughter, regarding it as a sort of trial run for Elizabeth who was also quick and intelligent. Since Margot herself had hated her short time at school, she had decided that both girls should be taught at home under her eye; for she had no intention of paying inefficient or bullying women to make life miserable for them. She took such care to find the very best governesses England and the Continent had to offer that Violet was much better educated than most girls of her time.

Violet's début into the rich and over-luxurious world of pre-1914 English society came too suddenly for her comfort. One day she was a child, treated as such, the next she was expected to behave as a grown woman and to understand the bewildering ways of adults. Such a violent transition from the schoolroom to the drawing-room had not happened to Margot. She had been part of the adult world since her birth and her coming out was no more than a gesture to convention and not a frightening step into a life of love affairs, gossip, intrigue and heartache for which nothing had prepared her. Margot understood the difference very well, so why did she allow this to happen to Violet? Perhaps because she recognized that Violet was conventional and hated to do anything out of the ordinary that would make her conspicuous. For one of Violet's nature to be lost in a crowd was security. Violet confessed that her first ball was torture and that to have to wear Charles's generous present—a diamond necklace—when every other girl of her age was wearing pearls, made her blush with embarrassment. Without in the least meaning to, Margot made Violet feel gauche and clumsy. It was her misfortune that in dealing with her stepdaughter she always seemed unsympathetic and worldly, because she was so well-dressed and self-assured and seemed to handle every contingency with such aplomb; Margot was also, according to Violet, too carefree and did not at all mind what other people thought of her. Violet was always on tenterhooks in her stepmother's presence, wondering in fear and trembling what sort of an impression Margot was making when she monopolized the conversation and put distinguished men in their place, although she knew them to be better educated and cleverer than she was.

None of this would have mattered had Violet not had set ideas on how a Prime Minister's wife should behave. For instance, it made her go hot and cold with embarrassment when visitors called and Margot would run downstairs, enter the drawing-room in a rush, shriek out a welcome, light a cigarette and begin a conversation that could be heard all over sacred No. 10. She disapproved, too, of the way Margot made acid comments in public about members of the Opposition and was often in agony in case such indiscretions might harm her father: she thought Margot ought to be more circumspect, more dignified and not treat everyone alike, but behave coolly and distantly towards servants in front of guests, for instance, rather than thanking them profusely for something they had done. Violet longed to tell Margot what to do but was afraid to say anything because, although she knew herself to be the better-educated (which Margot willingly owned), she also knew that her stepmother could run rings around her in argument and she minded this very much.

Margot's upbringing and background were a closed book to this young girl. She had been to Glen, listened to Margot's ravings about the magic and enchantment of the place (which Violet thought greatly exaggerated) and found it impossible to visualize for herself the things Margot talked about in the past. She could never understand that every time Margot entered the gates of Glen she saw in her imagination her mother, brothers and sisters waiting for her at the door and that the whole house still echoed with their laughter. That something of this lack in Violet seeped through to Margot is clear from her letters to DD Lyttelton[1], and sometimes she felt quite in despair.

It never occurred to Violet that the people who came to 10 Downing Street would not have come so often if Margot had been other than she was, and that Margot's seemingly light-hearted attitude to things Violet considered sacred was born of a confidence in herself that few possessed. Margot liked people and saw no reason why she should not show that she did. Full of good feeling for her stepdaughter, Margot gave her a charming little sitting-room on the ground floor, with a convenient door into the garden so that her friends could come and go without disturbing the rest of the household. Here Violet was able to entertain freely. Never once did Margot point out to Violet that it might be better if young Members of Parliament did not pop in to see her when the House was sitting late. Margot wanted her to feel free, yet Violet worried about whether it was right that Margot should allow her so much liberty—what would people think? She would have welcomed a little chaperonage, but except for accompanying her stepdaughter to the grander balls, Margot left Violet to make her own decisions, since to Margot chaperonage was no more than an absurd façade.

Life would have been much happier for these two women if Violet had only told Margot that she was grateful for so much trust. One word of appreciation would have sufficed, but Violet could not bring herself to say it, not even for the wonderful dress of white satin and lace made by Worth for her coming-out ball. A breathless few days in Paris was an extra treat, with M. Worth himself supervising the fittings, bringing out bale after bale of satin and testing it against her skin. The dress was moulded on her figure, every detail individual, for the couturier wanted to please his old client who was now the wife of the Prime Minister of England. Nobody asked Violet's opinion, and she resented it. She also hated the pantomime of Margot and M. Worth shrieking at each other in French (Worth was in fact English!), both pinching Violet in here and out there and passing such very personal remarks that she could not help blushing.

The transformation into womanhood was to be accomplished by 'a

large dinner party followed by a ball'. Violet wrote many years later, 'I
found the process for the rite bewildering and painful. For the first time in
my life the hair that dangled down my back was put up in a disfiguring
pile, I was laced into a white satin dress by Worth and feeling rather
breathless and a little cold I went downstairs to face the forty strangers
who had come to dinner.'[2]

Naturally Violet excited the curiosity of the press, but she did not
understand that it was not only as the Prime Minister's daughter that she
was the most photographed girl of the season but as the stepdaughter of
the famous Margot Tennant to whom no doors were shut. Perhaps that
was the reason Violet was 'a little breathless and cold'.

Violet worshipped her father, resented the fact that she did not come first
in his life and seized every chance to have him to herself. Because Margot
hated the sea, it was Violet who went with him on *Enchantress*. If Margot
planned a health holiday in the South of France (which bored Asquith), it
was Violet who accompanied her father to Archerfield on the East
Lothian coast. She loved the night express that whisked them so comfortably to Scotland and the hearty breakfast, eaten alone with her father, that
the housekeeper always prepared for the Prime Minister's arrival. In fine
weather they would spend the mornings playing golf on the perfect
private links that stretched down to the sea.

Margot deeply resented the unashamed delight that Violet showed
when she was about to go off alone with her father, but never said
anything about it to Henry for fear of upsetting him. It was to DD that she
poured out her indignation:

> . . . Don't show or tell anyone about my letter to you as in some ways I
> think I might be a little blinded by Violet. I feel as if by now the end of
> my keen youth must be over, I ought to have my own husband and my
> own children in a house of my own—I have only been alone with Henry
> and my children three weeks in nineteen years. This has got on my
> nerves; it is really physical and the more I control the longing or the
> showing of it, the iller I feel. We are always à trois—in shops, in the
> hills, on official occasions, round the fire and at the altar. I long to take
> the communion service with Henry alone.—I long to talk to him,—to
> be with him,—it would be so easy if she would marry . . .[3]

That was the trouble. Violet seemed to be in no hurry to leave home and have a husband and children of her own. Margot suspected that she was in love with Winston Churchill, who was married to someone very different. Churchill was the kind of young man Violet admired above all others: articulate, clever, energetic, bristling with ideas and full of a peculiar charm that many found irresistible. Next to her father, Violet wanted Churchill to do well in the world and whenever she could help him she did. In 1910, after the Agadir crisis was over, the question of a change in the Admiralty came up and Violet put all her weight on the side of the man she thought would fit the post better than anyone—Winston Churchill. In spite of being accused of being a 'barefaced partisan' and teased for showing 'gross favouritism and emotion' Violet worked on her father and Churchill got the job, although Asquith had probably decided to give it to him already. She may have tipped the balance in her longing for Churchill to have his heart's desire, 'because I felt sure that it was there that he would find his true vocation and his greatest self'.[4]

Violet was unhappy that Churchill did not get on with the rest of her family as well as she would have liked. She had seen for some time that Margot and Churchill were not compatible; two such strong characters were bound to disagree. Each thought the other was out to set a trap in order to topple self-esteem and it was true that Margot enjoyed bringing Winston low. On the rare occasions when the two met it did not take much to start the sparks flying, to Violet's dismay. With Churchill, Margot made a point of being, in her own words, 'brutally frank', which often meant being unkind, and naturally Churchill resented it. Sometimes when she saw what effect it had on Violet she was sorry, but she did not say so to Churchill, who probably would have readily forgiven her. It was as though she could not stop herself behaving rudely; once she half confessed as much to DD: 'I am so disagreeably constituted that I say brutal franknesses to people's faces without meaning to hurt them.'[5]

Margot and Violet never quarrelled openly, did not even bicker; there was simply a strong reserve amounting to disdain on the one hand and intense irritation and sense of failure on the other. Because of jealousy and a longing to have all Asquith's attention, neither was willing to meet the other half way. Each had too many fixed ideas about the other; Margot's despairing cry, 'I can't do anything with her because she thinks I am not clever enough about life',[6] was probably not true at all, any more than the disparaging things Violet said to her friends about Margot. Nevertheless these imagined criticisms were a barrier between them. Now and again Margot did find excuses for Violet: 'She has never known a mother—she values brains more than character. If only someone would say to her, live your life, don't waste it.'[7]

DD helped Margot all she could to understand Violet, since she saw what a bad effect constant irritation had on both of them. She sensed that if only Violet could be more affectionate and Margot more sympathetic most of their troubles would dissolve; for she knew from experience that Margot hated to be at odds with any member of the family and was responsive to affection. Margot was grateful for DD's efforts on her behalf and wrote:

> I am glad you had a good talk with Violet, though I always feel nervous for with the exception of her father who knows Violet's nature and mine and has helped me a hundred times, everyone who has tried to help either of us to grow accustomed to the world-wide difference of each other's natures has made hopeless mischief between us. I was a great fool to talk about her at all, as now both you and she will think it was 'nerves' on my part and this is just not true. Violet is iller than I am. As you say, the right man would help us all, but you must give gold for gold to find him and Violet has always given copper. She is brilliant, alas too brilliant . . .[8]

DD did some good for the gap seemed to close a little between the two women; at any rate, Margot thought it did, for she wrote to DD to beg her to

> make Violet see you several times and do just point out to her what a mess she is going to make of her life . . . it makes me ill to see her living from day to day and never seeing herself or life as it exactly is. Try a real talk on her future and on the want of resolution and earnestness she shows . . . she is born with so little reverence that when I am sad I can't bear to see her . . . I foresee with terrible clearness the clash of Elizabeth and Violet later on. So selfish to ask you but she is really fond of you that I really believe that you are the only person that can do it.[9]

There was a postscript: 'No one has ever touched Violet . . . , she would be a perfect wife if only she would give up a little for others . . .'

It was not until 1913 that Margot could bring herself to tell anyone that 'Violet has been on my nerves for many, many years',[10] but having shared the secret with DD, she felt the better for having done so. Her relief at the confession made up for what she called her 'disloyalty' in talking about her stepdaughter at all, and she was glad not to have it bottled up inside her any more. Margot thought DD had touched on the root of the trouble when she pointed out that Violet, although graceful and charming, was hard, and still immature at twenty-six. 'I am sure her character will progress a little towards her brains,' Margot replied.[11]

The saddest part about this stepmother business was the sense of failure it gave Margot. Henry's children had never accepted her as their father's wife and surrogate mother: 'Cis is the only one I have influenced' has a sad ring to it; '. . . none of his [Henry's] children have imagination, passion or compassion, but they have everything else, so one cannot grouse'.[12] Before she married, Margot asked herself the all-important question: 'Will I be able to love these children?' Now her question had become a wail: 'Why don't they love me?'

Of course it was time Violet left the nest, but she frightened men away by her sheer mental superiority which she never bothered to conceal. Yet Margot herself had been much the same and caused her parents similar worries, so why was she now preparing herself to accept the fact that her stepdaughter was going to be an old maid, hanging around her father and never letting Margot get a look in?

This prospect was so bleak that Margot sought help from above: 'I pray out loud . . . that I shall be relieved from looking at the mental and moral future and the failures of the present.'[13]

Quite suddenly everything changed. Not long after the outbreak of war Violet fell in love with Maurice Bonham Carter (known as 'Bongie'), her father's private secretary, who had adored her for years.

The effect on Margot was electric. She was ill with a cold when she heard the news and rose from her sick-bed to take Violet shopping for clothes: 'Such nonsense, all this talk about not having a trousseau, . . . you can't be married without a rag to your back.' Of course Margot paid all the bills; it made her happy to see that at last she could be of some use to Violet. During her engagement Violet was lethargic and half-hearted about everything and could not understand at all what had happened to her. Margot was reassuring: 'It's being engaged! Nothing in this world makes one feel so ill. When I was engaged to your father I felt like death and lost two stone.'[14]

Her words of comfort were taken to heart, for 'Beb' Asquith's wife, Cynthia, wrote in her diary that when she saw Violet shortly before her wedding, she thought she looked happy and serene: 'just absolute security and a kind of dependence on Bongie'. Yet Violet had been really ill and the wedding had to be postponed, which had a very bad effect on the bridegroom who, Cynthia thought, looked 'like a piece of chewed string'.[15]

Now that she was to leave home and family for a life of her own Violet began to realize how attached she was to everyone and how much her carefree existence meant to her. She saw Margot's good points too, and now that she had a man of her own her deep-seated jealousy of her stepmother abated a little and they became better friends than they had ever been before.

On a cold, grey November day in 1915 Violet and Maurice Bonham Carter were married in St Margaret's, Westminster with the full panoply of a society wedding. Elizabeth Asquith and her mother's niece, Kathleen Tennant, were bridesmaids and Winston Churchill's son, Randolph, one of the three pages. ('Randolph . . . looked quite beautiful in a little Russian velvet suit with fur. His looks made quite a sensation . . .' Clementine Churchill wrote to Winston.[16]) The church was packed and half London waited outside to catch a glimpse of the Prime Minister's daughter as she drove with her bridegroom to Downing Street for the reception.

Next day Margot was irked to read criticisms in the papers of such a perfect wedding. Apparently it was considered bad taste for the Prime Minister to marry off his daughter in such style while there was a war on.

CHAPTER 20

For Pure Cruelty Women Beat Men Hollow

IN JANUARY 1912, three years before Violet's marriage, Asquith and his friend Edwin Montagu, a large ugly man but full of wit and charm, went for a three-week holiday in Sicily. The two men were accompanied by Violet and her friend Venetia Stanley, daughter of Lord Sheffield, a handsome, intelligent girl of twenty-four, with a strong personality and mature beyond her years.

They travelled in a leisurely way by sea, and Asquith whiled away the time by persuading Venetia to teach him piquet, 'a quiet and useful resource for two people and a difficult game', he wrote to Margot, adding, 'I wish you were here, you would find some of the necessary horrors of sea travel, early morning noises, bad smells etc, but a cool clear air and for the most part bright sun. Above all the sense of being away from both the small and large worries of life.'[1]

Sicily enthralled him with its chequered history from classical times to the present, although he deplored the way the modern Sicilians lived like the Irish peasants with livestock of all kinds under the same roof. When the four went sight-seeing together it seemed natural for Asquith to take Venetia under his wing, pointing out places of interest and sketching the history of the island for her. Venetia was the ideal companion for a man tired and jaded after a strenuous parliamentary session, for she was a ready and sympathetic listener who possessed the ability to understand without saying too much herself. In this holiday mood Asquith lived up to Lady Diana Cooper's remark that he delighted in 'the young and the young's conversation and would talk of poetry and people and weddings and jokes and he wanted to hold one's hand and feel equal and comforted'.[2] (Duff Cooper, who was in love with the beautiful Diana, objected strongly and wrote furiously of Asquith: 'He is oblivious of young men and lecherous of young girls.'[3])

Before long Asquith was forgetting his responsibilities in the sheer enjoyment of Venetia's company and by the time he returned to London he was infatuated with his daughter's friend. Unaware of this, Margot congratulated herself on the improvement in her husband's health and looks and on her own wisdom in sending him away for a complete change. Asquith, on the other hand, seemed quite unaffected by the return to normal life. Still in a state of euphoria he settled down to enjoy this exciting experience certain that his affection was returned. Between 1912 and 1915 he wrote hundreds of letters to Venetia, at first mild and tentative as though he was afraid of a rebuff, later increasingly passionate Before long it became necessary to his peace of mind to write to her not only once but sometimes three times a day. In these letters Asquith poured out his soul with the sheer joy of being in love, forgetting that he was a married man and the Prime Minister of a country at war. He gave Venetia not only his love but Cabinet secrets as well ('Darling, I tell you everything'), an act of folly that might have cost thousands of lives. Whatever was happening, there was always leisure for the daily outpourings without which he was unable to work. They met every day too, and it was a common sight to see Asquith setting off for his afternoon motor drive accompanied by Venetia. When Parliament was in recess, Asquith often stayed at her parents' country-house in Wales, enjoying more of Venetia's company on the links and during long walks.

It has been said of Asquith that he was one of those men who needed a close friend outside marriage to confide in. For two years before the death of his first wife, it was Margot to whom he wrote long letters about matters of state, books and sentiments. Before that it had been Mrs Horner, and for a brief period Lady Scott, widow of the Antarctic explorer. After Venetia, there followed in quick succession her elder sister, Sylvia Henley, and Hilda Harrisson, a young war widow from Oxford. In his biography of Asquith, Mr Jenkins deals a little too sympathetically with his need for female confidantes when he says that for Asquith the writing of these letters was both a solace and a relaxation, interfering with his duties no more than Lloyd George's hymn-singing or Churchill's late night conversations.[4] In fact it did interfere considerably with his work (particularly during the first year of the war), and, as Mr Jenkins himself points out, the abrupt ending of the affair in 1915 was to shock Asquith so badly that he was shaken and muddle-headed when he should have been cool and collected.[5] Besides, Asquith took enormous risks, not only in his marriage but with national security. Venetia Stanley seems to have kept everything he told her entirely to herself, but very serious consequences indeed might have followed if, for instance, even one of his letters had been read by a servant and sold to a newspaper, or the Prime Minister blackmailed. It makes no difference that his confidence in her discretion was justified in the event: he could not guarantee that she would not inadvertently leave a letter lying about, and he knew that by telling her war secrets he was breaking a trust, for his own government had passed the Official Secrets Act only a year before his correspondence with Venetia Stanley began.

Luck favoured him. As his daughter Violet's friend, Venetia had been in and out of the Asquith homes for some time before the love affair started, so the household, and even Margot, thought nothing of it, and little attention was focused on them when they were together. Those who had eyes to see could guess the truth, of course, and surely Violet was among them? It is probably true that the love was never consummated. For all his frolicking with young girls Asquith was highly conventional, and knew very well the scandal that would ensue should he lose his head entirely. He could adore Venetia, put her on a pedestal and worship her, make her the recipient of all his secret thoughts, without taking her into his bed.

It was a great pity that Violet and her friends accepted her father as one of themselves. He was often to be found playing bridge with them (without Margot), enjoying the jokes and games that kept him away from wife and work. Many of the young people he mixed with lived in a fantasy world of their own that an ageing Prime Minister (he was now sixty-three) had no business to share with them, and thus allow himself to be distracted from his proper duties.

There is little to say of Venetia herself, who remains a shadowy figure. She was not a beautiful, seductive temptress but a big-boned, dark-eyed creature who according to several witnesses strode about in a masculine way and had the reputation of being a 'good comrade'.

Asquith's letters to her are either political or full of the literary allusions with which he loved to pepper his correspondence. But this does not mean that Venetia either understood the allusions or could reply in kind, and there is no evidence that she took the slightest interest in affairs of state before Asquith fell in love with her or that she was capable of giving him advice on Home Rule, Conscription or any of the other questions on which he asked her opinion. She showed not the slightest sympathy for Margot's sufferings—Margot's repeated complaints are proof enough

—and Venetia's unfeeling attitude deserves more condemnation than it has received. It was not her fault that Asquith fell in love with her, but it was her fault that she allowed the affair to drag on for three years.

At the end of 1912, after a long period of good health, Margot began to ail. Nothing organic was wrong, but her nerves were shaky, she was lonely and therefore depressed, and since she increasingly lacked the companionship of a husband she began to rely too much on the company of her only son. Old friends like Simon, Haldane and DD came often to lunch, tea or dinner and did all they could to encourage her to mix again in society and go out as she used to, but without much effect. As 1914 approached she began to feel that she was cut off from the world that mattered, the political world that she enjoyed and where she felt she belonged. She saw very little of Henry now, and although she never gave the merest hint to her family that she minded him spending so little time at home, she knew that his official duties did not occupy every hour of the day.

Such a thing had not happened to her before. Never in her worst nightmares had she believed that her husband could show such blatant disregard for her feelings. Asquith was always courteous to her, but it was plain that the centre of his interest was now elsewhere, and she sensed a coolness towards her that was deeply hurtful. She was under a considerable strain which she bore with courage and outward composure. She had not realized, because in some ways she was ignorant of that side of life, that when she left her husband's bed she was putting her marriage in jeopardy. Her doctors had told them both of the dangers of another pregnancy and Margot had accepted what this meant without envisaging the implications for a highly sexed man like Asquith.

There were those who said that Alfred Milner had been her lover, and that Asquith had only found this out after marriage and had turned against her. She had lent some colour to this by seeing Milner whenever he came to London and talking of him affectionately (some said with regret). Only her closest friends knew for certain that Milner had never been her lover, and even fewer knew of her deep-seated fear of physical love. Milner had discovered it in Egypt when Margot showed her repugnance by resisting his passionate embraces: '. . . You would frighten me if I did not know you so well.' When she left her husband's bed after only eleven years of marriage she did not suffer, nor did she feel anxious for the future, because to her physical love and affection were not synonymous. It was the loss of Asquith's confidence and regard that wounded her so deeply.

Margot's character, and the complete lack of evidence that she was ever unchaste, would make the whole question of whether she had lovers superfluous, were it not for a passage in Lady Longford's recent book *Pilgrimage of Passion* (pp. 296–8) which repeats Wilfred Scawen Blunt's assertion that Margot invited him to her bedroom at 35 Grosvenor Square and allowed him to seduce her.

There are several reasons why this story can be entirely discounted. In the first place, it is impossible to believe that Margot would so blatantly have betrayed her parents' trust under their own roof. Moreover, Blunt was a well-known lady-killer, a promiscuous man who liked to boast of his conquests. Margot was the one woman he particularly coveted because she was known to have yielded to no one. He clearly did not know her very well, for he says she asked his advice whether she should marry Evan Charteris or 'Henry' Asquith. There never was any question of her marrying Charteris, a man ten years younger than herself, whose short affair with Margot was quickly over and deeply regretted by her. The choice was between Milner and Asquith, two outstanding men. Besides, no one called Asquith 'Henry' until after the marriage, not even Margot herself until some time after the engagement. Until then all his friends knew him as 'Herbert', a name Margot did not like.

Margot made no known reference to this alleged incident, but she did once categorically deny that she had ever been any man's mistress. She wrote the following letter* to Arthur Balfour on 18 August 1920:

I have no *idea* where Evan [Charteris] saw his name & poem (a lovely little verse he wrote me years ago) or why he was furious because I never saw it but on hearing his name had appeared I wrote and apologized saying with truth as I had scratched his name out, I had scolded my publisher and he had apologized to me and chaffed him most mildly, he wrote back and said the poem was indecent which of course made me laugh. I said it was lovely and wondered what had offended his purity and that I thought it jolly of George Curzon to have told Maud Cunard and others (who repeated it to me) that nothing I had said of him was unkind and inaccurate, at which I get a letter of incredible Vulgarity and

* I am much indebted to Mr Paul Chipchase for drawing my attention to this letter, which is in the Balfour papers at Whittinghame.

Fury! He says one line compromises my girlhood and insinuates I was his mistress! When I knew Evan I knew *nothing* about anything but I was no man's mistress and never had a lover in my life and if I had been, this is the letter of a cad. I've never lied and I am not going to lie now. I would rather die than speak to him again. When Henry read it he said it was incredible that *vanity* should swamp breeding to such a degree.

This is as near a conclusive rebuttal as there is ever likely to be of a charge which is anyhow improbable in the highest degree.*

Asquith was too self-centred, too vain (a vanity that was mixed, where Venetia was concerned, with a strange humility) and too madly in love to understand that it was his love for another younger and prettier woman that made Margot tearful, short-tempered, nervous and in every way trying. No wife who loved her husband and had to suffer the agony of watching him becoming daily more enamoured of another woman could behave otherwise. A dozen years earlier she might have confronted him, and her very courage might have shown him how foolish he was to put his wife's health and devotion in jeopardy. But somehow the fight had gone out of her after so many painful pregnancies and so much ill health. Only once did she bring herself to upbraid him, and even then too timidly. In her own words, she was 'wounded, humiliated and bewildered'. Asquith replied at once in a coolly dishonest letter, accusing her of 'petty jealousies' and going on to say that:

> [my] fondness for Venetia has never interfered and never could with our relationship . . . but I admit I am often irritated and impatient and that then I have become curt and perhaps taciturn. I fear you have suffered

---

* The sequel to this letter is interesting in an entirely different context. Margot had written in the same terms to Mary Wemyss, who replied for herself and Balfour jointly on 19 August:

> You have never hesitated to express the most vehement criticisms in the most unrestrained language to your friends and about your friends. But you do it with such charm and your violence is so free from spite that I have no desire, except in your own interests, to enter a word of caution. But, believe me, it is very unwise to have wholly different canons of behaviour respecting what other people may say about you and what you may say about other people. 'Chartered libertines' must not abuse their privileges. No one values friendship more than you. Do not make it difficult.
>
> Yrs, Mary Wemyss, for M.W. and A.J.B.

from this more than anyone and I am deeply sorry, but believe me, darling, it is not due to want of confidence and love. Those remain, and will always, unchanged.[6]

True or false, this reply gave Margot a little brief happiness. She did not know that he was still writing to Venetia as 'the author and finisher of everything that is worth living in my life', 'the one incarnation of all that I worship', 'the pole and lode-star of my life'.[7]

Instead of giving way to her feelings, Margot made efforts to be natural and kind to Venetia Stanley when she came to No. 10, which she did quite often. The younger woman does not seem to have been in the least put out when she encountered her admirer's wife, and an additionally hurtful aspect of the whole business was that Margot suspected that Violet knew what was going on and had taken her father's side.

To friends she ascribed her low spirits to the fact that Puffin had recently gone to Summerfields, a preparatory school not far from Oxford. She was bound to miss him, but she would not have done so every hour of the day if her husband had not been in love with another woman. Strangely enough it was Margot who insisted on Puffin's going and his father who wanted to keep him at home. Asquith thought him too delicate to mix with young boys on an equal footing, and feared that the regime of a boarding school would be too severe. Margot had gone alone to interview Dr Williams, the headmaster, been shown over Summerfields, and returned convinced it was the right place for her son. Her arguments were sound: far better to mix with boys of his own age than to be all day closeted alone with a tutor. Besides, the regular hours, even the monotony of school life would be good for him and he might discover an appetite when he saw the other boys eager for food. It was heaven-sent that the school should have been so near Margot's new country home, The Wharf, a house on the Thames near Sutton Courtenay. She went regularly to see her child and watched the improvement in his health with amazement:

I was able to go every Saturday afternoon and watch him racing without a hat in the beautiful playing grounds . . . As he was forbidden by the doctors to go on the regular school walks, he and I spent most of our Sunday afternoons playing the piano, reading verses, telling stories and generally ending by saying our prayers in the garden before I motored back to join our guests at The Wharf.[8]

Margot adored this only son of hers, and was very proud of his sweet nature and talent for music. He was passionate about opera and had a large collection of records bought with his own pocket money.[9] At fourteen he could play Bach and Beethoven with amazing skill, practised the piano for hours and had tried his hand at composing: 'He's a real genius,' Margot wrote to Mary Drew, 'and I'm sorry you don't know him . . .'[10]

It was bad luck that, at the time of Puffin's departure for school, Elizabeth was developing teenage moods and rebellions and was no comfort to her mother at all. Margot found it impossible to confide in Violet, whose detached air brought an almost overwhelming desire to shake her in order to get a response: 'When I am ill and down a devil enters my heart and mind,' she told DD. 'I dream of her [Violet] hitting me or taking away all my things, absolute nightmares . . . and when she comes in gay and happy in the morning, I curse and hate myself.'[11]

Margot badly needed help and comfort from her family, but instead she got indifference. She began to look so pale and thin that even Henry was alarmed. One night when he returned home late, he went to her room and found her weeping silently into her pillow.

> He knelt down and kissed me. I told him that it would be best for me, as I was so tearful and rotten, to go right away from him for two months. He got up and said with such emotion 'Has it come to this?' The idea of hurting him deeply was so awful that I said 'Oh just to get well . . .' I asked him if at these times I did not get on his nerves? He put his arms round me and his eyes were wet as I clasped him to me. His love cheered me . . .[12]

Asquith was too clever, too used to the ways of women, not to know exactly what she meant, and just what was troubling her. He had not ceased to love Margot; it was only that he loved someone else more.

An invitation to Balmoral early in the year for the Prime Minister did not include Margot, much to her chagrin, for she had enjoyed her previous visit more than she had expected. By a lucky chance she had managed to penetrate King George's reserve by mentioning women's suffrage, a subject on which they both had similarly strong feelings. Both thought votes for women a lot of nonsense: 'They won't know what to do with them,' Margot once said, and the King had even forbidden his household to mention the word 'suffragette' in his presence. After this happy opening Margot had plunged into a description of how a group of well-brought-up women had broken the windows in Downing Street, tried to assassinate the Prime Minister and threatened the lives of her children, adding that she was now afraid to sit on a platform at a public meeting in case she should have a brick thrown at her. Fired by the King, Margot wrote to DD: 'It's as much as I can do not to pray that they won't have a vote in my life-time: reason has never governed women in times of political excitement. For pure cruelty women beat men hollow.'[13]

Now it seemed that this budding royal friendship had come to an abrupt end. She was not invited to Balmoral. She had not taken in the fact that George V had made it clear that business and pleasure were no longer to be mixed and that a serious discussion on Irish affairs could not be disguised as a social occasion.

Asquith's plan for Ireland—complete Home Rule with the imperial Parliament over all—did not find favour with anyone but the King. Bonar Law's gloomy prediction 'it will not do' was clearly echoed by many others, and Sir Edward Grey flatly refused to consider anything short of the exclusion of Ulster.[14]

Asquith returned from Balmoral empty-handed but with an excellent appetite given him by the bracing Scottish air and, alas, a few pounds' extra weight. Failure to agree about Ireland was not his only worry: the situation in Europe had deteriorated since he had been away and what he most dreaded—war with Germany and simultaneous civil war in Ireland —was, he feared, soon to happen. Margot was not able to offer much comfort: he would never do anything with Ireland, she warned him; the Phoenix Park murders in 1882 had convinced her that Ireland was not ready for self-government. She believed this strongly although it flew in the face of Gladstone's very different view: the murders proved to him that the Irish must be encouraged to govern themselves. Margot thought she had plenty to back up her theories: 'the Irish lack gratitude, purpose, vigour and loyalty'. A visit to Dublin with Henry in 1912 had done nothing to make her change her mind. The city was beautiful but dark with hidden traps. While they were riding through the streets a well-dressed young woman threw a scythe into the open carriage, cutting off one of John Redmond's ears and only missing Asquith by a hair's breadth.

After that narrow escape Margot saw nothing in the least beautiful about Ireland.

The atmosphere in Europe was becoming threatening and Irish affairs were worsening, but Margot had little idea how bad matters had become, although she read all the papers eagerly and discussed the prospect of war (still apparently remote) with her political friends. Asquith told her little. He refused, under any circumstances, to discuss politics in the home, while writing about them at length to Venetia Stanley. Margot was therefore astonished when, during a reception at the German Embassy, the ambassador told her that in his opinion Ireland was on the brink of civil war and that nothing but a miracle could prevent it. She hid her surprise and disbelief as well as she could and replied with some hauteur: 'Shocking as that would be, it would not break England.'[15]

But would it break Henry? She only half-believed what the ambassador told her and was not unduly worried. Nevertheless she was haunted by Lord Randolph Churchill's phrase, 'Ulster will fight and Ulster will be right'. No sober-minded Englishman seriously believed that when it came to the point the Irish would take up arms against the will of Parliament and that they would be supported by one of the great English parties.[16] Civil war belonged to history and not to the present day, so Margot believed the threats to be bluff and that Edward Carson was not to be taken seriously.

All through the autumn and winter of 1913–1914, Margot witnessed hysterical scenes whenever the Irish question came up in the House, with cries of 'traitor' coming from the opposition benches, accompanied by such rowdyism; on one occasion feelings ran so high that a copy of the standing orders was thrown at Winston Churchill's head. Accustomed as she was to displays of passion in the chamber, Margot was still appalled. In high indignation after witnessing a particularly unpleasant scene, she caught Bonar Law, the leader of the Opposition, as he was leaving the House and admonished him for allowing his party to behave so disgracefully. All she got in reply was a cold answer: it was his duty not to interfere.[17]

At Christmas 1913 Margot almost fainted as she sat down to lunch and had to be put to bed. Her doctor was called but diagnosed nothing sinister; it was her 'nerves' again, and more rest was prescribed. She was told to eat more red meat, but at meals she could only swallow a mouthful and so lost weight. Her friends were deeply concerned when they noticed how her clothes hung on her like a sack and that her smoking had increased, and they were amazed that Asquith continued to look so bland and sleek. Since they no longer shared a bedroom, he was quite unaware how little Margot slept and therefore did not realize that her insomnia was a sign of her anxiety over his affair with Venetia.

One day her friend Sir John Simon came to see her and was horrified to find her lying on her sofa, surrounded by books and writing her diary with her knees hunched up, looking the picture of discomfort. He scolded her for sitting so awkwardly and said he had just the thing to make her writing easier; otherwise she would add curvature of the spine to her other troubles. Next day, to her astonishment, a beautiful little mahogany writing table arrived, exactly the right size to take all her paraphernalia. Margot was deeply touched by his kindness; nothing like this had happened to her for a long time, all the family thought her too self-sufficient to need help or advice and so they never bothered to give any. The unexpectedness of the present, and Simon's spontaneous reaction to her unhappiness, did her more good than a hundred potions. She ended her ecstatic letter of thanks thus: . . . 'I can thankfully tell you that your very old table is one of the most genuine and rare pieces you could ever have given me. It is a real joy and I simply delight in it.'[18]

In January 1914 Margot developed a chest infection which left her with a cough so that her doctors ordered her to Cannes. She dutifully read all the French papers, but disregarded the warnings of war as Gallic excitability. She learned from the British papers that Parliament had agreed to strengthen the defences of the British Isles, but this had been Henry's plan long before there had been any talk of war and as far as she could gather relations with Germany were easier than they had been for years.

Henry wrote only short letters, and the first she knew of a serious rift in the Liberal Cabinet was an account in the Continental *Daily Telegraph* of an ill-advised interview Lloyd George had given deploring the folly of Churchill's proposals to increase expenditure on armaments at a time when the prospects of the world were never more peaceful. Margot promptly sent Henry a telegram asking for more information and two days later received this reply: 'The interview has set all Europe by the ears, not to mention the party here. Winston is still in Paris and maintains a dignified and moody silence.' On 20 June he wrote again: Lloyd George and Winston were still at loggerheads 'and it looks as though it might eventually come to a breaking point. If this were plainly inevitable, sooner than have a smash up and resignation I should probably dissolve Parliament and run the risk of the election'. Next day Henry reported that all was still not well; there were doubts that the quarrel could be patched up: 'It is curious what personal hostility Winston excites even in the most unexpected quarters.'[19]

Margot's instinct told her that an election at such a moment could be fatal, for the omens were all against the Liberals getting in if they went to the country now. Sunning herself on the terrace of the Villa Mimosa, she knew that she could not endure being left in the dark any longer. Without delay she telegraphed Sir John Simon, her closest political ally, begging him to let her know what was up, but received no reply. With many sighs she rattled off one of her long political letters, giving Simon what she thought was 'sound advice'.

> The election must be stopped . . . Can you all seriously intend a smash just now in our ranks? . . . Lloyd George has played a dog's trick on my husband. He once said that if times get tight he would try and have a smash which would be connected with his name in some way . . . if Henry dissolves and goes to the country does Lloyd George think we shall win? . . . does he want to smash the work Henry has given his life to? A general election which we shall surely lose and all our great work and fine ideas, dust and ashes. No Home Rule (it has always been the curse of our party) . . . , no Welsh disestablishment, no plural voting, nothing. Henry will go down in history as a man who allowed his most flimsy colleagues to smash him before he achieved one thing except old age pensions. People will say the renewing of [discussions about the] Lords' veto was a farce. I confess these are bitter reflections when I think of all Henry has done for others in a courageous career . . . Neither Lloyd George nor Winston care for anyone but themselves. I well understand your dislike of Winston's tall talk and even of high navy estimates. Personally I'm the most non jingo person in the world, but I am for a big navy, especially with foreigners increasing their armies . . . *do*, do stick to my husband and don't let him . . . be beaten by a quarrel of this kind.[20]

The next letter from Henry showed that the quarrel was still on and that there were no signs of it abating; in fact the situation was so bad that

Margot seriously thought of cutting short her cure and going home, a hasty act that was stopped by a more encouraging letter to say that after a long talk with Simon 'on this row with its perilous implications', Henry had decided to do nothing rash or in a hurry. Next day the Prime Minister made a strong appeal to the party not to split at such a time and on such a point.[21]

How Margot wished she had someone sympathetic with her to share her delight, but there was only Violet on a short visit. The poor girl had been appalled by Margot's audacity in writing to Simon at all. She should not interfere, she said, no good would come of it, it was none of her business and so on. They had had a short sharp quarrel in which both women gave vent to their feelings. Margot was unrepentant and thought Violet a bore. What did she know of her influence with politicians? She certainly had no idea that several times since her father became Prime Minister Margot had been consulted privately by one or other of Henry's Cabinet. Some good often came of this, for his colleagues were able to choose their moments to speak to her and she always told them the truth as she saw it. Leaving aside some of Margot's prejudices (her implacable dislike of Lloyd George, for instance) those who knew her well trusted her intuition. When it came to handling people and awkward situations, Margot's sure instinct often brought results where more orthodox methods failed.

Margot's father, Sir Charles Tennant, painted by J.S. Sargent in 1901

Mary Drew, daughter of W.E. Gladstone

Benjamin Jowett of Balliol College   Lord Curzon

Mrs Asquith as an oriental snake charmer, Devonshire House
fancy dress ball, July 1897

(Opposite above)
W.E. Gladstone with his wife and grand-daughter, Dorothy Drew,
at the Hawarden fête, summer 1894

'The Queen of the Liberal Party'

(Opposite: top to bottom and left to right)
Lord Rosebery; Alfred Milner; Alfred Lyttelton;
Winston Churchill, about 1904

May 1909. Margot's Downing Street dress show, to which she invited her friends, caused 'a good deal of comment'

(Opposite)
Margot and Puffin, *Tatler,* June 1903

(Left) 20 Cavendish Square today
(Below) 44 Bedford Square

(Left) 'A Notable House Party – Mr
Birrell and his guests at Phoenix
Park', *Tatler,* July 31, 1912.
'The above group, taken on the
occasion of Mr Asquith's recent
visit to Dublin, shows Mr Birrell,
the Chief Secretary for Ireland, and
his guests at the official residence in
Phoenix Park. The names, reading
from left to right, are (standing) Sir
Harry Verney, Mr R. Asquith,
Master of Elibank, Miss Elizabeth
Asquith, Mr H. Asquith, and Mr
Bonham Carter; (seated) Lady
Verney, the Prime Minister, Mrs
Asquith, Mr Birrell, and Miss
Violet Asquith'
(Far left) 'Mrs Asquith, the wife of
the Premier, and Miss Venetia
Stanley', *Tatler,* July 9, 1913

Elizabeth (Princess Antoine Bibesco) with her baby in about 1920

(*Left*) The wedding of Lord Glenconner and Miss Pamela Paget. Prince and Princess Bibesco with Asquith at Wells Cathedral, 1925

(Right) Margot in 1924, (Below) at a picnic, Winchester 1924 and (bottom) arriving at the wedding of Lady Ursula Grosvenor, St Mary's Church, Cadogan Street, Chelsea, July 1924

Golf at North Berwick, October 1926

(Opposite)
(Above) Asquith and Puffin at North Berwick, 1926
(Below) Asquith at The Wharf, August 1924

(Left) Family party at The Wharf, August 1926.
(Clockwise from left) 'Bongie' (Maurice Bonham Carter), Anne Asquith, H. Asquith, Violet, Mark Bonham Carter, Luke Asquith (son of Cyril and Anne), Laura Bonham Carter, Cressida Bonham Carter, Jane Asquith (in front), Margot

(Below left)
The Barn at The Wharf, June 1924

(Right) Margot with Asquith and Puffin, April 1927

(Below right)
Picnic at Glen, 1927

Margot at the marriage of her half-sister Nancy
to Captain Dugdale MP, September 1936

CHAPTER 21

Those Pulsating Days of Life

AT EASTER 1914 Asquith went off alone for a short holiday at Penrhos, the home of the Sheffields near Holyhead, to relax in the company of Venetia Stanley, while Margot stayed in London with the children, gloomy and depressed. Recently Henry had told her a little more of what he was doing, but she guessed, however, that after his return from Wales the influence of the younger woman would have begun to work again, and everything would be back to where it was before.

If there were troubles in the home, there was nothing outside to lighten her spirits. She had expected to enjoy chaperoning Elizabeth, who was now seventeen and ravishingly pretty, but Elizabeth lacked the sparkle that had made Margot so captivating at the same age, and her child's lack of enjoyment affected her too. She had taken Elizabeth to balls at Devonshire House, Crewe House and Stafford House, all now run on a reduced scale, which meant reduced fun. They had received far fewer invitations than formerly, too, and it took Margot some time to realize that Henry's Home Rule views were rebounding on her and his daughter. Many English upper-class families had estates in Ireland and strongly supported Sir Edward Carson in his determination to keep Ulster free. Cold stares and the marked drawing in of skirts were becoming usual in the Ladies' Gallery in the Commons. These wives did not exactly hiss when Asquith spoke on Home Rule, but remained so rigidly silent that their disapproval was obvious. This brought the worst out in Margot, and she was rude in return.[1]

The crowning disappointment was Elizabeth's attitude to her first season. Far more reticent than her mother, she had inherited her father's shyness, which she hardly tried to conceal. Tactlessly she made it known that she thought the young men ignorant and boorish and the girls not much better. She was not popular with her own age group and at first Margot did not realize it was because she was not good at hiding the fact that she was cleverer than they were. In Margot's day cleverness had not been something to hide; all her friends were proud of being well-read, familiar with the theatre and the opera and excellent conversationalists. Thirty years later standards had changed for the worse. The slapdash talk and unintelligible slang used by the young people Elizabeth brought home set Margot's teeth on edge. Even Elizabeth disliked modern jargon and never used it in her mother's presence. It comforted Margot to know that her daughter at least took her side; and she tried to impress on her that popularity was nothing and was generally enjoyed by those who had no strength of character and always fell in with the wishes of others.[2]

She was soon made to eat her words. In May 1914, George Curzon, one of Margot's oldest friends, gave a magnificent ball of the kind that had not been seen since 1910, to which the King and Queen and everyone who was anyone was invited. Elizabeth had recently done a 'vocation course' in Munich and Margot thought it a good idea to reintroduce her to people at this ball. Curzon was an admirer of Elizabeth's, liked her shyness and thought her both beautiful and clever; he told Margot that she reminded him of a white rose, 'pure and full of fragrance'. But when the time for the ball approached and no invitation had come, Margot asked Mrs Keppel why she and her family had been left out and was utterly astonished to be told that Curzon was so infuriated at Asquith's stubborn advocacy of Home Rule that he would not have them inside the house.[17] Frantic with rage, Margot remembered all the many kindnesses George Curzon had received both from her parents (he came to Glen as often as he liked) and from Henry and herself. The door of 10 Downing Street had never been closed to this old friend and it was not long since Curzon had unveiled a portrait of Asquith at Balliol and said: 'We do not carry our political differences to the point of obliterating personal friendship or public esteem. God forbid that such a day should ever come.'[3] That day had now come, and by his own will. But most of all Margot minded the unkindness to Elizabeth. It was her one chance to see a ball on the old lavish scale and for a change she was looking forward to it eagerly, for Margot had every right to expect that they would all be asked.

Unfortunately the Asquith family as a whole did not show that loyalty to Margot that was her due. Herbert Asquith and his wife Cynthia (who had frequently benefited from Margot's generosity) thought the ball would be all the better without her. It never occurred to either that in the circumstances it would be more seemly if they refused. Cynthia never missed an opportunity of denigrating Margot behind her back and her diary is spattered with spiteful references to her stepmother-in-law. This might have been nothing more serious than incompatibility of temperament gone a little too far, had not Cynthia repeatedly made use of Margot: she accepted money without a qualm (often complaining that it was not enough), new clothes and accommodation. Perhaps it was because she was so much in Margot's debt that Cynthia did her so much harm, and it is probably from her that many of the stories of Margot's tactlessness originated.

Margot's once enormous circle of friends was dwindling fast, as her rate of making new ones slowed down. It had been a great blow when in 1913 Alfred Lyttelton had died suddenly of peritonitis. One morning he complained of agonizing pains in his side and took to his bed, three days later he was dead; the last links with Laura were broken.

Not long before, Margot had had an unpleasant quarrel with Alfred's wife, DD, about Alfred's selfishness towards women and her sister, Charty Ribblesdale, in particular. The consequence of this was that a coolness sprang up between her and DD, and as a result Margot and Alfred never met again. Yet his death brought the two women together once more, and when DD decided to write Alfred's life it was to Margot that she appealed for stories and reminiscences of her husband before he married Laura. In turn Margot had to ask Mary Drew to help her because:

> . . . Alfred is not easy to write about, especially the years he was in love with Charty and almost lived with her . . . I kept no letters of his except one in Laura's prayer book which she put there and left me in her will . . . it would hurt DD . . . if I entered into the facts of Laura's character.[4]

Before DD wrote a word of the book Margot gave her one excellent piece of advice: 'Above all leave out all comment on Alfred's grief when Laura died.' That grief had been done, redone and even overdone so often that sensibly Margot felt the time had come to forget it. She had often tried to knock on the head the myth of Laura's saintliness too: 'Laura had a sense of humour,' she wrote, reminding DD that her sister was human, 'and a quick temper, although the "flame image" is quite true.'[5]

For Laura's sake Margot wanted to write a memoir of Alfred that was true to life, for she felt she knew his weaknesses and strengths even better than DD, but with Elizabeth still tied to her apron strings she was forced to provide endless chaperonage and could find no time for writing.

This was the first time since Elizabeth's birth that Margot had become really irritated with her daughter. Although she had gone through teenage moods of a sort with Violet, her own daughter's sulks and tantrums were far harder to bear. Besides, Elizabeth had a habit of touching her mother on her weaker spots and leaving a mark. How she wished that someone would take Elizabeth off her hands for a bit so that she could write the perfect piece about Alfred. Inspiration followed swiftly. Margot remembered Mrs Keppel, King Edward's former mistress who was now living in Holland. Elizabeth must go to her. At the very end of July 1914 Margot ruthlessly despatched her daughter (whose grumbles at the dullness of life in England were becoming louder every day) to stay with this old friend, praying that Elizabeth would find among Mrs Keppel's Dutch acquaintances some of the fun that seemed to be eluding her in England.

It is a little strange that Margot should send a treasured daughter to stay with a worldly woman like Alice Keppel, however kind, and with the added danger of war looming. Since Edward VII's death Margot would keep referring to Mrs Keppel as a 'plucky woman of fashion', whatever that may mean. In the past Mrs Keppel had certainly shown herself to be a woman who knew which side her bread was buttered, but she possessed a kind disposition and great generosity, a sure passport to Margot's heart. Moreover, she was Scottish and a staunch supporter of the Liberal party.

So to the flat plains of Holland went Elizabeth, accompanied only by her maid. By this one act alone Margot showed clearly that she did not expect war. It is even more surprising that Asquith, who knew the true facts, did not manifest some anxiety at his daughter going to a country which could be swiftly overrun should war break out. It is possible, of course, that he did not wish to arouse Margot's anxieties, but more likely that he simply underestimated the dangers. In her memoirs Margot writes that 'foreign affairs were not causing uneasiness to any of the people that I had seen'.[6] Could this possibly have included Asquith?

Three days after Elizabeth's departure, Margot read a report in *The Times* that alarmed her: On Monday 27 July Sir Edward Grey announced in the House that he had made a proposal to Germany, France and Italy to hold a conference with Great Britain, but that although France and Italy had accepted, no reply had been received from Germany. She telegraphed Elizabeth ordering her to return immediately. Ruefully Elizabeth told Mrs

Keppel that she must obey 'otherwise mother will row over for me herself'.[7]

Elizabeth brought back with her the surprising information that no one in Holland felt the slightest anxiety about the European situation. Nor, for that matter, did anyone in England, yet even with her daughter safely back under her roof, agitation seized Margot to such an extent that she repeated Cassandra-like warnings to all those friends who had children abroad and was mocked for her pains. It was only at the last minute that she managed to drag back her sister Lucy, who had one foot on the gangway of the cross-channel steamer bound for France where she was about to start a painting holiday. The astonished Lucy was entirely unaware that the sparks from the Continent could ignite a major conflagration at any moment, since she seldom read a newspaper.

Acute nerves gave Margot a strange sense of weakness in the limbs and she was unable to attend a single evening function without resting first. She said it felt as though she had weights on her head and fog in her brain, while all around her people laughed and talked and went about quite without a care in the world. Lying on her bed before dinner but with every nerve aquiver, she was sensitive to the slightest sound. It was as though muffled drums were playing through thick muslin. This had only happened to her once before and had been followed by a nervous breakdown. Suddenly she was petrified; if she collapsed now what would happen to them all? She need not have feared; events outside herself now swept her along with such rapidity that she had no time to think about her own feelings.

That same evening when Margot was wondering what the coming weeks might bring, Henry came to see her, looking graver than usual. He told her that he had sent preliminary telegrams to every part of the Empire informing all the government offices, navy, military, trade and foreign, that they must prepare for war. Two days later (1 August), Germany declared war on Russia. At once Margot's imagination began to rack her, making her nervous and shaky, for she was still not quite well. She did not see Henry all day for the Cabinet sat almost continuously, but longing for comfort she took Elizabeth to a communion service at St Paul's. She did not know exactly what she expected to find among the crowded congregation but she quickly realized with some relief that everyone was acting normally; the cool quietness of the Cathedral calmed her and she prayed fervently that if the worst happened her nerves would not let her down.[8]

The rest of the day was wasted, moving from room to room wondering what she should do for the best if war came. There were divisions in the Cabinet, she knew, but Henry had once told her that if Crewe and Grey stood by him, it mattered little if some of the others resigned. When in the course of their conversation Margot asked him if he would form a coalition if war was declared, Henry made no reply.[9]

A few days before, and without saying a word to Henry, Margot had written to John Redmond, a man she greatly admired, to ask him if he would set an example of patriotism to the Carsonites by going on Monday to the House and offering support to the Government. Fortunately these were still the days of Sunday posts and on her return from St Paul's Margot found Redmond's reply waiting for her—'I hope I may be able to follow your advice.'[10] Next day, 3 August, Redmond made a speech in the Commons, assuring the Government that they might safely withdraw their troops from Ireland and that 'armed Nationalist Catholics in the South would be only too glad to join with the armed Protestant Ulster men in the North'. Margot was thrilled but she had the sense to keep quiet about her part in Redmond's declaration.

The same day that the leader of the Irish Nationalist party was declaring his loyalty and that of his followers in the House of Commons, Germany declared war on France. On 4 August from her seat in the Ladies' Gallery Margot heard Henry tell a sombre House exactly what would happen if the reply to Grey's ultimatum to the German government was unsatisfactory. The House listened in silence, then to Margot's delight wave after wave of cheering burst out. As soon as she could get away she rushed to the Prime Minister's room where Henry waited looking grave and anxious.

'So it is all up,' I said.
He answered without looking at me: 'Yes, it is all up.' I sat down beside him with a feeling of numbness in my limbs and absently watched through the half-open door the backs of moving men. A secretary came in with Foreign Office boxes; he put them down and went out of the room. Henry sat at his writing table leaning back with a pen in his hand . . . what was he thinking of? . . . his sons? . . . My son was too young to fight . . . I got up and leaned my head against his. We could not speak for tears.[11]

That evening some of Henry's colleagues sat smoking and waiting in the Cabinet room at 10 Downing Street, waiting for the German reply. Margot came down from Puffin's bedroom, where she had prayed by the side of her sleeping son, to join them. 'The clock on the mantelpiece hammered out the hour and when the last beat of midnight struck it was silent as dawn.

'We were at War.'[12]

It was painful for Margot to take leave of old friends. She dreaded to think what would happen to the German Ambassador, Prince Lichnowsky and his wife, once back in their native land. These two staunch friends of Great Britain deserve to be remembered for the good-will they tried to generate between the two countries and for warning the Kaiser that the Germans would get the worst of a conflict with Great Britain, a warning to which the Kaiser had paid no attention. Agitated and upset, Margot rushed over to the legation in Carlton House Terrace where she found a picture of despair. Princess Lichnowsky was lying on a sofa, her dachshund in her arms, her eyes red and swollen with weeping, while her husband stared out of the window, his head bowed in grief. The two Lichnowskys had been her friends ever since they came to London and now Margot showed the depth of her affection by her spontaneous warmth and sympathy in their troubles, offering all the help she could. This display put some courage back into the ambassador and his wife. 'It will not last long,' Margot assured them, 'especially with Henry as Prime Minister and our well-equipped army.' But Lichnowsky shook his head; no one in England understood the strength of the other side.

Margot's four stepsons were much in her thoughts. All were of military age; two were married and had children. What would happen to them now? Cast down as never before, she was amazed by the cheering, flag-waving crowds in the streets, the people apparently welcoming war. The cheers went on far into the night, keeping her awake and increasing her misery. 'It was like rockets in the silent sky and I listened to snatches of God Save the King shouted in front of the Palace all night.'[13] For hysteria and false emotion, it was the Boer War all over again.

There was another problem Margot had to face quickly, but she had made up her mind before anyone mentioned the subject to her: she would not send her German governess away. This woman had been with her for years and was a much-loved member of the household. Every year Margot sent her back to Germany to visit her relations and every time she returned to England she told Margot the same thing—her links with her own country were loosening fast as her love for England and the English increased. The moment war broke out Margot's friends hastened to Downing Street to advise Margot to 'send that Hun packing', advice that she indignantly rejected.

PART THREE

War and the Aftermath

'Too much gloom lowered morale.'

CHAPTER 22

The Great Poster

BEFORE THE WAR was a month old one man's name was on everyone's lips: Kitchener. His face, with its piercing dark eyes and heavy black moustache, was reproduced on a poster, his finger pointing accusingly at his victim and underneath in large letters: 'Your Country Needs You'. It had a magical effect on recruiting. Elizabeth Asquith contemptuously christened Kitchener 'the great poster', and that is how he was known in her family thereafter.

On the outbreak of war, Kitchener was appointed not only Chief of Staff but to the Cabinet post of Secretary of State for War. Some members of the Cabinet thought Asquith rash in giving up the War Office and installing Kitchener there; Asquith himself noted: 'It is a hazardous experiment, but the best in the circumstances I think.'[1] When Margot heard of the appointment she was filled with disquiet: 'I said that . . . he had lived so much among subject races that I feared he would not get on smoothly with Europeans.'[2] Asquith had only met him once before. In 1912 *Enchantress* had stopped at Malta just long enough for the two men to have a conversation. From that talk alone Asquith had decided that 'Kitchener was the only soldier with brains since Wolseley'.[3] He backed his own judgement of the man against Margot's adverse opinion, yet he knew that Margot had been in Kitchener's company frequently on her Egyptian holiday in 1892: they had ridden together, played tennis together and held long conversations *à deux*. Kitchener had been delighted to escort Margot Tennant to fashionable functions when Alfred Milner was tied up with work. Nevertheless her opinion of him was clear—he was a man to avoid. She states her reasons for disliking him in her diary: 'He was suspicious, ruthless, cold and given to long silences.'[4] Her dislike—perhaps even fear—of him, hidden at the back of her mind for so many years, came to the surface when she heard of his appointment. She blamed Henry for not asking her what she thought of him; he had often praised her for giving him excellent advice in the past, intuitive though it was.

However, Kitchener's popularity with the British public was instantaneous. He was exactly what they imagined a great war leader to be: upright, suave, unsmiling, and strict, 'just the man to stand no nonsense from the Hun'. He even endeared himself to them when he let it be known that the war would be a long war, at least three years, unlike the newspaper forecast that it might be over in six weeks. Kitchener's public popularity affected Margot's opinion of him at the beginning of the war and her feelings about him fluctuated strangely. She could not help admiring his industry and single-mindedness, but in the end she knew that her first instincts had been right. He had been respected but feared in Egypt and his methods of dealing with men, learned when he fought with the French army in the Franco-Prussian war, had not altered. Writing to Alfred Milner at the end of the Boer War, Margot asked him why Colonel Kitchener (as he was then) was loathed by his men: 'Is it a sign of power or of weakness? Perhaps brutality would be a better word.'[5] She feared Kitchener would make mistakes. He very quickly made a big one when he refused to put Lord Haldane's well-trained Territorial Army into the field.[6] His stiff-necked attitude to innovation caused both resentment and confusion. New recruits were not treated much better. They flocked to London from all parts of the country full of patriotic fervour to join Kitchener's army, but there was no system of registration ready so they were forced to return home. However, Lord Kitchener's reputation stood the strain.

Milner had told Margot that Kitchener had one great defect: he was incapable of delegating work. He even took on duties which belonged to McKenna at the Home Office, leaving McKenna twiddling his thumbs.[7] It was a serious matter too that Kitchener did not get on well with the generals. Asquith could not understand why, but Margot knew: Kitchener continually criticized them and complained about them behind their backs. Margot wondered why he did not replace them with better men if they did their job badly and said so openly, but no one listened. Kitchener's lack of understanding of his colleagues and subordinates was to be a terrible handicap to the war effort.

Most of all Margot blamed Kitchener for snubbing the Irish when for once they showed goodwill. She complained to Henry that by refusing to allow the Irish to join British regiments Kitchener had undermined her hard work in winning Redmond round to the Allies' side. 'They would only bring their priests with them and start wholesale proselytizing,' Kitchener said.[8] One afternoon he called on Margot at Downing Street and with all the eloquence she could muster, she begged him to let the Irish have their priests, but he refused to listen. This obstinacy alarmed Margot. She was certain that this way of treating the Irish was a terrible mistake. In her opinion the Irish question was now far more potentially dangerous than either Kitchener or Henry suspected. Hurt feelings could grow and become explosive when it was a question of pride and patriotism. Margot guessed that Kitchener's attitude to the Irish was the result of a discussion with Carson as well as of his own deep-seated prejudices. Kitchener belonged to an earlier generation before self-determination was thought of, and would never recognize the legitimate desire for independence in Ireland, Egypt or India.[9] The very fact that he was in such a position of power weighed on Margot's mind. Asquith can be forgiven if he accused her of being obsessed by the man.

Margot was soon given a chance to see just how bewitched some members of the government were by the new War Minister. At a dinner party at Downing Street the talk turned on the new head of the War Office: how well he was doing, how splendid that the Prime Minister had placed him in such a key position, what calm, what sagacity and what popularity! Suddenly a voice was heard to say: 'How about making him Viceroy of India after the War?'—'An excellent idea!' With a great effort of will Margot remained silent, although she could not hide her expression of dismay. Next day she wrote to Lord Crewe who she knew had great influence with Henry:

> I wanted so much to talk to you about Lord Kitchener last night, just one word. I know him *very well*. He is a natural cad, tho' he is so remarkably clever. I know if you and Henry send him to India you will regret it all your days. Hardinge is the man to send and he is young and straight and a great gentleman. Never have dealings with a liar however clever. K's appointment would be looked on as a breakdown of the civil service system . . .[10]

She hoped her letter was incisive enough to spike Kitchener's guns. There was some satisfaction in hugging the secret to herself: she knew Crewe would not talk and India might have cause to be grateful.

Margot had great faith in Sir John French, that 'dear old man', as she always called him. The day before Sir John took the British Expeditionary Force to France, Margot gave him tea and cake and confidences in her drawing-room. They talked in a leisurely way for over an hour and French found his way to her heart by praising Henry—it was a good thing for the country that such known lovers of peace as Asquith and the Liberals were in power, otherwise the British people might not have accepted this war so readily. He praised the Prime Minister's speeches, which had inspired the whole nation. When they parted he kissed Margot on both cheeks and she wept a little on his shoulder, while French squeezed her hand to show he understood. She walked with him to the door, giving him a parting present: a small silver-gilt figure of a saint 'as a talisman'. In return she asked him to give her some personal trifle to remind her to pray for him. The shock of the war had sent Margot back into the secure past of the old Glen days with Laura, when praying for those in danger or misfortune was commonplace. Later French sent her his general's badges, cut from his horse cloth: 'it was the sort of thing you said'.[11]

French's appointment was popular, which pleased Margot since she had pushed so hard for him. She did not give a thought to his age; at sixty-two he was the same age as Henry, which seemed to her the prime of life. Nor did anyone remember that he had not distinguished himself in the Boer War and that one of his colonels (Douglas Haig) had said he was useless in a crisis. A crisis soon arose which shattered the complacent slogan 'over in six weeks and the Boche knocked into a cocked hat'. After a short encounter at Mons on 23 August 1914 French's army withdrew to the Marne. The news was a terrible shock, not least to Margot, who loyally defended the general to a white-faced Prime Minister: there must be some good explanation. There was, but it was not as good as Margot would have liked: the retreat was made to prevent the army falling into a trap which French only learned of at the last minute. A week later, when news came that French intended to retreat still further and entrench his army in the Le Havre peninsula, as Wellington had done at Torres Vedras, she told Henry in a voice of despair that perhaps the appointment of French was as much a mistake as that of Kitchener. In reply Henry delivered a short homily on the foolishness of jumping to conclusions —doubtless French had a plan which would reveal itself in good time.[12]

At first it had been disturbing to have unfamiliar khaki-clad figures everywhere and to hear the sound of marching feet, sometimes at night when all was quiet. Margot quickly got used to it, but she could never understand why the men looked so cheerful. She could see danger signs everywhere. The whole Cabinet had fallen under the sway of Kitchener's commanding personality as if they were a lot of raw schoolboys: he had made them believe that the war could not be carried on without him. Already his name was synonymous with victory and Margot feared that she was the only one who found such arrogance painful to look on. After listening to Henry singing his praises, she begged him not to regard the man as their saviour. He was flawed. Of course power went to his head, as Margot knew it would. On a mission to Paris to confer with French, Kitchener travelled in full Field Marshal's uniform instead of in civilian clothes, as befitted a War Minister, a reminder to all and sundry that French had not yet attained that rank. French was deeply offended and the Cabinet could not understand the failure of the meeting.

From her vantage point in 10 Downing Street Margot watched Kitchener like a hawk, hoping that he would overreach himself before he did irreparable damage. She was incensed by his casualness and his habit of keeping even the most vital information to himself. Late on 24 August, for instance, at the height of the anxiety over the fate of the British Expeditionary Force at Mons, Kitchener could not be found, although it was known that an urgent telegram from the Front had arrived at the War Office. He had gone off without telling even the Prime Minister that British casualties were lighter than feared and that French's army had managed to escape the threatened encirclement. Asquith's muttered 'this must not happen again'[13] had little effect on the great man, now well into his stride.

This time Margot said nothing to Henry, for she felt Kitchener had condemned himself and any words of hers would be superfluous. She knew that a bed and a bath had been installed in the War Office with someone always on duty so that in times of crisis the Secretary of State (whose whereabouts must always be known) could be contacted at once. Now, at the first emergency, neither of them could be found. Margot thought this the strangest thing to happen to a disciplinarian like Kitchener.

*

What sort of man was Asquith when war broke out? He had proved himself to be a highly successful peacetime Prime Minister—the Parliament Bill among his greatest achievements. With the right backing he might also have achieved much in Ireland. He was a man of peace who hated quarrels and conflict and because of this his talents were not suited to leading a nation in war. Up to the very last minute he had hoped that by some miracle peace could be maintained even as the Germans were advancing into Belgium, but he rejected as dishonest and cowardly any attempt to evade British treaty obligations. His great fear, like that of other Prime Ministers before him, was a war on two fronts—rebellion in Ireland at the same time as a major conflict with Germany—a terrible possibility which Kitchener's lack of political acumen almost succeeded in bringing about. Although sixty-two years old, Asquith seemed to be in excellent health. Trials and tribulations did not get him down easily; his daughter-in-law, Cynthia, frequently remarked with some astonishment as the horror on the Western Front mounted that the 'Pip Emma',* as she fondly called him, 'looked mellow and serene and as leisured as ever'.[14]

From 1908, when he succeeded Campbell-Bannerman as premier, Asquith had not had an easy time. One strike after another, all difficult to settle, Home Rule a perpetual thorn in his side, disputes galore about vital weapons for defence, reforms which meant increased taxation and the struggle with the House of Lords. All had taken their toll—how could they not?—while good living, heavy drinking, late hours and no exercise had all weakened him physically, although as yet he showed no outward sign of it. Always inclined to be self-indulgent, his consumption of alcohol had increased along with his responsibilities. It was a period of heavy drinking throughout society, especially of brandy and whisky, but as time went on Asquith's consumption began to be remarked. Arthur Benson recalls dining at the National Liberal Club one night when Asquith was also there: 'He ate, drank and smoked deep—5 or 6 cigars, much champagne, port and liqueurs.'[15] On another occasion in 1916 he drank several glasses of brandy after dinner and although unsteady on his feet, his head was perfectly clear.[16] He was able to hold his drink well, yet Margot worried and pleaded in vain for him to cut down, but he only laughed. In desperation she resorted to watering the brandy decanter, a trick he soon discovered.

* For P.M.—i.e. Prime Minister.

Physically Asquith was a heavy man who moved slowly like a dinosaur, turning his whole body and not just his head when he wanted to look round. His figure and the look of contentment on his face indicated ease and wealth. During the first years of the war his favourite forms of relaxation were a gentle drive in his motor car every afternoon, reading a favourite novel in the Athenaeum or playing bridge after dinner. It was his custom to go to his club after his drive, read and write letters and after a cup of tea emerge refreshed and ready to return to his onerous duties. Asquith was one of those fortunate people who could keep work and play in separate compartments.

This was all very well until war tension mounted. As British forces lost battle after battle and the Prime Minister's habits began to be known and criticized, the nation's confidence in him dropped steadily.

CHAPTER 23

A Rudderless Ship upon Unknown Seas

THE WAR WAS not going the way the nation expected: the German advance could not be halted and the hoped-for victories were few and far between in those early months. When Antwerp, the last of the Belgian towns to resist, was captured there was universal gloom. News of the number of casualties—17,000 in the early stages of the war—was received with horror-stricken disbelief, followed by a sense of bewilderment: Margot, for instance, was appalled and incredulous when told by General Sir John Cowans that 6,000 British casualties at the defence of Namur was small.

All the generals were welcomed by the Prime Minister's wife who was always prepared to give them dinner and a bed without prior notice. Whenever she could she questioned those home for a few days from the Front, and not one showed the smallest gleam of optimism. General Cowans told her that before the war ended the losses on both sides would be tremendous. When she asked 'How long will it last?', he and the others all now gave her the same answer—'a very long time'. Yet every day there were reports in the press of good progress by the British, so that Margot did not know what to believe until Henry enlightened her. She had gone to the country for a few days when he wrote to say that he was disgusted with the optimism of the newspapers. Margot bowed to his great knowledge but still thought that 'too much gloom lowered morale'.

When Puffin came home for the Christmas holidays she tried to keep newspapers hidden but he invariably discovered them, took them away to his room and devoured every word. He said little of what he thought to his mother. Puffin was working for his Winchester scholarship, but the war had made him lose interest in learning and he kept asking his mother how soon she thought he could join up. He longed to be in uniform like his brothers and he made Margot's heart leap with terror many times a day when he talked of guns and ships and wondered out loud whether the navy would suit him better. Margot's plan was to keep him away from London, especially Downing Street.

Recently the Wardenship of the Cinque Ports had become vacant and Asquith played with the idea of taking it for himself, but the King persuaded him not to incur the enormous extra expense: the upkeep of the grounds of Walmer Castle alone cost at least £800 a year. So the Wardenship was given to the Earl of Beauchamp, who kindly allowed the Prime Minister to use the castle whenever he liked. Walmer was just the place for an imaginative boy (the Duke of Wellington had used it often when he was Warden), but the guns from the Front could be clearly heard and Margot wondered if it was too close to the firing line for safety.[1] Puffin soon settled the matter by refusing to spend his holidays there. The sound of gunfire set his teeth on edge and stopped him working. Margot had been the same as a child and for that reason had refused to go out with the guns at her father's shoots. She did not want Puffin to endure the kind of secret phobia that had been with her for many years, ever since she had discovered that her favourite gardener at Glen had been made stone deaf by the guns in the Franco-Prussian war: for her to be shut into a world of her own would be torture.[2] The problem soon solved itself. In 1912 Margot had purchased The Wharf, on the Thames near Oxford. The new house, so near London and yet far enough away, became a haven of peace for jaded nerves. Here Margot kept open house for family and friends who needed a rest. At The Wharf comfort, good food and companionship were always to be found, and when war broke out Margot felt with some pride that she was doing something towards victory by sending people back to their work in London refreshed and in better shape.

If people looked askance at what they thought were her idle ways, Margot's own conscience was clear on this score, since she had chosen to do what she did best. She could neither sew, cook nor dress wounds, and in any domestic role she was useless. It had been suggested to her that she might like to help turn an Oxfordshire country-house close to The Wharf into a convalescent home for officers, but she had declined. She was quite the worst person for such a job since she had never arranged anything more exacting than a stall in a bazaar to raise money for charity. Then she had been young, did not know her own limitations and was full of crazy ideas that people thought clever.

In August 1914 Margot had been summoned to Buckingham Palace by Queen Mary, together with several wives of men in public life, to discuss what they could most usefully do to help the war effort. It was not a gathering to inspire anyone. The Queen was shy and stiff, spoke in a strange detached voice which held neither warmth nor enthusiasm, but covered up her embarrassment when faced with row after row of strange female faces. All she could think of to say was to ask whether any of the ladies present could do needlework for the soldiers. There was a long pause, and then Margot sprang to her feet to point out that it would not be a popular move to compete with the shops who were in for a hard time. She offered to make 'surgical shirts' which even the large stores did not sell. After the meeting dragged to a close, she rushed to a seamstress she knew and gave her a large order.[3] Margot had come to the conclusion that Queen Mary was one woman she would never get to know. She saw the Queen's many good points, admired her character and the way she never spared herself, but any attempt to get closer was repulsed. The Queen had not dropped her iron reserve for the whole two hours of the meeting. With so many relations in Germany, Austria and Russia, her sufferings at the thought of brother fighting brother were great and the more discerning side of Margot guessed her distress. She knew the Palace disapproved of her, yet she felt compelled to say something and as she made her departing curtsey she murmured: 'It may all be over very quickly, ma'am.'

More than once Margot had wondered why the Queen gave such á poor impression of herself. She knew her to be efficient and capable, likeable and sympathetic too, she had been told, yet whenever Margot spoke to her she was cold and unfeeling. How surprised Margot would have been if she had seen Queen Mary at a quite different meeting next day. She had called together on her own initiative a large number of unemployed women to give them real work and real wages for assistance in the war effort, with the motto 'Work not Charity'. Cool, yet kindly, she unbent as she talked of her plans and put them into effect at once.[4]

Of course Margot was criticized for 'doing nothing'. But, recognizing her shortcomings, she knew she was far more use raising the fallen spirits of the wounded than dressing wounds. When at Walmer, she never missed motoring with Henry to Lympne on the Kent coast, where the government had rented a house so that Asquith could confer with generals and interview men returning from the Front away from prying eyes. When Henry was busy in this way Margot visited the hospital and encouraged the wounded. Another useful job she undertook was to motor to Folkestone and Dover on a Sunday morning to visit and comfort batches of

bewildered refugees, sick at heart after losing their homes and possessions. Not a soul guessed that the war, talking to the severely wounded
and the dying and writing to their wives and girl friends afterwards,
strained her nerves and affected her sleep. She saw that her activities did
some good and never thought of stopping them.

All the Asquith and Tennant males of the right age were soon in
uniform and Margot did her best for every one of them, putting them up,
together with their wives, when on leave, and lending money if they were
short, so that they could have a good time. She called it 'lending' to avoid
hurting sensitive feelings, but she never expected to get a penny back, and
never did.

There was plenty of entertainment in London for those home on leave
who wanted to forget the horrors of the trenches. Theatres, concert halls,
cinemas were all doing excellent business, while the war had given a new
lease of life to restaurants, which were crowded night after night with
officers and pretty girls applauding the cabaret that had suddenly become
an essential part of an evening out.

Elizabeth Asquith was among those pretty girls who danced the night
away. She was also to be seen at the fashionable *thés dansants* that since
the start of the war had become popular. In one way Margot hoped very
much that her daughter was having the good time that she had missed
when she came out. Nowadays mother and daughter seldom met since
Elizabeth slept until noon or later and then was out for the rest of the day
and most of the night, always with a new companion; even Elizabeth
herself seldom knew their proper names. It was always Bunny, Pooky or
Bubbles or something Margot thought too ridiculous, like Jack Tar. It
made her sad that a girl as sensitive as her daughter should find in wartime
the fun that had eluded her as a débutante. Margot was thankful that she
herself had not had to grow up when life was artificial and moving too fast
for enjoyment.[5] In a burst of confidence Elizabeth had confessed that she
had no intention of falling in love with any of the boys she went around
with, it only made for unhappiness. Remembering her own carefree
youth, Margot felt profound pity for her young daughter and this helped
her to be more lenient with her and the strange ways of her friends.

Not all aspects of the war were hateful to Margot. She very much
enjoyed standing at the open window of her sitting room on a mild
autumn morning, listening to the military bands playing round the

recruiting tents on Horse Guards' parade, yet paradoxically she disliked the effect bands produced. At first she listened because they played cheerful tunes, later she would remember that they were there to do a job that led to destruction and death. Like the Pied Piper they called to entice the youth of Great Britain away—would they ever be seen again?[6]

When spring came Henry's two eldest sons were still in training camp in England, kicking their heels with nothing to do, bored and demoralized, forced into tedious duties that in no way improved their efficiency or prepared them for the sort of trench warfare that was blasting their friends to eternity.

The war had been going long enough for xenophobia to seize many of even the most reasonable people. When after the first battle of Ypres the casualty lists were published, it began to be said that if England had not foolishly opened its doors to the Huns (many of them now suspected of heinous acts of treachery) the war might never have started at all. By 1915 life was dangerous for those with foreign names, no matter who they were or how long domiciled in England. The first Sea Lord, Prince Louis of Battenberg, a patriot and a man of the highest integrity, was so hounded by the press that he was forced to resign, all his contributions to the navy counting for nothing because of his German origins. His place was taken by Lord Fisher.

This injustice shocked Margot profoundly. The treatment meted out to Prince Louis was the signal for many more decent citizens to vilify other decent citizens if their origins were German, no matter how many generations had been born in England. Windows were broken, slogans painted on the walls of houses, children bullied at school and whole families subjected to catcalls in the street. Many a small shopkeeper was ruined when his customers melted away, haughty with pro-British fervour.

Margot was furious at such shameful and cruel treatment of innocent citizens, built on unbridled emotion of the worst kind. She little knew that before long she too was to become a target of the same hate and derision. She had always been drawn towards people who like herself were outspoken and honest and (perhaps mistakenly) she had always encouraged her friends to tell her the truth. During her time in Downing Street as the wife of the Prime Minister, some of them unhesitatingly abused this privilege. One morning late in 1915 a deputation of her friends came to her, demanding to know why she did not send her German governess away, either to an internment camp, or better still back to Germany where she belonged. Did she realize that this woman might be a spy? The whole affair was so ridiculous that Margot could not help laughing, especially when they said that no one with a German name should be allowed to enter the doors of the Prime Minister's official residence.[7]

Because Margot refused to do what was asked, rumours now began in earnest . . . Her daughter was secretly engaged to a German (when things went badly at sea, her fiancé was said to be a German admiral), the Prime Minister had shares in the German armament firm of Krupps, Margot sent food-parcels to German prisoners-of-war in which secret plans of British movements at sea were hidden, she played tennis with German prisoners-of-war at Donington Hall and her servants were all in German pay. . . . Up to a point Margot was able to ignore such rubbish, but when a minor minister was hounded out of public life because his wife had gone to see an old friend's son, now a prisoner-of-war in England, she began to worry that if such absurdities were allowed to continue, Henry might be pushed out of office because of her. This thought upset her deeply —Cynthia Asquith put it mildly when she said Margot was 'very strung up about it all'.[8] In 1916 she courageously brought an action for libel against the *Globe* newspaper and was awarded £1000 damages, a large amount in those days.[9] This put a stop to the yellow press, but nevertheless she was deeply hurt that her friends could misjudge her enough to carry on a witch-hunt against her and other innocent families.

A new bitterness entered Margot's heart, hardened her and never completely left her. As a girl and young woman she had been idealistic, and this idealism had stayed with her, despite the cynicism of the society in which she lived. She could not understand and therefore found it hard to forgive the lack of trust between friends, especially those friends she liked and held in high esteem. The memory of her sufferings and that of so many she did not even know, was still fresh in her mind when she wrote in 1922:

Our treatment of our aliens was worse than that of our allies. We crushed their businesses, ruined their houses, boycotted their families and drove their wives into asylums. Not a voice was raised from Christian pulpits, but prelates were photographed on gun-carriages chatting to soldiers on the glory of battle.[10]

Margot bore hostile criticism bravely, never letting her enemies see how much they hurt her, although she could not ignore the injustice. If she was indifferent about herself it made her angry to have Henry attacked and before long she had to steel herself against this too. When the war went badly the government was assailed from all sides and Asquith was beginning to show the strain. The British fleet was not so invincible as people believed and when one of the glorious Dreadnoughts was sunk Margot lay in bed weeping for the beautiful ship, the men who went down in her and the widows and children left behind to cope with life alone. When Lord Fisher came to luncheon in Downing Street soon afterwards, Margot was not impressed: no man in his position should take his responsibilities so lightly. 'He was at his gayest and coarsest,' said Margot to Violet.[11]

From the moment Turkey entered the war on Germany's side in November 1914 the Cabinet was split between 'Easterners'—those who wanted to create a new front against Germany from the eastern Mediterranean —and the 'Westerners', who wanted all the troops they could get for the war in France. Winston Churchill's plan for an attack on Turkey through the Gallipoli peninsula carried the day, and one winter morning Margot and Violet went out to watch the King review his troops on the Downs before they embarked for the Mediterranean. Her stepson 'Oc' Asquith was one of those in the parade, and she was overcome with pride and patriotism.

But the initial naval assault on Gallipoli was a failure and Margot prayed it would not have repercussions for Henry. The same tormented feelings racked her when the shell shortage scandal burst on an unsuspecting public in May 1915. Gas had been used against the British forces at the second battle of Ypres; the casualties had been devastating, and Lloyd George blamed Kitchener for the shortage of British munitions. The attack was fuelled by the Northcliffe press and rapidly grew into an outcry against the government's conduct of the war. Margot ordered the papers to be brought to her room as soon as they arrived each morning, and at once began a feverish hunt for criticisms of the Prime Minister. If necessary she could produce proof positive that the shell shortage was not Henry's fault, for she distinctly remembered one day at Walmer Castle hearing him imploring French to postpone further frontal attacks until the arsenals in England were in a position to supply him with more munitions.

French's answer had been glib: Margot had heard him say the same thing often enough before—'they have sufficient for their needs; the operations that I contemplate are not extensive.' Now that he was proved wrong, it was Henry who was blamed: believing French, he had made a speech in an arms factory praising the workers for keeping up the supply of shells. So conscientious himself, he did not doubt for one moment that French's assertions were correct. Colonel Repington, military correspondent of *The Times*, seized on this speech as an excuse to quote letters sent home by men at the front, complaining bitterly of the shortage of ammunition. Some of these letters had been printed before, but Asquith had taken them for nothing more serious than natural grumbling. He held the firm belief (unfortunately so often proved unwise) that once generals had been chosen, it was the duty of the government to back them to the hilt. So the discontented letters and vague rumours were ignored.[12]

The newspapers did not waste a moment in taking up the cry 'our men cannot defend themselves', followed by heartbreaking stories of 'gallant soldiers in the trenches' exposed to crushing bombardment without being able to retaliate and ruthlessly sacrificed in attacks which for lack of ammunition could not be pressed home, while lethargic politicians sat in Whitehall obstructing those who saw the truth and were pressing for action.[13] Margot knew perfectly well that Henry never read criticisms of himself, but even so she tried to hide them from him 'in case', while each member of his staff devoured every word.

For a strong-willed, outspoken woman, Margot behaved uncharacteristically. She did not warn her husband of the dangers ahead, although she saw them clearly enough. Instead she did a thing she had never done before: she suffered in silence. In the past she would not have hesitated to urge him to get rid of French immediately, now that he had been proved untrustworthy, and not to allow the high command to remain as it was. Asquith did not act because he thought it might undermine morale —already very low—if he dismissed French, and because he did not know that French's popularity was sinking fast. French was later replaced by Haig, but before this he had received a tremendous dressing-down from Margot. Writing to her about it, he called it 'a terrible "Damning"', but did not say a word about her effrontery in taking upon herself the role of Prime Minister.[14]

The newspaper campaign about the shell-shortage fuelled the agitation in the spring of 1915 to force Asquith to agree to a coalition in order to make the direction of the war more effective. Margot hated the word 'coalition' and feared that the demand for it was a sign that people thought that Henry had failed and should be replaced as Prime Minister. Instead of telling him of her fears, she again behaved uncharacteristically and kept her worries to herself, becoming edgy and irritable in consequence. When asked by a friend why she disliked a coalition so much, she answered promptly 'because it does not suit Britain, it is unEnglish',[15] whereas deep in her unconscious mind lay the unvoiced fear that Henry was not any longer up to it and that others suspected this too.

In the small hours when she could not sleep, she thought out various schemes to circumvent what she saw as a 'plot'. As a prelude to this she begged Henry to silence Bonar Law, who was pressing for a coalition as the only recourse after such a disastrous year. Margot could hardly bear to see him so deflated, and wrote in high indignation to DD about 'a deliberate attempt by the press and certain persons to entangle the Prime Minister in a Machiavellian personal controversy'.[16] In an effort to help, she tried to enlist the support of friends to back Henry and the Liberal party, a self-imposed championship of the Prime Minister that was most unwise. Many of her letters for the period are so emotional as to be almost unintelligible, and the word 'plot' constantly occurs. In this excitable state she worked on Henry until he too saw the Liberal party and the Liberal movement dissolving under the pressures of war.[17] She knew who was the villain of the piece; it was the all-powerful Northcliffe (whose empire included the *Daily Mail*, the *Daily Mirror* and *The Times*), and she was enraged by odious hints in his papers that the Prime Minister was inefficient and slack. She resolved to fight to the last ditch to save Henry because (as she later told Sir John Simon) 'where his personal interests are concerned, he won't lift a finger. If it's to save a colleague from resigning . . . he will act at once, but for himself, never'.[18] If she could discredit Northcliffe as well as saving Henry, so much the better.

Here was a chance for Margot and Violet to join forces to defend the man they both loved, but each had different views on how this should be done. A cool temperament as well as good nerves were needed to fight in Violet's way, whereas the hot-blooded Margot could never think out tactics rationally when her feelings were roused, and more often than not hit out blindly. Violet thought her stepmother was going about things in the wrong way: she should be more reticent, not show her hand so openly. To this Margot retorted that her way was better than fiddling while Rome burned. However, she took Violet's warnings to heart, and the next batch of letters to politicians was written in a more relaxed tone, although the gist remained the same.

The shell scandal was at its height when on May 15 Lord Fisher—never won over by the Easterners—dramatically resigned in protest against the government's decision to send reinforcements to Gallipoli. Four days later Asquith yielded to pressure to form a coalition, and Bonar Law and the Unionists entered the Cabinet.

During these same critical weeks Asquith was distracted from his public duties by private anxieties: not, however, anxieties about his wife or children, but fears that he might be about to lose his confidante Venetia Stanley, to whom he had become so attached that it would hardly be too much to say that his mental stability depended on her. At this critical moment, Venetia wrote on 11 May telling him that she had become engaged to Edwin Montagu, now Financial Secretary to the Treasury. The suddenness and baldness of the announcement reveals Venetia's desperate need to be rescued from a situation that had begun to frighten her; there is no evidence that her affection for Asquith had lessened. It was a stunning shock and Asquith reeled from the blow: 'As you know well, this breaks my heart.'[19] The loss of Venetia undoubtedly shook Asquith's judgement during the critical days when he was grappling with a major political crisis, but before the day was out he had written no less than three times to her sister, Sylvia Henley, and was well launched into a correspondence of a similar kind to that which had just ended so abruptly.

Shortly before the affair came to its sudden end, Violet had decided to go to Alexandria to nurse. All the arrangements had been made and her farewells said when she returned home to find a note on her pillow from Asquith: 'Don't leave me now.' So devoted was she to her father, and so evident his anguish, that it only took her a moment to make up her mind to cancel her plans.

The extent to which private grief affected Asquith's public conduct is impossible to measure. An attempt has recently been made to minimize it,[20] but the language of his letters makes it difficult to believe that he was not at the least very seriously distracted during weeks when a host of problems with which he had not hitherto dealt energetically enough were clamouring for his attention. Asquith bowed to the demand for a coalition only a week after Venetia's thunderbolt struck him.

How much did Margot know of the Venetia affair? This was a question which those who loved her often asked each other, but they never asked Margot because they realized that she could only endure it by ignoring it, or at least seeming to ignore it. There is ample evidence that she did in fact know all about it, and that it hurt her deeply, but almost none of the evidence is to be found in her surviving letters for 1912–1915, numerous though they are, and it is a reasonable deduction that she was trying to give the impression that the affair was of little consequence to her. The letters betray her real feelings nevertheless, for they are far fuller of complaints of 'lowness' and 'sleeplessness' than ever before—the effect, quite obviously, of the nervous strain under which she was labouring.

Ever since her marriage Margot had known of her husband's liking for the society of young women, but at that early stage she was more amused than disturbed by what their circle called Asquith's 'little harem'. She liked to feel that she was broad-minded, and many years later wrote that 'no woman should expect to be the only woman in her husband's life . . . I not only encouraged his female friends but posted his letters to them if I found them in our front hall'.[21] As time went by, however, she could not fail to realize that the Venetia affair was different, since this was plain from her husband's changed attitude towards her. In March 1914, for instance, when the affair was some two years old, she wrote to Edwin Montagu complaining that Venetia was teaching Henry 'to avoid telling me things. I'm far too fond of H to show him how ill and miserable it makes me'.[22] In any case, Asquith could not have hidden the affair from her if he had tried; regular drives and daily letters could not have been disguised for three whole years.

That Margot wanted to restrict knowledge of the affair to the smallest possible circle and to put the best construction on it, is demonstrated by a remarkable memorandum she sent to J. A. Spender in 1932, just before he published his biography of Asquith and just after the publication by Desmond MacCarthy of Asquith's letters to Hilda Harrisson.* Publication of these letters caused a furore among Nonconformist Liberals, to whom this side of Asquith's nature was a complete revelation. In Margot's memorandum both Venetia and Sylvia Henley are mentioned (it was impossible to pretend to Spender that they did not exist), but only lightly

---

* Hilda Harrisson had succeeded in the 1920s to what had once been Venetia Stanley's position as *confidante*. This was an affair of his old age and was in a much lower key.

and in passing, preliminary to a lengthy discussion of the Hilda Harrisson friendship. The proportionate allocation of space tells its own tale: something had to be said, because of Desmond MacCarthy's book, but even at that late date Margot was anxious to suppress knowledge of the first and far more serious affair as far as possible. She succeeded remarkably well in protecting her husband's good name. Spender did not use the memorandum, and made no reference to the three women, and it was not until fifty years later that the publication of Asquith's letters to Venetia Stanley at last revealed the full extent of his infatuation—but by doing so showed how deeply Margot had been hurt.

The memorandum runs as follows:

I know nothing more important to the happiness of married life than the recognition of both husband and wife of their separate personal affections.

If a woman really loves her husband, she should not be surprised if other women—when of superior character—care for him also in the same way. The same may be said of men. Jealousy is natural to women of temperament, but it should be controlled if they wish to retain the devotion and confidence of their husbands.

I have observed in my own experience the women who from vanity and over-confidence in their own attractions have compelled their husbands to engage upon mild deceptions which when discovered have made both of them miserable. A little jealousy may be trying, but as against this, where there is none it may be humiliating. Unless a woman can keep her husband's interest and affection by her own personality, I do not think she has an exclusive right to it. She is in the strong position and therefore can afford to be jealous and the women I have seen who allow themselves one or even more male diversions while excluding their husbands from a similar privilege, have not enjoyed the full happiness and confidence of married life.

My husband told me that before he met me his life had been lived for the most part among interesting men and he had few intimate women friends. He had not the leisure or opportunity of meeting interesting women . . . and he did not care for anyone but his wife and her sisters . . . Nor indeed after he met me did he care for many . . . only those who were my earliest women friends and his own relations and therefore became part of our lives. Our sex are apt to be intellectual snobs. I watched with amusement our flimsiest female friends fluttering round my husband in the early days of our marriage without making much impression on him. But I was so anxious that he should share the enjoyment that I derived from a society that was not always intellectual that I begged him to be less critical and more responsive. The very fact that he did not care for women in the accepted meaning of the phrase made him attractive to them. It was not till fifteen years after our marriage that he formed the two friendships with women that gave him the most pleasure in his life. The first was Venetia Stanley—his daughter Violet's greatest friend—who before her marriage spent most of her holidays with us in Scotland and elsewhere. Her parents Lord and Lady Sheffield were intimate friends of ours and when I was ill the Asquith children had long visits to the Sheffield family at Penrhos. I suffered so much from my confinements that I seldom accompanied them but both Venetia and her sister Sylvia* became friends of mine and it was only years later that my husband developed a deep affection for Venetia. Her cleverness, enterprise and good humour, as well as her talent for writing letters and genuine affection [attracted him]. But when she married our secretary Edwin Montagu who joined Mr Lloyd George when we left Downing Street, she moved in a different circle and we saw little of her.

His other woman friend whom he saw and corresponded with till the end of his life was Hilda Harrisson. She lived near my sister Lucy Graham Smith at Easton Grey so we had every opportunity of meeting her. Mrs Harrisson's husband was killed in the war and she was left with two small children and little money. When she left Wiltshire she took a house near The Wharf at Boar's Hill, Oxford, and we saw her very often. My husband appreciated her devotion and her companionship was a refreshing rest from the turmoil of Downing Street. Her equability of temper, Liberalism and sincerity endeared her to both of us. They played bridge, and golf and chess together at a time when political events made us unhappy. I was only too glad to see the pleasure he took in her letters and companionship. H.H. always told me when she intended to go for motor drives or meet him in London and never at any time concealed from me her devotion to him. Neither she nor I took the smallest notice of those who in a misplaced desire to be loyal to me thought that their affection for one another was hurting his reputation.

*   Mrs—later Lady—Henley.

Rumour is always rife over a Prime Minister's reputation, but I have lived long enough in the world to see rumour wrong over almost every political person and event. I had always had intimate men friends of my own and though in the first years of our marriage my husband had taken exception to some of them, we knew, loved and understood one another [rest of sentence missing]. After the confidence he had shown in me in our early married life, I felt it would have been a lack of generosity on my part to have withheld mine when in his later years he developed a lasting affection for Hilda Harrisson.[23]

A good deal more of what she probably felt can be read between the lines of her contribution to a collection of essays by a number of women entitled 'Myself when Young' which Margot edited in 1924. She mentions no names but the clarity and precision of the phraseology strongly suggest that she had her own case in mind:

I think that jealousy is the cause of half the unhappiness in the world. It is more of a punishment than a crime, but worse than this, it distorts all sense of proportion, destroys the serenity of the soul and has marred some of the most promising married lives. If a woman has sufficient love for her husband she is selfish and vain to expect no other woman to care for him. She should welcome the friendships which give him pleasure, even if they are temporarily tinged by what is called 'physical attraction'. It is contrary to all wisdom to expostulate or enquire into every movement of the man you love. As his wife and the mother of his children, you will always be in the strongest position and if you are patient and keep him amused he will ultimately tire of his passing passion. If you do not conquer your jealousy you will prompt him to deceive you and alienate the affection which is the foundation of your home and without which your married life must be a failure: you would be a rudderless ship which sails dangerously upon unknown seas![24]

CHAPTER 24

The Principle of Give and Take

DURING THE DAYS when Asquith was forming the coalition his morale was at its lowest ebb. Sick at heart about the unhappy turn in his personal affairs, he did not like what he was doing and did not do it well. He always looked on the reorganization of his government as 'the most uncongenial job that it has ever been my lot to carry through'.[1] He had had to give way under pressure and in a letter to Sylvia Henley he described briefly what took place. 'They got together a meeting in one of the committee rooms which was attended by nearly all the good men on the back benches who expressed themselves with the utmost freedom. Duped by the government, treated like dirty ciphers etc etc.'*[2]

In the moment of crisis Asquith made many mistakes and showed callous disregard for his colleagues. He agreed to drop Churchill because the Dardanelles plan had failed and gave in to Bonar Law's demand that Haldane must go because the Unionists refused to work with him. Asquith never remembered that he owed it to his oldest friend to explain to him in person why he had to go; instead he left him to learn the news from others.[3]

Margot, who knew nothing of the manner of Haldane's going, was anguished that he was no longer working with Henry; while he was a member of the Cabinet she felt that at least he had one loyal defender. She gave Frances Horner a touching testimonial to Haldane's abilities, for like many others she was bewildered by what she mistakenly thought was his refusal to stay with Henry in his hour of need: 'He has made an expeditionary force more perfectly trained and equipped than any body of men that ever left our shores.'[4] Cynthia Asquith describes in her diary the awful effect the dropping of Haldane had on Margot: 'He was the best Lord Chancellor we ever had, but more than that he was her friend and

---

* This was one of the three letters Asquith wrote to Sylvia Henley on the day he received news of her sister Venetia's engagement.

now that he had gone, she lay on her bed and sobbed and appeared at dinner that night looking a wreck.'[5] Margot felt that Churchill too had been needlessly sacrificed to Tory prejudice and she was disgusted that none of his friends lifted a finger to defend him. Violet explained the meaning of the word 'coalition' bitterly to Churchill: 'It is the sacrifice of one's friends to the blind prejudice of their enemies—what is called the principle of give and take irrespective of quality or justice or even expediency.'[6]

Churchill had a brave and loyal wife who wrote to Asquith while anger was hot in her heart. It was a letter the Prime Minister never answered, nor did he show the slightest understanding of her feelings at the shock of hearing that her husband had been undeservedly sacked. Asquith had so lost grip on good sense and kindness, even decent feelings, that he told friends that Clementine Churchill's letter was that of 'a maniac'.[7] Ironically, when the same fate befell Asquith the following year, it was the turn of his wife to write frantically here, there and everywhere in a frenzy of indignation alerting friends to 'plots', 'enemies' and 'revenge' as she sought allies to get her husband reinstated. Although she did not get her wish, old friends answered kindly and in perfect understanding of this loyal reaction.

The coalition government began its task of trying to win the war with a violent attack on certain members of the former government by Lloyd George, now Minister of Munitions. He accused them of neglect in not increasing the supply of guns and shells, and threatened resignation unless the whole direction of the war was changed. The speech was greatly praised in the press, and although it contained no open abuse of Asquith, Margot thought she could read between the lines and feared the worst: Lloyd George wanted to chop Henry into little pieces.

Lloyd George's attack coincided with a series of reverses on the Eastern Front, where the Russians were being beaten back by the German troops. To Margot the Eastern Front was as far away as the moon, and it was only important to her because of the effect it might have on Henry's future. Asquith was a 'Westerner' and his decision that no troops must be moved from the Western Front was applauded in the press. That lifted Margot's spirits for a moment, but everywhere she went she heard Lloyd George's name spoken with praise and Henry's supporters seemed to be melting away. The King was said to like the fiery Welshman and the press had taken him up in strength. Among those still ready to come to Asquith's defence was Lord Haldane, who publicly answered some of Lloyd George's accusations against the Government. In answer to a note of gratitude from Margot, he called on her and told her bluntly: 'X—— and Co. are out to smash the Prime Minister.'[8] (When she published her autobiography in 1920 she could not print the name, but the inference is obvious.)

But Henry seemed to lack the will to defend himself. When he showed her the draft of a speech he was to deliver to munitions workers at Newcastle she thought it lacked the power the moment and the subject required. She told J. A. Spender: 'If his speech at Newcastle is not a punchy, fighting speech he will fail however fine, however wise, however perfect it may be. If he shows no indignation, no snap, he is DONE.'[9]

Lloyd George's bombast and Henry's refusal to stand up for himself maddened Margot. As far as possible she kept her fears to herself (Henry was now confiding only in Sylvia Henley) but it meant that she was living on her nerves again, as she was inclined to do in times of crisis, tearing herself to shreds, so that her judgement was affected and she could no longer think rationally. In the old days there would have been a large number of friends to console her and, what was more urgent, keep her on a steady course. Now she felt that she could trust no one.[10]

For some months Margot had been greatly perturbed by the uneasy feeling that someone was selling Cabinet secrets to the press, someone close to Henry, perhaps, who might be posing as a friend for the sole purpose of worming information out of him. She believed that the row about munitions had come about through some person or persons on French's staff 'falsifying the truth by supplying the press with misleading information'.[11] She would have been horrified if she had known that there were many who thought she was the guilty one. All they had to go on was the erroneous belief that those who enjoy talking can never keep a secret. They did not know that a secret was sacred to Margot; she had never betrayed a confidence in her life. Besides Henry told her nothing, not even trivialities now, and she no longer had close friends in the Cabinet. Curzon (with whom she was still cool), Lloyd George, Churchill, McKenna, Runciman all came to Downing Street, but all they wanted from Margot was her dinners: she had the best cook in London. Sir John Simon was still a close friend, but he was discretion itself and he had been so busy recently that she hardly ever saw him. Fortunately she never heard these calumnies and before long they died down and were forgotten.

Asquith was now paying the price for years of ignoring criticism. The patience of the British public was growing thin; not without a touch of bitterness Asquith called them a 'fickle lot'. First they welcomed the war and the quick victories they were sure would follow, then when positions fell and the losses mounted, they were startled and shocked and looked for a scapegoat. Asquith's phrase 'wait and see', which Margot insisted had been uttered in the Commons as a threat, quickly became a derisive catchword: newspapers quoted it, Members of Parliament quoted it, peers in the Upper Chamber quoted it, and so did the man in the street. Margot had heard a general quoting it in her presence. She felt sure it was all a widespread conspiracy to oust Henry from the premiership. Behind her back, her friends were shaking their heads and asking each other if the Prime Minister was losing his grip. They were already saying that he ran the war like a government department, from nine till six. J. A. Spender, Asquith's official biographer, makes rather too much of the extreme rapidity with which the Prime Minister worked, and defends his 'faculty of relaxing the strain' by playing bridge and golf while the fate of the country was in the balance; but he gives no evidence of his speed of work and forgets that it was the length of time Asquith spent on the golf course or at the bridge table which was noticed and commented on adversely.[12] If in consequence there were intrigues afoot he refused to notice them; Margot let it be known that she knew, but that Henry could rise above such things: 'My husband, although an excellent judge of men and events, despised suspicion and abhorred intrigue.'[13]

When Lady Tree asked him if he took an interest in the war, he laughed heartily and later repeated her remark as a good joke, but it never occurred to him to look on the remark as a warning. If he did his duty, he felt, it was his own business how he spent his leisure. More used to the ways of the world than her husband, Margot saw how mistaken this was, and feared for him. But instead of upbraiding him smartly she hotly defended him, and made the ridiculous assertion that they were both so worked off their feet with trying to win the war that some nights they never took their clothes off.[14] Needless to say no one believed her.

In twenty-one years of marriage they had never been so far apart. At Violet's wedding in November 1915 Margot tried her best to look as if she was enjoying herself, but her thin, white face told another story. She had little support from her daughter or stepdaughter.

A year earlier, in December 1914, Margot had undertaken a brief visit to the Western Front. She had met the King and Queen of the Belgians at Lord Curzon's country-house. The Queen had been incredulous at Margot's prediction that the war would last for at least two years. The King and Margot got on splendidly; he showed his surprise that she had such a thorough grasp of what was happening and invited her to come and see the 'fighting front' for herself.

It was a strange invitation and stranger still that Margot accepted and Asquith let her go. But he was so taken up with troubles in his Cabinet that—according to one friend of Margot's—he seemed to be unaware of what his family were doing.

One of Margot's fellow guests at Hackwood happened by a lucky chance to be Major Gordon, secretary to the Duke of Wellington, who was himself going to the Front shortly. He offered to escort Margot and she gratefully accepted. The two of them set off one bitter December morning, a day of sweeping rain and threatened snow, the worst weather for years, the papers said. The Admiralty yacht *Princess Victoria* that was to take them across the Channel soon ran into a gale and Margot was promptly seasick. The ship had to slow down because of enemy mines and take a serpentine route through the locks into Dunkirk harbour, which was followed by a long exposed wait outside the town. The only lodgings Major Gordon could find were comfortless and dirty, while mice and indigestion from her tasteless supper kept her awake all night.

When Margot emerged from her room the next day she looked a comic sight in what she told Major Gordon was her 'Glen' attire—short tweed skirt over leather breeches, thick jersey, woollen scarf and fur coat with a Belgian soldier's forage cap on her head: 'All very ugly but businesslike,' she remarked briskly to Gordon as she handed him one of her two brandy flasks. In her autobiography, Margot says both of them carried wooden crosses; Margot's for Lord and Lady Lansdowne's son who had been killed at Ypres, and Major Gordon's for the Duke of Richmond's son. Thus loaded, they piled into a shaky Ford car that was to take them on the next lap of their journey. There were many hardships ahead, especially for a delicate woman. It was intensely cold, there was little to eat and only hard beds in a wooden hut to lie on, but Margot had no difficulty getting to sleep that night, despite the continual sound of gunfire which mingled with a terrific storm blowing in from the North Sea. At daybreak they rose—Margot dressed by the light of a torch—drank tepid tea and were taken at breakneck speed along an icy road. It was depressing to see houses and churches either completely gutted or damaged beyond repair, trees and hedges burnt and whole fields churned up. All was desolate, deserted, forgotten. Tears sprang to Margot's eyes as she gazed at the wholesale destruction. Thinking of those lying dead all round her she understood the truth of something she had once said in irritation to Violet: 'Live your life, don't waste it.'[15]

This moment of weakness soon passed. While separated for a time from Major Gordon, Margot endured a taste of enemy fire with commendable courage: 'Two Belgian soldiers asked me if I was not afraid to stand in the open so close to the German guns. I said not more than they were.'[16] The King of the Belgians was quartered nearer the Front that she expected, living in wretched conditions, yet he did not complain as he told Margot that he wanted to live like his men, without luxuries or privileges of any sort.

She was thankful to be back in England but she believed her sight of the Western Front had changed her. The memory of what she had seen remained vividly imprinted on her mind. A year before she had opened at random the Bible which she always kept on her bedside table, and had found that she had picked on Revelation xii, 12: 'Woe to the inhabitants of the earth and of the sea! for the devil has come down with you having great wrath, because he knoweth that he hath but a short time.' She wrote in her diary:

This is an accurate description of what is happening today, in this frightful war with its aeroplanes, submarines, poison gas, grave digging, bombs and general massacre and mutilation. But are we so sure it is only for a short time? or that the devil was not among us before?[17]

Asquith too had crossed the Channel, to St Omer to visit the army camps. From Ypres he wrote to Margot: 'Through glasses one could see the English and German trenches running parallel, not more than 100 yards apart. Not a soldier was visible, and except for a little cloud of shrapnel in the sky pursuing an aeroplane, not a shot was fired.'[18]

Unlike Margot, Asquith travelled by train in comfort, able to read in the saloon and repose at night in a comfortable sleeping-car. The food too was excellent. Margot thought his journey very dull indeed and took a sly relish relating her adventures. The most extraordinary fact about her trip is one she does not mention—her ability to put up with hardship. Thin, frail and often ill, Margot nevertheless showed the real toughness of her constitution by cheerfully enduring discomforts without complaint. Everyone in her household was amazed, and it was only her husband who thought nothing unusual had taken place.

CHAPTER 25

Wait and See

BY NEW YEAR 1916 the look of London was changing. Margot noticed the difference suddenly when walking home one morning by herself: every fit man of military age was in uniform, and there was not a civilian in sight. The wounded too were everywhere, reminders of man's inhumanity to man, in wheelchairs, on crutches, many with bandaged heads, and some with a leg or an arm missing. On the whole they seemed cheerful enough, but Margot was quick to sense that more had despair in their eyes than smiles on their lips. Most affecting of all, Margot felt, were the new recruits, mere fresh-faced schoolboys, looking as though they had not yet started to shave. The wish to do something for these boys seized her, and immediately she was struck with an idea: why not take batches of them to the theatre or the cinema and give them tea at Downing Street? Charles Hawtrey was playing at Drury Lane and Gladys Cooper at the Haymarket, and if she could get tickets she would put her scheme into practice right away.

The first venture was a huge success: Margot enjoyed the performance as much as the men and it gave her real pleasure to watch them devour her excellent tea. Violet and Elizabeth were astonished to see how well Margot got on with these boys; her lack of condescension and natural manner at once did away with all shyness and she quickly got them talking as she moved among them, plying them with cake. Next time, by way of a change, she took them to a cinema, and flanked by khaki, she was able to nerve herself to watch a film of the first battle of the Somme. 'It was really horrible,' she told DD,[1] not without a note of satisfaction in her voice as she remembered that she had watched it without once closing her eyes.

The year 1916 started badly. Oscar Wilde's literary editor, Robert Ross, who was a friend of the Asquiths, was accused by Lord Alfred Douglas of indulging in homosexual practices. Ross was prosecuted and lost the case.

Douglas then demanded through a newspaper that Asquith should publicly denounce Ross and forbid him ever again from entering 10 Downing
Street. Asquith (probably pushed into it by Margot) organized a testimonial for Ross to which several well-known writers (Shaw, Garvin, Wells
and others) put their names, and in the next Honours list gave Wilde's
publisher a baronetcy. With her idealized view of friendship, Margot was
delighted by Henry's prompt action, which demonstrated to the country
that the Prime Minister was a man who stood by his friends. Douglas,
however, had more slights to pay off and had not done with the Prime
Minister and his wife yet. He published a satirical poem 'All's well with
England', a clever attack on Asquith's weaknesses, which was gleefully
read by all Asquith's opponents.

The best policy, Margot decided, was to shrug off the whole affair.
Everyone knew that Lord Alfred Douglas was mad. If they took him
seriously people really would begin to think that there was something in
his accusation. Asquith could not take the same light-hearted view and he
began to look white and strained, which in itself seemed like an admission
that Douglas was striking home. No one in the Cabinet mentioned the
matter but Asquith knew that this was not because they had forgotten it.
At the end of January Margot wrote to Sir John Simon, telling him that
Henry had taken the matter too much to heart and that it was having a
bad effect on him:

> Henry said to me with passion in his voice: all my colleagues lack
> imagination, they are all self-centred . . . it is very depressing and I
> confess it has been a shock. He looks old and I cannot forgive the bother
> and trouble he is having from newsmen . . .[2]

Unaccustomed to disappointment, unused to failure, Asquith had no idea
how to fight back, but stood bewildered and perplexed, surrounded by the
empty panoply of his former glory. Before January was out, he was taken
suddenly ill in the night. He called Margot, who found him looking
ghastly; indeed, she feared that he was dying. Her relief was overwhelming when the doctor told her it was nothing more than the strain of 'much
worry and heavy responsibilities'. After sleeping for thirty-six hours he
was back in harness but Margot could not throw off her anxiety and at
moments she was distracted with misery, afraid that Henry was suddenly
a spent force, afraid for herself, her family, her friends and the young men

who might soon be dead. So many of their friends' sons had died and she and Henry had cried together for them, yet 'people dared to say he did not care'.[3] Every hand seemed against them and Margot was full of self-pity, saying that even the strangely erratic course of the war was blamed on Henry.

Worse was to come. Serbia was overrun and her army chased into the mountains of Albania, just as Lloyd George and his fellow Easterners had predicted, and in December 1915 Asquith had reluctantly consented to the evacuation of Gallipoli. The manpower shortage was severe and the government was accused of doing nothing to alleviate it; conscription was advocated as the remedy and the old cry of discontent was heard again loud and clear: 'the government has no policy'. Some put it more personally—'the Prime Minister cannot make up his mind'. Margot knew that he found the idea of forcing young men to enlist repugnant. Kitchener was against conscription too, but for different reasons: conscripts would make bad soldiers, and more recruiting drives were the thing. The Church should do its bit with strong hymns like 'Onward Christian Soldiers' and patriotic sermons. When the Cabinet was forced to go forward with compulsory service whether they liked it or not, the result was several instant resignations: Simon, McKenna and Runciman would have nothing to do with it. Asquith was aghast at the thought of losing McKenna's support and Margot wrote to his wife Pamela, begging her to 'talk Reggie out of it'. Simon got a letter from her too. 'It is with the deepest regret I heard your decision is final. It seems so cynical that just when Austen [Chamberlain], Selborne and Curzon are threatening resignation because Henry won't go far enough, you should leave because he had gone too far . . .'[4]

Quite suddenly at Easter 1916 rebellion broke out in Ireland.

At first details of the uprising were hazy but it soon became clear that during the night of 20 April a German auxiliary disguised as a neutral merchant ship, carrying arms and ammunition to Ireland, was intercepted and sunk. On the same night Sir Roger Casement, a Dubliner who had devoted himself to the Irish cause since his retirement from the British consular service in 1912, was landed in Kerry from a German submarine. He was instantly recognized by a coastguard, arrested, and soon tried for treason. On Monday 24 April a body of Sinn Fein volunteers seized the post office and other public buildings in Dublin, looted and set fire to houses and murdered British soldiers in the streets. Reinforcements were rushed to Dublin and Belfast from England with Sir John Maxwell in command, and after six days of fighting the rebellion was suppressed and its leaders arrested.

The uprising came as a total surprise to Asquith, but he took it coolly: 'This business in Ireland, tho' it has a comic side is a real bolt from the blue . . .' he wrote to Sylvia Henley. 'The rebels seem to have plenty of rifles and will do a lot of sniping from windows and barricades. I am afraid it will be rather a bloody affair. . . .'[5] By the time Asquith went to Dublin to confer with General Maxwell and the Viceroy, Lord Wimborne, it was already too late for the Home Rule Act, Asquith's way of preventing the Nationalist movement going over wholesale to Sinn Fein. A number of executions had already taken place, causing him much disquiet, although General Maxwell thought himself lenient. The hastiness of the sentences might have caused a furore in England too, had not the Battle of Jutland on 31 May, with its heavy losses, temporarily removed Ireland from the picture. *The Times* gave great prominence to what it regarded as a naval disaster—hoping, Margot guessed, to finish the Prime Minister off at a stroke. When the number of cruisers and destroyers lost at Jutland was published, there was a violent national reaction, so intense and lasting so long that Margot began to feel in despair—would nothing go right again?

In the hope of settling the Irish question, Margot proposed that Sir Edward Carson should come over to England to thrash out the whole matter face to face, but Henry rejected this as 'foolish and a waste of time'. She wrote to Lewis Harcourt exasperatedly that Henry would not consider the idea for a moment: 'He says nothing would come of it . . . but it is the only way.' She sensed that he had thrown in his hand from the beginning and was saying to himself: 'Since nothing can be done, why waste nervous energy in trying?'[6]

Casement was found guilty of treason and Asquith signed his death warrant without a word to Margot. He could not face her scorn that it was inhuman to send such a man to the gallows. Liberality was needed here but Asquith showed little of it.

Asquith knew very well that Margot was passionately interested in everything that happened in Ireland, an interest that had begun in Gladstone's day when she had courageously argued with the one politician who might have made a difference to that unhappy land. But he never mentioned his Irish problems to her—instead he poured them all into the ears of Sylvia Henley, an intelligent enough woman but too young and unversed in the ways of the world and of politics to be able to give him wise advice. So Margot was never given a chance to persuade her husband to be merciful. Deeply religious, she did not believe in taking life and Asquith knew this, but he had the diehards in the Cabinet to contend with and thought he could manage Margot's wrath better than their fury. He did not see that he should have shown clemency in his own interests, if nothing else. When the news broke many Liberals were shocked and turned against him, and thus he sealed his own fate at the same time as that of Roger Casement. Some hint of this may have got through to him when it was too late. 'Ireland is a country of mirages, never more elusive than when you think you have her in your grasp,' he wrote to Sylvia Henley in May, 'therefore to any sensible politician caution is necessary. Tread carefully, must be the first thought of anyone who attempts to settle Irish affairs.'[7]

Margot herself never completely understood why Asquith sacrificed Casement when he had ordered General Maxwell not to put the rebellion down with too heavy a hand and only send to England those against whom there was a real case. 'I asked them all whether they had any complaint to make of their treatment in prison and they all said no, except one man who asked for a pillow,' he wrote to Margot.[8]

H. A. Gwynne made much of Asquith's 'awkward handling' of the rebellion in his paper the *Morning Post*, taking the line that it would not have happened in the first place if the Irish had been treated with more sympathy earlier on, and that Asquith's muddleheadedness was becoming a danger.[9] With a sinking heart Margot forced herself to read the article to the end. Its meaning was all too clear to her—Henry should step down and make way for somebody else better able to deal with these problems. She had not yet met Gwynne, nevertheless she could not let his abuse of her husband pass without comment, so she wrote to him. It was not a good letter: '. . . the Irish muddle is *pas rire*. Neither you nor anyone else need be afraid of my husband being a greater danger than what you have already.'[10]

Of whom was she thinking? Had she begun to fear Lloyd George in earnest? A year before she was already wondering if the little Welshman was out to replace Henry, and sooner rather than later.

CHAPTER 26

Things Will Straighten Out

SPRING WAS LATE in 1916; Margot could see no sign of it in her Downing Street garden as she looked out of the window of her sitting-room and longed for winter to end. How dreary life had become, the glitter and the glow all gone. There were Zeppelin raids over London, and watching one of these raids from her bedroom window Margot had been fascinated by the sight of shells bursting like stars, leaving behind white puffs of smoke in the sky. She had been told that despite the sinister noise they made as they whistled through the air, they did little damage.

That spring a cry arose that no one had ever expected to hear—Kitchener must go. Had the Prime Minister the nerve to remove this all-powerful man? The Secretary of State for War had become almost impregnable; he held so much power in his hands that if he went the entire Government might collapse. Despite criticism in Parliament, his prestige in the country was still immense, and the War Council too leaned heavily on him, believing with a kind of blind faith that Kitchener was the rock without which the army would crumble.

Kitchener's overbearing attitude was conspicuous even on social occasions. At luncheon at Downing Street he liked to dominate the conversation, crushing those who dared to argue with him by a look or a word. It was, Margot thought crossly, as if she and her guests were his generals, sitting round a table at a briefing when all they had to do was to listen respectfully and nod in agreement. She would have struck him off her guest list but Henry forbade it. At an informal luncheon with the whole Cabinet she noticed to her consternation that the moment Kitchener appeared, the entire lot became diminished and seemed to cower before him. Even Henry shrank to half his size and had little to say.[1] Such a state of affairs could not be right. Even when the Cabinet at last realized that Kitchener had outlived his usefulness to the nation, they could not steel themselves to action. So there he remained, an immovable machine, inefficient, outdated.

Henry's calm belief 'it will all work out for the best' was no comfort to Margot, who thought it the philosophy of despair. When by the spring of 1916 Kitchener became offensive to her, she complained to Henry that he behaved as though the Prime Minister's house was his own and she only the housekeeper. Henry replied wearily. 'Things will straighten out as they generally do, if you give them time and don't strike before the hour.'[2]

Would leaving Kitchener where he was, doing as he liked as though he were God, work out all right too? Margot thought angrily. She little knew how much more power he had wished to gather into his hands and had nearly obtained. In December 1915 Asquith told Sylvia Henley that he had had 'a curious talk' with Kitchener:

> If you were here I would go over the ground with you . . . He wants now to leave the War Office and become a kind of generalissimo with a world-wide range, Robertson as directing operations from here—this would solve a lot of difficulties if we could precisely define the functions of the G. [Generalissimo] and a very big G. I am most attracted by the idea.[3]

In May 1915 Kitchener had received an invitation from the Czar of Russia to visit his country in order to give some much needed advice on military matters, but it was not until June 1916 that he was able to go. Not a single member of the Cabinet raised a finger to stop him, indeed it seemed as though they were all holding their breath in case he changed his mind. No one said he could not be spared now. On the morning of 5 June he set sail in the *Hampshire*, one of the cruisers that had escaped damage at Jutland. That night the ship struck a mine and sank, and Kitchener was among those drowned.

Margot heard paper boys shouting the news on her way to a christening and could not believe it. It seemed impossible that anyone would dare. Naturally it was considered only good form to talk of 'England's terrible loss', shed tears and remember his good points. Henry and Margot went to Kitchener's memorial service which, Margot recorded, was beautifully done and in a way a man of his lack of religious faith would have liked.

Since the Zeppelin raids began, restaurants were half-empty of an even-ing, cinemas and theatres were suffering in the same way, while society had found a new form of entertainment—supper at midnight in the cellars with champagne and any extra goodies that could be found. It had become quite a craze. Margot loathed it: the damp, the sordid conditions and the horrible feeling of claustrophobia that had attacked her the only time she tried it put it beyond the pale for her at once.

The only bright spots for her were the week-ends at Walmer Castle which to her surprise she greatly enjoyed, now she was used to the noise of the guns and had been assured by the War Office that the Castle was out of range of shells. Henry too was cheerful when he remembered that his four sons were still in England, although Raymond (now transferred from the Westminster Rifles to the Grenadier Guards) was due to be posted to France at any moment. Over the years Margot had come to see what a remarkable young man Raymond was, and there seemed nothing he had not achieved at Winchester and Balliol. He was the last person in the world to be marked out for war service and Raymond never ceased to be amused at the idea of himself as a soldier. 'I am joining the army,' he had said in 1914, 'because the alternative is to spend the rest of my life in explaining why I did not.'[4] Academic success had come to him so easily that it had drained him of all ambition, and he had, without any particular eagerness, followed in his father's footsteps and become a barrister, with a vague idea that later on he might take up politics. Gradually he and Margot had become friends, despite arguments and criticisms on both sides, for Margot thought she saw Raymond as he thought he saw her, with a very clear eye. He was never quite sure whether she was laughing at him or not, and no one, least of all an Asquith, liked to have his self-esteem punctured too often. When left to themselves they enjoyed long conversa-tions together.

When he was at the front, Margot was the only one of the family to write to him regularly, except for his wife, Katharine. Her letters to him were different from her usual illegible scrawl and were composed with some care. She gave him family news, gossip about his friends and her own observations on people and events, which she hoped would amuse him. They evidently did, for the last letter he ever wrote to her (from the Ypres Salient on 5 July 1916) began: 'I was delighted to get your excellent letter . . .'[5] The mixture of boredom and discomfort in the trenches irked him more than the dangers, and Margot understood this, as she did the fatalistic view he took of life, like so many of his generation.

On 15 September 1916 the second big push on the Somme began. In the first wave of the attack Raymond was killed. It took two days for the news to reach The Wharf where the Asquiths were at the time. Dinner was over, bridge was in progress, and the war was for the moment relegated to the background. Puffin was home and Margot's thoughts were on his return to Winchester next day, rather than on the battlefields of France. When she was called to the telephone, Margot says, she had a premonition it was about Raymond and that he was dead. White and shaken, she had to find Henry and tell him as well as she could, but all she could say between sobs was 'terrible, terrible news'.[6] It was a blow from which Asquith probably never recovered. Although they were not close, he was proud of his son and in his heart loved him dearly: 'Whatever pride I had in the past,' he wrote some years later, 'and whatever hope I had for the far future, by far the largest part of both was invested in him. Now all that is gone.'[7]

After a short respite to collect herself after Raymond's death, Margot carried on as before and was much criticized for having her usual luncheon parties at Downing Street and week-end parties at The Wharf. Most of all she was censured for returning to her guests that same night and telling them what had happened in a flat, matter-of-fact voice, then immediately turning to a friend and asking him to amuse them with card tricks—so merciless is the world to those whose reactions to grief are different from the conventional. She herself saw the whole tragic episode differently: nothing could bring Raymond back, the agony of his loss had to be borne and so there was no sense in disrupting other people's lives because she and Henry were suffering. She had loved Raymond, and his death was a blow that she scarcely knew how to endure. In these circumstances she did her best to be normal. She showed her suffering to her friend DD. 'If you only knew how wonderfully fine . . . his life has been, you'd know what pain his death is to me.'[8] Later they were told that Raymond had been brought in mortally wounded to a field hospital where he was given morphia. He asked for a cigarette but never smoked it. He was killed in the traditional senseless way—leading his men over the top.

When everyone had gone, Margot buried her head in her pillow and sobbed 'what a waste, what a waste'. Cynthia Asquith, who had come to The Wharf next day for comfort, agreed with her: Raymond should have had a staff job where he could use his brains. But as she pointed out, at that stage in the war, no one of any sensitivity would take a staff job any more, so invidious had it become: 'All the best brains chucked away in the trenches.'[9]

'Lieutenant Asquith killed in action' was front page news; the House of Commons was particularly kind and Margot collected cuttings for Henry to read when he was less grief-stricken. Their first thoughts were for Raymond's wife, Katharine, but like many war widows she was 'inaccessible to any sort of comfort'. Margot was in despair for her and she sensed that Raymond was the kind of young man, popular and full of talk, who would be missed more than most. When he was alive, wherever he happened to be, life took on a rosier hue: 'Darling, brilliant, magically charming Raymond,' Cynthia wrote. 'How much delight and laughter goes with him. It seems to take away one's last remains of courage.'[10]

Lloyd George was to be Kitchener's replacement at the War Office. The announcement brought a loud shriek from Margot: 'We're out, rather Bonar Law than that little cad.'[11] Asquith, heavily backed by wife and family, wanted Lord Derby to replace the late Field Marshal: the fact that his graded scheme of recruitment had failed was no reflection on his abilities. Margot hoped that by procrastinating Henry could have slipped Lord Derby into the post as more congenial to everybody, using him as a 'kind of figurehead' while Henry did the real work and had the real power. She forgot that she was already complaining that Henry was overworked, so how he was to manage such an onerous job as well as all the other things he had to do, she does not say.

She invited Lord Derby to luncheon to sound him out and was astonished to be told that he did not want to be Secretary of State for War. He hated war-mongering and to follow in Kitchener's footsteps was not at all to his taste. Instantly Derby fell from favour; he had let Henry down. Such selfishness in times like the present was disgraceful. Without wasting a second she despatched a telegram to Lewis Harcourt who she knew would be staying with Derby in a day or two, pressing him to be Secretary of State for War instead. He too declined—after all the job had already gone to Lloyd George—but to pacify Margot he promised to speak to Derby, pointing out that he should not think of himself, and was rewarded by a somewhat cryptic telegram from Margot: 'Feeling disgusted with Derby—am truly sorry, congratulate you on your pluck.'[12]

As the year wore on Northcliffe steadily increased his vendetta against Asquith; there was no softening because he had lost his eldest son. He used *The Times* and the *Daily Mail* as his mouthpieces, but as Asquith made a point of never reading anything about himself—he merely skimmed the papers for small items of news—the worst of Northcliffe's abuse was lost on him. It was Margot who read and trembled with apprehension. She noticed that the closer the friendship between Northcliffe and Lloyd George, the more difficult did Lloyd George become with his Prime Minister. Lloyd George was a dangerous rival; she had sensed this from the beginning, but there was so little she could do to stop him. However, she thought of one thing and at once put it into action, although it was a very long shot. She wrote to her friend Lady Wemyss asking her if she could muffle Northcliffe through her admirer Arthur Balfour, who had replaced Churchill at the Admiralty. It was no use and the situation began to deteriorate rapidly.

It had always been Margot's custom to pay great attention to criticism. She had had plenty of it in her time and it often made her furious by arousing her most passionate feelings if she felt her critics were unjust; but she was too honest to disregard all of it and too self-assured to be ashamed, and because she was a strong character she never minded owning she was in the wrong. Once after a rebuff from Lord Selborne she wrote disarmingly that he was right of course, but 'unfortunately I am one of those unlucky women who don't ever improve . . .'.[13]

In one respect she could not improve; she was irritated by Henry's lethargy, the way he thought things were all for the best as they were, and now and again her exasperation spilled over. If she mentioned Lloyd George with a critical tone in her voice, he rebuked her for prejudice. If she related some gossip she had picked up when lunching with friends, he refused to listen. Nor would he pay attention when she told him that the loyalty of some of his colleagues was suspect. She accused him crossly of not wanting to face the issue because it presented him with too many problems. When she said she saw the writing on the wall, and begged him to do something, before it was too late, he accused her of being petty. 'There seem to have been several entries for the competition to replace my husband in 10 Downing Street, but I think it only fair to say that the victory was won by the favourite,' she wrote some years later.[14]

In being fair to Lloyd George and giving way to a false sense of loyalty, Asquith was unfair to Margot, whose warnings he dismissed as feminine nonsense. Lloyd George, he said, was well placed in the War Office, no one better 'because a man of his education and experience would understand . . . the mentality of military men'. The War Office satisfied him completely, he wanted nothing more.[15]

CHAPTER 27

No one is on My Side

AS AN UNMARRIED girl, Margot had said that to have a husband and home of her own did not attract her, but that if she should marry it must be to a man who was in a position of power, so that she could have a hand in the events of the day. This was not social ambition—that had been satisfied by the time she was twenty—but a strong desire to put her talents to good use. Gladstone had told her when she was engaged to Henry (tipped even in 1894 to become Prime Minister) that he knew of no one more suitable to be the wife of a leading politician, and Margot believed him. She saw herself as Henry's second pair of eyes, his most faithful and alert watchdog, supporting and encouraging him and keeping his spirits up in times of crisis. She welcomed the challenge, praying for one thing only, the blessing of good health.

Yet in some ways she was quite unfitted to be the wife of a man holding high office, since she had insufficient nerve to face with any degree of optimism the uncertainties of life. The power and the glory were meat and drink to her, since she understood through instinct and experience how to handle them—they never went to her head, although she drew every ounce of enjoyment from them. It was a different matter when it came to intrigue, quarrels, disloyalties and sudden shocks like dismissals or resignations, which she met with fear and trembling followed by a nervous malaise that lasted for weeks. When the coalition was formed in May 1915 she felt, like Henry, that it was the end of everything, and each of them reacted badly on the other. Because her distress showed on her face, the whole political world could see how the business had upset her. Thus instead of stiffening Henry's back she unconsciously weakened him by losing her nerve. At those times she blamed herself for her nervous reaction and knew that if it happened she was quite unable to control it. Nevertheless, the loss of nerve served as a useful excuse when her husband turned to other women for comfort and told them his fears and difficulties; she assured herself that it was natural that he should do so because she was emotionally involved, and they were not, and thus they could give him sounder advice. Henry would probably have agreed with her, had she been bold and discussed it with him, but both knew that to bring these 'friendships' out into the open was dangerous.

When conscription was fiercely debated in the Cabinet in November 1915 Asquith did not seek Margot's help but poured out his troubles into Sylvia Henley's ears: '. . . think carefully about what I told you,' he wrote, '(locked in your safe and secret bosom) of the big things that loom and call for discussion. . . .'[1] Sylvia was able to give him what he so badly needed, attentive sympathy without nervous reaction, for was she not his 'very dearest who makes the desert bloom like the rose'?[2] Those who knew of these friendships blamed Margot, but for quite the wrong reasons: she was, they said, too selfish, unsympathetic and self-centred for a man carrying heavy burdens.

By 1916 Margot's friends were disappearing fast, a sad fact which left her lonely, perplexed and anxious, yet paradoxically she did everything to antagonize the most loyal of her own circle. She had become worse than ever at concealing her thoughts and would blurt out home truths better left unsaid. What was just forgivable in a young and vivacious girl became most unattractive in a middle-aged woman, especially one in Margot's position, where tact and restraint were called for. That she behaved badly was often due to the fact that her nerves were frequently on edge from her incurable insomnia. Later when it dawned on her that she had been offensive, she would dash off disarming letters of apology: 'I am so sorry I was rude and hurt your feelings . . .'[3]

Unfortunately, few gave her credit for such candour; but many more bore grudges and spread stories against her, for she sometimes revealed a marked lack of plain common sense. It was most unwise, for instance, to tell Violet that Winston Churchill was a cocky young man, too boastful by half, for Violet got her own back by passing the remark on to Churchill, which of course widened the gap between him and Margot. Something in this remarkable young man irritated Margot and she could not stop herself needling him whenever they met. She could not forget that in her presence he had once said that he hated the sight of ugly women. It may be that he did not have Margot in mind, but she was certain that she was his intended target. All her life Margot insisted that looks mattered not at all to her, that it was brains and personality that counted,[4] yet in middle age she became sensitive about her appearance, though in fact her face combined with her unique dress sense set her apart as an unusual and elegant woman.

The fact that Churchill had a high regard for Lloyd George must have played a part in her dislike and whenever she disparaged the man whom she was soon to look on as the usurper of her husband's office, Churchill wickedly praised him to the skies. Nor had Margot failed to notice that Henry too was not averse to giving the young man a sharp kick now and again to remind him who was master, for Asquith increasingly distrusted Churchill's large and imaginative ideas, his energy, confidence and vitality in proportion as he himself became more plodding and pedestrian. It was Margot and not Henry who in moments of honesty acknowledged Churchill to be out of the ordinary, and once she wrote: 'You can do something with talent but nothing with genius, and Mr Winston Churchill has a touch of—what we all recognize but cannot define—genius.' She also saw what Asquith did not, that no matter how often he changed his political allegiance, 'he remains what he has always been, a dyed-in-the-wool conservative'.[5]

Margot did not get on much better with Clementine Churchill. Although she admired her beauty and praised her for being a good wife, sharp words often passed between them, for Clementine, very rightly, refused to be brow-beaten. For some reason it amused Asquith to see the two women fight, and he gave Sylvia Henley a short description of one fierce battle of words in June 1915:

> Clemmie came here before dinner and I gather from Margot's account they had a very bad and almost Billingsgate half hour. Before she left I inveigled her here in the Cabinet room and spoke very forcefully to her and we parted on good and even affectionate terms and I trust that I dispelled her rather hysterical mutiny against the coalition and all its works . . .[6]

Although he rather enjoyed relating these female squabbles to Sylvia, Asquith was frightened of Clementine's sharp tongue, and was relieved when Margot had taken the brunt of her anger at the way he had treated her husband. A peace-loving man who hated quarrelling himself, he had a cynical streak which expected females to quarrel when they got together. In August of the same year he mentions Mrs Churchill again: 'I sat next to

C.C., who was quite amicable and showed neither teeth nor claws.'[7]

Towards certain people who irritated him, Asquith could be far harder and less understanding than Margot. When Winston Churchill was in trouble, it was Margot who took his side. Soon after losing the Admiralty, Churchill resigned from the government, preferring to serve his country as a soldier, and was now commanding a battalion in the front line. Home on leave in March 1916, Churchill insisted against all advice—including that of the Asquiths, with whom he had dined the previous night—on making an attack in the House on the controversial navy estimates, a speech that did him much harm. The effect on fellow members was disastrous, and many felt that his career as a politician was finished. Violet had joined Margot in the Ladies' Gallery and was shocked when she heard Churchill virtually destroy himself. As soon as they could, she and Margot rushed down to Bongie Bonham Carter's room, fearful that Winston Churchill had ruined his political career. Everyone in that small group looked at Margot for the answer: 'For once,' wrote her stepdaughter, 'she tempered the wind to the shorn lamb. "He is young," Margot said, "and if he goes back and fights like a hero all will be forgotten." '[8]

Next day, crestfallen and crushed (if only for a moment) Churchill came to Asquith's room in the House of Commons to tell him that he was thinking of leaving the army. But Asquith urged him not to do this, 'it would be surrender'. A few days later he received a short letter from Churchill, written on his way back to the Front, asking to be released from his command, 'when this can be done without disadvantage to the service'. Asquith was furious and wrote to tell Sylvia Henley so: 'That unstable little cur Winston has evidently fallen again under evil influences since our interview . . . Well, I have done my best to save him from a colossal blunder which will ruin his own future, henceforth he must stew in his own juice.'[9] Asquith entirely failed to understand Churchill's sense of futility, his longing to be of use. The fatherly advice, so much needed at that time, was not forthcoming from the Prime Minister. Although she was glad to hear Churchill had been admonished, Margot did wish Henry would deal rather more cleverly with the man. She chided him for playing the headmaster, cane in hand, and told him that if such athing should happen again he should bring Winston home and let him talk his troubles out with tea and cake. It was a mistake to make him feel that he had 'as much judgement as a hen'.[10]

Margot was soon to learn that there were others nearer home who were disloyal. At a women's luncheon party at 10 Downing Street, Mary Drew had the audacity to praise Lloyd George in a loud voice to those who were only too pleased (so Margot thought) to listen to a daughter of the great Gladstone putting Margot down. Margot took it as a deliberate insult and quite justified her criticisms of Mary to DD Lyttelton that Mary was 'spiteful and not to be trusted', and that never again would she have anything to do with her. Of course these quarrels blew over and Margot forgot her strictures on Mary until the next time, when the pattern was repeated all over again and Margot once more complained to DD. 'I don't care to think of any one living like Mary Drew, the callousness and want of not only decent feelings gets on my nerves and makes me cold with rage.'[11]

In 1917 when her world was crumbling and her women friends were few and far between, Margot foolishly quarrelled with Mary over a most trivial thing. She heard that Mary had said that the Asquiths would be better off if they did not entertain so much. At the time Margot was indeed very worried about money and instead of letting such silly tittle-tattle pass unnoticed, in a highly combustible mood she wrote a silly offended letter to Mary to put her in her place:

What a curious being you are! When we entertain *you*! Don't spread evil things . . . many foreigners, Americans, French, Roumanians etc, come to us at the Wharf and all the tired officials. As for Henry it has saved his life. Though I count for nothing, he does. I've suffered a good deal lately of which you are hardly aware, I can see![12]

The real trouble that griped Margot was Mary's lack of appreciation of Asquith as Prime Minister. She resented Margot's husband being in her father's place (she might have thought otherwise had Asquith married somebody else) and Margot in her mother's, and consequently she could not help showing that she never really believed Asquith was up to the job and that he ought to hand over to someone who could do better.

Margot's quarrels with Mary threw her into the arms of the American Lady Astor, whom at first she found honest, open, warm-hearted and kind. But Nancy was a dangerous enemy, and when Asquith badly needed friends during the crisis of November 1916 Nancy helped to give him the final push out of office. She sincerely believed that Asquith was no longer the man he had once been, but when Margot heard that Nancy had said Asquith ought to resign or be kicked out, she seethed with anger and without finding out if it was true, she declared the friendship over—'How dare she!' she wrote to the long-suffering DD.

> Nancy never said anything about me that I minded. I don't care a d... about that. It is her lies and the cruelty of her lies about Henry that I can't forgive . . . She said that Henry never felt the war, with one son killed and another off his head with shellshock and the third maimed for life—was the kind of vile remark only a woman could make and a woman blessed with the thickest of nigger skins . . . She is a typical female of noisy and light material, without the instincts of a gentle-man . . . no two people were ever born so differing in nature as Nancy and I.[13]

What 'lies' had Nancy uttered? She was supposed to have said that Asquith was 'lazy, slow and played bridge while fine young Englishmen died'. To get even with her, Margot said in public that Lady Astor had no business to criticize anyone when her own husband did nothing in the war. Margot heard that Bonar Law was behind Nancy's insults, since he had said (with Asquith in mind) that it was not only necessary to be active, but to be seen to be active,[14] a simple truth that Asquith never properly understood.

Then in 1918 Nancy Astor disgraced herself by standing for Parliament and getting elected, thus becoming the first woman to penetrate that masculine holy of holies over which Henry had presided for so many years. Margot made a point of hearing Nancy's first speech and generous-ly admitted it was not bad. She went again and changed her mind: in the course of a debate, Nancy jumped to her feet and contradicted Henry, as though they were equals. She was very rude too, although Henry behaved with the utmost courtesy. Margot lingered behind to waylay Nancy to give her a piece of her mind but Nancy slipped out unnoticed and Margot was foiled.

Much later, in 1929, the House of Commons hung Nancy's portrait in the chamber; it was considered a very good likeness. Margot refused to believe this, until she had seen the painting in position for herself. The fact that it was there at all was to her a terrible outrage, as she told DD in an indignant letter:

I do think Nancy Astor's allowing herself to be hung in the House of Commons shows a vanity and vulgarity even I (who as you know think of her as the least spiritual being I ever met) could not have credited her with. I am shocked at all of you who love her, allowing her to make such an ass of herself.[15]

Nancy too wrote to DD: 'I have no doubt Margot resents it, but then she resents everything that happens to me. I really don't care in the least whether they put the portrait up or not and as far as I am concerned, I would personally rather it was not up and it is entirely a matter for the House of Commons.'[16]

During 1916 the attacks on Asquith in the Northcliffe press increased in ferocity; everything that went wrong on the Western Front was imputed to the inefficiency of the Prime Minister and the coalition. Here was a chance for Margot to show what she was made of: a long straight talk with Henry, nothing held back, might have helped him to make up his mind either to resign or to show the nation that he was quite capable of infusing new life and vigour into the war effort. But she could not bring herself to do this; her courage failed her when she thought of the shock this might be to him. That there were greater shocks in store she did not doubt, but that she might save him from these by being outspoken did not occur to her.

In these last weeks in Downing Street, Margot felt an acute sense of isolation; no one was on their side. Harcourt had assured her that Henry would stay the course: 'The Prime Minister is irreplaceable.' Crew and Grey told her solemnly that Henry was not being edged out, the trouble would all blow over, while Simon said lightly that the papers were only using him as a scapegoat. She saw they were only trying to comfort her and shook her head: 'I saw what was going on as clearly as fish in a bowl.'[17] She was sick and tired of reading that the war would be lost if a new spirit was not awakened in the government by someone who had the courage to take over. The Morning Post, kinder than some papers, printed General Sir William Robertson's defence of the Prime Minister but without giving it prominence. Robertson said that Asquith had done everything possible to increase the supply of recruits in 1916 when manpower was so short. Real sympathy and support was becoming so rare that when it happened it touched Margot to the heart: 'Poor nation, poor Henry, poor British army, if only they had listened to Robertson.'[18]

In November 1916 a secret memorandum presented to the Cabinet by the Marquis of Lansdowne, advocating negotiation with the enemy as the only way to prevent more useless slaughter ('we are slowly killing off the male population of these islands'),* was leaked to the press. The memorandum in no way represented Asquith's views, but there were many who believed it did and that Lansdowne was acting as his spokesman. Asquith seemed not to realize the significance of the leak and appeared as unperturbed and serene as ever, but Margot saw it as the writing on the wall, and was not at all surprised when the *Morning Post* came out strongly for a new direction of the war, alleging that the Cabinet was hopelessly divided, not only about the conduct of the war but whether to go on fighting at all. But she was quite unprepared for the Liberal *News Chronicle* to say openly that the Prime Minister ought to make way for Lloyd George.

According to J. A. Spender, during the last fortnight of November 1916 Lloyd George and Sir Edward Carson, aided by the press lords, Beaverbrook and Northcliffe, were engaged in a definite plan for taking the conduct of the war out of Asquith's hands and giving it the 'new direction' Lloyd George had so often advocated.[20] On 1 December Lloyd George formally proposed to Asquith a war council of three with himself in the chair. Unable to secure the support of the Cabinet, Asquith resigned and on 7 December Lloyd George became Prime Minister.

When Lewis Harcourt called to see Margot that terrible week he found her in an alarming state: hollow-eyed and pale, with her clothes hanging on her, she looked like a skeleton. He was amazed that Asquith did not seem to notice what was happening under his eyes. Harcourt was as kind and reassuring as he could be, but she refused to listen to his words of comfort and kept on asking for his 'help', though how best to give it he did not know. She complained bitterly of politicians cultivating Lloyd George while paying lip-service to Henry. He saw that she had convinced herself in the past that Henry was indispensable for victory and that no one but he could form a government capable of achieving it. Too late she realized her mistake. Her astonishment when she learned that many of Asquith's

---

* The following year, when Lansdowne wrote a letter to the *Daily Telegraph* on much the same lines, Margot commented: 'Peace just now makes me shudder. In my days in Downing Street we never heard the word mentioned. War in our day meant that the Germans were to be brought to their knees.'[19]

Liberal colleagues were willing to serve under Lloyd George was great, and she was as disillusioned as a child who had been told the truth about Father Christmas. When she heard that Edwin Montagu was one of them she wrote him a bitter letter; the wretched man was alleged to have said that he saw the crisis as the tragedy of two great men of England being slowly but surely pushed apart, a truthful description of the problem as he saw it, but one which did not suit Margot at all: 'I hear you are going with them,' she wrote angrily. 'Where is friendship, where is loyalty?'[21]

When the Cabinet called at No. 10 to say good-bye to their former chief, Margot cut a sad figure and embarrassed everyone by whispering to each in turn to remain loyal to their leader. Asquith was not the first Prime Minister to fall by the wayside, yet Margot turned his resignation into a disaster of the first magnitude and suffered terribly when she saw friends join the enemy ranks. In her misery she forgot that she had been proud of her studied attempt to win over Labour members like Henderson and Snowden, sensing that their support might be needed at some future date. When Cynthia called at Downing Street she found Margot packing feverishly, and talking of 'plots and intrigues' and of Northcliffe who, she said, had had his knife into Henry from the beginning. Did Cynthia know that the great newspaper magnate had been going to Lloyd George's house every day since the beginning of the war? She wanted the whole of Britain to be aware that Henry had been ousted by dirty work, and the best way to do this was to get hold of the newspapers. She said she knew a very influential editor and would write to him as soon as the new government was formed. In the New Year she did her best to enlist the help of H. A. Gwynne of the conservative *Morning Post*, whom she imagined was sympathetic, although she knew that he was among those who had been calling for Henry's resignation. Immediately after the resignation she had written hopefully to him, and although the letter had achieved nothing, she thought he was behind her: 'We live in cowardly, egotistical times,' she now wrote. 'What has the government done with our brain-power scheme? This was all shipshape when we were kicked out . . . there were only two things to do . . . Ireland Home Rule or Conscription. But we must . . . all stand together. Times are too serious.'[22]

Sir John Simon was a great comfort; he had the happy knack of saying just what Margot wanted to hear. He told her that the source of the trouble was Northcliffe and conscription combined.

But now what is happening will clear the air and leave the Asquith party standing on its merits, without being obscured by treacherous and scheming influences to which he [Asquith] has always been too indulgent. Lloyd George has no independent following in the House . . . Let us have a Liberal opposition, patriotic in the real Asquith sense and get the country out of this awful hole.[23]

Unfortunately, words of comfort so often hold little truth. Cynthia, too, was more sanguine than Margot expected; everything would work out for the best, and the Prime Minister would soon be back with a firmer seat in the saddle. Encouragement from this unexpected quarter cheered Margot and she glowed visibly, warmed by her daughter-in-law's tact and kindness. Some time before his fall Asquith had written an uncharacteristically revealing letter to Margot:

These last few years I have lived under a perpetual strain, the like of which has, I suppose been experienced by very few men, living or dead. It is no exaggeration to say that I have had a hand more often in half a dozen problems than a single one, personal, political, parliamentary etc . . . I do my best in the way of self-control but I admit I am often irritated and impatient . . . you have suffered from this more than anyone, I fear.[24]

to take it for granted that nothing was expected of her. Consequently she never bothered to do anything seriously, made little effort of any kind and let her talents run to seed. She felt that she did her share of war work by dancing with officers home on leave, selling programmes at charity concerts to raise money to buy comforts for the troops or standing in Grosvenor Square rattling a collection box for the Red Cross, which bored her very much. By choice, she preferred to read poetry to invited audiences in aid of the Star and Garter Fund. Like her mother she loved to mix with cultivated actors and once earned acclaim when she played in a charity matinée opposite Sir Gerald Du Maurier. Cynthia Asquith realized that Elizabeth was surprisingly talented: 'I thought she did amazingly well, she looked so pretty, really charming and her dress was lovely.'[1] Elizabeth's attitude to her sister-in-law was ambivalent, as Cynthia's was to her. Sometimes she was very much drawn to Elizabeth and at others the young girl's affectations irritated her and she dismissed her as 'hilarious'. But her fluctuating moods were well matched by Elizabeth's, who saw that Cynthia could be both grasping and spiteful and that she put too much emphasis on beauty. In Cynthia's more sensible moods they got on very well. Both Cynthia and Margot's great friend, the novelist Marie Belloc-Lowndes (sister to Hilaire Belloc), thought that Elizabeth, though beautiful and talented, was overshadowed by her mother and her past reputation, which many in London society had not forgotten; she was longing to be married and have a home of her own in order to escape.[2]

Margot wasted too much time wondering if Elizabeth loved her, when she should have been asking herself if her own overpowering love did not repress her daughter. It would have helped if Elizabeth had told her mother how much she was suffering: after the first shock, Margot might have understood. For instance, Elizabeth wished that her mother would not write rather personal articles for magazines which all her friends read.[3] She could not make up her mind if Margot did it for the £100 the publishers paid her or the sheer love of writing. She also very much wished Margot would not argue so often and so shrilly when defending expatriate Germans in public because she knew that her father disapproved of such 'openness'. She adored her father but, unlike Violet, saw faults in him. She disliked his habit of ingratiating himself with her friends and holding their hands. Equally irritating was his refusal to discuss the war with his family and his habit of spending too much time away from home. He was able to embarrass her even more than her mother did when he was too frank in answering a question. When he came to fetch her one day from the studio of the fashionable painter, McEvoy, where she was sitting for her portrait, he caused her to blush with shame when he criticized the artist's work just after she had told him that it was a perfect likeness and that her parents would love it.

Her stepbrothers were her heroes and she adored Violet, whom she looked on as a second mother. One of her greatest pleasures was to take Puffin to the theatre or to persuade her father to take them both to one of the musical comedies which were then so popular; long-suffering as he could be on occasions, the tone-deaf Asquith went with very bad grace: 'Crammed to suffocation,' he wrote in disgust to Sylvia Henley in December 1917, after seeing *Pamela* at the Palace Theatre.[4]

It was unfortunate that Elizabeth had a bad habit of being particularly hard and unsympathetic when her mother was worried. At the height of the crisis about her father's resignation, Elizabeth sauntered into her mother's bedroom one evening when Margot was resting before dinner and coolly announced that she was engaged to be married to Hugh Gibson, a young American diplomat assigned to the Embassy in London. Margot was outraged and made no attempt to hide the fact. America had not yet entered the war on the side of the allies and at that very moment the papers were accusing her of assisting the Irish gun-running. And here standing before her, quite unabashed, was the daughter of the man who had worked hardest to stop the traffic in ammunition, having the effrontery to say that she was engaged to one of these 'traitors' and, what is more, a man without a penny to his name. Cynthia, who was sleeping at No. 10 at the time, was as bitterly upset as Margot. She knew what it was like to be married to a poor man and could not see Elizabeth happy in that role: 'I had such high hopes of Elizabeth,' she wrote in her diary, 'this is really too much. To marry an American is bad enough, but a poor American!'[5] Margot refused to hear of the match. Elizabeth cried with chagrin, Margot with rage. Elizabeth tried to stand up to her mother, but Margot, on edge with political troubles, would brook no argument. Cynthia was more subtle and gained a great deal more when she made this love affair look ridiculous by parodying Hugh Gibson's name—did Elizabeth really want to be known as Mrs Libby Gibby?

When Gibson asked if he could marry Elizabeth, Asquith trotted out the age-old excuse: she was too young to know her own mind, he must come back when she was older. Meanwhile he must promise never to see

Elizabeth alone.[6] To everyone's relief, after many ups and downs, the affair petered out. Hugh Gibson's doctor diagnosed consumption; he had to go home for treatment and Elizabeth acquired another admirer of a very different kind.

Much to Margot's annoyance, Henry did not use the spare time that followed his resignation to work his way back into power, nor did he use what little influence he had left to blacken the name of those who had so disloyally supplanted him. In her heart Margot knew that to do what she asked was quite out of character and that she would never be able to persuade him. That is what irked her and she asked herself why it was always left to her to defend the family fortunes. On top of it all she was asked to accept defeat. This she would never do. Those who had betrayed the Prime Minister must be brought to justice. What she meant by this she does not explain, but she passionately wanted to see the coalition toppled and Henry back in his rightful place. She could not think or talk of anything else, but laid her feelings bare for all the world to see. Those who did not know her well misinterpreted her and concluded that she missed the power and the glory. Here they were unjust. She really believed that Henry was the only man who could bring the war to a successful conclusion. His fine principles, high moral fibre and sense of justice were needed now as never before when men everywhere were losing their heads. Already the country was forgetting what he had done. Did they remember that he was the man who had got rid of French and appointed Haig and Robertson, two of the ablest generals the fighting forces had yet seen?[7] Were they not grateful that it was because of them that the tide was beginning to turn at last? Now it was being said that it was all Lloyd George's doing.

The witch hunt against the Asquiths was still going on. They were now accused of siding with the enemy, and every day batches of anonymous letters full of vile abuse arrived through the post and were thrown into the fire as too ridiculous to notice. One writer accused Margot of signalling from some secret spot on the North Sea coast to the German submarine that sank the *Hampshire* with Kitchener on board. Contemptuously Margot pronounced the writer insane. It was all very well to dismiss rubbish of this sort but it was another thing that every time Asquith criticized some action of the Coalition's, it was hailed by the press as personal jealousy.[8]

By the end of the year money was tight and getting tighter. The loss of Asquith's salary as Prime Minister left a gaping hole and there were no savings to fill it. Although Margot tried to be careful (after her own fashion) money seemed to slip through her fingers. She lay awake at night deciding what little comforts she could do without, but as soon as daylight came she would forget all about those good resolutions and carry on as before. She had no idea how to retrench, for every servant, every luncheon party and her friendly gatherings at The Wharf seemed indispensable. All her life Margot had been saying that 'people who worry about money are not worth much' and 'there are no pockets in shrouds', phrases that slipped glibly off her tongue when she had a fat bank balance and a father to replenish it when she needed more.

They still kept a car, a chauffeur, a butler, a housekeeper, two private secretaries and hosts of other servants. Entertaining went on much as before. Margot felt this was necessary if people were not to forget Henry. It was for this reason that she urged him to speak in the House frequently, visit his constituents and other Liberal strongholds, go to the Front to see General Haig and to keep in touch with the Irish party. If he found it fatiguing travelling all over the country making speeches he did not say so. Occasionally Margot went with him, but not too often, for by staying at home she felt she was saving money on hotel bills; there were now few country-houses that offered to give them even a bed for the night.

Her lack of money was going to affect the whole family. In one way the Asquith children, although grown up, were still a liability. Beb (Herbert) and his wife Cynthia relied on her to put them up when he was on leave, and all the family had acquired the bad habit of looking to Margot for 'tips' as though they were still at school. Without the rent from 20 Cavendish Square (where they were now living again), these would have to be drastically cut down in future. The root of the trouble was that Asquith had no savings and now no income either: in those days there were no pensions for ex-Prime Ministers. The whole burden of the family finances fell on Margot, and their friends began to wonder how they were going to live.

It was to be expected that Margot would find less to occupy her than Henry, who had his books, speeches to write, constituents and former colleagues to see. Mr Jenkins describes Asquith's state out of office very aptly: 'No one could have been less unbalanced by set-backs than was Asquith. He lived amongst his relations and friends and books, and he lived agreeably. But he lived without power or public honour or real occupation.'[9]

Margot's restless spirit could not accept her new life so philosophically; she was burning with schemes to get Henry back in office. Unfortunately she had few resources to fall back on. From the day Henry became Prime Minister she had allowed all intellectual pursuits to lapse; even reading, once her greatest pleasure as well as a solace, she only indulged in by fits and starts. There were still some old favourites by her bedside, but when sleep would not come she would soothe her frayed nerves in writing letters, most of them on the same theme—Lloyd George's iniquities —until her head buzzed and her heart raced with anger. What would have happened if she had gone on like this can only be guessed at, but the whole house dreaded another nervous collapse.

Just as she seemed to have lost hope, her son came to the rescue with music and the theatre. It was a lifeline that he forced her to grasp by throwing aside his usual gentleness, and he produced two tickets for the Bach St Matthew Passion in St Paul's Cathedral. To her surprise she enjoyed herself and was so enraptured by the music that she did not need much persuasion by Puffin to get her to invite the great Joachim's nieces, Jelly d'Aranyi and Adela Fachiri, to give a violin recital at 20 Cavendish Square for their musical friends. The evening was a great success, and Margot was back on her old form. (Not so Henry, who was forced to attend from politeness. He grumbled to a friend that these famous violinists were nice women whose only fault was their addiction to fiddling!)

Encouraged by the improvement in his mother, Puffin came up from Oxford more and more often to take Margot to a concert or the opera, and in the vacation they did a round of theatre-going together. When he knew some of the actors Puffin would take her behind the scenes and introduce her, an interesting experience that was new to her. No longer did she read the papers merely to discover what trickery Lloyd George was up to, but she would turn to the entertainments page to see what new plays, operas, concerts were coming and then read the reviews of those she had not yet seen. She quickly discovered favourites: Gladys Cooper and Viola Tree headed her list, and she never missed anything in which they appeared. She held strong opinions on playwrights, Pinero, Shaw, Arnold Bennett, O'Neill and Synge all delighted her equally although so different, while Caradoc Evans' *Capel Syon* sent her into raptures; it reminded her so vividly of the people who lived in the villages that surrounded Glen. How stupid she had been all those years to wrap herself up in politics and not relax more watching some of England's cleverest entertainers, merely because if she ate late after a performance she could not sleep.

Since Margot did nothing by halves, she had to take up the theatrical world in a big way. She invited actors and actresses to The Wharf and her visitors' book soon held such names as Ivor Novello and Noël Coward, not then as famous as they were soon to become. To her delight Margot discovered that these guests needed no entertaining but played the piano, sang or discussed their next play with complete unselfconsciousness and at meals talked with as much vivacity as she did. She cast her net even wider and captivated Barrie, Kipling, Frederick Lonsdale and the theatrical journalist Desmond MacCarthy. Her son had opened up for her a more satisfying world than that of politics; he had reawakened her more intellectual side, dormant for so long, by bringing his Oxford friends to The Wharf, among them Lord David Cecil and a then unknown Polish Jew from New College, Harold Laski, whose advanced views Margot took in her stride. Here was a life she had forgotten existed, the life she had loved in her youth and early womanhood. She had only one regret: Henry would not join in but sat in his study alone with his books. His interests were narrowing and she did not quite know how to rouse him out of his lethargy. Secretly she had plans to get him back into politics—if only he would co-operate.

CHAPTER 29

Serve under Lloyd George? Never!

FROM THE DAY she left Downing Street in December 1916 Margot resolved to do everything in her power to reinstate Henry as the Queen's First Minister. She imagined it would not be difficult once she got started, for she had a plan which was bound to succeed if only she were resolute enough to see it through. This was to get the press on Henry's side again and make them see that he was the only man in the country to bring the war to a successful conclusion. She knew Geoffrey Dawson of *The Times*, not intimately perhaps, but well enough to write to tell him the true facts and evoke his sympathy, and she was endeavouring to cultivate a friendship with Gwynne of the *Morning Post*. She had never taken into account that Gwynne was a high Tory and that his paper had played no small part in forcing Asquith to resign. Gwynne was perfectly well aware too that Margot was trying to use him (her methods were so unsubtle) to reinstate the one man he was certain would lose the war, and it was not difficult for him to parry her attacks and thinly veiled pleas for help. In an attempt to bring this manoeuvring to an end he told Margot that her husband had done his bit and was worn out, and that the difficult times called for a leader 'of sufficient strength, knowledge and firmness to bring victory'.[1] By return of post Margot said that she quite agreed, since the qualities he mentioned belonged to Henry and to him alone. He must say so in his paper, where it would carry weight.

Of course Asquith had not the slightest idea that Margot was carrying on a correspondence of this kind with the editor of a Tory newspaper and he would certainly have put a stop to it if he had known; Margot was very well aware of this and therefore took pains to keep it secret. Many of her letters to Gwynne have a bold 'Confidential' or 'Most Secret' scrawled in large letters across the top or bottom of a sheet of writing paper though sometimes he could not imagine why, for she was saying to him only what she had said to a roomful of people not more than a week before. Every time she slipped out to post one of these letters (too precious to entrust to a servant) she felt like a conspirator, and a very delicious feeling it was: one day the whole country would thank her.

Her firm and unshakeable belief in the power of the press was so naïve as to be very endearing and Gwynne (who had never met her) wondered what kind of woman she could be. In 1918 she tried to use this supposed power to obtain a prominent post for her husband in the coming peace negotiations. For one who prided herself on her directness, her plan was full of twists and turns yet, at the same time, almost childish. She hoped that she could increase Gwynne's antipathy to Lloyd George and so turn him more and more to Henry. With some apprehension she awaited his reply to these tactics, which she imagined to be subtle and clever, but when it came it was not at all what she expected. Gwynne did not mention the peace talks, but he did have a suggestion to make: that Asquith could best use his talents by serving under Lloyd George—perhaps as Chancellor of the Exchequer? Margot was outraged, but she had the sense to suppress her feelings and consented to meet Gwynne and talk over the plan. Gwynne invited her to luncheon at the Bath Club. When the day came Margot felt unwell but forced herself to keep the appointment, mistook Lansdowne House for the Bath Club and walked up and down the pavement for an hour waiting for Gwynne, while he waited in vain at the Bath. Bitterly angry with Gwynne (she refused to own that the mistake was hers) she upbraided him immediately on returning to Cavendish Square: 'I wonder where your Bath Club is,' she began.

> I suppose where your non-political military dictator of glorious mind and character is; a man who will march us into Berlin and roll up the Hun before the Rhine . . . my husband is the least vain of men, this indeed is the skeleton in our cupboard. He cares much, much more about the war than any one else . . . his loathing of intrigue is so great that he never saw it seething round him. I saw it all as clear as fish in a bowl. You will be shocked to hear he never saw a pressman in his life . . . as I said my husband is not vain but he knows of no man of greater knowledge and strength of firmness than himself whom he could serve under.[2]

She had so wanted to tell Gwynne to his face that the greatest statesman of the day would never serve under Lloyd George and be a party to his intrigues, but that she feared that if 'duty' was sufficiently stressed Henry might be persuaded to accept. Such a contingency must not arise and Gwynne must understand this: 'It was not my husband's fault that we did not win the war in 1916,' she wrote a few days later, '. . . the lack of firmness you attribute to him is because he used the material given to him, Winston, Bonar, Balfour, Curzon and Carson. . . .'[3] She had begun to realize that Gwynne blamed Henry for certain mistakes in his handling of the war, but could not imagine what they were:

> Was it because he did not shout like Herbert Samuel: 'We've won the war and the enemy knows it'? . . . if you can send me any remark in a speech or private letter (Northcliffe boasts he can buy any private letters) of my husband's which is against this war and in favour of peace you will be a very remarkable man. What do you suppose he is in favour of . . . defeat? . . . You won't win the war by your national party, nor by swagger, nor by bluff.[4]

By Christmas 1917 the whole of England was feeling the effects of the discomforts and privations that must come with a long and exhausting war. Because fuel was in short supply Margot was forced to dine in hat and fur coat, a rug over her knees. Food now was both rationed and scarce, butter, sugar and meat were especially hard to come by, but with her bird-like appetite Margot did not mind. It irritated her far more when she could not match some material at Swan and Edgar's and when the only thing offered was of such poor quality that she refused to buy it. If this went on much longer, what would she do for clothes? There were hardly any assistants in the shops now, all the young were making munitions and the old, brought out of retirement by necessity, had to manage as well as they could. To a woman like Margot, used to having assistants cluster round her, all trying to please, there was no fun in shopping any more and she fulminated that soon she would be going around in rags.

The general public's attitude to the war had changed; it was not only uncomfortable, but wretchedly hopeless too. There was hardly a household left which had not suffered some bereavement, and many of Margot's own friends had lost as many as three sons. When she looked at her stepsons, she could hardly believe that they were the same as the arrogant, carefree young men who had amused and exasperated her only four years ago. One had gone for ever; Henry seldom talked of Raymond but Margot knew he felt his death bitterly. Arthur, the latest of them to be maimed, had recently been staying with them for several weeks. He had lost a leg and the artificial limb fitted so badly that it caused unbearable soreness and he had to remove it several times a day. Cis (Cyril) was as yet all in one piece, but there was time for something dreadful to happen to him too. Everyone was weary and wondering if peace would ever come; when it did come what would the peace be like?

Margot was not a weak woman, for all her 'nerves', and she could have put up with the privations if her mind had been easy about Henry. He was stagnating and showed little interest in public affairs, whereas not long ago politics were his whole life. Perhaps the break had been too sudden: her great fear was that if a call should come to lead his party once again, he would not be ready for it. With rest his health had improved, although his doctors had warned him to go carefully in order not to run the risk of repeating the kind of sudden illness brought on by overwork in 1915. Margot was quite certain, however, that they did not mean him to sit down and read all day long, and in the spring she persuaded him to visit the Western Front again and to go to Cassel to see General Sir Douglas Haig and hear at first hand what exactly was going on, for contradictory reports were making people confused and distrustful.[5]

In his own way Haig was having as bad a time as Asquith. Both he and General Robertson were Asquith appointments. Already Robertson had been elbowed out and replaced by General Wilson, a Lloyd George favourite, but Haig was made of sterner stuff and was harder to shift than Lloyd George reckoned. After Passchendaele, Lloyd George realized that he could not dismiss a general of Haig's standing without causing a political storm which he would not be able to ride, and he therefore tried to get the direction of the war into his own hands by creating a supreme war council in order to lessen Haig's powers.

Just at this moment the Germans struck. The first battle of the war had been on the Marne; now, more than four years later, another battle of the Marne in July 1918 turned out to be even more decisive, for it marked the end of the German offensive, their last great effort for victory. The Allied counterstroke made 8 August, in Ludendorff's phrase, 'the blackest day in the history of the German army', and opened the way to the armistice of 11 November. Margot followed this last stage of the war with the closest attention, her heart filled with thankfulness when she saw how Henry's choice of Haig ('the man whom Lloyd George tried to sack') was vindicated in full measure. What price now the Easterners' slogan 'we cannot beat the Boche on the Western Front'? She could never forget that Lloyd George had once been an Easterner.

Shortly before the second battle of the Marne, Asquith had taken Margot's advice and gone to France. He made a sad journey to Delville Wood where Raymond had been killed. Whatever his thoughts were he kept them to himself: a friend who went with him told Margot that he gave no sign of emotion but stood quite silent staring at the ground for some time.

All his life Asquith had kept his deepest feelings hidden and very few were allowed to glimpse the agonies he preferred to endure alone. Margot noticed on his return that he was very silent, and when she asked him if he felt unwell he did not answer but went to his shelves and began rearranging some books with his back to her. Then, in an expressionless voice, he told her where he had been when in France. Overcome by sudden emotion, Margot rushed from the room.

Later, when she was resting, she pondered on how alike the Asquith men were, especially Henry and Raymond: all emotion must be suppressed, to show affection openly was weak and a breach of good taste, especially between men. Cyril Asquith once explained to Margot that all the brothers hated any deviation from their usual cool behaviour towards each other and that it embarrassed them to show their feelings. In Raymond's case the harm suppression did was shown by his cynicism, his affected flippancy and the cruel wit that made him at times seem indifferent to the sufferings of others. Very rightly Margot thought that to keep such a tight rein on his feelings was bad for Henry, and she longed for him to give way. She wondered too if he was suffering from a sense of guilt at his neglect of Raymond. He never wrote to him once when he was at the Front, never sent him messages through her, and rarely mentioned him. Margot had sensed that Raymond had minded the omission very much and deeply resented it.

For a brief moment in May 1918 Margot had thought there was a chance to turn the tables on Lloyd George. General Sir Frederick Maurice, who until recently had been Director of Military Operations, wrote an astonishing letter to *The Times* giving confidential figures purporting to show that during the German offensive Lloyd George had wilfully held back reinforcements from the Western Front. (Maurice later told Margot that he wrote his letter to save Haig from dismissal.) Asquith immediately demanded a debate, but Margot's hopes that he would be able to use the Maurice letter to discredit Lloyd George were dashed when Henry made an ineffectual speech and was overwhelmed by Lloyd George's defence. Asquith mustered 108 votes against 295 for the Government; he lost prestige instead of regaining it, and Lloyd George never forgave those who had voted against him.

Margot herself came under attack immediately afterwards in what came to be known as the Pemberton Billing case. Billing had once been Independent MP for East Hampshire, and now edited the *Vigilante*, a paper that thrived on scandal. He alleged that there was a simple explanation for the Germans' success in the war: they were winning by 'propagating among British public men and their wives, sons and daughters evils which all decent men thought had perished with Sodom and Lesbia'. He made great play with an alleged 'black book' which listed the names of forty-seven prominent people (including members of the royal family) whom German agents had corrupted by means of homosexual vice, and particularly mentioned a young dancer called Maud Allen, who was appearing in Oscar Wilde's *Salome*. Mrs Allen prosecuted Billing for criminal libel. In the witness-box Billing implicated both the Asquiths, accusing Margot of being a lesbian.

None of Billing's allegations were true, of course, but such was the state of public hysteria induced by the German offensive that some of them were believed, if only on the 'no smoke without fire' principle. Margot came to feel that she was being spied on, her comings and goings carefully watched: a man in a black mackintosh lurking behind a tree in the square, a car parked opposite her drawing-room window. At St Dunstan's, where she worked with blind soldiers for several hours each week, she was certain she saw a man taking a photograph of her when she was helping a patient into a taxi and was sure it would appear in a foreign newspaper, above an unflattering caption like 'Mrs Asquith says goodbye to one of her pacifist friends'. On the other hand, she got a certain excitement from believing that she was taking part in some hidden drama and intrigue —perhaps it was the work of an international spy ring?—and in a curious way the Pemberton Billing case put new life into her; the wrong kind of life perhaps, but at least the affair made her and Henry the centre of interest again and gave her a chance to speak out. To be forgotten was the worst punishment of all for one of her temperament: 'We might as well be dead.'

In many ways the last three months had been the most trying of all. Time had hung heavy on her hands and Margot was at her worst with nothing to do. Feeling dreary and out of sorts, though she did not quite know why, she went to Mells for a few days to be with her old friend Frances Horner, whom she had not seen for many months. With remarkable fortitude and no complaints of any kind Frances and her husband Jack were trying to accept the cruel fate that had taken their two sons from them, deprived their daughter Katharine of a husband and their grandchildren of a father. This letter from Clementine Churchill to Winston Churchill after she had visited the Horners perfectly describes tragic Mells and its inmates:

> Both their sons dead, one lying in the little churchyard next to the house carried away at 16 by scarlet fever, the other sleeping in France, as does the husband of the best-loved daughter of the house, Katharine Asquith. Both their swords are hanging in the beautiful little Gothic church beside long inscriptions commemorating long dead Horners who died in their beds.[6]

The losses of the Tennant and Asquith families had been terrible too; the list had become so long that Margot had to consult her private roll of honour to discover who was dead and who still alive. The war had dragged on and on, leaving her feeling 'numb as an old piano with broken notes in it'.[7] Soon after the end of hostilities DD Lyttelton sent her an extract from her son Oliver's diary: 'When the last post sounded the soldiers were too dull and stupefied to rejoice. Everywhere the reaction was the same, flat dullness and depression.'[8] This roused Margot to the caustic comment: 'If the commanders in the field expected the war to continue until 1920 it is small wonder there was little enthusiasm left on either the German, British or French side.'[9]

When the war ended on 11 November 1918 Margot characteristically went to her desk and wrote three telegrams as though she was still the Prime Minister's wife. The first was to the King, the second to Queen Alexandra and the third to General Sir John Cowens, the Quartermaster-General, of whom Margot was very fond. Then she ordered every flag in the house to be hung out of the window and since it was a day to be magnanimous she included the Welsh harp. Afterwards, thinking it a duty, she walked out into the street where a complete stranger clasped her hand and another kissed her cheek and without a word disappeared into the crowd. 'It was more like a foreign carnival than what we are accustomed to in this country,' she wrote in her diary.

After a hurried lunch she and Henry drove slowly through the crowds to the House of Commons to hear Lloyd George read the armistice terms. Tears of joy came to Margot's eyes when the crowd greeted the former Prime Minister with cheers, and she saw by the way his face lit up that Henry too was delighted.

The terms of the armistice shocked her. She does not say what she expected, but it was certainly nothing as revengeful as that read out in solemn tones by Lloyd George. She did not reflect that if the Germans had won they would have imposed far harsher terms. Whatever her feelings it was unwise of her to turn to her neighbour and say in a loud voice as Lloyd George laid down his papers, 'Much too harsh'. Remarks like this when repeated often enough went a long way to revive those jibes about pro-German sympathies and there were unpleasant whispers behind her back.

St Paul's was packed on 19 November for a thanksgiving service. The Asquiths sang 'O God our help in ages past' with much emotion: Margot said a prayer of thankfulness that the war had ended before Puffin was old enough to fight. Her thoughts strayed to Raymond and to the thousands like him who were never coming back.

After an early tea she walked to Buckingham Palace to join the crowd in cheering the King and Queen who stood on the balcony waving and bowing, King George in khaki, Queen Mary glittering with jewels. That day Margot learned a useful lesson: in a crowd she was nobody. An officious WAAC roughly ordered Margot to get out of the way 'with that rudeness natural to women in authority'. Whatever war may have done for the dead it had not improved the living. Walking home in the fading light she reflected on the cruelty of fate that brought America into the war too late to keep Henry in his rightful place. If things had happened differently he would have been the one who stood today with their Majesties on the balcony, acknowledging an ovation from the crowd. It was bitter to see 'that little upstart' standing where Henry should have been.

A general election was fixed to take place immediately after Christmas. There was indignation at 20 Cavendish Square when the news broke; Margot declared it was nothing less than a confidence trick, to hold an election before the soldiers had come home from the Front, 'when men's hearts are tired, their minds confused and the flower of the nation still abroad'.[10]

There had been rumours of an election for some time and long before the end of hostilities Margot had written to Professor Gilbert Murray, congratulating him on an article in the *Daily News* asking for the election to be postponed: 'It will be war to the knife,' she wrote.

> Henry has been working very carefully over our programme and on the speeches he intends to make in September in Manchester. . . . Labour and Liberals sink or swim together . . . the idea of the government returning reinforced by more Toryism is intolerable.[11]

Although dead against an election at that time, Margot was encouraged by well-wishers who felt that now that the war was over Lloyd George's day was done, and came to think that with careful planning there might be a chance to get Henry back. It was a good sign that Henry's friends were rallying round him, many of them saying that instead of an election that could be dangerous the best solution would be for the official Liberals and Lloyd George Liberals to unite under Asquith. Margot pointed out that such an arrangement could never come about unless someone could persuade Lloyd George to forget self and put his country first.[12]

A clever agent would be absolutely essential. The Asquith Liberals must make a pact with Labour, and win over the north of England. Scotland was solid enough. 'We shall want perfect organization, female votes etc and immense energy,' she wrote happily to Gilbert Murray. 'Henry the wise goes into winter quarters, which will help us; it is stupid to flatter Labour and be so pessimistic and fruitless.'[13]

The whole country was plastered with posters, just as it had been at the beginning of the war, but this time it was not Kitchener with his accusing finger but the last of the Hohenzollern monarchs with the caption 'Hang the Kaiser'. He glared at Margot from trees and walls as she drove from London to Sutton Courtenay. Why were people so vindictive, she wondered? There was another poster that upset and angered her as she set about helping Asquith canvass for the 'coupon' election: it carried an excellent likeness of Henry and the caption: 'Asquith nearly lost the war, are you going to let him spoil the peace?'[14]

Christmas was spent at The Wharf and ought to have been a day of rejoicing that the war was over, but nerves were on edge and tempers short. Margot was worried about the outcome of the election, Cynthia about money, while Asquith was exhausted after travelling all over the country making speeches on behalf of Liberal members whose seats were shaky, neglecting his own constituency which he knew to be loyal. His heart was not in this election, for which his party was quite unprepared. The National Liberals and the Conservative coalitionists had partitioned the seats among themselves, giving their own side an unfair advantage over the Asquith Liberals although the whole Liberal party had supported the coalition government during the war. Those who had followed Asquith in the division after the Maurice debate found themselves opposed by coalition candidates.

Before December was out there was a pleasant diversion for the Asquiths when they went to a luncheon at the Mansion House in honour of President Wilson, who was to be given the freedom of the City of London. The President was in England to launch his League of Nations scheme, the league that was to end all wars. Margot sat close to Wilson and was able to observe him closely:

> I examined his lanky face, egotistical, slightly sensual and charming if too frequent smile, and noted the refinement of his brow and nostrils. He made an excellent if uninspiring speech . . . everyone could hear each word.[15]

Later when they were able to have some conversation together she found him easy to talk to and quick to take a point. Asquith thought he had a good intelligence and real personality—'he is a great and refreshing change'.[16]

No one guessed what an effort it was for Margot to appear cheerful and lively. The day before she had heard that Henry was to be given no part in the peace talks, despite the fact that he was the only one who could speak French and had a thorough knowledge of international law and finance. He had made it clear that the only service he thought he could render the country at that time would be to go to Versailles, where they would have to deal with the havoc war had created in all the foreign exchanges and fix new frontiers, jobs where his lawyer's training would be invaluable. Lloyd George had not taken up the suggestion and nothing more was said. 'Henry's omission is the country's loss,' Margot wrote to Gwynne, 'his qualifications alone make it worthwhile to create an exception. There is no one else with his knowledge and legal brain.'[17]

She would have liked to say something to President Wilson about this slight to Henry but there was only time for a brief word and a quick handclasp before she and Henry were walking to their car. But as she was leaving the Mansion House her keen ears had caught the words 'election results' and even before she reached her own front door she had heard a newsboy shout that McKenna, Samuel and Runciman had lost their seats. Suddenly feeling sick and trembling with apprehension she longed to get home. Were they all beaten, she wondered. Henry was calm: 'I only hope,' he said 'that I have not got in. With all the others out it would be the last straw.'[18]

Almost before the car stopped at 20 Cavendish Square Margot jumped out and flew into the house. She looked at the hall table; no message might mean bad news. It did. Seizing the telephone Margot called Liberal headquarters and feeling faint with dread forced herself to listen to the results. It was as she feared: Henry was out too.

CHAPTER 30

Leading Apes to Hell

THEY COULD NOT take it in—East Fife, for thirty years Henry's own constituency, disloyal! He had lost by 2,000 votes to the Conservative Sprott, a man Margot had written off as 'hopeless'. Both of them had been so sure that all was well that Henry had only been once to East Fife during the whole of the election campaign, feeling that his services were needed most where Liberalism was weakest.

The shock affected Margot, sleeplessness set in and she was advised by her doctor to have a short holiday in the South of France. She left at once, taking Elizabeth with her. From The Wharf, where he intended to stay until her return, Henry wrote to her encouragingly: 'I see no reason why we should not be happy. . . . I have not many grievances against Fortune. Few men have had a life more crowded with interests both big and small and none that I know has been so nearly blessed in his home.'[1] More comfort came from old friends. 'I feel humiliated at such a result,' Haldane wrote. The Master of Balliol spoke of a feeling of deep regret and shame. A remark of Augustine Birrell's made her smile: 'You surely are better out of it for the time being rather than watching Lloyd George lead apes to Hell.' Warm sympathy too came from Sir William Robertson, the former CIGS who had suffered at Lloyd George's hands. He mentioned those qualities which Margot had always admired in her husband: kindness, consideration, straightforwardness and courage.[2] These comments were soothing, but Margot could not rid herself of the feeling that there had been jiggery-pokery in East Fife and she refused to listen to those who told her to forget about it. Evil forces had been at work, otherwise good Scotsmen would not have turned traitor. A letter to Asquith from James Scott the Liberal agent seemed to prove her point:

For a week before the election we've had a swarm of women going from door to door indulging in a slander for which they had not a shadow of proof. This was used to such purpose as to influence the female vote very much against you ... With others who had been employed on munitions and in receipt of good wages, the pocket outweighed the principles. Again we had those who made a point of your absence from the constituency and did not hesitate to say that 'we never saw him and are not going to vote'.[3]

The very fact that Margot thought Henry had been right to oppose women's suffrage comforted her somewhat for the loss of the seat. How prudent Henry had been to hold fast against pleas that women should be given a franchise they did not know how to use. In his opinion women were not yet educated enough to make such decisions for themselves; they were too emotional, too swayed by feelings.

Asquith, like Margot, believed that there was truth in this story of James Scott's and he wrote to Sylvia Henley:

I have no doubt the result in my case and many others was due entirely to the women who appear to have ratted in droves. As one has always suspected, they were more susceptible to vulgar catchwords ('Hang the Kaiser' etc) than the average man in the street if possible, also more ignorant. As for the final result I am much more glad than sorry that I am out and nothing will induce me to look for a seat in this new house.

He added a postscript: 'Winston goes about saying the Asquith Liberals are totally smashed. Comment would be superfluous.'[4]

A little later when she felt calmer Margot wrote to Gilbert Murray with a show of bravado:

We are not the least worried though a trifle surprised. I agree with all you say, we shall beat them yet. Common sense and fair play will gradually emerge ... we must organize and stand together. Henry is in grand form and much relieved at not being in the H. of C. (which represents nothing that is rich or new) ... everyone yearns for what is clean and straight ... Henry sees all sorts of men tomorrow in London and we are settling our plans with activity and precision.[5]

Asquith still did not want to be entirely out of public affairs. President Wilson's idea of a League of Nations to prevent future wars had fired his imagination, but would the government take up an idea that seemed to be unpopular in America, France and Italy, even in Britain? Margot saw its enormous possibilities but said that it needed a man of extraordinary ability and forceful personality at the head (did she mean Henry?) to induce all countries to accept Germany as one of the League. She thought it very vindictive to say: 'Germany must be made to suffer' or 'We won't let America save Germany from the consequences of her mistakes', and quite failed to understand that such an attitude was natural after more than four years of war. It amazed her that nobody thought it essential that 'Germany must not be rendered impotent'.[6] Henry, too, felt from the start that the government did not like Wilson's League and was going to cold-shoulder it. Ten years later, when she was a widow, Margot brought the subject up in a letter to Gilbert Murray, a great supporter of the League:

> Henry was really sad when he realized that the government that succeeded him was profoundly unconcerned with the League of Nations. It is too easy to say that nothing will stop war. The same was said of duelling . . . and every great discovery. The only new thing that came out of the war with life was the League of Nations.[7]

In the summer of 1919 Margot had high hopes that with Gilbert Murray's help Henry could mould the League idea into a workable form, for the only hope for the peace of the world was for Great Britain and America to keep together. She was delighted, too, that Henry was so enthusiastic. Would Wilson play? 'I doubt his being a loyal colleague,' she wrote to Murray, 'but would not say so to anyone but you.'[8] It was important to keep in with men like Wilson who had ideas, Margot told Henry, who, because the League was proving difficult to get off the ground, had dropped it and gone back to his books, his rekindled ambition evaporating fast.

Yet Margot knew that his interest could be revived if he was sufficiently roused. He was stirred to action when Sir John French, now Lord Ypres, published a book of memoirs called simply *1914*. French said it was he who had prompted the campaign that had resulted in Asquith's downfall. He accused Asquith of misrepresenting the facts about the munitions situation and said that his speech at Newcastle in 1915* was too

* See p. 258

moderate for the Prime Minister of a nation fighting a war that was not
going well. Margot believed that the hand of Lloyd George was evident in
every line of French's book. She turned to Spender: 'Lloyd George says, I
can make England laugh at this man and prove that he cannot unite us in
war or peace and that I am the only man.'[9] French had hitherto always
been friendly, even affectionate, towards Asquith, and this bald statement, made in such a treacherous fashion, aroused him to fury. For a
moment not even his calm temper could hold against such insults and
Northcliffe's ridiculous cry 'Asquith must be impeached'.[10] He delivered
a slashing reply to French's slanderous attacks. But the revival was
short-lived, and he sank back into the life of retirement he had chosen.

For the first time in her life, Margot knew what it was like to have a man at
home all day, and although loyalty prompted her to say that she was only
too happy to have Henry with her so much, those closest to her guessed
that it was difficult for her to reverse the habit of a lifetime. It was not that
Henry was obtrusive: he shut himself up in his study with his books and
his writing and they often did not see each other for hours on end.
Nevertheless she felt constrained by his presence; it was as though the
house was not completely hers. She could not shake the feeling off,
although she knew it was unworthy of her, and not justified by Henry's
behaviour at all. The real cause of her unease went deeper. It was not so
much the presence of her husband in the house that she found disturbing
but the absence of his colleagues and their comings and goings that upset
her and gave her the frightening thought that Henry's day might be over
and done with.

One blessing during 1919 had come about without any intervention from
Margot: Elizabeth was engaged to the forty-one-year-old Roumanian
diplomat Prince Antoine Bibesco, and suddenly was radiant with happiness. Elizabeth was only twenty-two, but Margot thought the steadying
influence of those extra years in a husband was all to the good. In some
ways Elizabeth was mature for her age and in others inexperienced, while
Antoine was highly sophisticated and worldly; but this too Margot saw as
an advantage. She felt that her daughter needed protection, for she fell
easily in love and suffered dreadfully if she had to be unkind to a suitor. In
that way she was exactly like Margot's sister Laura at the same age.
Antoine had watched Elizabeth's fleeting love affairs with amused indulg-

ence, only occasionally showing his feelings when she seemed determined to marry Gibson. He told her then that he had decided never to set eyes on her again, and this made Elizabeth see him in a new light.[11] In a way Elizabeth had been attracted by him all along, but his continental manners had made her shy; before Antoine knew her very well he asked her if she was a virgin, deducing from her blushes that she was. He had put the question lightly in French, making it seem less indelicate.

Then one night, just as Cynthia Asquith wrote in her diary that Antoine seemed to be cooling towards her young sister-in-law, he proposed and was accepted. That year there were two portraits of her in the Royal Academy's Summer Exhibition, one by McEvoy and the other by Augustus John, both making her look dreamily beautiful and bringing the painters much acclaim. She lacked her mother's stylish elegance, but her English rose beauty dressed in soft clinging materials caused a sensation whenever she entered a room. In her total acceptance of an indoor life she was her father's daughter, for she disliked all sport and detested hunting, although she could ride well enough when she chose.

Some of her mother's friends, living in reduced circumstances since the war, said how lucky it was that Elizabeth had chosen a rich man, since she had not the slightest idea how to run a home. Like her mother, she could not cook, sew or care for babies and did not look as though she could ever learn. Married to Bibesco she would not have to. Margot had said often enough that she saw no reason why Elizabeth should learn the art of home management and the secrets of the kitchen any more than she had done herself, since to do so deprived many a good honest woman of a job.

Love changed Elizabeth. The remoteness and withdrawal into herself that had so irritated her mother vanished, and she was once again the sweet daughter of the house, kind, helpful and willing to fall in with every plan. She even accompanied her parents to Balliol to dine with the Master. Margot had not visited the place since Dr Jowett's death and she wondered what changes she would find. To her delight there were almost none.

Margot began to plan the wedding at once. She only had one regret —Elizabeth would not be marrying from 10 Downing Street—but when she remembered the unpaid bills in her bureau drawer she thought that it was just as well, although she was optimistic that things would improve as they always had in the past. In the old days when she had overspent on her hunters, for instance, some friend had always come along to pay the bills.

Her letters show that now she felt stronger than Henry and the whole family put together, for in her heart she fully expected that when she had succeeded in trampling the enemy underfoot, Henry would once more rise and lead the Liberal party back to the promised land.

In May 1919 Elizabeth and Antoine Bibesco were married in St Margaret's, Westminster. Even with money in short supply Margot refused to allow her only daughter to have a pinch-penny wedding, so it was lavish in every way and was talked about for months afterwards. Several relations, who grumbled to Margot that they could not accept her invitation to the wedding because they had nothing to wear, managed by a lucky chance to find just the things they needed at Reville and Rossiter's —and put them on Margot's account, meaning, of course, to pay her back later when their husbands gave them the promised cheque. When Margot's bills came in they were enormous and could hardly be met. As she was struggling with her accounts and wondering what she could sell to realize some money quickly, Henry broke the news that they could no longer afford to live in 20 Cavendish Square. Exhausted and missing Elizabeth, Margot burst into tears; but when, some months later, the agent took them to see 44 Bedford Square, a delightful house which had once belonged to Lady Ottoline Morrell, she saw at once that the move would be no hardship.

Nevertheless she was leaving the place where she had started her married life and where her children had been born. The dismantling of 20 Cavendish Square brought out an unexpected touch of masochism which forced her to follow the removal men from room to room to watch them pack up her possessions. She tried to explain her passion for houses by saying it was really because of the people who lived in them that she loved every brick, every nook and cranny, but this was not strictly true; the real reason was that they had been the scene of events which formed landmarks in her life. After a last nostalgic dinner-party the keys of 20 Cavendish Square were handed over to the agents and Margot slept her first night in less fashionable Bedford Square.

20 Cavendish Square was put on the market at £30,000 but was not sold for some time. This in itself was a strain on the Asquith finances. Never before had Margot had to count the cost of anything, and as the daughter of a very rich man she had had no lessons in thrift. Even her father had accused her of not knowing the difference between a penny and a

sovereign, and to have to think twice before she signed a cheque was a new and unpleasant experience. After settling the household expenses, first priority must be Elizabeth's and Puffin's allowances, but this did not leave anything like enough for the countless relations and friends who expected rich Margot to help out for a wedding, a confinement, a long illness, an operation, a holiday or even a dress for a special occasion. If she talked of increasing poverty (later she was to refer to herself as being 'dog poor') they only laughed and did not believe a word. She had always advised wealthy friends to spend before the state took all, and those who really cared for her had often tried to shake her out of this extravagance.

Sir Donald Maclean, leader of the 'Wee Free' Liberals and a close friend, was deeply concerned for his former chief and his wife and suspected that things were worse than they knew themselves. He begged Margot to find out exactly what happened to her income after he discovered that she did not seem to know where it all went. It was unfortunate that Margot misunderstood this kindly action and thought Maclean was accusing her of extravagance and of spending too much money on herself. She tried to explain to him exactly how heavy the demands on her purse were:

> I have paid for every confinement of Cis's children (paid for all extra food in the house when grandchildren came to stay). I don't want any of the family to contribute—kept three T.B. servants in Switzerland and Scotch sanatoriums in the last twelve years. Have helped members of the family . . . helped all my stepchildren with money at all times. My crippled sister Lucy Graham-Smith I have dressed entirely. I don't say this to boast, but it is not personal vanity or poverty or folly of any kind . . .[12]

On the whole she was not too down-hearted. Better days would come now she had settled in at 44 Bedford Square. Living in a smaller house gave her the feeling that she was saving money. Thus she thought she was justified in re-starting her luncheon parties in the new house. With Puffin now at Balliol there was no shortage of guests, for he frequently drove over to The Wharf from Oxford, bringing one or two friends. He had grown into a most attractive boy, slender and alert, and Margot loved showing him off to her friends. He was not very talkative, perhaps because he knew he could not compete with his mother whose conversation was as pungent as ever.

Lord David Cecil has described Margot's welcome on his first visit to The Wharf:

> She immediately gathered me into her arms and gave me an affectionate kiss. . . . Puffin, her son, had told her that I had become a great friend of his and that was enough to make her, regardless of convention, enfold me in a loving embrace. Her feelings easily and frequently found physical expression. If excited, she clutched one's elbow; if amused she squeezed one's arm; and, like a very young child, if she wanted to engage one's attention she had a habit of seizing one's wrist and keeping hold of it till she finished what she had to say.
>
> This could happen sitting next to her at meals; the consequence was to hamper one's use of knife and fork. If Margot's feelings were touched—and they were easily touched—she might lay her head on one's shoulder. This too could happen at meals, thus adding even more to the difficulty of eating. At such emotional moments, her eyes would fill with tears which soon began to trickle down her cheeks. It was, however, an April shower. Within minutes, even seconds, all was sunshine again, the causes of her tears forgotten, and she was discoursing gaily about her youthful adventures in the hunting field or expatiating with eloquence and severity on the weaknesses of the political colleagues of her husband. . . . I found her comic and disarming and winning.
>
> *The Observer* 20.12.81

When Puffin's friends were her guests, Margot had it all her own way, since they were too shy to interrupt her monologues (though Lord David Cecil soon discovered her 'inability to distinguish between reality and fancy' in describing the past). With older people the conversation was fast and furious, as Desmond McCarthy, literary critic of the *Sunday Times*, discovered to his bewilderment the first time he lunched at The Wharf:

> The atmospherics are terrific. Neighbour is not necessarily talking to neighbour, nor, except at brief intervals, is the conversation what is called 'general' . . . but resembles rather a sort of wild game of pool in which every one is playing his or her stroke at the same time . . . while

anecdotes and comments whiz backwards and forwards, cannoning or clashing as they cross the table.[13]

Invitations to The Wharf were much sought after, but friendship was not what it was before the war. Guests who had enjoyed Asquith hospitality often gave greatly distorted accounts of what went on there. Geoffrey Madan, who had been at Balliol with Henry, spent a few days at The Wharf one summer and afterwards put it about that the ex-Prime Minister's consumption of alcohol was prodigious and that Asquith was 'slack'. 'He seems entirely lazy and greedy and indifferent to public events,' Madan told Arthur Benson, 'but when a thing has to be said, he says it better than anyone else.'[14]

'We mean to live very quietly,' Margot had announced when Henry fell from power, 'only seeing the King and a few friends.' One night at a dinner party Margot sat next to the Prince of Wales (later Edward VIII) whom she had not seen since her visit to Sandringham when the prince was only fourteen. In those days he had been a thin and nervous boy who hardly said a word and Margot thought him unhappy. He did not look cheerful even now but, not in the least put off by his blank expression and air of boredom, Margot promptly asked him to dinner.

Without being snobbish, Margot was fascinated by the Royal Family and proud of being able to entertain royalty, and took the extra trouble involved in her stride: police outside and detectives in the hall, the menu submitted for approval in advance. She had heard that with the wrong choice of guests the Prince could be difficult and might contribute almost nothing to the conversation, and she picked her guests with care.[15] Elizabeth and her husband Antoine, the Portuguese Count Soveral, who was never at a loss for a word, the Macleans, who would be willing to fill any gap when conversation flagged—those headed the list. Afterwards she had second thoughts. Would the company prove too highbrow for the Prince? Perhaps a request to keep conversation on a low level would not come amiss.

On the night all went well. The food and drink were excellent, the talk banal but easy and the police outside unobtrusive. She did not suggest bridge after dinner (Edward was said not to care for it!) but continued to talk on topics he enjoyed: horses and hunting and his latest tour abroad. The Prince often referred deferentially to Asquith, who glowed with pleasure at comments to which, had they been uttered by a commoner, he would have paid scant attention: 'He talked amusingly of his visit to America,' Asquith wrote to his latest female confidante, Mrs Harrisson, 'the meal was a great success.'[16] For all their highly developed critical faculties, the Asquiths were no different from anyone else when it came to royalty. Unhesitatingly they endowed the Prince with unusual wit and perception, and they went to bed telling each other what a stimulating evening they had had.

will be a success.'[2] There was another snag; she did not want to use her
diary, it was her hostage against misfortune, the one thing that her
children might be able to turn into money. She was really writing it for
Elizabeth and Puffin—it was to be left to them in her will and they could
sell it when times were hard.[3]

It was not quite true that she had never thought of publishing her diary.
The year before she had written to ask Mary Drew to 'write a sketch of me
for posterity. A good many people have done it and are doing it and I think
yours would be great fun. I am not touchy about style'.[4] The character
sketch was to be a preface to her diary. Why she asked such a thing of
Mary is inexplicable. She was the one woman certain to be spiky about
Margot's personality, and flattery was not in her nature. The reason may
have been that Mary was one of the few who remembered her as a girl at
the height of her popularity. When the sketch arrived it was no more than
Margot deserved and although she half-expected it, she was cross: 'You
have always thought me fast and wicked,' she wrote reproachfully, 'but I
forgive you.'[5] Mary was always telling Margot that it was better to forgive
than be forgiven and this was Margot's way of showing that she could do
so even when mortally offended. She wondered if Mary had her knife into
her because she wanted to write seriously. In 1906 Margot had made an
attempt to write the life of her sister Laura and after completing fifty pages
she had sent it to Arthur Balfour for his opinion. But he had never
returned it and when Margot asked for the manuscript back, he remembered nothing about it, making Margot very irritated indeed. Ten years
later Mary Drew herself wrote Laura's life and Margot found it hard to
forgive her for doing it so secretly, without once asking for her views.

From the moment the idea of a book of memoirs was mooted Margot
secretly began to work out what form it should take. Autobiography was
something she was not familiar with, although by 1919 she had prevailed
upon Henry to begin collecting material for his reminiscences (later
published as *Memories and Reflections*) and he had written a few
chapters. Margot found them disappointing: they were flat and dull and
she was sure the book would not sell. No one but Violet would read it and
she only out of loyalty. Now that she had time to spare, Margot had
joined the London Library and thought she knew what the public wanted.
Annoyingly Henry refused point blank to brighten his pages with character sketches and anecdotes of the great. No one had been in a better
position to collect both, she said, and tried to persuade him that it was

absurd to throw away such a marvellous opportunity. Margot could not understand such short-sightedness at all. It made her quite angry when she thought how by listening to her advice he might contribute substantially to the family budget. She herself had no scruples of that kind at all and was already considering changing her mind about her diary; there was so much in it that would make society sit up and take notice. She would only use some of it, of course, and still leave the bulk of it for her children.

Both Asquiths had been greatly encouraged to write since they had heard of the huge sums others had earned from their books. Winston Churchill had been able to buy a modest country-house and eighty acres of land in Kent, and the author of the best-seller *If Winter Comes* had made £50,000 out of that one novel alone. Lloyd George refused to disclose the sum his publishers had given him to write his memoirs, but it was said to be 'fabulous'. Henry and Margot considered themselves just as clever and they had just as much material. Both agreed they could become rich with a little effort.

Dull though she thought *Memories and Reflections*, Margot buoyed herself up with the hope that it would sell because of the author's name. As yet he had no publisher, so Margot wrote to Newman Flower, literary editor of Cassell, whom Arthur Balfour recommended to her; he came post-haste to The Wharf to look at the book now nearing completion. His verdict was not promising. Politely he indicated that it was 'too meticulous and elaborate' in its present form. In high dudgeon Asquith wrote to Mrs Harrisson: 'I gave him no encouragement and said I must do it my way or not at all.'[6] Argument only made him more stubborn. In vain Margot cited cases she knew of where money had been made out of 'mere trifles': Mary Drew's life of Margot's sister Laura thirty years after her death was over-sentimental and not in the least like Laura (Arthur Benson rightly called it 'a clumsy little memoir'), but it was a best seller and had been bought by people who knew nothing of the Tennants; while Arthur Benson's brother had made a fortune out of *Dodo*. Since Dodo herself was supposed to be Margot it caused a sensation and went into many editions, despite the heroine being a 'pretentious donkey with the heart and brains of a linnet'. A month after publication day Alfred Lyttleton had tried to buy a copy in order to find out what the public saw in it and was told it was completely sold out.[7] Margot went on and on in her most persuasive manner, but it was no use.

Meanwhile Lord Esher produced his book on the Great War and

Margot wanted Henry to review it to refute some of the criticisms it made of him. Without telling Henry she wrote to H. A. Gwynne to secure the review in the *Morning Post* for him: 'I only write you one line to tell you I hope you will heed my husband's criticism of Lord Esher's book, which comes out in Pearson's in November . . . It made my blood boil with its inaccuracies and cheap writing.'[8] The account of Lord Esher's delicate mission to St Omer to give French the unpleasant news that General Haig was to take his place, annoyed Margot exceedingly because she thought she detected between the lines criticism of Henry when he was Prime Minister; it was 'base and wrong' and Henry must say so in public. But Henry would have none of this either, so washing her hands of her unenterprising husband, she stalked off to work on her own memoirs. For the first time the story of her 'glorious youth' could be told. It was to be 'an open, honest account of people and events' that the public would relish reading. There were some she could think of at once whose behaviour would not look too good in print: the 'cold and impenetrable Kitchener' and 'that little parvenu Lloyd George'. She could fill a volume about those two alone.

Words flowed out of Margot with ease and rapidity. Not for her those agonizing doubts and cruel self-criticisms that seize most authors of a first book. If only she had started writing years ago . . . but all she had managed was part of a small treatise on the education of children from birth to boarding school, something she felt had never been properly understood before. The social, moral and intellectual sides of this problem were of the greatest interest but she had become bored and never finished it. These memoirs were different; here she was dealing with real people, events that really happened and the three hours spent at her desk every morning (6.30–9.30 were her working hours) she found most stimulating. 'I deal with what I thoroughly understand,' she wrote to Mary Drew, 'human nature and character. . . .'[9]

A draft of the first volume was soon finished and Henry persuaded her to send it off to Newman Flower for his opinion before plunging straight away into volume two, for there was too much material to cram into a single book. He warned her that there might not be a market for such a book despite all her publishers had said, and as a lawyer he cautioned her about the laws of libel: it was a hazard that should not be forgotten, for it might still be libellous to state a fact even though it were true. If a publisher passed it then all was well. Both had heard that Newman Flower had a genius for publishing best-selling autobiographies; he hardly ever made a mistake and could be completely trusted. As Margot said, they had been so surrounded by untrustworthy people for the last few years that they had become over-suspicious. She supposed there were still some honest people left in the world.

She was rather pleased with her first draft. She had made good use of her diaries and of snippets of comments she had the foresight to jot down at the time or very soon afterwards; these had been stuffed into the corners of desk drawers and now came in useful to fill a blank space. When she wrote in the early morning she had a basket of these beside her as, tea in one hand and pencil in the other, she wrote for dear life. One thing surprised her, even shook her a little: how could she, with her good memory, have forgotten so much? In some cases she had even forgotten the intense emotion provoked by certain events which she knew must have burned through her like a fire.

Newman Flower was tact itself; he had to be, for it was his job to suggest many alterations, especially in Margot's descriptions of people. Her remark about Kitchener, for instance—still a revered figure in England—must be toned down: 'aggressive self-assurance' he wanted replaced by 'melancholy self-assurance', which Margot objected to, saying very rightly it was not the same thing at all. Flower wanted certain stylistic alterations too: 'No one can suspect the trouble I take in writing,' she told him. 'An amateur has difficulties in writing which are hard to resolve by critics who do not read books, and dislike authors.'[10] Not unnaturally, after the energy she had put into her book, her feathers were a little ruffled. She could not understand that all Newman Flower wanted was that the book should sell. The preface worried him too. He wanted a second opinion, but this Margot would not allow: only her eyes and his must see the draft: 'The proof must be shown to no one . . . if you send it to all sorts of people, it will never be finished.'[11] However, with tact and firm but sympathetic persuasion Newman Flower got his way, and although Margot had never expected so many changes—she had enjoyed writing straight off the cuff and had not thought any corrections necessary —when he showed her how much better it looked his way, she gave in at once. For the final draft (she had not understood she would have to revise her work, and was dismayed) Flower warned her to write more slowly, reflect more carefully, and pay greater attention to dates. At the end of a two-hour discussion between author and editor it was hard to tell which was the more worn out. Margot was showing all the signs of an author's sensitive feelings about a first book and she returned to Bedford Square white-faced and tight-lipped. When Henry offered to read the manuscript she said she would not let anybody see it, but secretly sent Flower's corrected version to Mary Drew, whom she trusted to give her an honest opinion.

Mary had plenty to say about it and did not mince her words; to read the book today is to feel that Mary was probably right in her criticisms. Margot took umbrage at her suggestions and wrote Mary a sarcastic letter in return for her pains: 'I am glad you think I have only a little work to do to make up for the lack of humour, and some intelligence to make up for being so stupid.'[12] Why had she been so weak as to let Mary see her work? Just as unwisely she sent it next to Edmund Gosse the literary critic. His comments were long, detailed, even fulsome:

> I cannot sufficiently thank you for the chance which has allowed me to read these beautiful, sincere and eloquent pages before the whole world unites in praising them. The record is of an extraordinary power and beauty. It will rank with the greatest autobiographies in literature if it goes on as it begins. You have achieved an impression of truth which is really thrilling, not a false note, not a silly touch of mock modesty, all is full, rich and vivacious—you have nothing to fear from criticism.[13]

Coming so soon after Newman Flower's uncomplimentary remarks, this overdone praise elated her, and having little or no self-criticism, she now felt able to snap her fingers at Flower's reiterated: 'I'm afraid, Mrs Asquith, this won't do.'

The *Daily Telegraph* bought the serial rights and about two weeks before publication they printed snippets from the book to whet the readers' appetite. But they merely succeeded in giving a false impression of all Margot had said, making it seem flat and tedious, a terrible disappointment to her friends who had felt that anything written by Margot would be scandalous or at least exciting. DD Lyttelton was first astonished and then upset when she read the extracts and told Margot that they were not well chosen:

They have done an incalculable disservice. There are a few things I wish
you had not said and of course these are prominent . . . the truth to you
is not always the truth to others. The book lacks cohesion—you are
frank in your criticisms and naturally these are resented.

But she ended her letter kindly, telling Margot that even these poor
extracts gave her a wonderful feeling of vitality. Margot's reply was short
and cool: 'I only claim to be extremely accurate.'[14]

Everyone felt free to criticize the book, such is the penalty of fame.
Margot had often been critical of Lord Esher, but he was far fairer to her
than some of her few close friends. Although he blamed the publishers for
allowing the extracts to appear, he wrote to Margot to say that her work
would have a permanent place in English literature. Arthur Benson noted
in his diary that it was 'an interesting record but ends in undiscriminating
egotism and self-glorification . . .',[15] but this of course Margot did not
see.

On publication day there was a rush to buy the book and Margot
records that 1500 copies were sold in six hours. Before the end of the
following day it was a best-seller. If the public looked for scandal, they
were disappointed; it was far milder than people expected. Very soon
Margot was in the bewildered state of not knowing whether to believe the
vitriolic abuse of some papers or the wild congratulations of others. It was
the same with her friends. John Masefield was among the admirers and
wrote, 'Surely you ought to do nothing else but write your life since you
are one of those people born to set down the likeness of old England that is
passing.'[16] Lord Crewe wrote of the 'power and brilliance of your
character writing'. Knowing Margot as well as he did, he warned her that
there would always be people who thought that 'one or two anecdotes
ought to have been omitted where the public interest was against publication'.

The bedroom sessions and the free life Laura and Margot enjoyed as
children and young adults were misunderstood, as Mary Drew had
warned her they would be. 'People have strange immoral minds' was
Margot's retort. Because they were quite innocent occasions, she refused
to understand why others should condemn them: 'Are these provincial
prudes worth worrying about? I've had dozens of letters daily thanking
me for my wretched book.'[17] Amongst the 'dozens' were delightful ones
from Queen Alexandra and Lady Dudley, both of whom loved it.

It was to be expected that Margot should get her first taste of professional jealousy. How could a woman without education or training of any kind produce a book that sold and sold and sold? Gwynne of the *Morning Post*, who liked Margot and heard a great deal of unjust abuse of her work, made a point of seeing Margot and giving her much helpful advice. Volume two was still to come and with great goodness of heart he showed Margot how it could be better arranged, gaining her confidence by praising the good bits in volume one and her courage in attempting it at all. In this way he did much to soothe hurt feelings: 'We agree well over my book,' she wrote to him after he had been with her for some time going over her work.

> Neither you nor I think it good [here Margot is putting words into Gwynne's mouth]. I didn't want you to, but it is true and this is why 11,000 copies were sold before the press with almost comic unanimity rushed at it like a bull at a gate . . . now the third edition's almost gone . . . it has one merit and one only, it is absolutely true. Katharine Asquith came to see me yesterday. She rocked with laughter over the stories which as she said I had put so mildly: 'Never mind the papers and the crabbers, Margot, . . . you should give it up if you expect to be praised by the press: you'll think me an awful bore but I advise absolute honesty.'[18]

For the second time in her life Margot was the personage in her own right. In a curious way she even enjoyed the criticism of her book, for it meant that she was not ignored. Then Edmund Gosse's review in the *Sunday Times* tore it to shreds. It was a terrible shock after his effusive letter of praise. She wrote for an explanation and back came the cool answer: 'That was my personal opinion: I wrote as a friend, the other I have written in a public capacity.'[19] Margot was bewildered and wrote angrily to Mary Drew:

> I have been hurt to the bone by Gosse, whose wonderful letter you saw and have got a copy of. Look at his review in *Sunday Times* . . . he leaves it to be thought by every reader that my book is poor stuff. Had I written even half of what I think about people and events my book would have been really alive. . . .[20]

By contrast, Winston Churchill reviewed it kindly for the *Daily Mail*. She was particularly pleased that he mentioned her 'superb horsemanship' and was delighted with the phrase 'a featherweight dare-devil'.[21] J. A. Spender, too, did a great deal to wipe out Gosse's cruelty with another favourable review. In thanking him Margot repeated what she had said much too often already—that every word in the book was true, as though that gave it extra merit and removed all faults. As so often, it was the bad reviews that stuck in the mind. In forlorn mood she wrote to Mary Drew, who herself had blamed Margot for her lack of tact but had asked for a copy for the Hawarden Library:

> I wish I had never written it, but as Tennyson said one must learn to be indifferent to critics. I am rather glad you say I have no humour in discussing myself, as I was always in earnest, but I have as a matter of fact laughed at myself all through life . . . Alas I do not pride myself on having no tact. I have not even that excuse. I am tactless on purpose . . . My book would be hopelessly out of place in your father's library for students and nothing will induce me to give it to anyone . . . it is far too improper I fear.[22]

To Margot's great joy the part about Laura had moved those who remembered her, including some who recalled her charitable work among the London poor. Mary Drew had particularly disliked the Laura part because she felt that only she had the right to tell her story, and complained that Margot should not have gone into such detail. Margot's reply was triumphant:

> I have had thousands of letters of praise and thanks which had I refrained I would never have had. I infinitely prefer the understanding of the East to the West End of London. Margaret Keynes and Colonel Lawrence think I ought to have been bolder and dealt with Balfour etc more forcefully and with less reticence. But Morley thinks I have been perfectly fair to Milner . . . it's all rather funny and fearfully unexpected the heaps of letters I get but I take no credit except for extreme industry and absolute truth.[23]

Whatever the tone of the reviews, no one could say they were not numerous, far more than Morley got for his life of Gladstone. Letters poured into 44 Bedford Square and Margot spent hours answering them.

When she and Mary next met they had a sharp argument about the amount of the advance Margot had received. Mary said it was £10,000 'for indiscretions'. Margot contradicted her, it was £25,000 'for real insight into character'.[24] It is doubtful if this was true; more likely it was merely said to startle Mary, which it certainly did. She had never dreamed that Margot was capable of earning such a sum; her face showed it and Margot got her own back at a stroke.

Margot had taken a great risk in not showing the manuscript to Henry and seeking his advice on the laws of libel. It was only a week before publication day when they were alone together at The Wharf that she placed the finished copy on his desk immediately before leaving for London. On her return late the next night she went straight to her room without seeing him.

> He came into my own bedroom the next morning and sat on my bed. He told me he had spent most of the night reading it and I looked at him with apprehension ... but all was well. He said he thought my autobiography was one of absorbing interest and literary distinction, which no one could have written but myself. After which I burst into tears.[25]

Read sixty years later the book seems mild in the extreme, and one wonders what the fuss was all about. While it contains some well-written passages, it is too diffuse, even confusing, as the author leaps from one subject to another, often without any sort of chronology. Yet it so easily could have been improved, and one wonders why this was not done. Perhaps Newman Flower was afraid of destroying the liveliness and spontaneity which are its greatest merits. Those friends who were fond of her were dismayed at the false and unsympathetic picture she gave of herself. In many cases she shows herself dealing clumsily with her stepchildren and in others to have little affection for them, yet their love and friendship were precious to her and in reality she was not so awkward as the book suggests. She was ill-advised to get her own back on George Curzon, of whom she had once been very fond, by criticizing his manners as a young man. Curzon promptly went into a sulk and never spoke to Margot again. She thought such a reaction very silly: what was plain speaking among friends? There were others, too, who read more into her words than she ever intended and shunned her for this reason. If she gained new friends through her book, she lost many old and loyal ones through her rough handling of their feelings. As a new generation grew up and took the place of old departed friends, there were few left to tell of Margot's dazzling past. Who can blame them for taking her as they found her and not making allowances?

There were compensations. As the author of a successful book she began now to lean more towards the literary world where she was soon held in high esteem, not so much for her talents as for her success, and many a struggling writer deeply envied her. Enid Bagnold, the playwright, became an instant friend and brought her fiancé Roderick Jones, who was to become the head of Reuters, to The Wharf. 'Chips' Channon brought Beverley Nichols, who in turn introduced Margot to Duncan Grant the painter. After a good review of her book in the *New Statesman*, its editor, Clifford Sharp, was another frequent visitor to The Wharf, where the presence of so many literary figures perceptibly raised the level of conversation. Margot was once again in her element, a little more didactic than of old, perhaps a little less inclined to be contradicted, but according to Sir Henry Channon, as crisp and lively as ever.

If she was still surrounded by admiration and new faces, there were moments when she longed for the old days before she had ever published a word and could attract people by her personality alone. She said this to Colonel House, the man who was supposed to be the power behind President Wilson, when she gave a luncheon party in his honour; Lord Crewe overheard her and noted the real pathos of the remark, for he saw that she was not speaking for effect, but really meant what she said. He realized suddenly that for all her public nonchalance she had been cut to the quick by the unkind remarks of friends and reviewers. Next day he wrote her an encouraging letter. '. . . I can't tell you how highly I rate it myself, and no one has contradicted me . . . how well you can tell a story when you try.'[26]

CHAPTER 32

A Practical Joke of the Worst Kind

VOLUME TWO OF Margot's book was coming along well. She was trying
to make it bolder than volume one; she was also trying hard not to make
mistakes, since rewriting almost drove her frantic with frustration. Newman Flower had discovered that she never read her work once she had
finished it and almost expected him to treat it as casually as she did. After
'lean' writing, 'spontaneous' writing was the thing and corrections ruined
the feeling of life that she was trying to convey, she told him. Harold
Nicolson promised to read the finished manuscript and make the corrections for her. He returned the first draft quickly with only a few pencil
marks, instantly giving Margot the feeling that she had learned a lot when
writing the first volume. She noted with some pleasure that his erasures
were only of insignificant things due more to carelessness than lack of
knowledge or style. She wrote humbly to thank him: 'It was really good of
you to read my manuscript. The mistakes are incredible . . . I can hardly
believe I have left them in. . . .'[1]

When the second volume was published, she was greatly surprised not
to be bombarded with invitations to write another book. She had to put
away the happy pictures of playing off one publisher against another, the
bidding reaching prodigious heights. On the other hand she needed a rest.

She seems to have made a considerable sum out of the first volume,
unless she had got her figures wrong. The advance for volume two was as
large as £30,000, she said, and volume one was still selling well. For some
extraordinary reason she did not look on this money she had earned as an
addition to her income, giving her the wherewithal to pay her debts, but as
an extra to fritter away as she pleased. Asquith does not seem to have
helped her here. Perhaps he felt that it was hers to do what she liked with,
while Margot was carried along by the delusion that there was a lot more
money to be got if she could only think of something to write about.
'Perhaps Vita could give me a plot?' she wrote to Harold Nicolson, whom

she had no qualms about bombarding with requests for ideas and offers of collaboration. 'We could write a play together, which would pay us like fun.'[2] Neither Vita Sackville West nor her husband took up the offer.

After much thought Margot came to the conclusion that it might be easier for her to take up journalism than to go on with serious writing. She began to try writing articles for newspapers, starting at three or four in the morning when she could not sleep and her mind was at its sharpest, so she said. Some time before she had published an article or two in *Pearson's*, but she forgot that she was then the wife of the Prime Minister and her name on the cover helped to sell the magazine. Of course she had not the slightest idea how much discipline and knowledge of current affairs would be required. The articles that she read for comparison looked so deceptively simple that she imagined she could knock off one or two a week with ease. Things did not quite work out as she intended. Her intelligence told her how it should be done, but confronted with a blank sheet of paper she felt empty of ideas and could not begin. When she woke in the night she would wrap herself in a shawl and try to scribble. After wasting much paper she at last succeeded, and by morning thought it good enough to send to 'dearest Harold' [Nicolson], who with the greatest good nature corrected it, improving it here and there. Yet even so it was rejected. She asked him to improve it further, saying that the 'only merit I have is to write well'.[3] In the end Harold Nicolson persuaded her that newspaper articles were too specialized and were not for amateurs, the professionals would beat her every time. He had an inspiration: what about short stories? Would they not be more suited to her imaginative type of mind? It was the very thing; it was such a good idea that she was amazed she had not thought of it herself. Each story would bring in a nice fat cheque, and in her mind she had written several already, with magazine editors clamouring for more. She thanked Harold Nicolson enthusiastically: 'You certainly are the best of friends . . . you will help me to be less sloppy which will be of value to me.'[4]

Before she could write even one short story she was diverted by an invitation which both terrified and fascinated her: to go on a lecture tour of the United States. She tried to resist the tempting offer, but circumstances were too much for her, the pressure too great, and in the end she went without counting the cost to health and nerves. Her New York publisher, Gerald Christy, was a determined man; Margot had no idea how to deal with him, when on a flying visit to London he said emphatically that a lecture tour of the USA was expected of her after her book had sold so well, and cleverly registered a certain measure of surprise that she had not taken it for granted. Besides, not a great deal was known in the States of English upper-class life, he said, but Mrs Asquith knew it all from A to Z, so her subject was ready made.

The first time Christy approached her she had a valid excuse—she was in the middle of volume two. After the second pressing letter she was more honest: 'I have no idea of lecturing and could never do it.'[5] He tempted her by increasing the fee and when that was no good he changed his tactics. He had heard Margot had once written short stories for the *Strand* and *Cornhill*—the tour, he wrote, could give her much copy for her short stories. When he was in England he had heard the Asquiths were not well off and at his first meeting with Margot he had seen at once that, properly exploited, she could be a real commercial success. He took no notice of Margot's plea that she was terrified of speaking in public; all new lecturers said this, there was nothing to it, he reassured her. She asked hopefully if it would be enough for her to read a chapter or two from her second volume, 'which nobody has yet heard. Reading it would help the sales enormously. I loathe pretentious female lecturers or orators'.[6] Ignoring such remarks, in his next letters Christy showed that he considered the matter settled, making Margot quake at the knees. She had never spoken in public, although she was used to sitting on the platform listening to Henry's speeches at political meetings. Every time she had wondered how anyone dared do it. Yet she was a far more audacious character than Henry, far more aggressive and outspoken than Violet. Her terror of public speaking helped her to fight Christy. 'I have no talent for this sort of thing,' she wrote again on a postcard. After that there was a six months' silence, but just when she was beginning to feel safe, a letter with a New York postmark arrived at The Wharf: Christy had struck again.[7]

It was April, and Margot's Oxfordshire garden showed the budding signs of spring. Even the air seemed to have a mellow feel about it, giving promise of a hot, dry summer of a kind that suited Margot's nervous temperament. She hated gardening herself, nevertheless she could appreciate the efforts others put into caring for her plants and shrubs. The garden at The Wharf had always delighted her and this year it seemed to hold a special beauty. She walked slowly all over it the day Christy's unwelcome letter arrived—nothing, she vowed, should take her away from 'all this' to cross the ocean and visit America. 'I am confined to bed with exhaustion,' she wrote untruthfully from 44 Bedford Square, 'and have lost over a stone in weight and am off to the country this afternoon to lie in bed and feed up. Sleep has departed from me.'[8] To this letter Margot's secretary added a postscript of her own: 'She doesn't mean to speak in public at all.'[9]

In the end Christy won, as he knew he would. He could not guess that one of the deciding factors was the Bibescos' move to the New York Embassy. Elizabeth missed her mother and had been urging her for weeks to come and see the baby Priscilla, who had been born in England. That was the tastiest bait of all. 'My grandbaby', as Margot called her, would not know her own grandmother unless they met soon.

On 20 January 1922 Margot, her secretary and maid set sail for the United States. There had been a large farewell dinner the night before at 44 Bedford Square and it had not broken up until the small hours when Margot suddenly remembered why the dinner was given and was at once plunged into despair. When daylight came her depression was deeper than ever. As she waited in the hall surrounded by the paraphernalia thought necessary for a long journey—trunks, rugs, wraps, baskets of books, writing pads and pills and potions for every emergency—she began to tremble at the thought of crossing the Atlantic Ocean in winter, and she longed to be struck down by some crippling but mysterious illness which would keep her in bed for weeks. It did not help her spirits that she had chosen to travel in deepest black as though in mourning, her satin highwayman's hat unrelieved even by the usual diamond pin, her small figure almost smothered in fox furs. The effect was startling and made her look amazingly grand. At Victoria Station heads turned to watch the guard conduct her to her carriage. Was she the widow of an Emperor or a King?

In these days when authors are only too glad to be given the opportunity to advertise their wares, Margot's panic seems greatly exaggerated, but in her case it was genuine. Not without some bitterness she noticed how eager her husband and stepchildren were for her to go, talking of 'the wonderful opportunity' she was being given and what a fool she would be not to take it up; it might never come again. She could not help but be resentful. Henry, she supposed, would not miss her much. His latest friend, Mrs Harrisson, lived almost next door to The Wharf at Boar's Hill and was only too willing to fill the gap.

Margot was not a natural tourist. People interested her more than places and books dealing with human nature more than travellers' tales. In her time she had known many travellers; some, like Wilfred Scawen Blunt, who travelled for pleasure, but more like George Curzon, who did so in the course of duty, yet however interesting she found them as people any recital of their travels sent her to sleep. She thought herself fortunate that people had come to her.[10]

Although it was winter, the sea was like a millpond, but even so Margot managed to be sea-sick on the crossing. She lay on her bunk in her cabin writing up her diary, missing all the fun on board, so that when they docked in New York she was in poor shape to meet the hordes of pressmen who awaited her on the quay. Still worse, she was immediately rushed off to see the hall in which she was to lecture that night, so vast and so empty of human faces that it seemed even bigger and more formidable, making her feel like a 'midge on a dreadnought'. It was, she says, a practical joke of the worst kind.[11] The result could have been foreseen: tired and dizzy, she lectured badly and her audience left the hall in disgust.

Next day she felt so ill that she was beyond nerves and was praised for her relaxed manner. 'We wish we could talk as she does, casually, leaning against a table', wrote the *World* newspaper, giving her high marks for clear diction and interesting style, and she was showered with flowers and invitations to dine after her next public appearance. Receptions and dinners always followed the lectures, when questions were hurled at her by curious Americans longing to know more about the English way of life. 'What do you think of flappers?'—'Tell us about Princess Mary's trousseau.' Only one man seriously annoyed her: he asked her to tell him about England's greatest man. Somewhat puzzled, Margot asked him if he meant Thomas Hardy or Kipling, and was taken aback when he replied 'Lloyd George'. She met with boundless kindness and was overwhelmed with presents so that her secretary was kept hard at it writing letters of thanks. Nevertheless she found much to criticize in the American way of life: in particular the amount of alcohol consumed in the land of prohibition shocked her. She wrote home: 'Americans thrive in rooms as hot as conservatories, sit up all night, eat candy and ice-cream all day and live to a great age.'[12]

While in New York she stayed with Elizabeth and Antoine at the Roumanian Embassy. She did not care for the life Elizabeth was leading: engagements all day, out every night with little or no rest, her child too much in the care of her nannie. Nothing, it seemed, was ever perfect.[13]

Despite the praise lavished on her by American journalists, Margot would keep insisting that the tour was a failure, adding that in the circumstances it was fortunate that hers was a temperament not easily knocked under. But by this, she really meant that all the kindness in the world could not make her like America or the whistle-stop tour. It was all too much for her, she said, and complained of the mad rushing about, the lack of rest and relaxation and the tiring night journeys from one town to another when she could not sleep. Yet when she returned to England she was not the wreck her family had expected from her letters, but alert, bright-eyed and in perfect health. She had left home clad in deep black; she returned a bird of paradise in a new plaid suit of vivid red checks. 'Jaunty' exactly described her. Life had been such a rush, she said, that there was no time to think of her health. Asquith confirms this in a letter to Hilda Harrisson: 'I went to Victoria at 5 this afternoon [24 April 1922] to meet Margot who was in excellent condition and is going tonight with Puffin to see the gloomy Christmas play [*Anna Christie* by Eugene O'Neill].'[14]

Home again, Margot spent her mornings writing up a narrative account of her trip from notes made at the time. It is not exactly a modest account but it is amongst her best-written work, because since it was not meant for publication, she felt free and unselfconscious, her 'lean writing' forgotten. No longer striving for effect it is a good, straightforward account of her life from day to day.

The publication of her autobiography stamped Margot as a successful writer and the American tour confirmed it. Everyone likes to know a best-selling author and Margot got more attention than most. One or two markedly cold glances from a few old friends who thought she ought to have mentioned them or were angry because she had done so too often, did not bother her at all. What is more she now began to look back on the tour as a landmark in her life. To be spoiled and fêted because she had had a book published amazed her, and although at the time she was inclined to think the adulation a bit too much, looking back she felt that she had earned it by endurance alone.

Nothing succeeds like success. There was not a morning when an invitation or two was not waiting on the breakfast tray. At the Mountbatten wedding in October 1922, just after the publication of her second volume, Margot caused a sensation in a stunning new outfit specially designed for her by Lucille. People craned their necks to get a better view as they whispered to each other, 'Why should someone so rich bother to write books, of all things?' while others wondered how she managed to do it all alone at her age and without any experience. Asquith was amused by the gossip and Margot not so indifferent as she liked to pretend.

In April 1923 the Asquiths occupied prominent seats at the marriage of Lady Elizabeth Bowes-Lyon to the Duke of York, and at the luncheon afterwards Margot was placed next to Winston Churchill who explained his own special housing scheme to her: 'Build the home round the wife and mother, let her always have water on the boil, make her the central factor, the dominating condition of the situation.'[15]

George V never forgot what he owed to Asquith's guidance in the first months after his accession, and invitations to functions at the Palace were regular if not frequent. Although Margot did not find the King and Queen a stimulating couple she was grateful that they were happy to talk of the old days when Henry was at the helm.

Country-house parties were now few and far between, but in the autumn of 1923 Lord Rosebery asked the Asquiths to spend a few days at Mentmore, his large Victorian mansion near Aylesbury. Dalmeny in Scotland Margot knew well—it was beautiful and filled with antiques, like dozens of houses of the rich all over the country—but Mentmore made her gape with wonder and surprise: it was an Aladdin's cave of fantasy and delight, like nothing she had ever seen before.

It was a regular museum of every kind of work of art and antiquity: Gobelin tapestries of the best period hung round the walls, representing the twelve months of the year. There were Titians galore, Sèvres milkmaids' pails which Marie Antoinette had had made for the Trianon.[16]

She could have added the gilt doge's chairs and furniture of the finest quality from England, France, Holland and Germany, while in every room there were the most superb examples of Boulle that she had ever seen. Margot proved a most appreciative guest. But it saddened her to watch Rosebery, now partially paralysed, carried up and down stairs in a chair.

Henry did not care for horse racing, so Margot left him at home when she went to the Derby as guest of the Aga Khan, and the following month she took Puffin to the Vanderbilt Ball—'the last word in American luxury'. In return she had to promise (somewhat reluctantly) to go with Puffin to Wimbledon, and to her surprise she loved every minute of it. The agility of the women players amazed her and she applauded the short skirts they wore.

If her book had done her harm in one direction, in another it had opened up life surprisingly: new faces, new ideas, everyone continually on the move, and now she was in the stream once again moving as fast if not faster than the rest. She loved it all, and all the more because she had done it by herself.

CHAPTER 33

Governed by a Lot of Reckless Gamblers

MEANWHILE, ASQUITH'S POLITICAL future had for a moment taken a rosier hue. Early in 1920 a vacancy arose through the death of the Independent Liberal Member of Parliament for Paisley. Margot saw the obituary and rushed into Henry's study waving *The Times*. Henry must take his place. It was a week or two before the local selection committee could make up its mind that it preferred Asquith to a Lloyd George Liberal, but at last he was able to write to Mrs Harrisson that 'the Paisley people have got down to the right side of the fence'.[1]

Asquith was not looking forward to the adventure because 'the issue is extremely doubtful', since in the last election the Liberal majority had been very small. For her part Margot was jubilant and filled with optimism as she tried to stir Henry into action, reminding him that Sir George Younger, once a Lloyd George Liberal, was now on their side and that he had great influence with the young susceptible Liberals who were not sure where their loyalties lay. She advised him to forget how in the coupon election Younger had backed Lloyd George to the hilt and had pulled every string he could to get rid of Asquith. With her practical mind she told him that it was the present that mattered. Who cared today that a year ago Younger had called Lloyd George 'the man of the moment', and now he was 'that little Welsh devil'? Politics was like that.

The moment the invitation came they hurried to Scotland together with Violet and Asquith's private secretary Vivian Phillips, and put up at the Central Station Hotel in Glasgow. It was comfortable enough, but in the old days the Liberal country-houses would have vied with each other to put them up. She confessed she missed 'the comfort, good food and encouragement, for an hotel is only an hotel however comfortable and not the same thing at all'.[2]

From Glasgow she wrote a long letter to Gwynne to contradict a statement in his paper that 'even the Asquith Liberals recognize that Mr

Lloyd George will be leading them in fact if not in name'. This was not true at all.

> It is one of the curiosities that Lloyd George and Northcliffe stated and spread that my husband was a fool who was too lazy to speak and too old & gaga to show energy etc. There never was a younger man though his hair has now been white since he married me. It turned white when I nearly died suddenly with my baby. His voice was never hoarse at all in spite of the newspapers. He has spoken three times a day since the first day of the election and travelled nearly 4000 miles, he is in great spirits . . . your newspaper, tho' against Asquith is the only paper that reports fairly . . .[3]

Scotland was Margot's native land, yet she did not feel at home in Paisley and canvassing was not easy. She made short work of the pro-German taunt after Asquith had said publicly that the peace terms were too harsh. She told everyone how Henry had been left out of these talks: 'In 1918 he was approached by men of every party and opinion who begged my husband to go to Paris; that he must overlook personal feelings and in such an emergency offer his services to the country.'[4] To their surprise Asquith did not lack canvassers. His most ardent followers were university students from Glasgow and many other young men from as far afield as the south of England.

Polling was on 12 February, and a fortnight later (the extra time was needed to allow postal votes to be received) Asquith was declared the winner. It was a matter of great pride to Margot that Henry had been victorious by sticking to his principles, that the fear of failure had not deterred him from denouncing the Versailles treaty, and that his statement about Ireland (that Dominion Home Rule was the only solution for that strife-torn country) won him many votes.[5] The night the poll was declared the crowds that escorted the successful candidate to his hotel were so dense that extra police had to be brought in to protect the new MP and his wife. The Asquiths were to catch the night train to London, and at the station the crowds again went mad. Margot was knocked on to the railway line and might have been killed had not a porter hauled her back on to the platform, to her amazement without injury of any kind. 'I found instead of the bruises I expected to see I had not received a single scratch.'[6] Relief and elation mingled together as they sped through the night to

London, every member of the party too worked up to sleep. As the train drew into Euston in the morning, Margot saw with a thrill that the platform was packed with enthusiastic supporters. The drive through the streets was a repetition of what had happened in Glasgow. When they reached 44 Bedford Square they were astonished to find a huge wreath of flowers fastened to the door welcoming them home, and inside stacks of letters and telegrams of congratulations.

It happened to be Elizabeth's twenty-third birthday and Puffin had come up from Oxford to join a family party for *Pygmalion* with Mrs Patrick Campbell and Marian Terry in the principal roles. The thunderous ovation the Asquiths received at the theatre touched her deeply. Nor did the enthusiasm stop there, but there were smiles and bows and shouts of congratulations as they waited for their carriage which even Henry seemed to enjoy. When she drove on 2 March with Henry to the House of Commons, where he was to take his seat after a year's absence, the entire route was lined with cheering crowds. It was quite like old times, Margot thought happily, and if she saw once again visions of Downing Street, who can blame her?

The atmosphere inside the chamber was as chilling as it was warm and enthusiastic outside. From her seat in the Ladies' Gallery Margot immediately sensed the hostility and became apprehensive. As her eye roved over row upon row of the dark clad figures below, she noticed old friends: Balfour, Churchill, Montagu, not one of whom spoke a word of welcome. Of course she had expected nothing from Lloyd George or Bonar Law, for Henry's return could only mean unease for these two and others like them; nevertheless the omission hurt Margot, as she remembered all Henry had done for these men and how they had both always made them welcome at 10 Downing Street.

There was another blow in store. When Asquith tried to induce Edward Grey to join him in an attempt to upset the coalition (which the whole country was sick of, Margot had been told), he put up excuses: his eyesight was failing; his health in general was not good; politics had changed so much he did not care for the House any more; he had found new interests in the country.[7] At first Asquith was hurt, but Margot tried to brace him: they must accept these reverses in a philosophical manner. But she only managed to sound bitter. Henceforth when anyone mentioned Grey's name in her presence, she was careful to hint that Grey was declining and only cared for chasing squirrels in Northumberland.

It was a big disappointment to Margot that Henry did not like the new House of Commons at all. During his year in exile it had altered drastically and all of it for the worse. The things that he had loved, that he had thought solid and unchanging, the camaraderie, the dignity and the feeling of strength that the House always gave him had vanished, and the bitter struggles going on between different sections of the government were barely veiled.

> Moderation and severity, coercion and conciliation, free trade and protection, were practised alternately and simultaneously by the same ministers as though they were the same things or it was a mere chance which came uppermost. But the greatest change was the frequent absence of the PM from the House.[8]

Henry's low spirits after his triumph of the election disturbed Margot and she tried to cheer him. When a few days later he told her that he had decided to fight for the one thing he longed to see, Dominion Home Rule in Ireland, she felt she had succeeded. This better mood did not last. Ireland was not a prominent subject any more, it seemed, few were interested and Asquith had lost what popularity he had by trying to hammer home its importance. No one was more acid in his comments on Asquith's plans for Ireland than Lloyd George—Dominion Home Rule was 'sheer lunacy', he said.[9] Margot was in the House when he ridiculed Henry's fine ideas, and she could hardly refrain from taking up the cudgels on her husband's behalf. When Lloyd George painted a lurid picture of Ireland under Home Rule, he saw it with a fleet of submarines sowing the seas with mines and providing bases for a hostile fleet; and he defended reprisals as a necessary means of dealing with Irish murders.[10] Margot admired the way Henry did not flinch before these jeers: 'Now that Lloyd George calls me a lunatic and Carson calls me a traitor, I begin to feel sure I am on the right lines.'[11]

'The Government is doomed,' Margot wrote to Gwynne:

> It is at loggerheads with each other [sic]—no two can agree about Ireland—the India Office is at war with the Foreign Office and the Foreign Office with the Prime Minister and his secretariat whom it accused of usurping its functions and acting without his knowledge;

Cabinet responsibility v. Mr Montagu, the secretary of India said was a joke.[12]

Although a passionate patriot, Margot was not displeased that the country was in a deplorable state and that there was grumbling on all sides at Lloyd George's lack of a proper policy and at his many mistakes—for (as she told Gwynne) 'when Lloyd George trips himself up, you will remind all Liberals that they have pledged themselves to supplant him'.[13] She searched the newspapers for evidence and found plenty to prove her point that 'there has been no Cabinet responsibility since Lloyd George became Prime Minister'. Henry was forced to agree, but she wished that he would either rouse himself to do something about the effects of misgovernment or rise above them altogether. Instead, he remained perpetually depressed but convinced that nothing could be done except lament that the country was being 'governed by a set of reckless gamblers'.[14]

By January 1922 Margot was sure that the days of the coalition were numbered, and predicted that the very self-assurance that had enabled Lloyd George to rise quickly to the top would be instrumental in bringing about his downfall. However, it did not happen overnight as she had hoped; the government took ten months to fall.

They were at The Wharf in the autumn of 1922, Margot very much absorbed with her second volume, when the Carlton Club revolt took place and the Tories withdrew their support from the government. Lloyd George was forced to resign and Bonar Law, who took his place as Prime Minister, immediately dissolved Parliament. At the General Election in November 1922 Asquith again stood for Paisley as an Independent Liberal, but his heart was saddened by the split in the party which meant that in many cases Independents were opposed by National Liberals, a strange state of affairs and difficult for the Asquiths to swallow. This time, encouraged by Margot, Henry took more willingly to electioneering, making excellent speeches, many with his old fire. Margot still did not understand that as a candidate for power her husband's strategical position was hopeless from the start, since there was no chance of the Independents ever getting a majority, but buoyed herself up with the hope that, however long it took, the Asquith Liberals would one day be in government again. As she had written to Gilbert Murray at Easter:

I know we can't get in in the next General Election but if we win 101 seats the Tories will be in a bad position and we only need to be very brave and patient to see the standards of Liberalism revived again. I and all who believe in truth and honour have suffered very deeply. So has Henry tho' he never shows it, even to me, but we must go the whole hog . . . and keep together without too much criticism of what goes on over the footlights.[15]

Lloyd George appealed to Liberals not to rock the old boat with fresh quarrels and put out feelers to discover whether Asquith would join a new government should the Liberals gain a majority in the House. Margot put her foot down—'Henry in a secondary position? Never!'

Asquith held Paisley by a mere 316 votes. 'A very narrow squeak,' said Margot, who could not help gloating over the corpses left on the battlefield by the Conservative victory, among them Winston Churchill and Edwin Montagu. Margot gave way to her feelings in her usual way: 'Serves them right,' she cried gleefully.[16]

With Henry back in Parliament, Margot became once again a very active politician behind the scenes: no Nancy Astor role in the forefront for her! She felt strongly that she had far more power standing at Henry's back, ready to give the necessary shove when spirits drooped and using her eyes and ears to his advantage, for she had noticed with alarm that Henry was now inclined to take up the attitude of the elderly and retired who find everything too much bother and prefer to sit by the fire and read.

Soon after the election Lloyd George appeared to be planning the formation of a new central party with himself as leader, and appealed to men of progressive outlook in all parties to act together. This gave Margot the chance to repeat to all who would listen (Dawson of *The Times*, Gwynne of the *Morning Post* and Professor Gilbert Murray among them) that Henry would never serve under Lloyd George. How could he be subordinate to a man who had made such a mess of the peace terms? Did people not remember that Henry had predicted that if they were too hard on Germany it would in the long run rebound on Britain? This was happening even sooner than Henry had expected, Germany could not pay the enormous reparations due under the Treaty of Versailles (Margot had said at the time that money could only be got out of a 'living enemy'), so France threatened to occupy the Ruhr instead. Margot insisted that since the mess was all Lloyd George's doing he ought to go and sort it out instead of Bonar Law, whom the Asquiths had taken up in a big way.

A leading article in *The Times* pointing out Bonar Law's talents for this delicate task might be a help, they thought, but great collector of newspaper editors as she was, Margot had not progressed very far with Geoffrey Dawson, who was not easily dictated to. Her chance came when his newspaper said that there were complications in the Paris talks and a possibility of war with France. She promptly invited Dawson and his wife to The Wharf, and the visit was a great success. In the comfort of her drawing-room Margot explained to him how the present troubles between France and Germany were all the fault of France: 'Europe is threatened with collapse and it is humiliating to be dragged at the heels of an insolent, ungrateful French government.'[17] Asquith did not think for a moment that English newspapers could prevent the French marching into the Ruhr; he had no faith in them and was gloomy when it happened. He made a speech in the Commons urging that an appeal for quick intervention be made to the League of Nations.[18] The speech, though short, was given wide coverage in the papers. Margot was immensely pleased; she had long held the view that to be reported in one of the big national newspapers was far more important than being heard in the Commons. She would have liked to back up the speech with a leading article, but could not risk a snub by asking Dawson directly, and a hint produced no result. The reason she worked so hard to enlist Dawson's support was that she was convinced (without any evidence) that he was a great power, even manipulator, behind the scenes. She could not have known that Dawson had once disliked Asquith very much indeed (and probably still disliked him) and that in 1916 he had sided with Northcliffe and Beaverbrook. By 1923 there was not much he did not know about Margot's views on politics, but there was still very little she knew about him.

On 22 May 1923 Stanley Baldwin replaced Bonar Law as Prime Minister. To many people, and Margot was no exception, Baldwin was the personification of John Bull, the solid backbone of England with a whiff of the land about him, although in fact his origins were not rural but industrial. Margot took to him because there was something about the way he looked that reminded her of Henry, square-cut and rock-like. Despite the fact that he was a true blue Tory, she felt the country would be safe with him. Appearances mattered to Margot. If Baldwin had been thin and undersized, she would have harped endlessly on the terrible misfortune of having a Conservative Prime Minister and the mess the government would make of things if they carried out their threat to bring in Protection. Baldwin's pipe and his solid frame went a long way towards winning her confidence. Even more vital to her happiness was the hope that he would keep Lloyd George out for years. Baldwin was 'the salt of the earth',[19] so humane and caring as to be almost a Liberal, even though in his very first speech he spoke of the need to get rid of Free Trade.

In the autumn of 1923 Baldwin dissolved Parliament. This time Asquith could stand as the candidate of a hastily reunited Liberal party. It was as though in a dream (and not a pleasant one) that Margot found herself sitting on a platform at Paisley with Henry, Violet, Lloyd George and his daughter Megan. Margot and Lloyd George had had a short conversation before entering the hall and both had been the soul of politeness. Of course she would never admit it, even to herself, but Margot much enjoyed talking to this witty and clever man who she sensed enjoyed her own special brand of wit and humour. What is more, he gave her all his attention, never once letting his eyes wander, but keeping them fixed on her the whole time, something that Margot was beginning to appreciate. When Sunday came round Asquith and Violet went with Lloyd George and Megan to a service in a Baptist Church while Margot drove to Glasgow to canvass for her brother, Jack Tennant, who was contesting the central division.

Next day Asquith and Lloyd George again appeared on the platform together as though the best of friends. It was Asquith's turn to speak, and to Margot's dismay the speech lasted a mere quarter of an hour. But when it was Lloyd George's turn, he spoke for nearly an hour and with so many histrionics and so much verve that it seemed merely five minutes. Asquith thought Lloyd George's speech 'ragged and boisterous but with quite a good assortment of telling points'.[20] Between them, however, they rallied the Liberals enough to ensure that Asquith retained his seat.

When the Commons met, no party had a sufficient majority to govern alone, and Asquith played a prominent part in the decision that it should be Labour and not the Conservatives who took office in 1924. But Ramsay Macdonald's government soon ran into difficulties, and another election was necessary within the year. At the age of seventy-two, Asquith had to face another campaign, this time against a new and more dangerous opponent, Rosslyn Mitchell, whose tactics included obstruction and rowdyism. Margot had decided views about him ('Mitchell is better dressed than Peter Flower, is highly educated and no more Labour than

you are,' she wrote to Lord Islington, 'an orator, windbag and dangerously courteous with a face like the actor John Hare, only handsomer. He
may run us very close'[21]), and feared that her husband had no stomach for
the fight, for he had said that he was getting too old for such capers and
that for two pins he would have given up the idea of standing again
altogether. He did not seem to notice that his speeches lacked the old fire,
and she could see that he was pretending an enthusiasm he did not feel.
Slowly it was dawning on Margot that in the four elections Henry had
fought at Paisley he had not strengthened his position at all. Unemployment and the Labour vote were, she believed, proving too strong for him.
In his daughter's words '. . . a new generation of young men who had
ripened into voters, almost it seemed since the last election, were determined to give a solid class vote to Labour, no matter what we said . . . or
what we did'.[22]

Unhappily, Violet's forebodings were borne out by the event. Asquith
was beaten by over 2000 votes. Margot and Violet were at his side when
the results were declared, both looking white and tense. Violet records
that with great gallantry Margot said a few words to their supporters, yet
it was difficult for them not to break down when the Liberals sang
mournfully 'Will ye no come back again?'.[23] The last of the Romans had
gone down for ever, and the two women could tell by his face that he knew
it.

CHAPTER 34

Some things cannot be got round

ON 4 NOVEMBER 1924 the King offered to confer a peerage on Asquith. 'It would be a matter of the greatest satisfaction to me,' George V wrote in his own hand. Asquith asked for time to think about taking such a final step. Margot certainly did not want him to do so until he had got away from the political scene altogether for a time, so the King agreed to let him postpone the decision for the moment.

Gradually Asquith was starting again to listen to Margot's advice and he quickly took up her suggestion that he, accompanied by his son Cis (who knew the East), should visit Egypt, Palestine, Syria and the Sudan, while Margot stayed behind at The Wharf. Apart from her dislike of travelling, she knew that if she went with him there would be far too many political post-mortems which would be bad for both. Thus it came about that in the spring of 1925, Henry was exploring Jerusalem while Margot planned a holiday with the twenty-two-year-old Puffin who had just left Oxford.

It was not easy for Margot to accept the fact that Henry's days in the Commons were over: she had always imagined him as a second Gladstone, dying at his post. But she recognized that at seventy-two he could claim to have done his bit, and that for him the glamour and excitement of politics had disappeared. Even before his return to England, Margot got a letter to say that he had decided to accept the King's offer, news which Margot took philosophically. She saw compensations in his elevation for her too; each election took something out of both of them, canvassing had become more of a burden than formerly, and it was a chore she would be glad to be rid of. Looking back, she realized that they had never understood properly that Paisley was an uncertain seat, 'full of fervour for Scotland' and caring nothing for the bigger issues of the day. Scottish nationalism was increasing and, Scot to the backbone though Margot was, she never felt at home among such people. Like Asquith himself she had begun to think that perhaps a peerage was the best way out.

There was one further disappointment in store, and one that hit Margot hard. Henry was not elected Chancellor of Oxford University. Although she had at first thought him the favoured candidate, the Conservative candidate, Lord Cave, polled many more votes. Margot minded this slight more than she dared admit. To her the Chancellorship was a prize worthy of Henry and if it had been a choice between a peerage and the Chancellorship, she would have urged the latter every time. Short of the Mastership of Balliol, she wanted this for him more than anything in the world. Later she heard that many Oxford graduates had decided that 'their consciences would not permit them to vote for the author of the Parliament Act, Welsh disestablishment and other enormities'.[1] Nevertheless Asquith still had his defenders. Lord Birkenhead (F. E. Smith), who had been his lifelong political opponent, came quickly to his defence and in a letter to *The Times* which touched Margot deeply he referred to Henry as the 'greatest living Oxonian. To reject him because he is a Liberal is to admit partisan prejudices, as narrow as they are discreditable'.[2] Sensing Margot's deep disappointment, Harold Nicolson wrote her an understanding letter that gave her so much pleasure that she replied to him the same day:

> . . . as you say there is nothing so narrow as the clergy and the inhabitants of a university town. We have been for so many years both abused and vilified but I feel happy that the world begins to realize what Henry has done in his life. He has one great quality, he is without vanity and self-centredness and most men of his calibre have both.[3]

Sir John Simon made it plain that he thought Asquith's defeat at Oxford an outrage: his letter brought tears to her eyes and she answered him affectionately: '. . . You have shown real loyalty and love over Henry's candidature for Chancellor of Oxford and we both thank you.'[4]

There was, however, one consolation in store for a woman whose life had become so bound up with her husband's: the King offered Asquith the Garter, an honour he had declined in December 1918. Margot was delighted, yet the rejection by Oxford still rankled.

In recent years Donald Maclean had become a close friend and it was to him that Margot told her unhappiness that Henry's active political life was finished for good. She wrote pathetically: 'It is the end of politics in the real sense of the word for both of us.'[5]

By the autumn of 1925 the Asquiths felt empty, as though everything had been taken from them. Margot was the better able of the two to pull herself together; she rapidly got down to some work and suggested that Henry should do the same, otherwise they might sink for ever.

So while Henry shut himself into his study at The Wharf to struggle with his *magnum opus*, *Fifty Years of Parliament*, Margot set to work on her novel, *Octavia* (Octavia was her favourite girl's name because it had been her sister Laura's). Writing this novel brought her far more pleasure than the writing of her autobiography, since in the best traditions of the romantic novelist she could allow her imagination full play. To sit at her desk and scribble away just as she felt inclined without having to consult her diary or remember dates and other tiresome facts, gave her immense pleasure, even put new life into her. With certain embellishments the plot of this novel is more or less a romanticized version of her own life; the heroine Margot herself, but an idealized Margot, confident, beautiful ('her eyes were like pebbles at the bottom of a burn'), always brave, loyal and free. Of course, Octavia was the centre of attention wherever she went, just as Margot had once been. Nothing is left out: the hunting, the dancing, the falling in love, the friendship are all there. Much more can be learned about Margot from the novel than from any of her other writing.

Margot makes it plain that if Octavia had been a man she would have been in politics and an influential member of the Cabinet, but since she is merely a woman she is made to say and do insufferable things; she swaggers, she is a braggart, and does not mind saying loudly in her insensitive way that she is intolerant of people who have not got the courage to live. This boasting is meant to be part of Octavia's charm, which is very great indeed.

Greville, the hero, appears thoroughly unlikeable, but to Margot he is fascinating, the exact image of Peter Flower: tall, lean, hawk-faced, selfish but daring, accepting impossible wagers, but triumphant all the same. He is Margot's idea of a man no woman can resist. The end is very conventional: Octavia softens him by her winning ways.

Margot's sheer enjoyment in writing this kind of lush romance shines through on every page and makes the book readable. Unhappily most of her writing is very different. In her essay 'Men and their Books', written later, Margot is painfully didactic, and lays down the law on how to write: 'There is a certain order in style which gives it dignity,' she writes, 'a chaste economy and severe restraint preclude purple passages.' Rashly she goes on to say that it is possible to read a man's character by his style![6] But of course she never follows her own advice. She must be free to put her thoughts down just as they occur and in the way she thinks best. The style of her writing in *Octavia* is neither lean nor chaste, but verbose and sentimental, only redeemed by the vivid colours which give it life.

Trembling a little, she gave her manuscript to Henry for comment as soon as she had finished it, and was thrilled when she noticed he could not put it down. When a little shyly she asked if he had enjoyed it, he had nothing but praise. It was posted off to Newman Flower who unhesitatingly gave Margot the £10,000 advance she asked for. She was amazed she could earn such large sums so easily and enjoyably, and with the cheque in her hands she wove dreams about her future not only as a great novelist but as a rich one. Deeply grateful to Newman Flower for accepting the book without asking for one alteration, she invited him to The Wharf for a few days. He accepted and she wrote at once to say how delighted they were that 'you can come to see the little home I created in the country for Henry when he was Prime Minister (he needed rest and isolation from colleagues, worries and war)'.

> . . . For the first time since I finished it [the book] . . . Henry's praise has given me enormous hope that it will be a success. I was amazed at what he said. You do not know (since I am neither vain nor shy) people don't realize that I am fundamentally humble . . . if I had begun earlier I might have written a really good novel. I was so keen to be fresh and simple that I know I could improve it. I am much touched by your courage and your kindness.[7]

Before the book was published, Margot saw a good deal of Newman Flower and began to realize that he was a most delightful man; tactful but firm, earning her respect by refusing to let her get away with anything. He taught her a valuable lesson that poor stuff churned out at a great pace for money would kill her popularity stone dead. She begged him to try and persuade her obstinate husband to change his style for something less sober, a miracle even Newman Flower could not work, although as soon as Henry saw him as a man and not as a publisher they got on very well.

Quickly he became a regular visitor to The Wharf, and even Henry learned to tolerate his refusal to make a four at bridge. Newman Flower was so entertaining, charming and helpful that Margot's conscience began to prick her: was she greedy in asking for £10,000 advance? Suppose the book did not make much? She needed the money badly but she could not rest until she had written to Flower to find out what he really thought:

> I wish I thought my novel was worth many times what you are giving for it. All I can say is I have taken trouble . . . Had I not been fifty [she was sixty-five] and hard up, I could never have asked so much. But Sir Ernest Williams would have given me the same. He was a great friend of mine and over-praised me always. He offered me £6,000 for my little 'Lay Sermons'.[8]

She wanted to dedicate her novel to her daughter Elizabeth, but the wording of the dedication worried her unreasonably. She wrote to Flower for advice: 'Should it be: "I dedicate this first novel to Elizabeth" or should I just put "To Elizabeth"?' She had lost so much confidence that small things played on her mind. In the old days she would have pleased herself and been content that whatever she did was right. Now she was uncertain.

But it was only trivialities that worried her now. The General Strike in 1926 affected trade, and the kind of soft wool she found it essential to wear next to her skin in winter was unobtainable. She worried that if she did not have her special wool combinations she might become ill. Recently she had paid a visit to a country-house and had been given linen sheets, which her doctor Sir John Williams had told her she must always avoid. She had not slept a wink all night wondering what the consequences would be.

She felt the need to lean on someone for comfort and advice, someone stronger than herself, but there was no one. Long ago Henry had slipped out of this role, and now it was Margot who had to strengthen and reassure him. In some ways he had become very trying. Every day she had to listen to his grumbles about the House of Lords, which he found most uncongenial. A Parliamentarian to his fingertips, he was at home in the Commons in a way he never could be in the Lords, where the standard of speech-making was deplorably low, the pace unbearably slow. He could feel the cobwebs collecting round him as he listened to platitude after platitude, he told Margot in an attempt to pass off his irritation as a joke. He was not enjoying writing, although Margot encouraged him all she could. He told her that he could never get the same enjoyment from it that she did, the same thrill at seeing his words in print, nor the satisfaction Winston Churchill derived from a well-turned phrase. Asquith's stiff and stilted style bore no resemblance to the speeches he had delivered in the past, nor could it have anything like the same impact. His chief pleasure was reading by the fire at The Wharf, undisturbed except for his memories. Margot saw that he was getting old, and it made her sad.

Both found a measure of compensation in their children. Puffin was in America with his sister Elizabeth, and Margot loved their letters with stories of the Hollywood stars. They were staying with Mary Pickford and Douglas Fairbanks, so that when in the following year *Octavia* was published in America she sent a telegram to Mary Pickford asking her to use her influence in promoting it. The sales were dropping in England and she could not bear the thought of Newman Flower losing money because of her, although he had tried to comfort her by pointing out that there were times of the year when people did not buy books.

> I am terribly distressed [she wrote] to hear that the London season is not a time when anyone reads anything. All my friends say: 'I'm keeping it to read in the country, but what a success you've had etc.' As I only expected to sell 8,000 copies of my book, I thought 17,000 enormous . . . shall I wire the following telegram to Mary Pickford?[9]

Mary Pickford did not think the request at all unusual and did her best. When she came to London two months later Margot repaid her kindness by helping her promote her own book (she had recently written her life story), gave a large party for her, and arranged a Foyles luncheon in her honour with herself in the chair.

As an economy measure Margot had recently learned to drive a car, and after the luncheon she drove Mary Pickford to Denham to watch Puffin at work on a film. All this she enjoyed with her old zest. The year before, when she had discussed the question of getting rid of their chauffeur, they had both come to the conclusion that they were too old to learn to drive. Yet she had done it, thereby giving herself a wonderful sense of freedom, and although she drove recklessly and had little idea of the rules of the road, she somehow managed never to have an accident. Henry flatly refused to learn and Margot did not try to persuade him. She knew now that he was too unadaptable and minded not having a chauffeur and being forced to make economies far more than Margot did. It was to Margot's great credit that she never once blamed Henry for expecting her to keep the home fires burning.

Part of Asquith's improvidence and his lack of willingness to economize was due to a conviction that the country ought to provide for him and his wife in their old age. The idea was not unreasonable, since many of the chief generals had been given lump sums at the end of the war as a mark of the country's gratitude. Why should not retired Prime Ministers be similarly treated, as (according to Margot) Pitt, Chatham, Fox and others had been in the past?[10] Perhaps the thought that Margot was very rich gave the government the feeling that a pension for Asquith was not necessary. Asquith hated arguing about money; it was bad enough having to question Lloyd George about his Liberal Party funds (a considerable sum of money) which he clung on to regardless of the fact that the Independent Liberals were penniless, whereas Lloyd George Liberals could call on this fund whenever they liked, despite Asquith's insistence that the fund was meant for all Liberals.

Margot was grateful for Geoffrey Dawson's friendship. It had started slowly, but once he and his wife had been to The Wharf, it had steadily progressed, even though Dawson knew that Margot was deliberately attempting to cultivate him and would try to use him whenever she could. He liked this strange, outspoken woman who still radiated a certain charm he had never met with before. Stories of her sharp tongue and unkindness were common talk in London society, but as soon as he got to know her he understood that they were greatly exaggerated. That she could be exasperating he acknowledged to his cost when she bombarded him with urgent requests to put this or that into a leading article, but he quickly got the measure of that through a mixture of tact and firmness, and never hesitated to tell her when she was wrong. Margot had always appreciated what she called 'honesty'—that is, telling the truth without embellishments—and on the few occasions when he used her own methods against her she had taken it like a lamb and even admitted her fault. There was only one thing he kept from her: that he had been thankful when Asquith was forced to resign in 1916. Margot had guessed this but liked Dawson so much by that time that she forgave him, after letting him know that she knew: '. . . Your paper did more to kill us during the war than even Lloyd George—and yet it is the only paper. You had nothing to do with this.'[11] This did not prevent her, however, from telling him all the details of the peace talks and how Henry could have prevented this or that, as though he had not heard it all before. But he liked her and was sorry for her, knowing she had a lot to put up with.

Margot was grateful to him because he prevented her from making silly mistakes in her writing and impressed on her that to say what was true was not always the best method of attack. He allowed her to use him as a father confessor, keeping her confidences and bracing her when her spirits were low: 'I don't know why I say all this to you,' was her bewildered refrain, but she did know: it was because Dawson never rebuffed her.

In some ways Margot was old-fashioned; she had not kept up with the modern usage of first names and for a long time addressed Geoffrey Dawson as 'dearest Mr Dawson'. In October 1927 she took the plunge: 'If you don't think it cheek I should like to call you Geoffrey. New friends are such a joy to me that you cannot imagine the pleasure I have had in getting to know you.' As so often this kind of letter might be followed by a very different one in which she poured out her grievances to him relentlessly:

> . . . Our best friends turned against us and said we were doing nothing in the war. If they had taken the trouble to come and see me, 4 a.m. or any hour, they would have found me and my husband had not even taken our clothes off. Nancy Astor has said that she had gone continually to 10 Downing Street on matters of vital importance—a lie, as she only came once to ask for a vulgar fellow to be made a bishop—and was shocked to see how little we felt the war. Coming from her whose husband had never fought—about a man whose eldest son was killed . . . was what I never forgive. The war took all my brother's sons and I have never got over it and never will. P.S. It is not very nice of me to say of Nancy Astor her husband never fought in the war. So scratch out this bit.[12]

Writing to Geoffrey Dawson was a solace, and so was writing to H. A. Gwynne, another exceptionally patient and kindly man. These letters gave Margot the feeling that she was still in affairs, which was important to her morale.

Recently Margot had met Philip Snowden and had taken to him greatly. 'He is the only one [of the Labour party] with any intellect,' she wrote to a friend. He reminded her vividly of those clever men (where had they all gone?) whom she had known and conversed with in her youth. That he was a prominent member of the Labour party and a Fabian only enhanced him in her eyes, for she had heard that the members of the Fabian Society were rather like the 'Souls' of her youth, among whom political opinions of all colours were tolerated. She had been much taken with Arthur Henderson when she had first met him, but although this friendship had blossomed at first, he had now become 'a stupid selfish man'. Ramsay Macdonald too had turned out to be a disappointment, for although they were both Scots there was nothing in him that appealed to Margot, no common ground on which they could meet, converse and argue. She thought him a 'doomed man', always in pain, which she supposed he could not help and 'always surrendering', which he could.[13] Some time before, Margot had written off Winston Churchill and Arthur Balfour as 'hopeless'. She did not encourage them to call; quite why is not clear, for she missed their lively conversation and wit very much, although she had never found Winston Churchill exactly congenial.

Yet there were signs that Margot was mellowing, and sometimes she preached 'tolerance towards one's enemies'. On one occasion at least she showed that she meant it, for one spring day in 1925 the unbelievable was seen on the very steps of 44 Bedford Square: Lloyd George handing Dame Margaret out of their motor car, a festive air about their dress. They had been invited to lunch to meet the Queen of Roumania. It went against the grain for Margot to invite the enemy to her table and converse with him as though she took pleasure in his company (which undoubtedly she always did, though loyalty to Henry prevented her from admitting it). But Henry hoped—vainly as things turned out—that the invitation might help to heal the breach between him and Lloyd George over the Liberal party finances. On one thing she had insisted: Dame Margaret must accompany her husband. She had always admired Mrs Lloyd George's dignity and restraint in her difficult position and hoped that in her own troubles she too had appeared in a good light. Unfortunately the tension between the two men made it a dreary meal: neither Margot nor the Welsh wizard shone, Henry seemed oppressed and for once Margot herself could think of little to say. Afterwards she found plenty. The luncheon reminded her of an old grievance and she wrote to H. A. Gwynne that very evening. 'The coalition called Lloyd George the greatest man since Pitt . . . Lloyd George has not got a tooth in his head. He was always a bright amusing little fellow, a good servant and he showed spunk, but he has no statecraft and he lied. . . .'[14]

It was the same old song and Gwynne had heard it all before, but at least it was lively, whereas Asquith's letter to his friend Mrs Harrisson told her nothing: 'We have just disposed of the Queen of Roumania, who came to luncheon when we had Lloyd George, Desmond (MacCarthy), Violet and others . . .'[15]

At the height of the acrimonious controversy over the Lloyd George fund in May 1926, Asquith decided he must get away somewhere to rest his strained nerves and think in the peace and quiet of the country. He decided on Castle Howard in Yorkshire, owned by Mr Geoffrey Howard, 'a very sound Liberal' and an old friend.

In October 1926 he wrote a memorandum on this notorious fund which Lloyd George refused to let out of his grasp: 'Lloyd George regards the accumulated fund as at his own disposal to be given to or withheld from the central office of the party as a dole upon such conditions as he thought fit to impose.'[16] Not only the fund but the question of the leadership of the Liberal party was given prominence in the press all that summer. It was up to the Liberals themselves to choose their leader, one paper declared on its front page, Lord Oxford and Asquith or Mr Lloyd George. It was unfortunate for Asquith that in disputes of this kind Lloyd George's pen and tongue were both sharper and more honeyed than his rival's and far better calculated to dazzle and confuse the party man. As J. A. Spender put it, Members of Parliament who elected their own chairman found themselves in the unhappy position of being called upon suddenly to choose between their two leaders.[17]

Later on, Margot felt it her duty to give Geoffrey Dawson the benefit of her opinion, which he might find useful as the basis for an article in *The Times*. While reading her batch of newspapers the morning before, it had struck her that even those that had once been favourable to Henry no longer considered him in the running now that he had become a peer. Since his energy was lessened, she felt it was up to her to keep the Liberal flag flying—Henry's Liberal flag—and not let those with short memories forget. 'I can tell you exactly what the Liberal papers are at,' she wrote.

They think Lloyd George will lead the Liberal party and that if they can prove that Asquith and the whole of his family are rotters, full of spite, self-indulgence and thwarted ambition, they will prove to the world that their hopes with their hero have been maligned. That he was the man who won the war and that he is the only man also to save the country. Lloyd George is a discredited man among people who are educated and know that except for the *Morning Post*, he is doomed. . . . the gaping public do not realize he is the biggest bluff, a dangerous bluff, ever to put across the country . . .[18]

Chapter 35

Great Moments which Small Things Produce

THE ASQUITH HOMES, although never exactly serene, had always a bright welcoming air about them; the coming and going of friends, colleagues and relatives, and lively talk in comfortable surroundings where warm hospitality abounded. Recently there had been a subtle change. The talk and the bustling life were subdued and an air of gloom seemed to pervade 44 Bedford Square and The Wharf. It had all happened imperceptibly, creeping in unobserved, well established before it became noticeable.

In the old days Margot and Henry hardly knew what it was like to be alone, but since friends were the breath of life to both, they did not miss the peace and quiet of an evening together. Strangely enough Margot hardly noticed the change: she says she felt tired, old and worried about Henry, who seemed to take no interest in anything. There were times when to see him so listless and changed made her irritable and she could not prevent herself snapping at him for doing so little to help himself. What use was it asking friends to come and cheer him up when he seemed not to want to be cheered? Even bridge no longer attracted him.

On his return from Castle Howard in May 1926 he suffered a slight stroke. At first Margot was not very alarmed for it was not dissimilar to the 'attack' he had had in the night in 1916 before his fall from power. From that illness, the first she had ever known him have ('my husband is a mixture of iron and leather' had been her proud boast), he had completely recovered. This time too he was soon himself again. But on 12 June he suffered another and more severe stroke and became so unwell that he was unable to attend the annual meeting of the National Liberal Federation at Weston-super-Mare. This time he was incapacitated for three months, walking was difficult, he looked drawn, sometimes very pale, at others flushed, and he complained of feeling seedy. Nevertheless he got better, but minor problems which once would have passed over his head preyed on his mind. His book, too, had to be put on one side, and soon it was overdue at the publishers. Briskly Margot pointed out that he could never get it finished if he checked and re-checked every reference so carefully and rewrote sentences until they dazzled and shone like diamonds but added nothing to the sense. The truth soon dawned on her; his interest in writing, never very strong, had gone completely. She bravely tried to revive it by reading passages aloud to him to prove how excellent it was. He did not seem to care.

On 15 October 1926 he announced his resignation of the Liberal leadership, and that night Margot travelled with him to Greenock to bid farewell to a small band of the faithful. In his speech Asquith made the message clear: the mission of Liberalism was not exhausted. The younger ones must carry on the torch and keep the faith.[1] The short visit was a success but the strain on them both was very great.

Christmas that year was spent at The Wharf and was not as sad as Margot expected, for Henry's interest in his book had been revived by a visit from his publisher on 16 December. It had been a cold, grey day that had given Henry a cold, grey mood, yet so infectious was Newman Flower's enthusiasm that when he left Henry declared that he would finish the book after all and that he was looking forward to a morning spent at his desk. That night Margot wrote a grateful letter to Flower:

> There are great moments in life which quite small things produce; you and I have just gone through one. My husband's conscientious desire to rise to the occasion and receive his publisher worried him, but now he is happy and only wants to make his book perfect for me. . . . I will read it all and add things . . . and you should let me know how many more words we need. I have a fine memory of the diary and so has he . . .[2]

If only the cold and the damp did not affect Henry so much, she thought. If he looked out of the window in the morning and saw an overcast day he would dress but refuse to go downstairs, stayed where he was and became depressed. Otherwise Margot thought she saw some improvement in his general health. Her hopes were short-lived. Just before Christmas, while at luncheon, he suffered yet another stroke. Just as he was rising from the table he felt a loss of power in one leg and although the 'numbness' seemed to pass off it soon recurred, forcing him to use a wheel-chair for a short time. Yet with Margot's help he got better, did not need the wheel-chair and even played a little golf when they took a holiday at North Berwick.

A visit to Whittinghame, only a few miles away, gave them both a jolt. There, in excellent shape, they found Arthur Balfour, six years Asquith's senior, and enjoying a game of tennis. He was pretty well, he said, except for slight deafness in one ear. He attributed his good health and spirits to the keen Scottish air. The air braced Margot too, who played eighteen holes of golf at Muirfield—'a long and exacting course'—not in the least hampered by most unsuitable clothes, a black 'afternoon' dress and satin toque. But the climate did nothing for Asquith: 'I have not adventured out on the links yet,' he wrote to Mrs Harrisson, ''tho' I think my powers of locomotion are developing.'[3] In December 1927 they went again to Castle Howard for Asquith to receive the freedom of the city of York, an occasion he seemed to enjoy with a little of his old zest. Indeed he felt so much better that he went to see an exhibition in Norwich with Mrs Harrisson and on the way back he spent a night with Venetia Montagu at Beccles. What memories, it may be wondered, were evoked by this meeting with a woman who had once consumed his whole being with love and the joy of living? Now they met for the last time.

Back at The Wharf Asquith went straight to his desk, determined to finish his book, and even talked of starting another. Just as he seemed in better spirits than for some time, he caught influenza from a guest and was cast down as never before; Margot had her work cut out to try and make him see illness as merely a temporary setback. She wrote to Newman Flower:

> For me it is terrible seeing the man I love lose his spirits and hope. It is no use saying to someone: 'Why be afraid you are dying when you know quite well you are not. What does it matter you are walking feebly as long as you can read and write,' unless you can make him believe this . . . Intellectually he is as acute as ever, even more alive than I have known him, but he has lost his calm hope. As he has never been ill, he says to himself, 'I am too old to recover so what does anything matter?' It is curious how those who have been giants of health all their lives . . . lose their faith . . . I would hate you to lose out of his book (if he never finished it) so you must let me pay you out of my novel . . .[4]

Antoine Bibesco's term as Roumanian Minister to the United States was coming to an end and Elizabeth wanted to stay with her mother while awaiting the new posting. Normally this would have delighted Margot, but instead she was frantic with worry in case Elizabeth might be shocked at the change in her father, which now, unhappily, was plain for all to see. Recently his voice had taken on a flat tone, the tone of a man who knows that whatever is happening in the world of politics, the outcome cannot affect him in the slightest.

Ever since the birth of her baby, Elizabeth had looked frail. Margot sensed she was not happy in her marriage either, and had no idea what to do about it. Her husband Antoine lived in the glittering social world that was part of his job and that had regained its glamour very quickly after the 1914–1918 war. He adored beautiful women (why otherwise had he married Elizabeth?), enjoyed their admiration and possessed the money to indulge his whims. As a diplomat he felt he had to be seen and photographed at smart social gatherings, mixing with people of importance in whatever country he happened to be serving. Once Margot had thought this the ideal life for her girl, giving her the opportunity to write her poetry and plays. But her writing had ceased with her marriage and all Margot's encouragement could not persuade her to take it up as seriously as would be necessary for her to make her mark. Last time they had come over Margot noticed with dismay that Elizabeth was drinking far more than was good for her and that it had begun to affect her health.

When Elizabeth did come to The Wharf late in 1927, she was thinner, paler and more remote than ever. Margot invited Geoffrey Dawson and his wife to stay so that Elizabeth could meet them. They arrived two days before Elizabeth, and Henry at once seemed more cheerful, talked better and roused himself to be pleasant, so that Margot had high hopes that Elizabeth's visit would pass off well, especially since she had warned the Dawsons to say nothing of Henry's serious condition. Somehow this was one of those small and intimate house-parties which promised much but fell flat for no particular reason, unless it was Elizabeth's refusal to enter into things with anything like her old enjoyment. Nevertheless the Dawsons took to her and invited her to their home.

No sooner had her guests departed than one of Margot's letters followed them by the next post, for she had been unable to talk privately when the Dawsons were at The Wharf.

You saw Elizabeth and said little of what I told you. She is both very old and very young for her age and has no idea really of the situation here, though she is infinitely tender and understanding. Nor do I want her to, as I feel it may last several weeks as Henry was made by God to last 100 years. He has nothing that has in any way deteriorated nor any kind of stroke but the blood vessels are all worn and slack, feeding the arteries and brain unevenly and perversely. He is sometimes quite [word illegible] about his old colleagues and full of intellectual scorn for Lloyd George . . . sometimes quoting Bacon on judges or Pope or Marvell, often laughing at life's little vanities and the cowardice of the Liberals and confusion and lethargy of the Tories etc. Then at times far away from me and very very unhappy.

Tues. 3. I did not finish this as I am so seedy myself that I hardly know why I write to you. Only you are the first person I told (I believe it will be a much longer thing than I thought) and you are so affectionate and understanding—let Elizabeth tell you anything she likes but don't tell her anything . . . No one outside a very small circle knows he is seriously ill and I open letters every day asking him to speak and lecture in the summer and autumn.[5]

When she had faced the inevitable fact that Henry could not recover, she was troubled that never now could he score off his enemies. She wanted revenge in some concrete form and with Henry incapable she could not do it alone. She longed for a strong arm to lean on, to encourage her and keep her spirits up. In Henry's presence her behaviour was as cheerful and normal as she could make it. Even on one of her bad days when she was 'seedy' she tried to be bright. There was nothing in particular wrong with her, only the effects of worry and loneliness.

One night when she was sitting with Henry in the dark and hoping he was asleep, he suddenly said: 'You know quite well I'm not dying, I'm dead.' Another evening his mood had changed and he seemed quite brisk: 'I must give Baldwin a word of advice, he is letting his great opportunities slip through his fingers and he is assisted in this folly by second-rate men. I don't know who advises him.'[6]

Without warning Sir Donald Maclean turned up, having driven himself from London 'at a great pace'—an average speed of twenty-five miles an hour! In case he was rebuffed (there were rumours in London that Margot would not let anyone see Henry) he had not announced his coming. However, he was greeted rapturously by Henry and Margot, and his visit not only enlivened a dismal winter afternoon but left a glow that lasted several days. Afterwards Margot wrote to tell Maclean how much they had enjoyed his unexpected visit and that her heart was full of gratitude for the 'natural way' he accepted Henry's illness:

> My suffering has been so great . . . that if it were not for Puffin I feel I must throw myself into the river. I don't mean *now*, nor as long as I can do anything for the man I love, but when it is over . . . what shall I have to live for? I am brave and gay when I am with him, but I crawl over here [to her own bedroom] like a beaten creature and look out of my window to see if he turns his light on . . . Henry has lost confidence to a degree I could not believe. His sensitiveness has always been beyond other people's understanding and he is a man of tremendous emotion hidden by vast self-control.[7]

In January 1928 Sir John Simon called at The Wharf but was not allowed to see his old chief. Even before he could get a foot over the threshold he was told that Asquith was too ill to see visitors. Margot was in London at the time but two days later she wrote full of contrition:

> He had such a poor night that when he fell asleep just before you came they did not want to wake him . . . I was in London arranging the new building (to avoid him having to use the high stairs in Bedford Square) . . . I had got a sort of 'flu and gave it to him but I think he is going on steadily. . . .[8]

Why did she hope to throw dust in the eyes of even close friends? He was not 'going on steadily', but declining fast. The doctors had told her that the end could not be long delayed, yet she could not face it, and pushing reality further away made the inevitable easier to bear.

That winter of Henry's last illness Margot had none of the family with her. Puffin was in America, Elizabeth in Paris, and Cynthia and Violet too busy with their own families. Sad and forlorn, on Christmas Eve she had sent Gilbert Murray a belated card with a short letter: 'He is very ill . . . it may last six to eight weeks, but if you love us as I know you do, I beg of you to say nothing . . . if he saw it in the papers it would kill him.'[9]

Shortly after Christmas Henry's illness had taken a new and terrible turn. He began suddenly one day to rail at Margot, accusing her of being against him, saying she was his jailer and The Wharf his prison, where she was keeping him against his will. Silent tears poured down Margot's cheeks when she heard those dreadful words shouted at her with malevolence. She wrote to Geoffrey Dawson:

> I don't think the end will come soon, but I would like you to talk to Baldwin who really loves me and Henry (he withdrew the Tory in the tragic Paisley election to help us) . . . It is nice of you to say that the Liberal press, which I loathe, won't cavil over Westminster Abbey . . . I would not want Elizabeth or any living soul to know I had suggested Westminster Abbey . . . I had no idea such anguish could happen to any of us which has happened, to see a man whose genius for sanity has been his great distinction asking me why I am here and why after all his love I am against him and in ten seconds talking as though he was still in Downing Street, is more than I am able to bear. Yet his memory (for things in the past) is prodigious . . . I am so nervous when he gets on to politics and steer him on to books but in a few seconds he is miles away and asks me why I don't knock the wall down. I let the committee (the doctors) come in to decide once and for all if he is mad or if all of us are. He never opens a book or a paper now and is very weak.[10]

The seriousness of Asquith's illness—hardening of the arteries—had never been fully explained to her; all that Sir John Farquhar Buzzard had said was that the delusions and his detachment from life were all part of his malaise, and she must take no notice of it.

The end came sooner than Margot expected. On 15 February 1928 it was all over. Margot kept vigil to the end, sitting by the bedside watching the man she loved and admired become confused and giving way to delusions. When the doctors explained to her what was happening, she no longer wished his life to be prolonged, for his sake she hoped death would come soon. It took him from her so quietly that although she was sitting by his bedside holding his hand it was some time before she knew he had gone.

Next day she wrote to Geoffrey Dawson:

> The anguish is over for me and so is the joy. He became unconscious Sunday morning at 7 o'clock and died at 7 yesterday. After what I asked you (about Westminster Abbey) it was a disappointment to find a little

written statement in his will: 'I shall probably be buried at Wanborough but wherever it is I desire the utmost simplicity. I do not want anything in the nature of a public funeral.'[11]

PART FOUR

Widowhood

'I am not exactly poor, only very, very lonely'

CHAPTER 36

Friendship Made of Spun Glass

MARGOT WAS NOW alone, a widow with no one close at hand with whom she could discuss her troubles and whose advice she trusted. At first there was too much to do for the void in her life to be experienced to its fullest extent. The relief she had felt when she knew that Henry was out of pain, distress and delusion had not lasted more than an hour or two. All too quickly it was replaced by total weariness when her legs felt leaden, her heart beat fast and trying to get out of bed in the morning was torture. She had passed through the funeral rites as though in a dream and might have been a sleep-walker for all the emotion she displayed. Dry-eyed and deathly pale, she gave the impression of being amazingly composed as she stood erect by the graveside in deep mourning, a widow's veil covering her hat but not her face, holding the arm of her stepson Beb Asquith. Elizabeth stood a little behind her mother, alone and unsupported, in floods of tears. The grey winter's day did not help, nor did the simplicity of the short service in the small Wanborough church; if only Henry had been willing for Westminster Abbey, the grandeur and solemnity of those magnificent surroundings and the public nature of the occasion would have carried her through the ordeal, but at least Margot had the comfort of knowing that she had fulfilled Henry's wishes in every detail.

The long obituary notice in *The Times* did not meet with her entire approval. On the night after the funeral Margot sat by the fire at The Wharf, pad and pencil on her knees, busily composing a second obituary which she felt was nearer the mark than the long official one. It is very much on the lines of those character sketches which are such a feature of her autobiography and for which she had a special talent. Among the many things she said of her husband was the remarkable way he was able to scorn personal quarrels; that he treated press misrepresentations with dangerous indifference, and that although he disliked publicity he never shrank from public danger. She ended her little piece with a phrase she had often used before when writing of people she liked. 'His mind was big enough for trifles to look small in.'

She sat up half the night writing hard, fell asleep towards morning and woke stiff and chilled. Re-read in the cold light of day, her version seemed to her better than she thought, so she sent it off at once to Geoffrey Dawson: 'Will you put this in your paper? I would so much like to have this side of Henry in a paper . . . do you mind? It is quite true. I was in the House of Commons every day since we married in 1894.' Geoffrey Dawson sent it back, but with such a kind and tactful letter that Margot accepted its return without a murmur, telling him that of course he was perfectly right, it would not do: 'I was foolish but somehow they all write such rubbish about Henry, also my description was better written.'[1]

It was some comfort to open the hundreds of letters of condolence, but the one she liked best was from Newman Flower, which arrived inside an enormous bunch of hothouse roses. There is something unaffected and simple in her reply: 'I can never thank you enough for your very wonderful generosity and sympathy. I assure you he and I often spoke of it. You gave him a great deal of pleasure and for this I shall always love you.'[2]

Asquith did not leave much money, only about £3000, and to Margot he gave a mere token amount. Mrs Hilda Harrisson, the confidante of his declining years, was left £2000, each of his seven children £1000, and his butler, chambermaid and his housekeeper £50 each. Even Margot, with her poor head for figures, could see that these bequests came to more than £3000. Where was the extra money to be found?[3] The bequests leave many questions unanswered. Did Asquith know how little money he had in his account? Did he expect Margot to make up the full amount out of her own pocket? Had he the least idea how much of her money Margot spent on him and the family, including her stepchildren? He had often heard her complain about the decreasing value of her income and how she had turned to writing because she was 'dog-poor', but he may not have taken much notice of her grumbling. He had long been in the comfortable habit of leaving the management of their finances entirely to her, and Margot had surprisingly shown that she fully accepted responsibility for earning the extra money they so badly needed. Her trouble was not lack of initiative, but an inability to account for the rapid disappearance of the large sums she had earned from her books. Asquith's biographer, Mr

Stephen Koss, is mistaken in saying that Asquith gave his wife license to spend freely.[4] This he could not do, for the money was Margot's own, but placed in a joint account by her own expressed wish and against her father's warnings. From the day of her marriage Margot had subsidized her husband's political and private activities as well as the education of his children by his first wife. In the event, Margot accepted responsibility for filling the gaps in the will as a sacred trust, the one last thing she could do for Henry, although there was no legal obligation for her to do so. She told Marie Belloc-Lowndes that her conscience obliged her to carry out his commitments.

She immediately decided to write a new book, for this was the only way she knew of raising sufficient money. But she could not think of anything to write about and journalism was not her style: topical subjects bored her and the past was not in vogue. Besides there was not enough money in it for her purpose. Then suddenly an idea struck her which lightened her spirits at once. She informed Geoffrey Dawson that 'the day will come when you people will have to have a little chit-chat column and when it does you must give me a £1000 a year to do it for you'.[5] With her letter posted the £1000 was as good as earned and her mind a little more at rest, but Dawson failed to take the bait. In the small hours, when sleep had fled, she thought up another bit of literary nonsense, a series of imaginary love-letters; *Pearson's Magazine* bought them, but they were so dull, unrealistic and unromantic that the magazine soon discontinued them. After this setback she was depressed, but still not without hope.

The task of sorting Henry's papers to see what was suitable for the official life, kept her fully occupied for weeks. He had not kept a diary but had recorded some of his thoughts and feelings in a commonplace book. It made Margot's heart ache to read the House of Commons of 1919–1922 described as 'the worst in which I have ever sat. I myself when I came back in 1920 was treated by the coalition rank and file with studied contempt'. Again and again Margot read the word 'deserted' and there was much condemnation of colleagues who met his idea for Dominion Home Rule for Ireland with derision. Amongst these thoughts there was a short and poignant obituary on his political career:

I am now in my 75th year. I have been for the best part of half a century in public life. I have been Prime Minister for a longer time than anyone during the last hundred years and for a still longer time I have been leader of the Liberal Party. During the whole of that time I have given my time and strength without stint or reserve to the services of the party and the state. From the principles of Liberalism as I have always understood them . . . I have never swerved either to the right or to the left and I never shall.[6]

Henry's book *Memories and Reflections* was to be published in the autumn of 1928 and Margot was very exercised in her mind about the choice of person to review it. She informed Geoffrey Dawson that she wanted him to ask Winston Churchill to review the book for *The Times* 'and offer him a proper sum to do it'. No sooner had she posted this request than she had second thoughts: 'I hear Winston is furious so why not ask Lord Crewe who has nothing to do and does not need money . . . don't ask Winston, ask Crewe.'[7]

Now that she was alone, many grievances that had been festering for years came to the surface—Beaverbrook, Rothermere, Bonar Law, Lloyd George were all devils, miserable sly cowards and fiddlers. The only one without blemish was Henry. She would not see reason about these 'enemies'—because they had injured Henry and she imagined that if his book fell into the wrong hands for review, they would take the opportunity to harm him still further. Geoffrey Dawson got the full blast of her vehemence and began to be seriously worried about her. Was she losing her reason? Newman Flower reassured him: the only way of keeping her quiet was to lavish praise on her husband, but there were few left who could do so in quite the way she insisted on. The key to her erratic behaviour was her loneliness: her friends were melting away fast because if ever they so much as hinted that Henry was not perfect she became angry. After they had gone away she would justify her outburst by telling herself that they were all followers of Lloyd George and always had been in secret.

It was 1916 all over again, when Margot damned everyone who dared as much as smile in Lloyd George's direction. Even her husband had found her defence of him desperately trying and had seen how she was antagonizing all her friends, but had done nothing about it. She had written in despair to Sylvia Henley, Asquith's former confidante, the one person she sensed would not want to rebuff her: 'It is a terrible blank and blow when you see devoted friendships break as though they were made of spun glass instead of steel and no one minding in the least.'[8]

When Henry's book was published she was the first to receive a finished copy, as Newman Flower was careful to tell her, at the same time making her feel needed by asking her opinion and showing that he had listened to her suggestions.

After reading the first chapter, she was bitterly disappointed, for it seemed so much less inspiring than when she had read it in Henry's own hand. 'I wish we had more politics' she told Newman Flower, 'I wish there had been a photograph of myself and of all my children. . . .'[9] Flower had taken infinite pains to make it attractive; the printing was beautiful and the binding dignified, but the preface she had written did not please her: it ought to have been longer and she should have explained more fully 'all the things people did not understand about Henry'. She sat up all night reading the book and in the morning wrote a sad little letter to Newman Flower: 'So great a personality going out of this world with all his love and his counsel as well as his conversation, has left me very lonely.'[10]

It seemed to her that from the day Henry had given up politics there had been a decline in public morals. She thought Baldwin's resignation honours list cynical in the extreme: how could a sensible man like Baldwin reward Arthur Greenwood, now deputy leader of the second Labour Government, and leave out Lord Stamfordham, 'that splendid royal servant'? 'I've written to Baldwin but he will never be Prime Minister again after this foolish list of honours,' she told Geoffrey Dawson.[11]

The idea of Labour ruling the roost was as distasteful to her as ever: there was only one gentleman in the whole bunch, the erstwhile Liberal, Wedgwood Benn ('he has a delightful even noble side to him . . .').[12] What really astonished her about the 1929 election was the ease with which Labour won, despite the opposition of 'the press Lords'. Believing Beaverbrook and Rothermere to be omnipotent, she was perplexed that 'all the great papers in England are against the Socialists, yet they have won'.[13]

She had a grudge against Sir John Simon too, though they had once been close friends. It had started when Simon had 'shown the cloven hoof', that is, had begun to break away from the Asquith Liberals (or 'us', as Margot put it) when he had backed Baldwin's India policy and had made a speech that had disgusted her: 'In the fullness of time,' Simon had said, 'we look forward to seeing her in equal partnership with the Dominions.'[14] India was the one and only subject on which she and Winston Churchill agreed: both believed that Baldwin was willing to give away 'our brightest jewel'. She saw that country as a romantic, mysterious land, much more glamorous than Egypt which she associated with bed bugs, dysentery, lumpy mattresses and Kitchener. The Star of India was the only decoration she ever coveted. While entirely ignorant of British rule in India, she held fast to her opinion that India was better off and happier as part of the British Empire than trying to govern herself.

Margot gave her friendship or withheld it according to her prejudices. She allowed India to come between herself and Sir John Simon because she said 'he will not be happy until he has given it away'. So incensed did she become that she told an amused Geoffrey Dawson in all seriousness that she infinitely preferred Lloyd George ('at any rate he is a gay little blackguard') to Simon, who had become very dull.[15] When one day she heard a (wholly unfounded) rumour that Winston Churchill was about to join forces with Simon to get rid of India, Simon immediately became 'vulgar, noisy, mischievous, pompous, dangerous and sly'. But, as she told Geoffrey Dawson, truth getting the better of her: 'Though he is not exactly a sly man but has a very fine nature . . .'[16]

The first Christmas after Henry's death was naturally very painful. Elizabeth was still in Paris with Antoine, Puffin was making a film in Berlin, and Violet's children were ill, so she was alone, just as she had been the year before. Pathetically she spent the day writing to Geoffrey Dawson about Asquith: 'Henry led because he was sane, simple and brave. I see no one quite like him, do you?'

One easy source of comfort Margot disdained. Although to those who did not know her, she seemed a mass of contradictions, there were certain qualities in her character that were rock-like and immovable. The strongest was the moral fibre which she derived from a religion as firm and alive as it was unorthodox. Her belief in God and in eternity never wavered, despite the fact that she lived through a period of proliferating cults that gripped the imagination of many people of less strong beliefs than hers. Phrenology and spiritualism (the latter with Sir Oliver Lodge as its evangelist) swept through the country, taking into its grasp many clever men and women, among them Margot's favourite brother Eddy and her close friend DD Lyttelton.

Eddy Tennant had hidden his growing fascination with the occult from his sister, knowing full well how she would disapprove. It was a terrible shock, therefore, when she discovered his secret. In 1920, as he lay dying at Glen, he confessed to Margot how much spiritualism had come to mean to him, and how happy he was in the belief that he would be able to keep contact with her after death through séances. Margot wrote indignantly to DD, who was steeped in the same faith and quite beyond recall:

> Eddy's death and everything connected with it has given me a profound shock . . . I did not know the spook world peering through man and not through God into the unknown had quite such a devastating effect on the human heart, and my soul revolts at everything I see and hear here. I suppose now we who are left will have the terrific tosh that the dead speak.[17]

Margot yearned for occupation but did not know where it could be found: she longed for a directive and one did come to her briefly. Sir Henry ('Chips') Channon thought boredom and loneliness were at the root of her bad temper and sharp rejoinders, so he persuaded her to go to the Ladies' Gallery in the Commons again, and half-reluctant she tried it. Once inside, recognized by the doorman, shut into the creaking old lift and entering the familiar gallery, she saw friends she had not bothered with for ages, who smiled a welcome and made room for her, and she began to feel the old excitement creep down her spine. That night she wrote a happy letter to Dawson: '. . . Lloyd George made an excellent speech that I never thought I should live to hear . . .'.[18] To her surprise Margot began to look forward to Lloyd George's speeches and to applaud them vigorously. Moreover she was very annoyed when she missed one through a 'seedy' bout or another engagement. When Protection once more became a major issue she told Dawson that Lloyd George's defence of free trade was the best she had ever heard. In the autumn of 1931 she heard Lloyd George make an election speech and shouted 'hurrah' with the rest when he thundered that if the Liberals had any guts they would sweep the country as they had done in 1906.[19] She was delighted at the way Lloyd George had improved, and thought him now full of good sense; it did not occur to her that it was she who had changed.

In the spring of 1931 she went to Paris for a few days, and although money was short she ordered a dress from Worth, long, flowing and black, worn with a matching turban. Immediately the material was draped over her she knew that she had made the right choice. In future, if only for economy's sake, she would wear no other colour. Monsieur Worth had been dead for some time but the establishment had not changed and Margot might still have been the rich Miss Tennant from the amount of fuss made of her. Her new clothes made quite a sensation at a reception given by Sir Henry Channon, who noticed with amazement that every new guest who had not met Margot before asked to be introduced to her.

At the end of July she went to North Berwick to rest and play golf. She felt so much better that she prolonged her holiday until October and only reached London just in time to vote. Wholly missing the point of the economic crisis she told Geoffrey Dawson that this was an election 'to satisfy the foreigners that we are a united people behind a national government'.[20] She went to a political lunch and called Baldwin a gambler, Ramsay Macdonald a foghorn and Simon a traitor, then wondered why they avoided her.

In February 1932 she witnessed a political rally in Hyde Park for the first time and was appalled: had the Communists taken over? Surely everyone knew that Hyde Park was sacred to children and dogs? Soon every square would have its tub thumper, standing on an upturned box, waving his arms about, preaching the kind of politics she hated. Indignantly she ordered Geoffrey Dawson to put a stop to this nonsense immediately and an article did appear in The Times 'protesting feebly' (Margot's words) against the practice. Nevertheless the outrage continued.

After her first visit to the Commons at the beginning of the new session, she noticed one young Member of Parliament she very much wanted to take care of. Paradoxically, this was James Maxton, the only Communist MP, but he did not want to be under anyone's wing and preferred his independence.

During the previous autumn Margot had been asked to luncheon at Buckingham Palace. Queen Mary remarked how sad it was to see her alone without her husband and the King clasped her hand warmly in sympathy while making the kindest remarks. But she soon discovered that His Majesty had gone downhill and had become a Protectionist. 'Keep the damn foreigners out,' he said, then embarked on the advantages of a self-sufficient empire 'and all the billowing bosh we know so well.' 'The difference between royalty and ourselves,' she told Dawson, 'is the difference between animals in the zoo and animals in the jungle.'[21]

CHAPTER 37

Dead Men can't Defend Themselves

SOME TIME BEFORE Asquith's death, opinions were canvassed as to who was the most suitable person to write the official Life. According to Margot, Henry was not consulted, nor did he express any views himself. In 1928, after many family conclaves with some close friends present, J. A. Spender, the historian and editor of the *Westminster Gazette*, was chosen, with Cyril Asquith as his assistant. Margot thought well of Spender, but she did not consider her stepson able enough for the job. She argued that Cyril did not understand the art of 'lean' writing and therefore might spoil the effect they all wanted to achieve. Although there was some truth in her remark that Cyril liked long, involved sentences, Margot should have had the sense to keep quiet. She had always got on well with Cis, her youngest stepson, who was only two years old when his mother died and had been happy to allow Margot to take her place in his life. After much unpleasantness, Margot was told as kindly as possible that there were 'other qualities' needed and these Cyril had, but her angry words drove a wedge between them which was never completely removed. Unfortunately she also gave the impression that she herself had a natural right to the job and when it became clear that none of her stepchildren had thought of her, she was deeply hurt. Spender tactfully explained to her that she was too involved emotionally to give a clear picture, although of course perfectly suitable in other ways. This mollified her somewhat, but one grievance was quickly replaced by another: no one had consulted her about the publisher. She had taken it for granted that Newman Flower would get the book for Cassells, and now she was afraid that he would lose prestige if it went to another firm. But guided by Spender the family chose Thornton Butterworth, who had published Margot's autobiography and with whom she had since quarrelled. She felt some explanation was due to Flower and was anxious to assure him of her regard: 'I do not think you know how deeply I felt the family not giving you the official Life. I cried when I heard it but it had nothing to do with me. I consider that you did everything for me and the man I love. . . .'[1]

Margot urged Spender to publish the official Life quickly: people had short memories when it was a question of right and wrong. She also wanted the Life to be on a canvas big enough to encompass the man for whom the adjective 'massive' seemed to have been specially designed.

Whether or not Spender wanted her help, she was determined to give it. She immediately set about collecting everything she had ever written about Henry's distress at the treachery inflicted on him in 1916 and his refusal to fight back. There were so many points which she wanted Spender to get straight, trivial in themselves but which when massed together would give a clear picture of Henry's personality. For instance, readers might wonder why she had hesitated for so long before marrying him. Would it not seem strange that she had not jumped at the chance of sharing her life with a man whose mind was so much larger than her own?[2] Without many details of this nature the book would be incomplete, and only she could provide them. It did not take her long to guess that Spender had never had the slightest intention of consulting her and she was convinced that he never even looked at the papers she sent him.[3]

It soon transpired that many documents were missing. Her own letters to Henry before their marriage were among those that could not be found. She came to the sad conclusion that Henry had burned these, along with other papers, including most of Hilda Harrisson's letters. One night she had happened to go to his study to find him tearing up papers and throwing them into the fire. She had tried to stop him, begging him to keep those he had not yet thrown away, since she was sure Mrs Harrisson valued his letters and would be hurt if she knew how little he valued hers. This secretive side of her husband was something Margot could not understand. Why did a figure so much in the public eye wish to be so private?

Generously she offered Spender her diaries, hoping that they would fill the gaps. She had them typed especially for him and made careful corrections. In these pages lay the truth and she wanted Spender to know it:

Since you are the only person who can write of Lloyd George and Northcliffe bravely and this must be done. I am much to blame as I warned Henry too often that Lloyd George was a disloyal little fellow and a wife becomes a bore if she says tiresome things too often.

At the end of January 1932, after much reflection, she wrote Spender a short but firm letter: 'I should not like the Life of my husband to be written without some contribution on my part.'[4] As well as her diary she sent him the long and carefully composed memorandum, already quoted,* in which she explained her attitude towards Asquith's need for a close relationship with another woman outside marriage, and the pain it had caused her.

In the late 'twenties and early 'thirties a large number of books and diaries were published about the Great War by both politicians and soldiers. Margot ordered them all from Hatchards and read them in order to find out what they had to say about Henry, for the fifteen years that had elapsed since his resignation had done nothing to wipe out the feeling of injustice that burned within her. Margot marked all the good (that is, flattering) bits about Henry in red pencil and made comments on adverse criticism which got more acid as dawn approached and fatigue began to tell, for the greater part of her reading was done at night.

In the late spring of 1931 the first volume of the Beaverbrook diaries of the war was published and Margot saw at once that it was full of errors. The resignation of Asquith in December 1916 was dealt with fully but 'not in the right light'. Quite naturally Beaverbrook presented 'that little blackguard' Lloyd George as a national hero who had saved them all from perdition. Henry, with his simple faith in human nature, would never agree that the man who had supplanted him was as cunning as Margot claimed. She began to wonder whether, if she had protested to him often and loudly, he might have listened to her. But it was now too late.

Margot's criticisms of the Beaverbrook diaries were treated contemptuously by the family; when she said 'diaries can be cooked' they merely felt that Margot was off on her hobby horse again. The knowledge that they did not believe her drove her on: 'Only fools could take serious notice of his [Beaverbrook's] revelations,' she wrote to H. A. Gwynne, 'dead men can't defend themselves . . . If you knew all my husband and I had to

* See pp. 253–5

put up with during the war; Kitchener and French hated one another, also Beatty and Jellicoe.'[5]

Twenty years later, when Margot was dead, her 'nagging' was vindicated with the publication of Middlemass and Barnes's biography of Stanley Baldwin. The book proved that she was far nearer the truth than either Asquith or his colleagues realized. How happy Margot would have been to read of the close conspiracy, the leaks to the papers whose support Lloyd George needed, the muffling of the rest of the press, the discussion of Cabinet secrets with Beaverbrook and Rothermere, the prostitution of judicial office and the sale of honours.[6] All these crimes Margot had proclaimed loudly, yet no one had listened. How lacking in love and confidence Asquith had become in old age! Never once did she have the satisfaction of hearing her husband say: 'You may be right.'

A year later, in 1932, the second volume of the Beaverbrook diaries was published. When the *Morning Post* gave it a good review Margot told Gwynne coldly that she never expected to see such disloyalty to herself in his paper. Violet tried to persuade her stepmother not to comment on reviews, it was undignified and no one read them anyway. Constant post-mortems on her father's resignation upset Violet as much as Margot but she believed that silence was the only answer. As always when any discussion arose between the two women in which Asquith was involved, old jealousies and antagonisms would rise to the surface and although Violet was able to keep her feelings under control, Margot could not. This time Violet did manage to cool Margot's anger somewhat, reminding her that Gwynne had been kind to her and that she might need him some time in the future. Even so her letter sounds sharp enough:

Your paper does not come out well in the Asquith–Lloyd George controversies of 1914–18. In the Maurice debate you call Lloyd George a winner—are you sure you backed the right horse? You would have preferred Asquith to Lloyd George had you known him.[7]

This was certainly a great deal more restrained than the hysterical letter she had written at three o'clock one morning the year before, after the publication of volume one of the Diaries, in which she damned Bonar Law (whom she really liked), and told Gwynne that he was 'harnessed to his own ambition which sat uncomfortably on his inferiority complex'.[8]

She was becoming more intolerant of friends who did not think as she did, hold the same opinions, admire and hate the same people. Only with her daughter Elizabeth had she learned to tread carefully; Elizabeth hated politics and did not want to hear about them. Margot was always most careful not to transgress, in case Elizabeth should sulk and leave her letterless. Sweet-tempered and dreamy, Puffin possessed a very different nature. Margot adored him and liked to pretend that he still needed her. But this son was quite self-sufficient and did not need anyone, not even a wife. By 1931 Margot began to think he would never marry, and if that turned out to be the case, he would make his home with her. She was always on the lookout to do him a good turn. When his film *Shooting Stars* was about to be shown in London, she asked Geoffrey Dawson if he would be willing to give it 'a little bravo' in *The Times*: 'If it is wrong of me to ask you this, take no notice . . .'[9]

By the end of 1931 Margot was forced to face the unpleasant fact that she might no longer be able to afford to run two houses and The Wharf would have to be sold to pay her debts, which were becoming bigger and more unmanageable every week. Ever optimistic, she was still hopeful that she could earn enough money by her writing to keep up both. Unfortunately writing no longer gave her any pleasure, but rather had become a heavy burden.

Misguidedly Gwynne advised her to continue with her writing, so by return of post Margot sent him a large batch of articles for which she asked £50 to £100 each, according to the amount of effort she had put into them. This was her criterion of excellence, and when told that an article was not worth much because no one was interested in that particular subject any more, she would reply sharply: 'But it took me hours to write.' All these articles were political, many harking back into the past and all overlaid by Margot's personal bias. Over a period of years samples had been sent to numerous editors in order to tempt them to buy her wares. Some were probably libellous (and the last thing she could afford was a lawsuit) for although she had been married to a lawyer she had no conception how wide and how devious were the laws of libel. Many of the articles were merely variations on the same theme: 'Henry was too concerned about the war to bother about his personal position, therefore he had been a sitting duck for Lloyd George and co.'[10]

She had already started to write *More Memories*, a book of essays enlarged from her autobiography. She said that Newman Flower offered her £10,000 advance for it, but later admitted that she asked for that amount but only managed to squeeze £6000 out of him. It was well received, and at the Austrian Embassy where she attended a musical evening a few days after its publication, she was overwhelmed with praise. 'I feel pretty sure I will make your fortune,' she told Newman Flower. She began to boast that she had made the book indiscreet on purpose to boost sales and was caught out when she next met Mrs Keppel, who in a furious voice said she would not allow Margot to mention her name in her books: Edward VII had never told her a Cabinet secret in her life, she said, and Margot had got her into endless trouble with George V. Margot only listened when the Marquess of Crewe took her aside and advised her that if the book went into a second edition she ought to modify her remarks about King Edward and Lord Kitchener, for although what she had said was true, it had caused offence. Yet Margot knew very well that it was her indiscretions (or 'honesty', as she preferred to call it) that sold the book so well and that those who asked her to delete them knew this. However, she was weary of all the criticism and feeling her age; the book would have to be altered. 'I shall keep my promises to all those old friends,' she told Newman Flower, who thought it an amazing statement for her to make when the book was making money. 'Send me the new manuscript when it is typed . . . it would not matter if I felt well, but I don't and I'm dog poor.'[11]

Some time in the late 1930s Newman Flower offered Margot a regular allowance in return for an occasional article which he could pass on to a magazine or newspaper. Margot refused this kindness saying she was too old and too tired and was short of ideas. To Flower she told the truth, but to her friends at large she talked of being worked to death writing articles for newspapers:

Every day of my life I am asked to write more. I write for hours every morning for the *Daily Sketch*. They do not publish the articles except very occasionally. I am not vain, I do not mind, but it is a great waste as I prefer to publish them.[12]

Did she really write these articles? She says she received 'a mild salary' for them, which probably meant that Newman Flower had managed to find a way to persuade her to accept an allowance, without hurting her feelings. But it is far more likely that she only wrote bits of articles on scraps of paper and since her memory was no longer good, she could have forgotten that she never completed them. Since she worked so hard it angered her that she was underestimated as a writer. She had never forgotten that Virginia Woolf and the historian H. A. L. Fisher had both said her work was undervalued and that 'if they were publishers they would force me to write more. Publishers do not appreciate writing like mine'.

There was still one place in London where Margot was warmly welcomed, and this was at the Belgrave Square home of 'Chips' Channon. There was hardly an important luncheon or dinner party there to which she was not invited, for 'Chips' had never forgotten that when he was an unknown American, Margot had introduced him to all her friends and included him in her parties.

Few people enjoyed dissecting their own characters as much as Margot, who found an infinite variety of things to say about herself—it was a never-ending and absorbing topic. But she did not discover during those lengthy self-analytical sessions that her frequent mistake was not to take enough time to reflect before writing about others. Too often she was in a mental flurry, the speed of her mind outran prudence and she could not resist the temptation to draw blood with the cutting edge of her intellect. Her impulsiveness increased with age and went hand in hand with a candour which was not wholly endearing. Self-absorbed though not self-satisfied, she never understood the effect of her words on other people and was in turn hurt and mystified when in consequence she was given the cold shoulder. Lord Rosebery, for instance, never quite rid himself of his resentment that Margot did not contradict rumours of their alleged engagement in 1892, nor did George Curzon forgive her for the very personal criticisms she made of him in her autobiography. When a chance came to pay her back, both did so without mercy. Not surprisingly, even the easy-going Stanley Baldwin resented her calling him a 'benevolent fumbler' behind his back, although she was sincerely fond of Baldwin and admired his leadership. When in later life invitations did not come so readily as of old she blamed everyone except herself. But the habit of mind that could sum up everything with lightning speed and with the sharpest wit had its funny side too. Who but Margot could call an indifferent painting 'A mouse's sneeze' or describe the fussy food at Taplow Court as

'. . . you know the kind of thing, salad decorated with the Lord's Prayer in beetroot'?

But Chips admired her still, and knew that she possessed a kind heart in spite of her sharp tongue. After a large dinner party in 1936 he wrote in his diary that Margot was '. . . rude, dictatorial and magnificent. She is the cleverest woman I know and is a terrific character . . . her crisp, penetrating phrases are rivetting'.[13] On another similar occasion she arrived 'looking like a death mask' but had not been in the house five minutes before she galvanized rather a slow party into life.[14] Chips's friends upbraided him for encouraging her, especially at bridge when she never stopped talking. It was all part of her restlessness. She had to do everything at a furious pace, in order to give her the feeling that she was getting the most out of life, although this constant activity made her bones ache and took away her sleep. She would climb into her high bed feeling drowsy and then become wide awake after putting out the light, when her worries took over.

rich woman since J. M. Barrie had left her all his money; now it was Margot who needed 'tips', but none were forthcoming. She complained bitterly to all who would listen that wealth had made Cynthia touchier than ever. Stories about Margot and her malicious remarks now abounded and it is not difficult to see how they came about. She happened to comment at the wedding of Cynthia's second son Michael on the plain looks of the bride as she had a few days before on Beb's drinking and the conduct of Cynthia's autistic son John: distinctly ill-advised remarks, and Cynthia made the most of them.

Old and relatively poor though she was, Margot still had the power to make Cynthia jealous, since it was she whom the new King Edward VIII asked to dine soon after his accession to the throne in 1936, so that Margot was among the first in London to meet Mrs Simpson. She dressed for the occasion with great care, only to find at Buckingham Palace a new informality into which she did not fit at all. A number of Americans were present, and their raucous voices and free and easy manners grated on her. She thought Edward a boring little man who encouraged his guests to treat him as one of themselves, a terrible mistake, Margot thought.

Wherever she went now the King's new companion was the main topic of conversation: Margot wished she had paid more attention to Wallis Simpson when they met at dinner. All she remembered was that she was a very ordinary little woman, with nothing special about her at all.

Although Edward VIII had made a favourable impression on the public, Margot felt that she had formed the right idea of him when she met him at Sandringham as a boy. As she told Geoffrey Dawson in 1929: 'When I look at the Prince of Wales' poor anxious little fretful face and ever restless body, I feel he will be a very poor successor, mulish and nervous and badly surrounded.'[4] Nevertheless, in 1936 she kept her opinions to herself and did not wish to hear about the King's liaison: no one in her circle had ever speculated about Mrs Keppel, but had taken her for granted. Margot stubbornly refused to believe that Edward meant to marry Mrs Simpson, nor did she think that the King was her 'absolute slave' and would go nowhere if Wallis was not welcome.

As the wife of the Roumanian ambassador in Paris Elizabeth was in a good position to pick up endless snippets about the King, and in the spring of 1936 she told her mother that she herself had seen them together at Cannes, while friends of hers had seen them in Vienna and Budapest, often walking arm-in-arm. Margot told Elizabeth sharply that Kings had

had mistresses before, and it was only the awful inquisitiveness of the present-day press that made a meal of it.

However, on her walks from the Park to Bedford Square Margot was shocked to see Edward's car regularly outside Mrs Simpson's flat in Bryanston Square: how foolish it was for him to be so indiscreet. She tried to draw comfort from Nancy Astor, but Nancy gloomily predicted that there was trouble brewing. Dining at Lady Cunard's one evening, Margot took a good look at Mrs Simpson's jewels and concluded that they were the sort an ordinary woman could only possess if they were given to her by someone fabulously rich and in love. Chips Channon showed no surprise; he had recently seen Mrs Simpson 'literally smothered in rubies'.[5] Margot was severe: 'She should not draw attention to herself in this way.'

In July 1936 the King again invited her to dine, this time at St James's Palace. It was a large party and immediately she entered the room she saw that Mrs Simpson had not only come without her husband but that her jewels outshone those of every woman present. When in the autumn a discreet paragraph in the papers announced the Simpson divorce Margot did not at first see it, but when Elizabeth came shortly afterwards she could talk of nothing but the royal romance. The King had spent the summer with Mrs Simpson cruising on the *Nahlin*, and wherever they went they were besieged by photographers, journalists and crowds of sightseers. This too Margot dismissed as pure continental hysteria. That the American papers were in full cry was almost proof that there was nothing in it: it was mere anti-British sensationalism of the kind America loved.

Soon after Elizabeth's arrival, Geoffrey Dawson lunched with mother and daughter at Bedford Square. Immediately Elizabeth poured out all she knew of the Simpson affair, while Margot remained uncharacteristically silent. That night Dawson was told why:

I did not want to say more about Mrs S. before Elizabeth and so I did not listen much to what she said (for fear of betraying confidences) . . . [I] warned her not to believe anything she heard . . . Elizabeth said that someone had told him [the King] that *The Times* intended writing a leader on the subject and as *The Times* is the Empire this hurt him very much . . . I said that your paper had not printed any form of gossip and certainly never would. I can't think who could have spread this fantastical idea that you said 'the King must be stopped, something must be done'. But how do you propose to stop it? Perfect silence is all that is obligatory now, the talk is already dying down. After all if it was not Mrs S. it probably would be someone much worse . . . neither the King nor Mrs S. have the slightest idea of marriage. She told me that she wanted to . . . be divorced in America but that H.M. and her husband would not hear of it. She is going to the South of France staying with old friends during the ten days of the coronation. She said with real emotion that fond as she was of him he was both childish and obstinate and that alas! she could never alter him, it was part of his nature . . . people should realize that he values the kingdom and will never fail in public duty . . . we should all back him and leave Mrs S. alone to wrestle with his mulishness.[6]

This letter was written on 26 November, only ten days before the final crisis; Dawson had been discretion itself, for although he had seen Margot frequently that autumn he had not given her the slightest hint of the real truth. At the time Margot wrote her letter he already knew that matters had gone too far for this.

When the news of the abdication burst on a startled nation, Margot was shocked by the King's self-indulgence: Edward had done the one thing she believed Kings never did—put private life before public duty. She was so upset that she had not the strength to be cross with Geoffrey Dawson for allowing her to go on in a fool's paradise, but praised him for his loyalty to the throne. Over and over again she repeated 'Can't he see she's unsuitable?'[7]

Because of her unbending attitude to change, she did not find it possible to start afresh like Lucy Baldwin who in a crisp letter to Margot's half-sister Katharine gave some sound advice: 'Now what we have all got to do is to set to work and repolish the throne.'[8] Edward VIII had let them all down and Margot never mentioned him again.

The coronation was fixed for 12 May 1937. George VI was one member of the royal family Margot hardly knew. Shy and retiring, he had played no part in the kind of society gatherings that Margot frequented. Nevertheless this would have been Margot's third coronation, and she would have liked a seat in the Abbey, if only for old times' sake; but all she could hope for was a position by one of the windows overlooking the Mall. In order to prepare herself for disappointment, she said she was too old to dress up for such occasions now, and seldom had the energy to stir from home. Yet her friends noticed that once she did make the effort, the chance of meeting new people soon galvanized her into life and there was no more talk of fatigue. That she still retained much of her buoyancy is well attested in these two extracts from the diary of the actor and playwright Sir Basil Bartlett, both dating from July 1936:

There is a small family party here [Herstmonceux Castle], and Margot Oxford. The old girl is, as usual, in tremendous form. She told me this evening all about . . . her hatred of Lloyd George, and the glories of the late Victorian fancy-dress parties. . . . She is an old horror, but has beautiful manners and great vitality and is, in general, very stimulating except at the Bridge table, where she becomes a menace. . . .

I dined with Margot Oxford in her delicious little house in Bedford Square. I know of no house in London in which I should prefer to live. She is awfully broke—'we all live by our wits here,' she said—but she has some lovely things, and the food is good, and the general atmosphere very peaceful and friendly. Puffin was there. 'Anthony Pick-nose Asquith' as we have always called him. A strange little fellow. But most intelligent. And a brilliant host. . . .

CHAPTER 39

She did nothing in particular, but did it very well

AT THE FEW functions Margot attended in 1937 she had been greatly alarmed by what she called senseless talk against Germany. The papers were full of Churchill's speeches with their thunderings against Germany's re-armament policy and 'other things' which were too uncomfortable to think about. Even Baldwin, whom she admired on account of his sound sense, surprised her: they had had a quiet luncheon together at Bedford Square and he had said that if Germany were to continue to increase her armaments it would be a terrible thing, since England's defences could not match Germany's in any way. Margot scolded him roundly for saying such a thing. Competition in arms was the way to start a war.

Puffin was filming in Berlin and came home for a short holiday in June 1937. Margot was amazed to find that even a non-political person like her son admitted that he had seen 'strange things' in the streets that had made him uneasy. He was no longer happy in Germany and was thinking of coming home to make his next film. On a recent visit Elizabeth had not been much comfort either. She had spent the previous few months travelling between Paris and Bucharest and one evening when alone with her mother she spoke vehemently on the necessity of fighting Communism; it was the root of all evil. On and on she rattled, but it was as though she was repeating word for word the phrases that had been dinned into her. Margot found it difficult not to lose her temper but she had to content herself with saying coldly that she had never expected a daughter of hers to be taken in by such 'tall talk'. There was less Communism and class revolt in England now than when she was a girl in the 1880s; she should have seen the riots then. Elizabeth's own father had once defended the revolutionary John Burns, who became thoroughly respectable when put in a position of authority. It was just the same with Ramsay Macdonald. That was what happened in England. But Elizabeth had, Margot felt, become rather opinionated and would argue with her mother, who came to the conclusion that Elizabeth had lived abroad too long to understand that 'fear is the fore-runner of all evil'.[1]

In May 1937 Neville Chamberlain took Baldwin's place as Prime Minister. Margot had known all the Chamberlains for years and had long before come to the conclusion that Neville had no leadership quality; in 1936 she had told Geoffrey Dawson that 'although Neville is good at his job he has no sort of vision'.[2] If he had had vision he would not believe in protection, for of all beliefs this was the most foolish for 'an island whose prosperity depends upon trade'. She had another grudge against him too: he never listened to a word she said, for like a lot of quiet men he was stubborn, and therein lay his weakness. A Prime Minister, Margot said, should listen to everyone who preferred advice before he made up his mind. Baldwin always did. Margot believed that in the many amicable arguments they had had together she had persuaded him to see that protection might not after all be the best policy. She had enjoyed these talks so much that she had come to look on him as more of a Liberal than a Conservative. How strong, too, Baldwin had been in comparison with Chamberlain, whom Margot quite unfairly blamed for the incorporation of Austria into the Reich and for the seizure of Czechoslovakia the following year. The Nazis would not have dared had Baldwin still been at the helm.

When Chamberlain flew to Munich for the third time in September 1938 to negotiate with Hitler she praised his energy and resourcefulness to Marie Belloc-Lowndes. The two ageing women sat together over the fire in Margot's sitting-room, apprehensive and filled with fear for their children. Margot hoped that Elizabeth would be 'protected by some sort of diplomatic immunity', but Marie feared for her numerous relatives in and around Paris. What would be their fate if the Germans overran France? When they heard on the radio of Neville Chamberlain's return from Munich, waving a piece of paper and proclaiming 'Peace in our time', they were overwhelmed with relief. But when Margot read in *The Times* that the Prime Minister had given the dictators all they demanded and had thrown Czechoslovakia to the wolves, she was shaken. The account of Chamberlain's capitulation made painful reading.

Gilbert Murray's letter in *The Times* condemning Chamberlain's action in the roundest terms frightened her badly. She trusted Gilbert and

could not rest until she had asked him for an explanation. He replied by
return of post:

> As far as I understand Chamberlain I think him fundamentally wrong. I
> spoke at Geneva to representatives of practically every small nation in
> Europe. They all dreaded and hated Germany and asked anxiously
> whether England would protect them. I believe they would still stand
> together to protest against German aggression if England and France
> would give them the lead. But of course they won't . . . The more I think
> things over the more I see the general extinction of Liberalism as a
> world disaster.[3]

When they met shortly afterwards, an irate Murray told her that Chamberlain had poured contempt on the League of Nations and there was
nothing more to say. A coolness sprang up between them and it was not
until 4 March 1939 that Margot, who had been ill, could find enough
energy to answer his letter of five months before. '. . . cursing Chamberlain is not a policy', she wrote:

> You say you do not think him a cynic. Does anyone? I never met a more
> modest man. He has no charm and is shy, but he is the least vain I have
> ever known. He has never varied by one hair from his convictions and
> thinks as I do that there is only one way of preserving peace in the world
> and getting rid of your enemy, that is to come to some sort of agreement
> with him and the viler he is the more you must frighten him with the
> opposite weapons from his. I have been and still am very unhappy that
> our own great party should be so very short-sighted as to refuse to face
> facts. The greatest enemy to mankind is hate. I think that it is the very
> height of disloyalty to make foreigners think that there is a party here
> that is against the Chamberlain peace party.[4]

In May Elizabeth came to see Margot, bringing her daughter Priscilla with
her. Margot noticed at once that Elizabeth was very changed. She was
silent and *distrait*, ate almost nothing but drank too much. It was painful,
too, for Margot to find that she could not get near her daughter. The
moment the time and place seemed right for a confidential talk, Elizabeth
had letters to write or an old friend to see, blatantly putting up artificial
barriers to keep her mother off forbidden ground. Remembering her own

superhuman efforts to be loyal to Henry, she wondered if her child was enduring the same misery and thought it disloyal to confide even in her mother. It was ominous that she did not once mention Antoine's name. Margot longed for someone to help and advise her, to show how best she could help her daughter. She was shy of turning to Geoffrey Dawson or Newman Flower, since both thought so highly of Elizabeth and Margot did not want to let them know she was unhappy.

The great joy of this short holiday was in Margot's love for the nineteen-year-old Priscilla. She had let the young girl accompany her on her walk one morning through the park, and when they came across workmen digging what she took to be a grave Margot was outraged to be told that they were constructing air-raid shelters to protect the citizens of London from German bombers. It was Priscilla who told her grand-mother that her father had been ordered back to Roumania and that her mother was to follow him there from London, while she herself continued her course at the Sorbonne. Margot was so upset that she had to turn aside to hide her face. If war broke out Elizabeth might not be able to come home until it was over, and by that time Margot herself might be dead. To let Elizabeth go back to Paris was agony but she did her best to look calm and unconcerned, although tears streamed down her face as she watched the taxi disappear. She went straight to bed and lay for hours, not crying but shaking from head to foot, racked with misery and apprehension.

Shortly after the Bibescos' departure, Margot went to Mells Manor to stay with the Horners. Margot could never look at Katharine, the widow of Raymond Asquith, without a feeling of sorrow. Though attractive she had never remarried but had devoted herself to her three children. With the threat of war hovering it was impossible not to remember how much they had suffered all those years ago. At North Berwick, where Margot went next, the imminence of war could not be hidden. The golf links were dotted with pill-boxes, while along the whole of the coast workmen were building other fortifications.

Mindful that war always came in the autumn when the harvest was gathered in, Margot changed her mind and did not prolong her stay, but was back in London by late June. Everywhere she saw again preparations for war, even sandbags and barrage-balloons in the Park. In order to reassure herself she went about telling people that there was not going to be a war, just as she had once said the King would never marry Mrs Simpson. When the ultimatum expired on 3 September, Neville Chamberlain told the nation almost in the same words Henry had used twenty-five years earlier: 'We are at war.'

Like many other people she expected to be annihilated by German bombs almost at once and bravely prepared herself for her fate. She had refused to collect her gas mask saying that claustrophobia would kill her before gas; authority had brought it round to her house even so. Nor would she go into a shelter 'to be buried alive'. If she was to die, she would prefer it should be at home in her own bed with her possessions around her.

Her long-standing passion for everything German, dating from those halcyon Dresden days before her marriage, again gave people the impression that she was pro-German and she unwittingly made many enemies. Margot did not understand why friends no longer asked her to their houses, so one afternoon Marie Belloc-Lowndes marched over to Bedford Square in order to enlighten Margot on the horrors of the Hitler regime: concentration camps, torture, the elimination of the Jews, old people, cripples and other abominations, 'which altered her views entirely', Marie told her daughter with some satisfaction.[5]

After having braced herself for the worst, she told herself that she must try to live as normal a life as possible, but she found black-out regulations tedious and ration books mystified her. Occasionally she lunched out, went to her bridge club for a rubber or two, walked in the Park (which she hardly recognized) or watched soldiers marching, the faces of the boys just the same as those of 1914–18, young and innocent and not long out of school. She was frightened lest she should be knocked down by a car in the black-out and not killed outright: to be crippled and dependent at the age of seventy-five was a fearful thought. For the first time in her life Margot was housebound with little to distract her. Rations did not provide enough food to entertain, and she missed the company of other people more than she dared own, for solitude made her turn in on herself and led to morbid moods. Puffin's return home just before the outbreak of war—he was hoping for an intelligence job—put new heart into Margot, but he brought the ominous news that he had not heard a word from Elizabeth. Every night, kneeling by her bed as she had done since childhood, Margot prayed as she had never done before that Elizabeth should be safe: 'Let me live just long enough to see her once more.'

When the Battle of Britain started, she would stand at her window with her field glasses watching Spitfires and Hurricanes in the distance twist and turn. One night a bomb fell very close to Margot's house, not a direct hit but near enough to cause considerable damage and to leave a huge hole in the roof. The place was unsafe and authority ordered her out, much to her indignation. A flat was hastily found for her in Cornwall Gardens, off the Gloucester Road, but she hated it at once. 'This unfindable flat is too far away for anyone to come here,' she wailed. Miserable though she was, she had no idea what to do about it. 'I have not an engagement in the world,' she told Major Radcliffe, a new acquaintance she had much taken to. 'I long for human companionship.'[6] She had too much time on her hands, and her thoughts were bleak: 'When I lie cold, awake, I ask myself if I have made anybody happy. Have I laughed, have I prayed, have I loved? If I can say "Yes" to these questions I feel at rest, I am prepared to die.' She felt old and unneeded. Brisk and helpful as ever, Marie Belloc-Lowndes offered a solution. Margot was to move into the Savoy Hotel, where there was a vacant room on the sixth floor and a large and roomy air raid shelter. Puffin was already living there and she would be 'near my friends in Fleet Street'.[7]

Once settled in Margot was reasonably happy. With regular meals (she was only too thankful to hand over her ration book) and cheerful company she began to pick up and some of her old energy returned. An urge to write came over her and she thought she would like to continue with 'Twelve Prime Ministers I have known', but now since Winston Churchill's elevation to that position she would have to make it thirteen. She was surprised to find his speeches comforting, so open and honest. Yet despite his popularity she felt sure he could not last, he was 'too unreliable', and she doubted whether he was 'capable of making a secure and enduring peace'.[8] She would never forget what a nuisance he had been to Henry. The one to look to was Stafford Cripps: 'Our hope lies in his return,' she told Gilbert Murray. 'Do you think if Winston were to fall, Stafford could form a Government?'[9]

She could only work in fits and starts now. It occurred to her that it would be more enjoyable to write a short book of personal reminiscences about Henry. Perhaps Gilbert Murray would help, and she wasted no time in asking him: 'Would you write me a letter . . . and say what you thought of Henry? It would be the making of the book. Spender did not know him nearly as well as you did.'[10]

The new book that Margot had in her head was to supply everything that Spender had left out of his massive two-volume life. Did she ever start it? She said she spent hours each day writing hard, but all she probably did was to think back and reflect on her Downing Street life, go off to sleep and think again. Living in the past was far pleasanter than living in the present.

After just a year of the Savoy Margot was tired of living in an institution which, for all its comforts, was a luxury hotel, not a home. On a day of heavy raids she impulsively moved back into 44 Bedford Square 'to live in four rooms'. But it was too dusty, desolate and cold as well as unsafe, so she bought a house in Thurloe Place, Kensington ('another lovely house', the homeless Marie Belloc-Lowndes told her daughter). It was to be Margot's last home. She no longer got out of bed for raids now no matter how heavy, but stopped her ears with cotton wool to cut down the noise and as dawn broke made herself tea and tried to write.

There had been no word from Elizabeth since she said good-bye to her mother in 1939. Margot was terrified to think of her in enemy-occupied territory, or perhaps even dead and buried she knew not where. Then one morning in March 1945, when at last the end of the war seemed in sight, she received a letter from the Red Cross to say Elizabeth was alive and well and coming home. Margot was delirious with joy and rushed all over the house, collecting Elizabeth's favourite prints to put on the walls of her room, her books and everything she had not taken with her when she went to live abroad with Antoine. Margot sang to herself as she telegraphed the good news to Puffin, asking him to get leave to come home. It was the last happiness she was ever to know. Early in April she received another letter from the Red Cross: Elizabeth would not be coming home after all. She was dead.

It was a mortal blow. Margot was completely crushed. At first she was too old, ill and suffering to take it in properly; numb with shock, she would sit for hours without moving in her armchair, staring at nothing and looking like a corpse. Friends and acquaintances wrote, Puffin came home, but Margot had no feelings left in her now. One letter did rouse her a little. It was from Gilbert Murray who knew Elizabeth and appreciated her many talents.

A few days later, although still very weak, she wrote this old friend one of the saddest letters of her life:

I knew that you would be thinking of me, dearest Gilbert. I remember your quotation but I was glad to read it again. I have had three hundred letters about my Elizabeth. They all say the same thing, how brilliant, young and kind she was . . . as you say, she deserved a better fate . . . the long separation has been intolerable to us both. When the news came that she would be back, Puffin and I sent her a long telegram through the Red Cross. I do not suppose she ever got it, do you? Nothing but death in the newspapers and in our hearts.[11]

What was there to live for now? 'Her mind has been affected,' Marie Belloc-Lowndes wrote to her daughter.[12] Semi-starvation probably did contribute to her decline, but the real cause was the shock of Elizabeth's death. Her last hope—the return of her daughter from Bucharest alive and well—had been taken from her. She had never been afraid of death and now, in suffering old age, she welcomed it. Except for Puffin, who had made his own life, she had nothing to live for. Margot took to her bed and died on 28 July 1945. She was eighty-one years old.

On 4 September there was a memorial service in St Margaret's, Westminster, where Elizabeth had been married. It was poorly attended and a far cry from the scene Margot had so often imagined at St Paul's or Westminster Abbey, packed to the door with friends.

From earliest youth obituary notices had always fascinated Margot and several times she had tried her hand at writing those of friends, but they always turned out too pungent, too true to life and too uncomplimentary to be well received by their subjects. She was strictly forbidden to send them to *The Times* to be filed until the right day came, so she had to content herself with stuffing them away in her overcrowded bureau. She had toyed with the idea of writing her own, and spent many happy hours composing suitable versions. However, on the whole she decided it was more seemly for some well-known person to have the honour and had fixed on George Curzon, until they quarrelled. Virginia Woolf was her second choice ('she will make me famous'). A few weeks after Asquith's death, she took up this occupation again, wrote the last word on herself and sent it to Dawson. It was a poorly described and dispirited picture of her life and activities that Margot had sent him out of the gloom of her early widowhood.[13] By the time Margot died in 1945 Dawson had forgotten all about it and wrote a tender and feeling obituary himself on a 'vivid and brilliant woman'.

Marie Belloc-Lowndes, who had been at the graveside in Wansborough when Margot was laid at Henry's side and who knew her in later life much better than most, summed her up very aptly: 'She was a child of nature; she could not conceal what she was feeling and she was wholly lacking in the capacity to behave with what may be called that hypocrisy without which life could scarcely be carried on.'[14]

REFERENCES

MANUSCRIPT SOURCES

BIBLIOGRAPHY

REFERENCES

Chapter 1

1. These passages are based on Nancy Crathorne, *Tennant's Stalk*
2. *The Autobiography of Margot Asquith* (1922), i, 15
3. *ibid.*, 16
4. *ibid.*, 18
5. *Tennant's Stalk*, 164
6. *ibid.*, 123
7. *ibid.*, 124
8. Masterman, 268
9. Benson, *Diary*, vol. 25, 77
10. Masterman, 268
11. *Autobiography*, i, 31
12. *ibid.*, i, 42
13. Chandos, *Memoirs*, 3/1
14. *Autobiography*, i, 63
15. Chandos, 2/32
16. Rose, *Superior Person*, 180
17. *ibid.*, 181
18. Chandos, 5/1
19. *Autobiography*, i, 13
20. Chandos, 5/1
21. *Autobiography*, i, 23
22. Rose, 164
23. *Autobiography*, i, 23
24. *ibid.*, i, 13
25. *ibid.*, i, 23
26. *ibid.*, 32

5. Liddell, *Notes from the Life of an Ordinary Mortal*, 226
6. Chandos, 6/1/8
7. Liddell, 227
8. *Autobiography*, i, 35
9. *ibid.*, 35
10. Mary Gladstone Papers, BL Add Ms. 46270
11. *Autobiography*, i, 229
12. *Letters and Journals of Mary Gladstone*, 268
13. *Autobiography*, i, 126
14. Chandos, 5/1
15. Mary Gladstone Papers, BL Add Ms. 46238
16. Masterman
17. Chandos, 5/1
18. *Autobiography*, i, 76–7
19. *ibid.*, 75
20. *Tennant's Stalk*, 172
21. *Autobiography*, i, 185
22. Blunt Papers
23. *Autobiography*, i, 57
24. *More Memories*, 222
25. Chandos, 1/6/3
26. *More Memories*, 236
27. Benson, *Diary*, vol. 158, 44
28. Balfour, *The Tennant Family*, pp. 329 and 341

Chapter 2

1. *More Memories*, 52
2. Mary Gladstone Papers, BL Add Ms. 40270
3. *More Memories*, 53
4. *Tennant's Stalk*, 173

Chapter 3

1. Chandos, 6/1/3
2. Chandos, 5/1
3. *Autobiography*, i, 162
4. Balfour 393; *Tennant's Stalk*, 173
5. *Autobiography*, i, 158

6. Chandos, 5/1
7. *Tennant's Stalk*, 173
8. Mary Gladstone Papers, BL Add Ms. 46238

Chapter 4

1. *Autobiography*, i, 38
2. *Tennant's Stalk*, 181
3. *Autobiography*, i, 37
4. Chandos, 6/1/3
5. E. Lyttelton, *Alfred Lyttelton*, 129
6. *ibid.*, 124
7. Chandos, 6/1
8. Benson, *Diary*, vol. 1, 15
9. Lyttelton, 134
10. Chandos, 6/1/A
11. Lyttelton, 136
12. *ibid.*, 137
13. Mary Gladstone Papers, BL Add Ms. 46270
14. Chandos, 4/1
15. *ibid.*, 4/4
16. Rose, 424
17. Rose, 169
18. *Tennant's Stalk*, 182
19. *Autobiography*, i, 41
20. *ibid.*, 44
21. *ibid.*, 46
22. Mary Gladstone Papers, BL Add Ms. 46238
23. *Autobiography*, i, 48–9

Chapter 5

1. *Autobiography*, i, 55
2. Chandos, 5/1
3. *More Memories*, 19
4. Chandos, 5/1
5. *ibid.*
6. Mary Gladstone Papers, BL Add Ms. 46238
7. Chandos, 4/2, Lyttelton 150
8. Chandos, 4/2
9. Mary Gladstone Papers, BL Add Ms. 46238

10. Chandos, 5/1; *More Memories*, 68
11. Chandos, 5/1
12. *ibid.*
13. *ibid.*
14. *ibid.*
15. *Tennant's Stalk*, 183
16. Chandos, 5/1
17. *ibid.*
18. Violet Bonham Carter in the *Listener*, 30 October 1947
19. Balfour, 252
20. *More Memories*, 147
21. Balfour, 232
22. *Autobiography*, i, 52
23. Balfour, 233
24. *Autobiography*, i, 120

Chapter 6

1. Chandos, AL 160
2. Chandos, 5/1
3. *ibid.*
4. *ibid.*, 5/33
5. *ibid.*, 5/1
6. *ibid.*
7. Chandos, 4/1 and Mary Gladstone Papers, BL Add Ms. 46238
8. Chandos, 5/1
9. Mary Gladstone Papers, BL Add Ms. 46238
10. Lyttelton
11. Mary Gladstone Papers, BL Add Ms. 46238
12. Chandos, 5/1
13. Chandos, 5/37
14. Mary Gladstone Papers, BL Add Ms. 46238
15. *Autobiography*, i, 171, and Chandos, 5/1
16. Mary Gladstone Papers, BL Add Ms. 46238
17. *Autobiography*, i, 172
18. *ibid.*, 173
19. *ibid.*, 164
20. *ibid.*, 166–8

Chapter 7

1. *Autobiography*, i, 91
2. *ibid.*, 99
3. *ibid.*, 100
4. Jowett Papers
5. *ibid.*
6. *Autobiography*, i, 101
7. *ibid.*
8. *ibid.*
9. Jowett Papers
10. *Autobiography*, i, 104
11. Jowett Papers
12. *Autobiography*, i, 102–3
13. *ibid.*, 116
14. Jowett Papers
15. *ibid.*
16. *ibid.*
17. Faber, *Jowett*, 421
18. *Autobiography*, i, 113–14

Chapter 8

1. *Autobiography*, i, 193
2. *ibid.*, 194
3. *ibid.*, 198
4. Milner Papers, Dep. 1, 36–9
5. Chandos, 2/33
6. Asquith, *Off the Record*, 11
7. Milner Papers, Dep. 1/1
8. Benson, *Diary*, vol. 1, 31
9. Milner Papers, Dep. 1/1
10. *ibid.*, Dep. 1/1–10
11. *ibid.*, Dep. 1/54–7
12. *More Memories*, 106
13. Margot Asquith, unpublished Ms., 1
14. *ibid.*, 12
15. *More Memories*, 110
16. Margot Asquith, unpublished Ms., 10–11
17. *ibid.*, 13–14 and *More Memories*, 110
18. Milner Papers, Dep. 1/18–20
19. Mary Gladstone Papers, BL Add Ms. 46238
20. Margot Asquith, unpublished Ms., 23

21. *ibid.*, 23, 26
22. Milner Papers, Dep. 1/27–32
23. *ibid.*, 1/90–93
24. *ibid.*, 1/33
25. *ibid.*, 1/61–4
26. *ibid.*, 1/34–5

Chapter 9

1. *Autobiography*, i, 221
2. *ibid.*, 222
3. Margot Asquith, unpublished Ms., 14
4. *Autobiography*, i, 220
5. *ibid.*, i, 222
6. Spender and Asquith, i, 98
7. *Autobiography*, i, 228
8. Spender and Asquith, i, 102
9. *ibid.*, i, 101
10. Milner Papers, Dep. 1/95
11. *ibid.*, i/61–4
12. Spender and Asquith, i, 105
13. *Autobiography*, i, 111–12
14. *ibid.*, i, 107
15. *ibid.*
16. *ibid.*
17. Spender and Asquith, i, 107
18. *ibid.*
19. *ibid.*
20. *ibid.*, i, 108
21. Chandos, 5/1
22. *ibid.*

Chapter 10

1. Spender and Asquith, i, 109
2. Chandos, 5/1
3. *ibid.*
4. *More Memories*, 129
5. *Autobiography*, i, 227
6. Spender and Asquith, i, 110
7. Jolliffe, 20
8. *ibid.*
9. Milner Papers, Dep. 1/72–3
10. Spender and Asquith, i, 108

11. Spender and Asquith, i, 109
12. Chandos, 5/1
13. *ibid.*
14. *ibid.*
15. *ibid.*, 2/33
16. Spender and Asquith, i, 110
17. Ponsonby, 281
18. *Autobiography*, i, 225
19. Mary Gladstone Papers, BL Add Ms. 229
20. Harcourt Papers, Dep. 75

Chapter 11

1. Chandos, 5/1
2. Mary Gladstone Papers, BL Add Ms. 46238
3. Chandos, 5/1
4. Mary Gladstone Papers, BL Add Ms. 46238
5. Spender and Asquith, i, 227
6. Osbert Sitwell, *Great Morning*, 211
7. Spender and Asquith, i, 105
8. Milner Papers, Dep. 1/74–7
9. *ibid.*
10. Chandos, 5/1
11. Milner Papers, Dep. 1/74–7
12. *ibid.*
13. *ibid.*
14. Mary Gladstone Papers, BL Add Ms. 46238
15. Chandos, 5/1
16. *ibid.*

Chapter 12

1. Benson, *Diary*, vol. 1, 179
2. *Autobiography*, i, 109
3. Milner Papers, Dep. 1/74–7
4. Chandos, 5/1
5. Spender and Asquith, i, 111
6. Milner Papers, Dep. 1/83–4
7. Margot Asquith, unpublished Ms., 80
8. Jenkins, *Asquith*, 91
9. *ibid.*, 92

10. Spender and Asquith, i, 101
11. *Autobiography*, i, 266
12. *ibid.*, 62
13. *ibid.*, 228
14. *ibid.*, 270
15. Chandos, 5/1
16. *ibid.*
17. Spender and Asquith, ii, 119
18. *Autobiography*, ii, 106
19. Chandos, 5/1
20. *ibid.*

Chapter 13

1. Milner Papers, Dep. 206
2. *Autobiography*, ii, 14
3. *ibid.*, 18–19
4. *ibid.*
5. *More Memories*, 131
6. Chandos, 5/1
7. *ibid.*
8. Milner Papers, Dep. 206
9. Esher, *Journals and Letters*, iv, 307
10. Chandos, 5/1
11. *ibid.*
12. Mary Gladstone Papers, BL Add Ms. 46238
13. Chandos, 5/1
14. Mary Gladstone Papers, BL Add Ms. 46238
15. *ibid.*
16. *ibid.*
17. *More Memories*, 85
18. *ibid.*, 89

Chapter 14

1. Chandos, 5/1
2. *Autobiography*, ii, 35
3. *ibid.*
4. Mary Gladstone Papers, BL Add Ms. 46238
5. *ibid.*
6. Joliffe, 108
7. Milner Papers, Dep. 206
8. *ibid.*, 207

9. Jenkins, 106–7
10. Milner Papers, Dep. 29
11. Gollin, *Proconsul in Politics*, 55
12. Milner Papers, Dep. 32
13. Spender and Asquith, i, 139
14. Milner Papers, Dep. 207
15. *ibid*., Dep. 216
16. *ibid*., Dep. 213

Chapter 15

1. Chandos, 5/1
2. *ibid*.
3. *ibid*., 1/91
4. Milner Papers, Dep. 217
5. Gollin, 39
6. Milner Papers, Dep. 216
7. Gollin, 64
8. *ibid*., 42
9. Selborne Papers, Dep. 79
10. *ibid*., Dep. 71
11. Mary Gladstone Papers, BL Add Ms. 46238
12. Chandos, 5/1
13. *ibid*.
14. Selborne Papers, Dep. 79
15. *Autobiography*, ii, 46
16. Jenkins, 145–6
17. *Autobiography*, ii, 55
18. Spender and Asquith, i, 172
19. *Autobiography*, ii, 63
20. Spender and Asquith, i, 229
21. Chandos, 5/1
22. *ibid*.
23. Selborne Papers, Dep. 71
24. Margot Asquith, unpublished Ms., 80
25. *ibid*., 81
26. Chandos, 5/1

Chapter 16

1. Spender and Asquith, ii, 193
2. Chandos, 5/1
3. Spender and Asquith, i, 195
4. Chandos, 5/1

5. Jenkins, 179
6. Spender and Asquith, i, 196
7. *Autobiography*, ii, 73
8. Milner Papers, Dep. 207
9. *Autobiography*, ii, 79
10. Randolph S. Churchill, *Winston S. Churchill*, ii, 243–4
11. *Diaries and Letters of Mrs Belloc-Lowndes*, 220
12. Chandos, 5/1
13. Nicolson Papers, Eng. Litt. e 141
14. *ibid*.
15. *Autobiography*, ii, 81
16. *ibid*., 82
17. *More Memories*, 240–43
18. Grey, 157
19. *ibid*., 151
20. Spender and Asquith, i, 152

Chapter 17

1. Spender and Asquith, i, 254
2. Soames, *Clementine Churchill*, 51
3. Spender and Asquith, i, 254
4. Chandos, 5/1
5. *Autobiography*, ii, 85
6. Benson, *Diary*, vol. 145, 17
7. Spender and Asquith, i, 255
8. *Autobiography*, ii, 87
9. Spender and Asquith, i, 261
10. *Autobiography*, ii, 85
11. Jenkins, 200
12. *Autobiography*, ii, 93
13. Selborne Papers, 79, fols 29–30
14. *Autobiography*, ii, 100
15. *Autobiography*, ii, 101
16. *ibid*., 103
17. *More Memories*, 288
18. Spender and Asquith, i, 281

Chapter 18

1. *Autobiography*, ii, 108
2. *More Memories*, 6–7
3. Jenkins, 223
4. Simon Papers, Dep 48, fols 15–18

5. *ibid.*
6. *More Memories*, 239
7. *Autobiography*, ii, 112
8. Spender and Asquith, i, 314
9. *Autobiography*, ii, 113
10. *ibid.*, 115
11. *ibid.*, 116
12. Harcourt Papers, Dep. 421
13. *ibid.*
14. *ibid.*
15. Grey, *Twenty-Five Years*, 240
16. Selborne Papers, 79, fols 29–30
17. *Diaries and Letters of Mrs Belloc-Lowndes*, 153
18. Joliffe, 33

Chapter 19

1. Chandos, 5/1
2. Violet Bonham Carter, *Winston Churchill as I Knew Him*, 217.
3. Chandos, 5/1
4. Bonham Carter, 255
5. Chandos, 5/1
6. *ibid.*
7. *ibid.*
8. *ibid.*
9. *ibid*, 11, 3/1
10. *ibid.*, 5/1
11. *ibid.*
12. *ibid.*
13. *ibid.*
14. Bonham Carter, 413
15. Cynthia Asquith, *Diaries*, 44 and 50
16. Soames, 134

Chapter 20

1. Spender and Asquith, ii, 13
2. Cooper, *The Rainbow Comes and Goes*, 105
3. Ziegler, *Diana Cooper*, 100
4. Jenkins, 258
5. *ibid.*, 363
6. Brock, 548
7. Brock, 588–9 and *passim*

8. *Autobiography*, ii, 181
9. Grahame Papers, Bodleian Library, Eng. Misc. D 530
10. Mary Gladstone Papers, BL Add Ms. 46238
11. Chandos, 5/1
12. *ibid.*
13. Chandos, 5/1
14. Spender and Asquith, ii, 37
15. *Autobiography*, ii, 119
16. Spender and Asquith, ii, 15
17. *ibid.*, ii, 219
18. Simon Papers, Dep. 49
19. Spender and Asquith, ii, 76
20. Simon Papers, 50, fols 27–8
21. Spender and Asquith, ii, 77

Chapter 21

1. Chandos, 5/1
2. *ibid.*
3. *More Memories*, 179
4. Mary Gladstone Papers, BL Add Ms. 46328
5. Chandos, 5/1
6. *Autobiography*, ii, 118
7. *ibid.*, 119
8. Chandos, 5/1
9. *Autobiography*, ii, 127
10. *ibid.*, 124
11. Spender and Asquith, ii, 93; *Autobiography*, ii, 144
12. *Autobiography*, ii, 145
13. Chandos, 5/1

Chapter 22

1. Spender and Asquith, ii, 105
2. *More Memories*, 135
3. Spender and Asquith, ii, 18
4. *More Memories*, 132
5. Milner Papers, Dep. 213
6. *More Memories*, 135
7. *ibid.*
8. *Autobiography*, ii, 131
9. *ibid.*, ii, 131

10. Nicolson Papers, Eng. Litt. D 183–5
11. *Autobiography*, ii, 150–57
12. Chandos, 5/1
13. *Autobiography*, ii, 154
14. Cynthia Asquith, *Diaries*, 16
15. Benson, *Diary*, vol. 44, 20
16. Jenkins, 412

Chapter 23

1. Milner Papers, Dep. 350
2. Chandos, 5/1
3. Mary Gladstone Papers, BL Add Ms. 46238
4. Pope-Hennessy, *Queen Mary*, 492
5. Milner Papers, Dep. 250
6. Chandos, 5/1
7. *ibid.*
8. Cynthia Asquith, *Diaries*, 35
9. *Autobiography*, ii, 109
10. *ibid.*, ii, 196
11. Violet Bonham Carter, 345
12. *More Memories*, 8
13. Spender and Asquith, ii, 41
14. *Autobiography*, ii, 173–4
15. Chandos, 5/1
16. *ibid.*
17. Spender and Asquith, ii, 166
18. Simon Papers, Dep 51, fols 83–4
19. Brock, 593
20. Brock, 454–5, 598–9; Jenkins, 363–4, takes the opposite view.
21. *Off the Record*, 121–2
22. Brock, 13
23. Spender Papers, British Library, June 1932, Bl Add Ms. 46388
24. *Myself when Young*, 12–13

Chapter 24

1. Spender and Asquith, ii, 165
2. Asquith–Henley Letters, 12 May 1915
3. Spender and Asquith, ii, 167
4. *Autobiography*, ii, 129
5. Cynthia Asquith, *Diaries*, 26

6. V. Bonham Carter, 403
7. Soames, 122–3
8. *Autobiography*, ii, 173
9. Spender Papers, BL Add Ms. 46388
10. Chandos, 5/1
11. *Autobiography*, ii, 173
12. Spender and Asquith, ii, 177
13. *Autobiography*, ii, 171
14. Chandos, 5/1
15. *ibid.*
16. *Autobiography*, ii, 162
17. *ibid.*, 165
18. Spender and Asquith, ii, 173

Chapter 25

1. Chandos, 5/1
2. Simon Ms., 53–4
3. Chandos, 5/1
4. Simon Ms., 53–4
5. Asquith–Henley Letters, 22 May 1916
6. Harcourt Papers, Dep. 205
7. Asquith–Henley Letters, 22 May 1916
8. Spender and Asquith, ii, 216
9. Gwynne Papers
10. *ibid.*

Chapter 26

1. Chandos, 5/1
2. Asquith–Henley Letters, 20 April 1916
3. *ibid.*, 7 December 1915
4. Spender and Asquith, ii, 127
5. *Autobiography*, ii, 187
6. *ibid.*, 188
7. Asquith, *Memories and Reflections*, ii, 158–9
8. Chandos, 5/1
9. Cynthia Asquith, *Diaries*, 223
10. *ibid.*, 217
11. Chandos, 5/1
12. *ibid.*
13. Selborne Papers, Dep. 44

14. Chandos, 5/1
15. *ibid.*

Chapter 27

1. Asquith–Henley Letters, 26 November 1915
2. *ibid.*, 1 December 1915
3. Chandos, 5/1
4. *ibid.*
5. *More Memories*, 65
6. Asquith–Henley Letters, 9 June 1915
7. *ibid.*, 19 August 1915
8. Bonham Carter, 447–8
9. Asquith–Henley Letters, 12 March 1916
10. *ibid.*, 4 and 11 March 1916
11. Chandos, 5/1
12. Mary Gladstone Papers, BL Add Ms. 46238
13. Chandos, 5/1
14. Spender and Asquith, ii, 230
15. Chandos, 5/1
16. *ibid.*
17. *Autobiography*, ii, 191
18. Gwynne Papers
19. *ibid.*
20. Spender and Asquith, ii, 264
21. Gwynne Papers
22. *ibid.*
23. Simon Papers, 53, fols 1–2
24. Spender and Asquith, ii, 230

Chapter 28

1. Cynthia Asquith, *Diaries*, 54
2. *Letters and Diaries of Mrs Belloc-Lowndes*, 29 February 1916
3. Cynthia Asquith, *Diaries*, 149
4. Asquith–Henley Letters, 16 December 1917
5. Cynthia Asquith, *Diaries*, 244
6. Asquith–Henley Letters, 4 May 1917

7. Spender and Asquith, ii, 191
8. Jenkins, 465
9. *ibid.*, 482

Chapter 29

1. Gwynne Papers
2. *ibid.*
3. *ibid.*
4. *ibid.*
5. *ibid.*
6. Soames, 187
7. *Autobiography*, ii, 244
8. Oliver Lyttelton Diary, 107, in Chandos, 5/1
9. *Autobiography*, ii, 208; Chandos, 5/1
10. Gwynne Papers
11. Gilbert Murray Papers, 12, 17 May 1918
12. Gwynne Papers
13. Gilbert Murray Papers
14. Spender and Asquith, ii, 216
15. *Autobiography*, ii, 206
16. Asquith–Henley Letters, December 1918
17. Gwynne Papers
18. *Autobiography*, ii, 297

Chapter 30

1. Spender and Asquith, ii, 321
2. Asquith Papers, Box xxiii, fol. 26
3. *ibid.*, fols 29–31
4. Asquith–Henley Letters, 31 December 1918
5. Gilbert Murray Papers
6. *Autobiography*, ii, 237
7. Gilbert Murray Papers, 19 February 1928
8. *ibid.*, 7 June 1919
9. Spender Ms., BL Add Ms. 46388, 15 May 1919
10. Spender and Asquith, ii, 326
11. Cynthia Asquith, *Diaries*, 418–23

12. Maclean Papers, Dep. c 468, fols 90–97
13. Spender and Asquith, ii, 380–81
14. Benson, *Diary*, vol. 154, 50
15. Chandos, 5/1
16. MacCarthy, *Letters to a Friend*, i, 122

Chapter 31

1. *More Memories*, 203
2. *ibid.*, 205
3. Mary Gladstone Papers, BL Add Ms. 46238
4. *ibid.*
5. *ibid.*
6. MacCarthy, *Letters to a Friend*, ii, 38
7. Mary Gladstone Papers, *ibid.*
8. Gwynne Papers
9. Mary Gladstone Papers, *ibid.*
10. Newman Flower Papers
11. *ibid.*
12. Mary Gladstone Papers, *ibid.*
13. Gwynne Papers
14. Chandos, 5/1
15. Benson Diaries, 179, 14–15
16. Nicolson Papers, Eng. Litt e 183, fol. 15
17. Mary Gladstone Papers, *ibid.*
18. Gwynne Papers
19. *ibid.*
20. Mary Gladstone Papers, *ibid.*
21. *Tennant's Stalk*, 191
22. Mary Gladstone Papers, *ibid.*
23. *ibid.*
24. *ibid.*
25. *More Memories*, 11–12
26. Mary Gladstone Papers, *ibid.*

Chapter 32

1. Nicolson Papers, Eng. Litt. e 141 (n.d.)
2. *ibid.*, 142
3. *ibid.*, 183

4. *ibid.*, 186
5. Bodleian Library Ms., Eng. Litt. d. 183, fol. 15
6. *ibid.*, fol. 20
7. *ibid.*, Eng. Hist. d. 395, fols 157–8
8. *ibid.*, Eng. Litt., fol. 22
9. *ibid.*, fol. 27
10. *Persons and Places*, 78
11. *ibid.*, 80
12. Chandos, 5/1
13. *Persons and Places*, 78
14. MacCarthy, *Letters to a Friend*, ii, 52
15. Chandos, 5/1
16. *ibid.*

Chapter 33

1. MacCarthy, *Letters to a Friend*, i, 123
2. Gwynne Papers
3. *ibid.*
4. *Autobiography*, ii, 329
5. Spender and Asquith, ii, 331
6. *More Memories*, 276–7
7. Gwynne Papers
8. Spender and Asquith, ii, 331
9. *ibid.*, 385
10. Gwynne Papers
11. Spender and Asquith, ii, 336
12. Gwynne Papers
13. *ibid.*
14. *Letters to a Friend*, i, 209–10
15. Gilbert Murray Papers
16. Gwynne Papers
17. Dawson Papers
18. Spender and Asquith, ii, 341
19. Dawson Papers
20. *Letters to a Friend*, ii, 85
21. Jenkins, 504
22. Diary of Lady Bonham Carter, quoted in Spender and Asquith, ii, 349
23. *ibid.*, 350

Chapter 34

1. Spender and Asquith, ii, 356
2. *ibid.*
3. Nicolson Papers, Eng. Litt. e 141
4. Simon Papers, Dep 58, fol. 125
5. Maclean Papers, Dep. c 467
6. *More Memories*, 249
7. Newman Flower Papers
8. *ibid.*
9. *ibid.*
10. Dawson Papers
11. *ibid.*
12. *ibid.*
13. Gwynne Papers
14. *ibid.*
15. *Letters to a Friend*, ii, 141–2
16. Spender Papers, BL Add Ms. 46388, Memorandum by Asquith, 108
17. Spender and Asquith, ii, 367
18. Dawson Papers, 25 November 1927

Chapter 35

1. Spender and Asquith, ii, 373
2. Newman Flower Papers
3. *Letters to a Friend*, ii, 197
4. Newman Flower Papers, 16 December 1927
5. Dawson Papers
6. *ibid.*
7. Maclean Papers, Dep. 468, fols 90–91
8. Simon Papers, Dep 61, fol. 108
9. Gilbert Murray Papers
10. Dawson Papers, n.d.
11. *ibid.*

Chapter 36

1. Dawson Papers
2. Newman Flower Papers, 26 February 1928
3. Dawson Papers
4. Koss, *Asquith*, 93
5. Dawson Papers

6. Spender Papers
7. Dawson Papers
8. Asquith–Henley Letters
9. Newman Flower Papers
10. *ibid.*
11. Dawson Papers
12. *ibid.*
13. *ibid.*
14. Middlemass and Barnes, *Baldwin*, 506
15. Dawson Papers
16. *ibid.*
17. Chandos, 5/1
18. Dawson Papers
19. *ibid.*
20. *ibid.*
21. *ibid.*

Chapter 37

1. Newman Flower Papers
2. Spender Papers
3. *ibid.*
4. *ibid.*
5. Gwynne Papers
6. Middlemass and Barnes, 98
7. Gwynne Papers
8. *ibid.*
9. Dawson Papers
10. Gwynne Papers
11. Newman Flower Papers
12. Letter to Sir Ernest Cassell, Newman Flower Papers
13. Channon Diaries, 116
14. *ibid.*, 179

Chapter 38

1. *More Memories*, 92 n.
2. Gilbert Murray Papers
3. Newman Flower Papers
4. Dawson Papers
5. Channon Diaries, 73
6. Dawson Papers
7. *ibid.*
8. Middlemass and Barnes, 1017

Chapter 39

1. Dawson Papers
2. *ibid.*
3. Gilbert Murray Papers
4. *ibid.*
5. *Diaries and Letters of Mrs Belloc-Lowndes*, 182
6. Radcliffe 2, 13 October 1941
7. Radcliffe 3, 23 October 1941
8. Radcliffe 1, 11 October 1941
9. Gilbert Murray Papers
10. *ibid.*
11. *ibid.*
12. *Diaries and Letters of Mrs Belloc-Lowndes*, 262
13. Dawson Papers
14. *Diaries and Letters of Mrs Belloc-Lowndes*, 262

MANUSCRIPT SOURCES

British Library:
> Mary Gladstone Papers
> Spender Papers

Bodleian Library, Oxford:
> Dawson Papers
> Newman Flower Papers
> Gilbert Murray Papers
> Grahame Papers
> Gwynne Papers
> Harcourt Papers
> Maclean Papers
> Milner Papers
> Nicolson Papers
> Ponsonby Papers
> Selborne Papers
> Simon Papers
> Spender Papers
> Asquith–Henley Letters

Balliol College, Oxford
> Jowett Papers

Churchill College, Cambridge
> Chandos Papers

Magdalene College, Cambridge
> Benson Diaries

Fitzwilliam Museum, Cambridge:
> W. S. Blunt Papers

Private:

Hon. Emma Tennant: Unpublished Ms. of Margot Asquith
Sir Basil Bartlett: Extracts from his diary
Mrs Maud Radcliffe: Letters of Margot Asquith

BIBLIOGRAPHY

(place of publication London unless otherwise stated)

Abbot, Evelyn and Campbell Lewis: *Life and Letters of Benjamin Jowett*, 1897
Arthur, Sir George: *Life of Lord Kitchener*, 1920
Asquith, Lady Cynthia: *Diaries, 1915–1918*, 1968
Asquith, H. H.: *Memories and Reflections*. 2 vols, 1928
Asquith, Margot: *Autobiography*. 2 vols, 1920–22
—— *Places and Persons*, 1925
—— *Lay Sermons*, 1927
—— *More Memories*, 1933
—— *Myself when Young*, 1938
—— *Off the Record*, 1943
Balfour, A. J. (ed. Dugdale): *Chapters of Autobiography*, 1930
Balfour, Lady Frances: *Ne Obliviscaris*, 1930
Belloc-Lowndes, Marie: *Diaries and Letters, 1911—1947*. ed. S. Lowndes, 1970
Blake, Robert: *The Unknown Prime Minister: The Life and Times of Andrew Bonar Law*, 1955
Bonham Carter, Mark (ed.): *The Autobiography of Margot Asquith*, 1962
Bonham Carter, Lady Violet: *Winston Churchill as I Knew Him*, 1967
Brock, Michael and Eleanor (eds): *H. H. Asquith: Letters to Venetia Stanley*, Oxford, 1982
Chandos, Viscount: *Memoirs*, 1962
—— *From Peace to War, a Study in Contrasts*, 1968
Channon, Sir Henry: *Diaries*, ed. R. Rhodes James, 1967
Churchill, Rt Hon. Winston Spencer: *The World Crisis, 1911–18*, 6 vols, 1923–31
Cooper, Lady Diana: *The Rainbow Comes and Goes*, 1959
—— *The Light of Common Day*, 1953
Crathorne, Nancy, Lady: *Tennant's Stalk. The Story of the Tennants of the Glen*, 1973
Curzon of Kedleston, Marchioness: *Reminiscences*, 1955

Esher, Viscount: *Journals and Letters*, ed. M. V. Brett. 4 vols, 1934–8

Faber, Geoffrey: *Jowett*, 1960

Falls, Cyril: *The First World War*, 1960

Fulford, Roger: *Votes for Women*, 1957

Gardiner, A. G.: *Life of Sir William Harcourt*, 2 vols, 1923

Gilbert, Martin: *Churchill*, vol. iii, 1971

Gollin, H. M.: *Proconsul in Politics. A study of Lord Milner in opposition and power, 1854–1905*, 1964

Goschen, Edward: *Diary, 1900–1914*, ed. C. H. D. Howard, 1980

Grew, E. S.: *Field Marshal Lord Kitchener. His Life and Work for the Empire*, 1916

Grey of Fallodon, Viscount: *Twenty-Five Years*, 2 vols, 1925

Haldane, Viscount: *Autobiography*, 1929

Horner, Lady Frances: *Time Remembered*, 1933

Hutchinson, H. G.: *Portrait of the Eighties*, 1922

Hyam, Ronald: *Britain's Imperial Century, 1815–1914*, 1976

Jenkins, Roy: *Asquith*, 1964

—— *Mr Balfour's Poodle*, 1954

Jolliffe, John: *Raymond Asquith, Life and Letters*, 1980

Kennet, Lady: *Self-Portrait of an Artist*, 1949

Koss, Stephen: *Asquith*, 1976

Liddell, A. G. C.: *Notes from the Life of an Ordinary Mortal*, 1911

Liddell Hart, B. H.: *The First World War*, 1930

Longford, Elizabeth, Countess of: *A Pilgrimage of Passion. The Life of W. S. Blunt*, 1979

Lyttelton, Edith: *Alfred Lyttelton*, 1917

Lytton, Earl of: *Wilfrid Scawen Blunt*, 1961

MacCarthy, Desmond: *Portraits*, 1931

—— (ed.): *Letters to a Friend* [H. H. Asquith to Mrs Hilda Harrisson]. 2 vols, 1933–4

Macmillan, Harold: *Winds of Change, 1914–1939*, 1966

Magnus, Sir Philip: *Kitchener*, 1958

Marlborough, Laura Duchess of: *Laughter from a Cloud*, 1980

Masterman, L. B. (ed.): *Diaries and Letters of Mary Gladstone*, 1930

Middlemass, Keith and Barnes, John: *Baldwin*, 1969

Milner, Alfred: *Egypt in England*, 1892

—— *The Milner Papers*, ed. Cecil Headlam. 2 vols, 1933

Newsome, David: *On the Edge of Paradise*, 1980

Nicolson, Sir Harold: *George V*, 1952

Norwich, Viscount (Alfred Duff Cooper): *Old Men Forget*, 1953

Pakenham, Thomas: *The Boer War*, 1979

Ponsonby, Arthur: *Henry Ponsonby, Queen Victoria's Private Secretary*, 1942

Rhodes James, Robert: *Rosebery*, 1963

Ribblesdale, Viscount: *Impressions and Memories*, 1929

Rose, Kenneth: *A Superior Person: A Life of Viscount Curzon and his Circle*, 1969

St Clair Erskine, Lady Angela: *Memories and Base Details*, 1922
—— *Fore and Aft*, 1932

Simon, Sir John: *Retrospect*, 1952

Sitwell, Sir Osbert: *Great Morning*, 1948
—— *Bright Morning*, 1942

Soames, Mary: *Clementine Churchill*, 1979

Spender, J. A. and Asquith, C.: *Life of Henry Herbert, Lord Oxford and Asquith*. 2 vols, 1932

Terraine, J.: *The Smoke and the Fire*, 1980

Warwick, P. (ed.): *The South African War*, 1980

Wemyss, Countess of: *A Family Record*, 1895

Ziegler, Philip: *Diana Cooper*, 1981

BIOGRAPHICAL NOTES

BIOGRAPHICAL NOTES

(HHA = Herbert Henry Asquith, Earl of Oxford and Asquith)

Asquith, Anthony ('Puffin') (1902–1968). Second child of HHA and Margot. Film director.

Asquith, Arthur ('Oc') (1883–1939). Third son of HHA by his first wife.

Asquith, Cynthia (d. 1960). Daughter of eleventh Earl of Wemyss. Married Herbert Asquith, 1910.

Asquith, Emma Alice Margaret (Margot), later Countess of Oxford and Asquith (1864–1945). Sixth daughter of Sir Charles Tennant.

Asquith, Herbert Henry, cr. Earl of Oxford and Asquith, 1925 (1852–1928). Scholar of Balliol, 1870–74; Called to the Bar, 1876. Married Helen Melland, 1877. MP for East Fife, 1886–1918. QC, 1890. Home Secretary, 1892–5. Married Margot Tennant, May 1894. Chancellor of the Exchequer, Dec. 1905–Apr. 1908, then Prime Minister to Dec. 1916.

Asquith, Herbert ('Beb') (1881–1947). Second son of HHA by his first wife.

Asquith, Raymond (1878–1916). HHA's eldest son by his first wife. Called to Bar, 1904. Married Katharine Horner, 1907. Killed in action, 15 Sept. 1916.

Asquith, Violet (Baroness Asquith of Yarnbury), cr. Life Peeress, 1964 (1887–1969). HHA's fourth child by his first wife. Married Maurice Bonham Carter, July 1915.

Astor, Nancy (1879–1964). American wife (married 1906) of William Waldorf, first Viscount Astor.

Baldwin, Stanley (1867–1947). Conservative MP, 1908; Financial Secretary to the Treasury, 1917–21; President of the Board of Trade, 1921–2; Chancellor of the Exchequer, 1922–3; Prime Minister, 1923–4, 1924–9 and 1935–7; Lord President of the Council, 1931–5; cr. Earl, 1937.

Balfour, Arthur James, first Earl (1848–1930). Conservative MP, 1874–1922; President of Local Government Board, 1885–6, Secretary for Scotland, 1886–7, Chief Secretary for Ireland, 1887–91, Leader of the House of Commons, 1891–2 and 1895–1902; Prime Minister, 1902–5; First Lord of the Admiralty, 1915–16; Foreign Secretary, 1916–19; Lord President of the Council, 1919–22 and 1925–9; cr. Earl, 1922.

Balfour, Edith (DD) (d. 1948). Second wife of Alfred Lyttelton.

Barrie, Sir James (1860–1937). Playwright.

Battenberg, Admiral Prince Louis of; Marquess of Milford Haven, 1917 (1854–1921). Eldest son of Prince Alexander of Hesse, lived in England from boyhood; married Princess Victoria of Hesse, granddaughter of Queen Victoria. Naturalized and entered Royal Navy, 1868; first Sea Lord, 1912–Oct. 1914.

Beaverbrook, William Maxwell Aitken, first Baron (1879–1964). Conservative MP, 1910–16; cr. Baron, 1917; Chancellor of the Duchy of Lancaster and Minister of Information, 1917; newspaper proprietor.

Belloc-Lowndes, Marie (1868–1947). Writer.

Benson, Arthur Christopher (1862–1925). Eton master 1885–1904, Master of Magdalene College, Cambridge, 1916–25. Diarist.

Benson, Edward Frederick (1867–1940). Author. Brother of A. C. Benson.

Bibesco, Prince Antoine (1878–1952). Roumanian diplomat. Minister at Washington, 1920–26, Madrid, 1926–31.

Bibesco, Elizabeth (1897–1945). Daughter of HHA and Margot. Married Antoine Bibesco, 1919.

Billing, Noel Pemberton (1880–1945). MP. In 1918 alleged that German agents had corrupted members of English society by playing on sexual weaknesses.

Birkenhead, Frederick Edwin Smith, first Earl of (1872–1930). Conservative MP, 1906–19; Solicitor-General, 1915; Attorney-General, 1915–19; Lord Chancellor, 1919–22; Secretary of State for India, 1924–8; cr. Baron, 1919, Viscount, 1921, Earl, 1922.

Bonham Carter, Maurice ('Bongie') (1880–1960). HHA's Principal Private Secretary. Devoted to his chief, whose elder daughter, Violet, he married (July 1915).

Campbell-Bannerman, Sir Henry (1836–1908). Liberal MP, 1868–1908; Secretary of State for War, 1886 and 1892–5; Leader of the Liberal Party in the House of Commons, 1899–1908; Prime Minister, 1905–8.

Carson, Sir Edward Henry (1854–1935). Conservative MP, 1892–1921; Solicitor-General, 1900–06; Leader of Ulster Unionists, 1910; Attorney-General, 1915; First Lord of the Admiralty, 1917; Minister without portfolio in the War Cabinet, 1917–18; Lord of Appeal in Ordinary, 1921–9.

Casement, Sir Roger (1864–1916). Entered British consular service and served in Africa and South America. Knighted, 1911. Extreme Irish Nationalist. Sought German aid for this cause in 1914. Captured en route to Ireland, 1916, and hanged for treason.

Chamberlain, Joseph (1836–1914). Liberal MP, 1876–86; Liberal Unionist

MP, 1886–1906; President of the Board of Trade, 1880–85; Secretary of State for the Colonies, 1895–1903; resigned office to conduct tariff reform agitation, 1903.

Channon, Sir Henry ('Chips') (1897–1958). American, naturalized British. Conservative MP, 1935–58. Knighted, 1957. Diarist and host.

Churchill, Clementine (1885–1977). Wife of Sir Winston Churchill.

Churchill, Lord Randolph (1849–1894). Third son of sixth Duke of Marlborough. Conservative MP, 1874–94. Secretary of State for India, 1885–6, Chancellor of the Exchequer, 1896. Father of Sir Winston Churchill.

Churchill, Winston Leonard Spencer (1874–1965). Conservative MP, 1900–03; Liberal MP, 1903–22; Conservative MP, 1924–63. Under-Secretary of State for the Colonies, 1906–8; President of the Board of Trade, 1908–10; Home Secretary, 1910–11; First Lord of the Admiralty, 1911–15; Chancellor of the Duchy of Lancaster, 1915; Secretary of State for War and for Air, 1918–21 and for the Colonies, 1921–2; Chancellor of the Exchequer, 1924–9; Prime Minister, 1940–45, 1951–5. KG 1953.

Collins, John Churton (1848–1908). Author and essayist. Professor of English at Birmingham University, 1904–08.

Cooper, Alfred Duff (1890–1954). Created Viscount Norwich, 1952. Married Lady Diana Manners, 1919. MP, 1924–9 and 1931–45. Secretary of State for War, 1928–9 and 1931–4; First Lord of the Admiralty, 1937–8. Ambassador to France, 1944–7.

Crewe, first Marquess of (1858–1945). Viceroy of Ireland, 1892; Lord President of Council, 1905; Secretary of State for Colonies, 1908; Lord Privy Seal, 1908–11 and 1912–15; Secretary of State for India, 1910–15, for War, 1931.

Cripps, Sir Stafford (1889–1952), Knighted, 1930, C.H., 1951. Solicitor General, 1930–1, Ambassador to Russia, 1940–42. Minister of Aircraft Production, 1942–5.

Cunard, Maud, later 'Emerald' (1872–1948). American. Married (1895) to Sir Bache Cunard, heir to the shipping fortune.

Curzon of Kedleston, George Nathaniel Curzon, first Marquess (1859–1925). Conservative MP, 1886–98; Under-Secretary of State for India, 1891–2, for Foreign Affairs, 1895–8; Viceroy and Governor-General of India, 1899–1905; succeeded as Baron Scarsdale, 1898; Viscount Scarsdale, 1911, and Earl Curzon of Kedleston, 1911; Lord Privy Seal, 1915–16; President of the Air Board, 1916; Lord President of the Council, 1916–19; Leader of the House of Lords, 1916–24; cr. Marquess, 1921.

Cust, Harry (1861–1917). Political journalist and man about town. Unionist MP, 1890–95 and 1900–06.

Desborough, Countess of ('Ettie') (d. 1952). Married Lord Desborough, 1887. Famous Edwardian hostess.

Douglas, Lord Alfred (1870–1945). Third son of Marquess of Queensberry. Poet. Intimate friend of Oscar Wilde from 1891 until Wilde's death in 1900. Appointed editor of the *Academy* periodical by Sir Edward Tennant (later Lord Glenconner) 1907, but unsuccessful. Imprisoned 1923 for libelling Winston Churchill.

Dawson, Geoffrey (1874–1944). Private Secretary to Milner, 1901–05. Editor of *The Times*, 1912–19 and 1923–41.

Esher, Reginald Baliol Brett, second Viscount (1852–1930). Liberal MP, 1880–85; Lieutenant and Deputy-Governor of Windsor Castle, 1901–28; Permanent Member of the Committee of Imperial Defence, 1905; Governor of Windsor Castle, 1928–30; private adviser to Edward VII and George V; co-editor of Queen Victoria's Letters, First Series.

Fisher, John Arbuthnot ('Jacky'), first Baron, cr. 1908 (1841–1920). Served in Baltic Fleet during Crimean War. Controller of Navy, 1892–7; Second Sea Lord, 1902; first Sea Lord, 1904–10 and Oct. 1914–May 1915: Responsible for Britain's lead in 'all-big-gun' battleships and battle-cruisers (Dreadnought launched, 1906). Flamboyant, the creator of greatly needed changes and of much discord.

French, Sir John (1852–1925). Cr. Viscount, 1916; Earl of Ypres, 1922. After success in Boer War, Lt.-Gen. and KCMG, 1902. Inspector-Gen. of Forces, 1907; CIGS, 1912; Field Marshal, 1913. Resigned after Curragh 'Mutiny', 1914. C.-in-C., British Expeditionary Force, 1914, till superseded, Dec. 1915.

George, David Lloyd (1863–1945). Liberal MP, 1890–1945; President of the Board of Trade 1905–08; Chancellor of the Exchequer, 1908–15; Minister of Munitions, 1915–16; Secretary of State for War, 1916; Prime Minister, 1916–22. Cr. Earl.

Gladstone, Mary (Mrs Henry Drew) (1847–1927). Third daughter of W. E. Gladstone. Married Reverend Henry Drew, 1886.

Gladstone, William Ewart (1809–1898). Conservative MP, 1832–45; Peelite MP, 1847–65; Liberal MP, 1865–95; Junior Lord of the Treasury, 1834–5; Vice-President of the Board of Trade, 1841–3; President of the Board of Trade, 1843–4; Secretary of State for the Colonies, 1845–6; Chancellor of the Exchequer, 1852–5 and 1859–66; Leader of the Liberal Party, 1867–8; Prime Minister, 1868–74, 1880–85, 1886, and 1892–4.

Glenconner, first Baron (1859–1920). Edward Tennant, seventh child of Sir Charles Tennant and brother of Margot.

Gosse, Sir Edmund (1849–1928). Poet, man of letters and literary critic.

Haig, Douglas (1861–1928), cr. Earl, 1919. Staff Officer to Sir John French, Boer War. Summoned by Haldane to work on military reorganization, 1906. Commanded First Corps, BEF, Aug. 1914; First Army, Jan. 1915. Commander-in-Chief, December 1915–19.

Haldane, Richard Burdon (1856–1928), cr. Viscount, 1911. Barrister. Entered Parliament, 1885. Secretary of State for War, 1905–12; Lord Chancellor, 1912–15.

Hamilton, Gen. Sir Ian (1853–1947). ADC to C.-in-C., India (Roberts), 1886. Distinguished service in Boer War. Commanded anti-invasion forces, 1914–15, Dardanelles army, Mar.–Oct. 1915.

Harcourt, Lewis (1863–1922). Son of Sir William. Liberal MP, 1904–17. First Commissioner of Works, 1905–10, 1915–17. Secretary of State for the Colonies, 1910–15. Created Viscount, 1917.

Harcourt, Sir William George Granville Venables Vernon (1827–1904). Liberal MP, 1868–1904; Home Secretary, 1880–85; Chancellor of the Exchequer, 1886 and 1892–5; Leader of the House of Commons, 1894–5; resigned leadership of Liberal Party in House of Commons, 1898.

Harrisson, Hilda. First World War widow from Oxford and close confidante of HHA in his declining years.

Henderson, Arthur (1863–1903). MP, 1903. President of the Board of Education, 1915–16, Paymaster-General, 1916, Minister without Portfolio in War Cabinet, 1917. Home Secretary 1924, Secretary of State for Foreign Affairs, 1929–31.

Henley, The Hon. Mrs Sylvia (1882–1980). Second daughter of Lord Sheffield. Married Anthony Henley, 1906. For some years HHA's chief correspondent and confidante.

Horner, Frances, Lady (1858–1940). Daughter of William Graham, India merchant, Liberal MP, and friend of Pre-Raphaelite painters. Married, 1883, John Horner of Mells, Somerset. 'Jack' Horner became KCVO, 1907. Raymond Asquith married their daughter Katharine in the same year.

Jameson, Sir Starr (1853–1917). Qualified MD, 1887, and practised in Kimberley, South Africa. Became a close friend of Cecil Rhodes and active in helping to found Rhodesia. CB, 1894. Led Jameson Raid on Johannesburg in December 1895 to assist an expected rising there, but captured by Transvaal government. Later Prime Minister of Cape Colony and promoted Union of South Africa. Created baronet, 1911.

Jellicoe, Adm. Sir John (1859–1935) cr. Earl, 1925. Controller of Navy, 1908; Second Sea Lord, 1912. C.-in-C., Grand Fleet, Aug. 1914. First Sea Lord, Nov. 1916–Dec. 1917.

Joffre, Gen. Joseph Jacques Césaire (1852–1931). C.-in-C., French armies, Western Front, Aug. 1914–Dec. 1916.

Jowett, Benjamin (1817–1893). Regius Professor of Greek at Oxford, 1855. Master of Balliol College, 1870–93.

Kaiser, The. Wilhelm II, German Emperor and King of Prussia (1859–1941). Grandson of Queen Victoria. Succeeded father, 1888. Abdicated 1918.

Keppel, The Hon. Mrs Alice (1868–1947). Married, 1891, third son of seventh Earl of Albemarle. Edward VII's intimate friend during the last twelve years of his life.

Kitchener, Horatio Herbert; cr. Earl Kitchener of Khartoum, June 1914 (1850–1916). Successful campaigns in Egypt and Sudan (battle of Omdurman, 1898). Roberts's Chief of Staff, then C.-in-C., Boer War. C.-in-C., India, 1902–09, British Agent and Consul-General, Egypt, 1911–14. Secretary of State for War, Aug. 1914 to death on HMS *Hampshire*, June 1916.

Knollys, Sir Francis (1837–1924). Private Secretary to King Edward VII as Prince of Wales and as King, 1870–1910; to George V, 1910–13. Created Viscount, 1911.

Law, Andrew Bonar (1858–1923). Conservative MP, 1900–23; Parliamentary Secretary of the Board of Trade, 1902–06; Leader of the Opposition, 1911–15; Secretary of State for the Colonies, 1915–16; Chancellor of the Exchequer, 1916–18; Lord Privy Seal and Leader of the House of Commons, 1919–21; Prime Minister, 1922–3.

Lichnowsky, Prince. German Ambassador in London, 1912–14.

Londonderry, Marchioness of (1879–1959). Edith, daughter of Viscount Chaplin. Married seventh Marquess of Londonderry, 1899. Most brilliant of the Tory hostesses.

Lyttelton, Alfred (1857–1913). Son of fourth Baron Lyttelton. Married firstly, Laura Tennant, 1885; secondly, Edith Balfour, 1892. Barrister. Secretary of State for the Colonies, 1903–05, MP (Liberal Unionist, then Unionist), 1895–1913.

MacCarthy, Sir Desmond (1878–1952). Dramatic and literary critic.

MacDonald, James Ramsay (1866–1937). Labour MP, 1906–18 and 1922–31; National Labour MP, 1931–5, and 1936–7; Prime Minister and Secretary of State for Foreign Affairs, 1924; Prime Minister, 1929–35; Lord President of the Council, 1935.

Maclean, Sir Donald (1864–1932). Liberal MP, 1906–22. Chairman of the Parliamentary Liberal Party, 1919–22.

Manners, Constance ('Con') (d. 1920). Constance Fane, married third Lord Manners, 1885.

Manners, Lady Diana (1892–   ). Daughter of the eighth Duke of Rutland. Married Alfred Duff Cooper, later Lord Norwich, 1919.

Manners, John Thomas Manners (1852–1927). Third Baron Manners, known as 'Hoppy'.

Mary, Princess Royal (1897–1965). Only daughter of George V.

Maurice, Major General Sir Frederick (1871–1951). Director of Military Operations, War Office, 1916–18.

Maxwell, Sir John (1859–1929). Service in Egypt, 1882–1900, 1906–12, 1914–16. South Africa 1900–02. Commander-in-Chief, Ireland, 1916.

McEvoy, Ambrose (1878–1927). Fashionable portrait painter.

McKenna, Reginald (1863–1943). Barrister. Entered Parliament, 1895. President, Board of Education, 1907; First Lord of Admiralty, 1908. Married Pamela Jekyll, 1908. Home Secretary, 1911–15; Chancellor of Exchequer, 1915.

Miles, Marguerite (1868–1943). Daughter of C. W. Miles of Malmesbury. Married Sir Charles Tennant as his second wife, 1898.

Milner, Alfred, first Viscount (1854–1925). Chairman, Board of Inland Revenue, 1892–7; Governor of the Cape of Good Hope, 1897–1901; Governor of Transvaal and Orange River Colony, 1901–05, and High Commissioner for South Africa, 1897–1905; Minister without portfolio, 1916–18; Secretary of State for War, 1918–19; Secretary of State for the Colonies, 1919–21; cr. Baron, 1901; Viscount, 1902.

Montagu, The Hon. Edwin Samuel (1879–1924). Liberal MP, 1906–22. Private Secretary to HHA when Chancellor of Exchequer and Prime Minister. Under-Secretary for India, 1910–14; Financial Secretary to Treasury, 1914–15; Chancellor of Duchy of Lancaster, Jan. 1915; Minister of Munitions, 1916; Secretary of State for India, 1917–22. Married Venetia Stanley, 1915.

Moore, George (1852–1933). Novelist.

Morley of Blackburn, John, first Viscount (1838–1923). Liberal MP, 1883–1908; Chief Secretary for Ireland, 1886 and 1892–5; Secretary of State for India, 1905–10; Lord President of the Council, 1910–14; cr. Viscount, 1908.

Mountbatten of Burma, Earl (1900–1979). Son of Admiral Prince Louis of Battenberg (changed name to Mountbatten 1917). Married Edwina Ashley, 1922. Admiral of the Fleet. Supreme Allied Commander, Southeast Asia, 1943–6, Viceroy of India, 1947.

Murray, Professor Gilbert (1866–1957). Regius Professor of Greek at Oxford, 1908–36. Chairman, League of Nations Union, 1923–38.

Nicolson, Sir Harold (1886–1968) Diplomatic Service, 1909–29. MP, 1935
    –45. Author.
Northcliffe, Alfred Harmsworth, (1865–1922) cr. Baron, 1905; Viscount,
    1917. Father of modern popular journalism. Proprietor of *Daily Mail*,
    1896, *The Times*, 1908, and other papers. Campaigned before 1914 for
    compulsory military service and gave warnings of Germany's warlike
    intentions.
Novello, Ivor (1893–1951). Actor-manager and composer.
Pembroke, George, thirteenth Earl of (1850–1895). Married Gertrude,
    daughter of Earl of Shrewsbury, 1874.
Redmond, John Edward (1856–1918). Irish Nationalist MP, 1881–1918;
    supported Parnell, 1890, and led Parnellite group after 1891; Leader of
    re-united Nationalist Party, 1900–18.
Rhodes, Cecil (1853–1902). Managing Director of British South Africa Co.,
    1889 and founder of Rhodesia. Prime Minister of Cape Colony, 1890
    –96.
Ribblesdale, Thomas Lister, fourth Baron (1854–1925). Married Charlotte,
    daughter of Sir Charles Tennant.
Roberts of Kandahar, Field Marshal Earl (1832–1914). cr. Earl, 1901.
    Served Indian Mutiny. Commander-in-Chief, India, 1885–93; South
    Africa, 1899–1900.
Rosebery, Archibald Philip Primrose, fifth Earl of (1847–1929). Lord Privy
    Seal 1885; Secretary of State for Foreign Affairs, 1886 and 1892–4;
    Prime Minister, 1894–5.
Rutland, Violet Duchess of (d. 1937). Married eighth Duke of Rutland, 1882.
    Artist.
Sackville-West, Vita (1892–1962). Novelist and poet. Daughter of third
    Lord Sackville. Married Harold Nicolson, 1913.
Salisbury, Robert Arthur Talbot Gascoyne-Cecil, third Marquess of (1830
    –1903). Conservative MP, 1853–68; succeeded to Marquisate, 1868;
    Secretary of State for India, 1874–8, and for Foreign Affairs, 1878–80;
    Leader of Conservative Party in House of Lords after death of Beacons-
    field; Prime Minister and Foreign Secretary, 1885–6, 1886–92 and
    1895–1900; Prime Minister and Lord Privy Seal, 1900–02.
Sassoon, Siegfried (1886–1967). Poet and author.
Selborne, second Earl of (1859–1942). Succeeded father, 1895. Liberal MP,
    1885–95. Under-Secretary for the Colonies 1895–1900, first Lord of
    the Admiralty, 1900–05. Governor of Transvaal and High Commis-
    sioner to South Africa, 1905–10.
Simon, Sir John (1873–1954). Barrister. Liberal MP, 1906–40. Solicitor
    General, 1910–13, Attorney General, 1913–15, Secretary of State for

Home Affairs, 1915–16 and 1935–7, for Foreign Affairs, 1931–5, Chancellor of the Exchequer, 1937–40, Lord Chancellor 1940–45. Created Viscount, 1940.

Simpson, Mrs Wallis (1896–   ). Married Duke of Windsor (Edward VIII), 1936.

Sinclair, Sir Archibald (1890–1970). Private Secretary to Winston Churchill at War Office and Colonial Office, 1919–22. Liberal MP, 1922. Secretary of State for Scotland, 1931–2, for Air, 1940–45. Created Viscount Thurso, 1950.

Sitwell, Sir Osbert (1892–1969). Poet, essayist and novelist.

Snowden, Philip (1864–1937). Labour MP, 1906. Chancellor of the Exchequer, 1924, 1929–31. Cr. Viscount, 1931.

Spender, J. A. (1862–1942). Editor, *Westminster Gazette*, 1896–1922. Biographer (with Cyril Asquith) of HHA.

Stamfordham, Lieutenant-Colonel Sir Arthur John Bigge, first Baron (1849–1931). Assistant Private Secretary to the Queen, 1895–1900; Private Secretary to King George V as Prince of Wales and King, 1901–30.

Stanley, Beatrice Venetia (1887–1948). Youngest child of Edward Lyulph Stanley (who succeeded as Lord Stanley of Alderley, 1903, and as Lord Sheffield, 1909) and of Mary Katharine, daughter of Sir Lowthian Bell, Bt. Close friend and correspondent of HHA. Married, 26 July 1915, Edwin Samuel Montagu (who d. 1924).

Strachey, John St Loe (1860–1927). Journalist. Editor of *The Spectator*, 1898–1925.

Symonds, John Addington (1840–1893). Historian and essayist.

Tennant, Laura (1863–86) Fifth daughter of Sir Charles Tennant. Married Alfred Lyttelton, 1885.

Tennyson, Alfred, Lord (1809–1892). Poet Laureate, 1850.

Tennyson, Lionel (1854–1886). Second son of the poet.

Wemyss, Mary Countess of (d. 1937). Daughter of Hon. P. S. Wyndham. Became Lady Elcho by marriage to the future eleventh Earl of Wemyss, 1883, and Countess of Wemyss on her husband's succession to the earldom, 1914. Famous hostess.

Wilson, Field-Marshal Sir Henry Hughes, Bt. (1864–1922). Director of Military Operations, 1910–14; Assistant Chief of General Staff to General French, 1914; Chief of Imperial General Staff, 1918–22.

Wilson, Woodrow (1856–1924). President of the USA, 1913–24. Instigated foundation of League of Nations.

GOVERNMENTS AND PRIME MINISTERS,

1880–1945

1880–5	Liberal	Gladstone
1885–6	Conservative	Salisbury
1886	Liberal	Gladstone
1886–92	Conservative	Salisbury
1892–4	Liberal	Gladstone
1894–5	Liberal	Rosebery
1895–1902	Unionist	Salisbury
1902–5	Unionist	Balfour
1905–8	Liberal	Campbell-Bannerman
1908–15	Liberal	Asquith
1915–16	Coalition	Asquith
1916–22	Coalition	Lloyd George
1922–3	Conservative	Bonar Law
1923	Conservative	Baldwin
1924	Labour	MacDonald
1924–9	Conservative	Baldwin
1929–31	Labour	MacDonald
1931	Coalition ('National')	MacDonald
1932–5	Coalition ('National')	MacDonald
1935–7	Conservative	Baldwin
1937–40	Conservative	Chamberlain
1940–5	Coalition	Churchill

FAMILY TREE OF THE
TENNANTS AND ASQUITHS

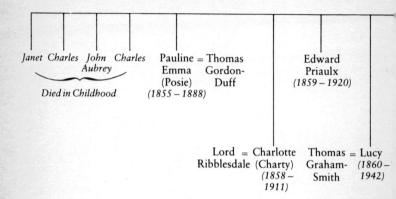

Janet Charles John Charles
　　　　　　　Aubrey

Died in Childhood

Pauline = Thomas
Emma Gordon-
(Posie) Duff
(1855 – 1888)

Edward
Priaulx
(1859 – 1920)

Lord = Charlotte
Ribblesdale (Charty)
*(1858 –
1911)*

Thomas = Lucy
Graham- *(1860 –
Smith 1942)*

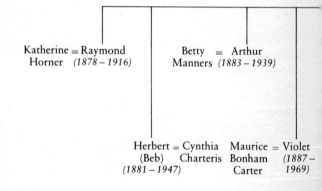

Katherine = Raymond
Horner *(1878 – 1916)*

Betty = Arthur
Manners *(1883 – 1939)*

Herbert = Cynthia
(Beb) Charteris
(1881 – 1947)

Maurice = Violet
Bonham *(1887 –
Carter 1969)*

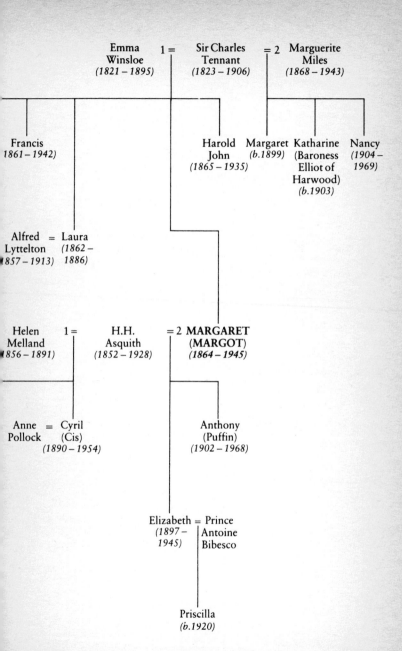

Emma Winsloe *(1821 – 1895)* **1 =** Sir Charles Tennant *(1823 – 1906)* **= 2** Marguerite Miles *(1868 – 1943)*

Francis *(1861 – 1942)*

Harold John *(1865 – 1935)*

Margaret *(b.1899)*

Katharine (Baroness Elliot of Harwood) *(b.1903)*

Nancy *(1904 – 1969)*

Alfred Lyttelton *(1857 – 1913)* **=** Laura *(1862 – 1886)*

Helen Melland *(1856 – 1891)* **1 =** H.H. Asquith *(1852 – 1928)* **= 2** **MARGARET (MARGOT)** *(1864 – 1945)*

Anne Pollock **=** Cyril (Cis) *(1890 – 1954)*

Anthony (Puffin) *(1902 – 1968)*

Elizabeth *(1897 – 1945)* **=** Prince Antoine Bibesco

Priscilla *(b.1920)*

INDEX